T0294618

MUSEUM
ADMINISTRATION 2.0

About the Series

The American Association for State and Local History Book Series addresses issues critical to the field of state and local history through interpretive, intellectual, scholarly, and educational texts. To submit a proposal or manuscript to the series, please request proposal guidelines from AASLH headquarters: AASLH Editorial Board, 1717 Church St., Nashville, Tennessee 37203. Telephone: (615) 320-3203. Website: www.aaslh.org.

About the Organization

The American Association for State and Local History (AASLH) is a national history membership association headquartered in Nashville, Tennessee. AASLH provides leadership and support for its members who preserve and interpret state and local history in order to make the past more meaningful to all Americans. AASLH members are leaders in preserving, researching, and interpreting traces of the American past to connect the people, thoughts, and events of yesterday with the creative memories and abiding concerns of people, communities, and our nation today. In addition to sponsorship of this book series, AASLH publishes *History News* magazine, a newsletter, technical leaflets and reports, and other materials; confers prizes and awards in recognition of outstanding achievement in the field; supports a broad education program and other activities designed to help members work more effectively; and advocates on behalf of the discipline of history. To join AASLH, go to www.aaslh.org or contact Membership Services, AASLH, 1717 Church St., Nashville, TN 37203.

MUSEUM ADMINISTRATION 2.0

Hugh H. Genoways and Lynne M. Ireland

Revised by Cinnamon Catlin-Legutko

ROWMAN & LITTLEFIELD
Lanham • Boulder • New York • London

Published by Rowman & Littlefield
A wholly owned subsidiary of The Rowman & Littlefield Publishing Group, Inc.
4501 Forbes Boulevard, Suite 200, Lanham, Maryland 20706
www.rowman.com

Unit A, Whitacre Mews, 26-34 Stannary Street, London SE11 4AB,
United Kingdom

Copyright © 2017 by Rowman & Littlefield

British Library Cataloguing in Publication Information Available

Library of Congress Cataloging-in-Publication Data
Names: Genoways, Hugh H., author. | Ireland, Lynne M., 1953- author. |
    Catlin-Legutko, Cinnamon, editor.
Title: Museum administration 2.0 / by Hugh H. Genoways and
    Lynne M. Ireland; revised by Cinnamon Catlin-Legutko.
Other titles: Museum administration.
Description: Lanham, MD : Rowman & Littlefield [2016] | Series: American
    Association for State and Local History
Identifiers: LCCN 2016015151 | ISBN 9781442255500 (cloth : alk. paper) |
    ISBN 9781442255517 (pbk. : alk. paper) | ISBN 9781442255524
    (electronic)
Subjects: LCSH: Museums—Management. | Museums—United States—
    Management.
Classification: LCC AM121 .G465 2016 | DDC 069/.068—dc23
LC record available at https://lccn.loc.gov/2016015151

Printed in the United States of America

This second edition is dedicated to my husband, Larry, and my son, Jacob, who are always supportive when I take on new projects and opportunities. And patient ... very, very patient.

—Cinnamon Catlin-Legutko

CONTENTS

PREFACE TO THE FIRST EDITION

"A leader is best
When people barely know he exists,
When his work is done, his aim fulfilled,
They will say:
We did it ourselves."

—Lao-Tzu, sixth century B.C. Taoist poet

"The best executive is the one who has sense enough to pick good men to do what he wants done, and the self-restraint enough to keep from meddling with them while they do it."

—Theodore Roosevelt, twenty-sixth president of the United States, 1901–1909

"Details are not my thing. You wouldn't expect the captain of a ship to go down and fix the boiler, would you?"

—Jesse "The Body" Ventura, governor of Minnesota, 2001

Although these quotes give excellent insight into the leadership that administrators must provide to their organizations, they do not describe the complexity that administrators in museums will encounter. Indeed, museum administrators will find themselves in a position, unless they work for a few of the largest museums in the country, where they need to fulfill many roles because there may be no one else to do the job. They may well need to go and "fix the boiler" or else expect to be cold. And after fixing the boiler, they may well need to scrub the toilet prior to reading a budget report, calming a stressed-out volunteer, and giving a personal tour to a potential donor. We hope this book will give students and those taking on new administrative duties some of the knowledge they will need to meet these challenges.

This book is the outgrowth of our teaching a course in museum administration and management in the Museum Studies Program at the University of Nebraska-Lincoln each year since 1991. It has been prepared partly as a textbook for use in similar courses, but we also believe it will be useful to individual readers who are interested in increasing their knowledge of museum administration as they grow in their professional careers.

Throughout this book material has been set aside in special boxes to enhance the understanding of the subject being covered. Many boxes highlight practical knowledge gleaned from relevant sources. Additionally, three types of boxes contain materials that give the reader special insight into or opportunity for applying the concepts discussed in the text. Case Reviews are brief summaries of real situations that have occurred in museum-related organizations that pertain to particular topics under consideration. These offer insight into how real-life scenarios develop and evolve, devolve, and are eventually resolved.

Case Studies are fictitious situations presented for the reader to analyze and resolve. Readers looking for the "correct" answers to the case studies will be disappointed. We use case studies as the basis of class discussions and we tell our students the "correct" answers are those that they can concisely state and defend. Many issues with which museum administrators must deal, and the appropriate response to them, will depend upon the circumstances under which they arise. No answer will work in every situation. We want our readers to learn to think analytically, to develop their basic administrative philosophy, and to be able to state the issues and their proposed courses of action succinctly.

Exercises, as their title implies, will provide readers an opportunity to practice preparing documents, statements, and policies they will need in administrative positions.

The unifying theme and activity throughout this book and our course is a project to plan a new museum (see pages 339–340) and to prepare all of the documents and policies the institution would need to operate. The first edition is arranged in the general order in which we would expect the documents to be prepared, beginning with a mission statement and bylaws and ending with a code of professional conduct. The final three chapters (13–15) discuss legal and philosophical issues that all museum administrators need to consider.

The semester-long planning project in our course is always done in small groups of four to seven people. It is so organized because we believe that the ability to function in small groups or teams is critical to successful work in the museum environment. Observing the functioning of these groups has been fascinating. All have successfully completed the assigned task, but in many cases the experience has been very uncomfortable. Our educational system does not promote and recognize team or group achievement; rather notice and "glory" go to the individual whose performance is exemplary. This is not a good background for museum work. Today's museum staffers must be willing to submerge their desire for personal recognition in the effort to attain recognition and success for the institution. We urge anyone using this book as a text to emphasize the team approach in every aspect of coursework and professional work. Students need the experience; and all of us have more to learn about effective work in groups.

Hugh H. Genoways
Lynne M. Ireland
December 2, 2002

PREFACE

When asked why she chose to be in museum administration, the newly retired Ellen Rosenthal (former president and CEO of Conner Prairie) said it was "because I had the idea that I could pull together everything I learned and experienced from twenty-five years working in museum and business realms. I believed I could create a successful museum, both in terms of mission and financial sustainability. I could only do that if I was in charge. And, by golly, it worked!"[1] Throughout this second edition of Museum Administration, you will see how being able to assemble the museum's "moving parts" and relying on experience and your peers will make you a capable administrator. As a result, your museum will be strengthened by solid administrative practice and policy.

The first edition of this book was the outgrowth of Hugh and Lynne's teaching of a course in museum administration in the now-closed Museum Studies Program at the University of Nebraska-Lincoln in the 1990s and early 2000s. The book was prepared partly as a textbook for use in similar courses, but it is also useful to individual readers who are interested in increasing their knowledge of museum administration as they grow in their professional careers.

Throughout this book material has been set aside in special boxes to enhance the understanding of the subject being covered. Many boxes highlight practical knowledge gleaned from relevant sources. Additionally, three types of boxes contain materials that give the reader special insight into or opportunity for applying the concepts discussed in the text. Case Reviews are brief summaries of real situations that have occurred in museum-related organizations that pertain to particular topics under consideration. These offer insight into how real-life scenarios develop and evolve, devolve, and are eventually resolved.

Case Studies are fictitious situations presented for the reader to analyze and resolve, but some are not far removed from real museum circumstances. Readers looking for the "correct" answers to the case studies will be disappointed. Case studies are great for class discussions as well as staff meetings; the "correct" answers are those that you can concisely state and defend. Many issues with which museum administrators must deal, and the appropriate response to them, will depend upon the circumstances under which they arise. No answer will work in every situation. Readers are to learn to think analytically, develop their basic administrative philosophy, and be able to state the issues and their proposed courses of action succinctly. And when needed, do more research, read more books and articles, and learn from you peers.

Exercises, as their title implies, will provide readers an opportunity to practice preparing documents, statements, and policies they will need in administrative positions. Each chapter concludes with Guiding Questions, good for both classroom and break room discussions. For professors, the Appendix includes the framework for a semester-long classroom exercise you may consider using with your classes.

To add texture and currency to this edition and to verify current trends in the field, I conducted over forty interviews with colleagues working in museums as employees and consultants, or as museum association affiliates. I am grateful for their talent and the time they gave to answer my questions. They are Katie Anderson, Tanya Andrews, Dina Bailey, Eloise Batic, Bob Beatty, Jenny Benjamin, Niki Ciccotelli Stewart, Anita Durel, Steve Elliot, Janet Gallimore, Jim Gardner, Brenda Granger, Andrea Grover, Jackie Hoff, David Janssen, Trevor Jones, Sean Kelley, Janice Klein, Wade Lawrence, Amy Lent, Allyn Lord, Wyona Lynch-McWhite, Kate Marks, Tonya Matthews, Nicolette Meister, Hassan Najjar, Trina Nelson Thomas, Carl Nold, Sarah Pharaon, Alex Rasic, Faith Revell, Nathan Richie, Cynthia Robinson, Ellen Rosenthal, Jill Rudnitski, Deborah Schwartz, Lauren Silberman, Janet Stoffer, Scott Stroh, Robert Trio, Janet Vaughan, Tobi Voigt, Phyllis Wahahrockhah-Tasi, and Larry Yerdon.

A special thank you goes to Hugh and Lynne whose original work I revised and updated for a new generation of administrators. The organization of their book and the advice contained within are evident in this edition. They've also made contributions to this edition, which I have credited when appropriate. And also thank you to Charles Harmon with Rowman and Littlefield and to, again, Bob Beatty with the American Association for State and Local History who have helped me make tough decisions for this second edition.

With this revision, my intent is to provide updates and enhancements that broaden the presentation and make it current. The chapters are organized with a "first things first" mentality combined with the priority of work that top-level museum administrators will encounter. For example, the COO of a large museum will likely spend more time working with finances and legal issues before she would be knee deep in collections care. That's not to say that no one is working in collections care or that collections aren't at the core of museum work, but it's more likely that a registrar, collections manager, or curator will have the lead on those improvements and issues and will work it up the administrative channels when needed.

The book uses director, executive director, president/CEO, and CEO interchangeably. All of those titles are possible names for museum leaders. Administration is certainly not limited to those title holders. Hopefully, whether you work in the collections division or facilities management division and you have administrative duties, this book will be relevant. I've also taken great pains to make sure small museums are represented alongside larger museum examples, and that that ideas and solutions offered may be scaled to any size of board, staff, volunteer base, and community.

A great debt of thanks goes to the numerous museum and nonprofit professionals and friends who have inspired me to do my best work and helped me "see the way" many a time. My late mentor, Margaret "Peggy" Hoffman, is at the top of every gratitude list I write. She is soon followed by a list of other great people who have pushed me to be the best human and museum professional possible: Sandy Alter, Tanya Andrews, Bob Beatty, Jamie Bissonette Lewey, Sal Cilella, Ted Donosky, Anita and John Durel, Tim Grove, Kitty Haffner, Kim Harty, Cathy Fields, Chris Fogg, Nancy Johnson, Cheryl Keim, Stacy Klingler, Fran Levine, Tony Loudermilk, Kate Marks, Rebecca Martin, Tonya Matthews, Evelyn Murphy, Trina Nelson Thomas, Bonnie Newsom, Carl Nold, Dennis O'Toole, Dale Petrie, Darren Ranco, Alex Rasic, Susan Reed, Nathan Richie, Laura Roberts, Donna Sack, Dean Smoll, Gail Stephens, Scott Stroh, Kristen Watson, Sandy Wilcox, and the incredible team at the Abbe Museum. I'm so lucky to know you.

Cinnamon Catlin-Legutko
Mount Desert Island, Maine
March 12, 2016

NOTE

1. Rosenthal, interview.

❶

MUSEUMS AND ADMINISTRATION

Imagine the graduate student or even the high school student, dreaming of the day she becomes an administrator. While administration is not your typical career goal, it is easy to imagine a student dreaming of leadership and increasing responsibility as she moves up in seniority at the museum of her dreams. As careers develop, administrative duties will always become a growing realm of responsibility. And the smaller the museum, the more likely administration and a list of other duties (education! collections care! facilities management! cleaning bathrooms!) will land on the work plate.

Anyone seeking a professional position within a museum must expect that a certain amount of time will be devoted to administrative duties. Even the smallest project will involve a plan of work, the assignment of someone to do it, and a budget to pay for it. The manager of that project will be expected to see the work done, done well, on time, and within the confines of the allotted budget. The office manager procuring and maintaining supplies for use by the staff; the staff artist determining the need for, purchasing, and monitoring use of materials for museum exhibitions; the registrar negotiating a loan; the educator scheduling volunteer docents—may be functioning as administrators.

So this book is not just for museum directors or department heads, but for all members of the museum staff who have administrative duties. (And that's just about everyone.) Although originally conceived as a textbook for graduate students in museum studies, this book will help museum staff members just entering the profession or moving ahead in their careers.

Yes, that is correct! If "moving ahead" or "moving up" is the museum career plan, it's the expectation that administrative duties increase and the amount of time devoted to these responsibilities will increase as well. Anyone entering the museum profession (or for that matter any profession) should expect a career filled with ever-increasing administrative and management duties. It is important to study and to improve administrative skills, as well as museum knowledge, throughout a museum career. Many people reach a plateau in their professional development beyond which they are not able to succeed; most often this involves some failure in administrative responsibilities because the person has not adequately developed the skills the position requires.

Rochelle Steiner, currently professor of Critical Studies at the University of Southern California Roski School of Art and Design, has deliberately pursued an administrative career path. "After many years as a curator, including roles that included management of junior staff, budgets, contracts, and commissioning, I took the role of chief curator and then the directorship of a small not-for-profit and then the dean of an art school. I found that as much as I love working with artists, I also excel with administration—and actually enjoy it as critical to the support of artists."[1] Janet Gallimore, executive director of the Idaho State Historical Society, even gushes a bit when asked why she chose museum administration: "I love administration. It is gratifying to consider how all of the unique elements of a museum—from collections stewardship, to audience development, to strategy can be brought to bear synergistically to deliver results and value to the public."

Although written centuries before museums developed as the institutions we know today, Chaucer's observation is apt: "The life so short, the craft so long to learn." Hopefully this book will serve as a starting point for a long life of learning about how to make museums work.

WHAT IS ADMINISTRATION?

"Administration" comes from the Latin *administrationem*, "aid, help, cooperation, direction, management." "Manage" has as its root the word, *manus*, or hand. It seems fitting to us that administration and management are fundamentally "hands-on" words, because making things happen is what administration and management are all about. To administer is "to help, assist; manage, control, guide, superintend; rule, direct,"[2] and it is this responsibility and authority that makes administration satisfying, worthwhile, and even fun. Museum administrators make choices, developing and executing plans so that museum collections can be preserved and so that museum visitors can have compelling experiences with the artifacts and specimens from those collections. A far cry from the mere paper-pushing that gives administration a bad name.

That's not to say that putting things in writing isn't important. In fact, the preparation of plans and documents is a major component of the museum administrators' purview. Creation of a mission statement and a strategic plan are the most vital; these two documents define the museum's niche in both the not-for-profit and museum worlds and determine how these roles will be filled. Other guiding documents and policies that must be written (or reviewed and revised if already in existence) and then implemented include:

Bylaws
Articles of incorporation
IRS 501(c)3 or similar status
Code of professional conduct
Organizational chart
Budget and accounting
Policies related to collections management, personnel, facilities, and
    public
Interpretive plans
Development, marketing, and public relations plans

Administration of an organization requires skill in conflict management, interpersonal relations, budget management and monitoring, and staff supervision and evaluation. Managers must also set legal and ethical standards and maintain involvement in the museum profession. Certainly all of these issues are very important, but budget management and staff development should be at the top of the list. Financially sound museums are the only ones that have the opportunity to fulfill their stated missions. Financial stability is no accident, but the result of active budget management. Effective staff development assures the maximum utility of the museum's most important asset, the time, and skills of its staff. The most innovative and exceptional mission statements and strategic plans come to naught if the financial and human resources are not managed well.

What the etymology of administration does not address are the critical elements of leadership and vision, but these are qualities museum administrators, particularly directors, are expected to embody. These are difficult attributes to define and instill, partly because notions of what leadership is and how it should be exercised are shifting. Leadership is no longer perceived as the solitary province of the person "in charge," rather it is exhibited by every staff member who has the ability to institute change, and does so, however minor that change might be. Similarly, visionary institutions are those that have found new mechanisms for community involvement and ownership, over those that have merely realized some particular project. Another meaning of administration's Latin root *ministere* is "to serve"; visionary leadership in museums in the twenty-first century is revealed by an institution-wide commitment to this fundamental meaning.

Strategic planning is one way to move the discussion of leadership and vision from the ethereal to the concrete. A bottom-up process that engages a broad representation of museum audience, supporters, staff and board can develop a common, vibrant vision for the museum. This shared vision guides the museum administrator's leadership and informs the work of administrators throughout the organization.

WHAT IS A MUSEUM?

The American Alliance of Museums (AAM) broadly defines what a museum is: "a museum (is) organized for educational and aesthetic purposes . . . and it owns and uses tangible objects and exhibits these objects on a regular basis through facilities it owns or operates."[3] AAM's membership is open to all museum types—nonprofit and for profit, virtual and location-based—and their museum definition aligns closely with the Institute for Museum and Library Services (IMLS) definition.[4] Per IMLS, a Federal agency, a museum uses "a professional staff, is organized on a permanent basis for essentially educational or aesthetic purposes; owns or uses tangible objects, either animate or inanimate; cares for these objects; and exhibits these objects to the general public on a regular basis (at least 120 days a year) through facilities that it owns or operates."[5] For obvious reasons, IMLS further restricts its focus to the fifty states in the United States, territories, and the District of Columbia. The International Council of Museums defines a museum more narrowly. "A museum is a non-profit, permanent institution in the service of society and its development, open to the public, which acquires, conserves, researches, communicates and exhibits the tangible and intangible heritage of humanity and its environment for the purposes of education, study and enjoyment."[6]

Objects are at the core of traditional institutional activities, such as education, collection, preservation, and exhibition. While the AAM and IMLS definitions recognize types of institutions that do not collect, such as art centers, children's museums, nature centers, planetariums, and science and technology centers, as museums, collected objects are typically the defining characteristic of museum. Collecting institutions can be broadly divided into those that hold nonliving collections (art, anthropological, history, and natural history museums) and those that maintain living ones (zoological parks, aquariums, arboreta, and botanical gardens). An alternate approach to museum practice, as demonstrated by science centers and children's museums place people at the core of museum practices, using objects to engage visitors in the mission.

Expanding technology is raising new questions about what constitutes a collection, and whether "objects" can exist solely in electronic form. Museum professionals differ on their opinions of how museums should be defined and why; funders have to determine grant eligibility based on their organizing principles or legislation. At their core, twenty-first century museums are focused on their communities, educational value, and their audiences, guided by their individual mission and purpose.

Text Box 1.1 Case Review: What's in a Name?

The museum definitions presented by AAM and IMLS differ from ICOM's in that AAM and IMLS include noncollecting organizations, such as nature centers and science centers. This aligns with the belief that the primary characteristic of the modern museum is its educational function using objects in hands-on, active, or inquiry-based programs.

If noncollecting museums can fall under these definitions, can a "museum" be extended to include nonexhibiting institutions as well? If "education using objects" is the most important issue, why is "exhibits open to the public on a regular basis" a critical defining characteristic? Can museums be educational without exhibits? Is the more narrow ICOM definition more appropriate?

We see virtual museums appearing online, which exist without a physical location. Do these institutions have "collections"? Do online images qualify as exhibits? They are certainly available to the public on a regular basis. Should these organizations be considered museums? Many are definitely trying to educate the public.

(continued)

Text Box 1.1 Case Review: What's in a Name? (continued)

Some university-based natural history museums have major collections of specimens and artifacts, but they do not have exhibits that are open to the public on a regular basis. This may make them ineligible for funding from IMLS. However, they use the specimens in their collections for educational purposes in a variety of other ways. Research based on the study of these collections is published, adding to the total body of knowledge of humankind. This new knowledge informs a wide variety of educational programs, including the programs of other museums. The specimens and artifacts are used in classroom and laboratory education, which is hands-on, active, formal education at the undergraduate or graduate levels. These museums also provide educational opportunities through tours of the collections; staff answer inquiries from the public, write popular and semipopular articles and books, and present public lectures. Should exhibition of collections on a regular basis be the critical factor to determine eligibility?

Take a moment and visit the following websites. How do you think "museums" should be defined?

VIRTUAL MUSEUMS

1. Trans-Mississippi Theater Virtual Museum
   civilwarvirtualmuseum.org
2. The Virtual Diego Rivera Web Museum
   www.diegorivera.com
3. The Food Museum
   www.foodmuseum.com

UNIVERSITY MUSEUMS

1. Museum of Southwestern Biology, University of New Mexico
   msb.unm.edu
2. Biodiversity Research and Teaching Collections, Texas A&M University
   brtc.tamu.edu
3. Museum of Vertebrate Zoology, University of California, Berkeley.
   mvz.berkeley.edu

All sites accessed November 14, 2015.

TYPES OF MUSEUMS

Museums holding nonliving collections can be divided into categories based upon such criteria as users, disciplinary focus areas, parent organizations, and governance structure. Children's museums are defined primarily by their principal users—children. Disciplinary emphases identify art, anthropology, history, natural history or science museums, and historic sites and houses. Many museums are classified as general museums because of the breadth of their collections and programs, whereas others are considered specialty museums because of their narrow focus on particular topics, like halls of fame, sports, automobile, and technology museums. Institutions with living collections that are considered museums include aquaria, arboreta, botanical gardens, and zoos.

Many museums are operated by a variety of government entities, including federal, state, county, and city units. Universities and colleges operate another large group of museums. Some museums are operated by for-profit companies, often through a nonprofit subdivision. Another large group of museums is operated by parent not-for-profit societies and organizations. Museums operated by historical and zoological societies fall in this category. Finally, there are museums operated as nonprofit organizations by freestanding, often self-perpetuating, boards of trustees.

In reading museum literature, one will often see references to "public" museums or "private" museums. These terms are sometimes mistakenly thought to refer to the funding sources for museums, but in reality they distinguish the type of governance of the museum and the parent organization, if there is one. Public museums are under the control of public or governmental entities, such as federal or state agencies, public universities, county government, or city parks departments. Private museums are under the control of private boards or private companies. Generally, public museums receive the majority of their funding from public sources—for example, federal, state, or county budgets. Private museums generally receive the majority of their funds from private sources, such as corporations, endowment returns, and individual contributions. Yet public museums may receive some funds from endowment returns or funds raised from private individuals, and private museums may receive public funds from government grants or direct budgetary allocations from a governmental entity. Finally, both public and private museums can earn income from entrance fees, museum stores, educational programs, or many other sources. Regardless of category, almost all museums exist for some public purpose. But the somewhat confusing terms public and private will be often seen in museum literature.

THE MUSEUM PROFESSION

Although we talk about "the museum profession," there is not uniform concurrence that such a beast exists. The controversy extends back at least as far as the 1930s. Alexander Ruthven, museum director at the University of Michigan, wrote, "A museum man is a professional zoologist, botanist, geologist, archaeologist, business man, teacher, editor, taxidermist, or some other kind of specialist, working in a museum and having a knowledge of methods of gathering, preserving, demonstrating, and otherwise using data which should be saved. He cannot be a professional museum man, for his institution can only serve the world through the efforts of specialists, in particular fields of knowledge."[7] Albert Parr, director of the American Museum of Natural History, echoed these same ideas in the 1950s and 1960s.[8]

Laurence Coleman countered this idea in *The Museum in America* (1939), arguing that museum work was a discipline of its own.[9] Later, Edward Alexander also supported this idea in his 1979 *Museums in Motion*: "The paramount essence of the museum profession is a common cause and goals."[10] (The same sentiment continues in the 2008 updated version by his daughter Mary Alexander.) Even into the late 1980s, Stephen Weil questioned the existence of a museum profession: "Some believe that American museum workers have already succeeded in achieving this status. Others doubt that they ever can. . . . I think that almost everybody, however, would agree that many important improvements in American museums themselves have come about as a by-product of this struggle by museum workers to gain professional identification."[11] Victor Danilov, after citing the pundits above, concluded in 1994, "Museum work may or may not be looked upon as a profession, depending upon one's interpretation, but there appears to be little doubt that many aspects of museum work are professional in nature and require specialized training and experience."[12]

The belief that there is a museum profession and that this profession initially can be identified by its adherence to a common set of values is described in chapter 10. There is a diverse range of specialists who work in museums and reflect equally diverse backgrounds and training. But if standards are applied that define a profession in conjunction with these common values, the shape and existence of the museum profession becomes obvious.[13]

Eileen Hoffman, in Danilov's book, suggests several standards that define a profession. The first is "intellectual activities after long, specialized education and training."[14] Everyone would agree that museum work is essentially intellectual, but is there uniformity of training? An expanding number of museum studies and related programs provide long, specialized training for an increasing number of the people entering the museum profession. Some individuals still take a discipline-based route into the museum profession and adhere to the common values of their particular specialization; they just happen to be performing their work in a museum environment. Thus it can be concluded that not all people working in museums (even some who have been employed by museums for long periods of time) are members of the museum profession.

Hoffman's second criterion is that the work of a profession is service-oriented and not for personal gain. This is the essence of museum work and clearly the basis for the common values of the museum profession. The third marker of a profession is that it "sets its own standards, adopts a code of ethics, and has a strong closely-knit professional organization."[15] The activities of the AAM surely have set the standards for the profession through peer- and self-assessment programs and accreditation of museums. And the field has accomplished the third criteria by developing a broad system of museum best practices along with its professional organizational peers such as the American Association for State and Local History (AASLH), Association of Art Museum Directors (AAMD), and more.

"Such controversy notwithstanding, a professional structure is now in place with national and international representation, numbering thousands of institutions and individuals who communicate regularly among themselves through publications and programs and it has resulted in a de facto profession."[16] The museum profession may still be considered young, but it is well established and there will be no returning to the preprofessional days.

ACADEMIC PROGRAMS

Museum professionals are coming into the field through a variety of academic programs on the undergraduate and graduate level. Graduate work is possible in historic preservation, history, anthropology, archaeology, archives management, animal husbandry, natural history, science, biology, Native American studies, and even further afield. For example, a development professional may bring to the museum job an English degree. Or, a CEO's background includes an MBA and an exhibit fabricator holds an MFA. While the museum team may collectively hold a variety of training backgrounds, adherence to the mission and purpose of the museum will help the team gel and use its assets to benefit the museum.

Museum Studies

"Museum studies" refers to academic programs designed to prepare students for professional positions within museums. Museum studies programs include applied history, arts management, collections management, museum education, conservation, decorative arts, historical administration, historic preservation, nonprofit management, public administration, public affairs, public history, and public horticulture. Most museum studies programs offer MA or MS degrees, although there are at least six institutions in the United States that offer programs at the baccalaureate level. There are no doctoral-level programs in museum studies in the United States, but there are some in the associated areas of public history, preservation studies, and arts administration. Some institutions offer only a few courses in museum studies, while others provide minors in museum studies as part of a degree in a subject-matter discipline. Certificate programs are another option. These are generally one or two years in length and are usually taken in conjunction with, or following, another graduate degree.

AAM's website lists 150 museums studies or related programs, in nearly forty states. And there are eight in other countries.[17] While a solid understanding of theory, hands-on practice, and other coursework is essential, there is no substitute for experience. In the past, the primary path into the museum profession was not academic; individuals with disciplinary expertise would be hired by museums and allowed "to work their way up through the organization," learning the profession as they progressed in their careers. This system has developed many excellent professionals who are leading world-class museums today. The prime benefit to be seen from museum studies programs is that they can greatly reduce the time it takes to learn the basics of the museum profession—from eight to ten years of on-the-job learning down to approximately two years in a program. Of course classroom work cannot replace real-world experience, which academic programs help provide by requiring three- to six-month museum internships for their students.

Museum historian Edward Alexander notes the roots of museum studies programs extend back as far as 1908–1910, when three programs were initiated. Sarah Stevenson started a high school diploma program at the Philadelphia Museum of Art to prepare students for work in art museums. At the Farnsworth Museum at Wellesley College, Myrtilla Avery started a course combining museum and art library skills. At the University of Iowa, Professor Homer Dill began a program that resulted in a minor in museum studies to go with a four-year degree in natural science. This program included taxidermy, exhibit techniques, freehand drawing, and modeling. Of these three programs, only the one at the University of Iowa survives today.[18]

John Cotton Dana and Paul J. Sachs started two famous early museum training programs. Dana's at the Newark Museum provided a year of apprenticeship for groups of post-baccalaureate students who were given lectures in addition to work in various programs within the museum. Sachs's one-year graduate program at Harvard University combined course work in museum studies and art history with experience at the Fogg Art Museum.[19]

Following World War II, there was slow development of museum studies programs in the 1950s and 1960s, but the 1970s saw explosive growth in new programs, mirroring the eruption of new museums nationwide. The majority of today's academic training programs in museum studies had their origins between 1970 and 1979. New programs have continued to appear, indicating a bright future for this developing academic field and reflecting a continuing and expanding need for trained museum professionals.

Public History

Many individuals looking to enter the field of public history pursue a graduate degree, and can choose from at last count more than seventy graduate programs in the United States.[20] The National Council on Public History (NCPH) is located in Indianapolis, Indiana, and is "dedicated to making the past useful in the present and to encourage collaboration between historians and their publics."[21] NCPH defines public history as "the many and diverse ways in which history is put to work in the field." Individuals working in public history may be "historical consultants, museum professionals, government historians, archivists, oral historians, cultural resource managers, curators . . . historic preservationists, policy advisors," and more.[22]

Archival Education

The Society of American Archivists (SAA) has approved guidelines for a graduate program in archival studies. With these guidelines, SAA "endorses the development of coherent and independent graduate programs in archival studies."[23] Across the United States there are more than forty colleges and universities that are providing archival academic training, both housed in library sciences programs and the broader academic community. These programs offer certificates and minors or majors with MA, MS, and PhD degrees through such departments as history, public history, and information science.[24]

MUSEUM ASSOCIATIONS

When you enter the museum profession, you are joining a group of national and international members. Museum workers have formed professional associations to share their ideas and further their mutual interests. In the United States, the primary professional museum association is the American Alliance of Museums, located in Arlington, Virginia. AAM holds annual meetings and publishes the magazine *Museum,* covering current issues in the profession; *Aviso,* an electronic newsletter that carries notices, career opportunities, and service advertisements; specific "how-to" guides and research; and books on museum issues. AAM advocates for national issues that further the interests of museums and museum professionals and offers continuing education through its workshop series. The Alliance's Accreditation Commission sets "the gold standard" and grants accreditation to museums that meet its rigorous criteria. And it fosters the Center for the Future of Museums, which publishes an annual *TrendsWatch* report that is useful for museum strategic planning efforts.

The Council of Affiliates of the AAM is a group of more than two dozen other museum-related associations, generally representing more specialized groups of museums and interests. These affiliates are a "source of information in policy deliberations that may have impact beyond the Alliance's immediate membership." Professional staff members working in these areas will find advantages in joining the appropriate associations.

- American Association for Museum Volunteers
- American Association for State and Local History
- American Federation of the Arts
- American Institute for Conservation of Historic and Artistic Works
- American Public Gardens Association
- Association for Living History, Farm, and Agricultural Museums
- Association of Academic Museums and Galleries
- Association of African American Museums
- Association of Art Museum Directors
- Association of Children's Museums
- Association of Tourist Railroads and Railway Museums
- Association of Science Museum Directors
- Association of Science-Technology Centers
- Association of Zoos and Aquariums
- College Art Association
- Council for Museum Anthropology

- Council of American Jewish Museums
- Council of American Maritime Museums
- International Association of Museum Facility Administrators
- International Museum Theatre Alliance
- Museum Computer Network
- Museum Education Roundtable
- Museum Store Association
- Museum Trustee Association
- National Association for Interpretation
- Natural Science Collections Alliance
- Society for the Preservation of Natural History Collections[25]

To further serve its members and strengthen the museum field, AAM has organized twenty-two Professional Networks (formerly known as Standing Professional Committees) around job responsibilities and common interests. Some of the networks offer fellowships, awards, and funding opportunities, while others are more focused on formalizing a professional network of colleagues and institutions. These committees offer an excellent opportunity for new professionals to be involved in "the museum business." The following list and descriptions are borrowed from the AAM website:

- Asian Pacific American: the study, discussion and presentation of Asian Pacific American issues through museums
- CARE: audience research and evaluation and the voice of the visitor in all aspects of museum operations
- COMPT: professional preparation, training, and development of museum staff
- CURCOM: curatorial practice and collections research, care, and exhibition
- DAM: development, fundraising, and membership
- DIVCOM: the advancement of diversity and inclusion
- EDCOM: the advancement and understanding of learning theories, educational practices, and programming
- Historic House Museums: issues common and unique to historic houses
- Indigenous Peoples Museum Network: fosters engaging and inclusive dialogue on the range of issues relevant to museums and indigenous peoples
- Latino: for the needs of Latino and Latin American professionals and the interests of those professionals who work in interpreting Latino issues

- Leadership and Management: leadership, governance, administration, finance, and human resources.
- LGBTQ Alliance: the range of issues relevant to the lesbian, gay, bisexual, transgender community and museums
- Media and Technology: use of media and technology to meet museum's public mission
- NAME: exhibit development and design
- PACCIN: proper care, handling, packing, crating, and transporting of museum collections
- PIC Green: environmental sustainable practices in museums
- PRAM: public relations and marketing
- Registrars: registration and collections management
- Security: security, fire, health, and safety issues
- SMAC: the advancement of small museums
- Traveling Exhibitions: the specialized area of traveling exhibitions
- Visitor Services: making service to visitors a core component of museum operations[26]

In addition to this national alliance, there are regional museums associations across the United States that support museums in similar ways. These associations hold annual meetings and produce newsletters with job notices and technical information. The regional associations also sponsor professional development workshops.

- Association of Midwest Museums (Illinois, Indiana, Iowa, Michigan, Minnesota, Missouri, Ohio, Wisconsin);
- Mid-Atlantic Association of Museums (Delaware, District of Columbia, Maryland, New Jersey, New York, Pennsylvania);
- Mountain-Plains Museums Association (Colorado, Kansas, Montana, Nebraska, New Mexico, North Dakota, Oklahoma, South Dakota, Texas, Wyoming);
- New England Museums Association (Connecticut, Maine, Massachusetts, New Hampshire, Rhode Island, Vermont);
- Southeastern Museums Conference (Alabama, Arkansas, Florida, Georgia, Kentucky, Louisiana, Mississippi, North Carolina, South Carolina, Tennessee, Virginia, West Virginia, Puerto Rico, and U.S. Virgin Islands); and
- Western Museums Association (Alaska, Arizona, California, Hawaii, Idaho, Nevada, Oregon, Utah, Washington, the western provinces of Alberta and British Columbia, and the Pacific Islands).

Nearly every state has its own state museum association. Their programs vary greatly, but they all offer an excellent opportunity for new museum professionals to become involved in the museum community.

The American Association for State and Local History (AASLH) is another very important museum-related organization. This nonprofit professional organization of individuals and institutions has the mission to provide "leadership and support for its members who preserve and interpret state and local history in order to make the past more meaningful to all Americans." Based in Nashville, Tennessee, AASLH encourages the highest quality expressions of state and local history through publications, exhibits, public programs, and professional development activities. The AASLH publishes *History News*, a quarterly magazine that includes practical how-to information and in-depth professional articles; *Dispatch*, a monthly electronic newsletter that reports on training programs, exhibitions, publications, and career opportunities; and *Technical Leaflets*, practical instructional guides for museum tasks from constructing exhibit mounts to the proper storage of photographs and documents. The organization also publishes books of interest to the profession in partnership with Rowman & Littlefield (this book is a product of this partnership). AASLH offers quality workshops at sites around the country and online, holds annual meetings, offers scholarships, advocates for museums and historical organizations, and co-produces the Seminar for Historical Administration, a top-flight leadership training program. It is also known for two signature programs, Visitors Count!, a visitor research program, and StEPS, a standards and excellence program for history organization, which dovetails with AAM's best practices and standards program. StEPS's distinguishing characteristic is that it is an incremental, self-paced excellence program designed solely for small- to mid-sized museums.[27]

Institutions with living collections are represented by two major organizations in North America. Established in 1924, the Association of Zoos and Aquariums (AZA) "provides its members with the services, high standards, best practices and program coordination to be leaders in animal welfare, public engagement, and the conservation of species." AZA has adopted conservation of the world's wildlife and their habitats as its highest priority. Accreditation of institutions was enacted on a voluntary basis in 1972; today, all institutional members must be accredited by the AZA. In addition, members pledge to follow the Code of Professional Ethics that was adopted in 1976. AZA offices in Silver Spring, Maryland, provide the monthly magazine, *Connect*, as well as communication materials designed to support the conservation goals of its members.[28]

The American Public Gardens Association (APGA), based in Kennett Square, Pennsylvania, is the professional association for public gardens and arboreta in North America. It publishes a monthly newsletter and the quarterly journal, *Public Garden*, and sponsors regional and national conferences each year.[29]

The Society of American Archivists (SAA) is the oldest (founded in 1936) and largest national professional association for archivists. The SAA publishes a semiannual journal, *The American Archivist*, a bimonthly newsletter, *Archival Outlook*, and books on a variety of archival topics. It sponsors an annual meeting, workshops, and continuing education opportunities.[30]

The International Council of Museums (ICOM), based in Paris, France, represents the international museum profession. ICOM publishes *Museum International* and has working groups focused on museum careers and global issues. ICOM and AAM have a joint committee to conduct business of mutual interest; regional and national museum associations in every part of the globe partner similarly with ICOM.[31]

IT'S ONLY AN INTRODUCTION

As the listing of definitions, issues, and resources illustrate, everyone entering the world of museum administration is becoming part of a complex profession. So even with a dozen chapters, this text is only an introduction. Readers will recognize after a quick glance at the topics covered that each of them has been the subjects of hundreds, and in many cases thousands, of books. Marketing, public relations, accounting, budgeting, personnel management, interpersonal relations, and the law—these are the focus of entire professions. People devote whole careers to understanding and contributing to each of these fields. So it is inevitable that the discussions here are merely "introductions" to the many topics museum administration touches in some way.

What does the inclusion of all of the disparate subjects in this text mean? In order to function effectively in their positions, museum administrators need to develop basic skills in all these areas. "Jack-of-all-trades, but a master of none" may be an apt description of many neophyte museum administrators, but the authors believe that after reading the book, working through the many discussions, exercises, and case studies found throughout, the reader will be on her way to a career as a museum administrator. She will have entered the "novice class."

To move closer to "master of some," read most or all of the references cited and become familiar with museum publications. Familiarity with these resources, when coupled with actual museum experience, will enable the reader to pass from "novice" in administration to the intermediate level.

Besides basic mastery of the facts and concepts of these professional areas, museum administrators, particularly museum directors, must set ethical standards and must be capable of giving the museum a vision and displaying leadership. How does one become a visionary and a leader? These can be intangible qualities. Chapter 6 introduces a framework for developing leadership skills, but it only scratches the surface on the publications and techniques that help one become a leader. Ultimately, experience is the great teacher.

At least ten years of administrative experience is needed to reach the level of "expert" in museum administration, and several of these years should be served as a museum director (or major department head in larger institutions). What's so challenging about museum administrative positions that such a long preparation and contemplation period is needed for mastery? The authors believe that these positions are some of the most complex jobs in the nonprofit sector.

One of the greatest challenges faced by museum administrators is matching expectations with resources. The director, and in turn the middle managers in the museum, will be faced with the sizable and sometimes contradictory expectations of the board, staff, and the public. Given the skills of the staff and the funds provided by the board, which probably were raised from the community, are there enough resources to meet the expectations? Is there a shared vision of what these resources will produce?

It is the responsibility of the director and other museum managers to plan, organize, and bring to bear all of the skills of the staff to accomplish the task, whatever it may be. Many museum tasks require teamwork among groups of staff. "Team building is among the key leadership tasks. The essence of team building is establishing a balance of skills and competencies; agreeing on common aims; and fostering creative discussion."[32] Individual egos and the need for individual recognition must be put aside, so that the success of the team and the museum becomes the ultimate goal. Teamwork is not easy under the best of circumstances and is even more difficult under the pressure of understaffing, funding shortages, and tight time schedules. Chapter 6 also offers ideas on how to develop a great museum team.

These circumstances, combined with the high and possibly conflicting expectations of museum constituents, make museum positions quite stressful, especially for managers and directors. The "burnout" rate is fairly high and the average length of service of a museum director in a position is less than four years. Given the long time period that goes into making many museum projects reality, such turnover creates considerable instability. Stress is hazardous when you do not deal with it openly and constructively; skills in stress management must be added to all of the other skills museum administrators need to learn.

Continuing education is also a fact of life for museum administrators and can be obtained through such programs as the previously mentioned Seminar for Historical Administration at the Indiana Historical Society; Museum Leadership Institute held at the Claremont Graduate University and supported by the Getty Leadership Institute; the 21st Century Museum Leadership Seminar led and supported by The George Washington University and Smithsonian Affiliations; the American Law Institute-Continuing Legal Education (ALI-CLE) annual "Legal Issues in Museum Administration" course; Bank Street Leadership in Museum Education courses; or the Campbell Center in Mt. Carroll, Illinois, among others. National organizations regularly sponsor workshops and webinars on administration topics. Not only do these programs provide continuing study, but they allow for contemplation and discussions with professional colleagues. And they provide an important opportunity to recharge batteries run low by the challenges of museum administration.

CONCLUSION

This introductory chapter has shared some of the challenges facing museum administrators and the wide range of knowledge and experience museum workers need, but it's also offered a sampling of resources available to help museum professionals acquire the mental equipment to respond effectively to the changing museum environment. Museum work right now is as filled with promise as it is fraught with problems. No matter what position in a museum, each staff member will be expected to perform some administrative duties, and every day presents another set of opportunities to make something happen.

Museum administration may be overwhelming, but take it from the authors—in their combined eighty years of experience in museum administration, they have been aggravated, consternated, exhilarated, frustrated, and stimulated, but they have never been bored. Perhaps that's because at the base of it all, beneath the budgets and the charts and the legalities, is their belief in the power of objects to affect the people who interact with them. This remarkable relationship between people and the objects in which they find meaning is why museums exist, and it is made possible by effective museum administration.

Please use this book as quick reference, inspiration during challenging times, and a jumping off point to dig into deeper and more complex topics. Good luck following the path to museum administration!

Text Box 1.2 Guiding Questions

1. In what ways has the museum field changed in the past fifteen to twenty years?
2. How have you charted a career path in the museum field? If you didn't, and you've "fallen" into it, what resources have helped you get up to speed?
3. Keeping in mind that many levels of museum positions can demonstrate and/or exercise leadership (not just those at the top), why would you choose to lead? Or, why not?

NOTES

1. Steiner, interview.
2. Harper, "Administration."
3. American Alliance of Museums.
4. Vaughan, interview.
5. Institute for Museums and Library Services.
6. International Council of Museums.
7. Ruthven, *A Naturalist*; Danilov, *Museum Careers*, 26.
8. Parr, ". . . Museum Profession?"
9. Coleman, *Museum in America*, 418.
10. Alexander and Alexander, *Museums in Motion*.
11. Weil, "Ongoing Pursuit," 31.
12. Danilov, *Museum Careers*, 15.
13. Ibid., 12.
14. Ibid.
15. Ibid.
16. Hein, *Museum in Transition*, 41.
17. American Alliance of Museums.
18. Alexander and Alexander, *Museums in Motion*.
19. Alexander, *Museum in America*, 212.
20. National Council for Public History.

21. Ibid.
22. Ibid.
23. Society for American Archivists.
24. Ibid.
25. American Alliance of Museums.
26. Ibid.
27. American Association for State and Local History.
28. Association of Zoos and Aquariums.
29. American Public Garden Association.
30. Society for American Archivists.
31. International Council of Museums.
32. Fleming, "Leadership," 98.

2

START UP

Museums' traditional purposes are to collect and preserve all manner of human-made artifacts and natural specimens (living and nonliving), and to exhibit, interpret, and educate in order to expand our knowledge about ourselves, our society, and our world. It is the aim of museums to be a resource for humankind and to foster an informed appreciation of our diverse world. And museums are about respect. Respect for the real, the authentic. Museum work demonstrates the "respect for the things we decide are worth making a part of humanity's heritage."[1] 'Many types of museums today, although diverse in their individual missions, have in common a commitment to education and public service.

Creating a new museum or improving an existing one is a complex process requiring a clear sense of purpose and compliance with state and federal regulations. The organizers and promoters of a new museum must take time for careful planning because decisions made in the initial stages will determine the future operations of the museum and the success of its programs and activities. And in the era of shrinking resources and public demands, the need for a new museum must be considered.

Best advice to a group seeking to form a new museum? Don't! A survey of museum leaders concludes there are few reasons new museums should form. Amy Lent, executive director of the Maine Maritime Museum explains, "There are already far too many museums and too many of them are underfunded, understaffed, don't have strong boards and don't have a compelling case or an engaged audience. I am having a hard time imagining a situation in which it would be a good idea for a new museum to form, rather than direct those resources (collections, financial support, leadership) to an existing institution. A fewer number of stronger institutions is preferable to a multitude of weak organizations."[2] A museum should form only when a community can specify the need for it and plan a solid business model for its sustainability.[3] Lauren Silberman, deputy director of Historic London Town and Gardens in Edgewater, Maryland, sums up the issue in a perfect analogy: "There's an old tradition that you are supposed to ask a Rabbi three times before you can convert to Judaism. [This] is to discourage someone considering conversion superficially, since Judaism is not an evangelical religion. I think that forming a museum should follow the same tradition. Don't do it unless you've explored every other option first. And then don't do it until you explore those options again and start looking at how to make this idea truly permanent. And then maybe think about it one more time. Creating a sustainable museum is not impossible, but it's pretty darn close."[4]

Whether a brand new museum or one that has been in operation for decades, all museums need a well-defined mission statement, written bylaws, articles of incorporation, and IRS tax-exempt status. In addition, the museum should be mindful of museum best practices and have a plan to embrace them.

MISSION STATEMENT

Wyona Lynch-McWhite, executive director of the Fruitlands Museum in Harvard, Massachusetts, believes that a mission statement is an institutional promise made to the public. Formed through discussions with internal and external focus groups, Fruitlands' mission is "to inspire and educate through the heritage, nature, and art of New England."[5]

Mission statements can also express a cause and a call to action, notes Scott M. Stroh III, executive director of George Mason's Gunston Hall in Mason Neck, Virginia. With the mission "to utilize fully the physical and scholarly resources of Gunston Hall to stimulate continuing public exploration of democratic ideals as first presented by George Mason in the 1776 Virginia Declaration of Rights," Gunston Hall clearly articulates its operational purpose and indicates how the visitor can engage with the historic site.[6]

The American Alliance of Museums (AAM) considers the mission statement one of the five core documents that define a museum. Many funding agencies, including the Institute for Museum and Library Services

(IMLS), evaluate museums on the effectiveness with which they fulfill their mission. "A mission statement is the beating heart of a museum. It articulates the museum's educational focus and purpose and its role and responsibility to the public and its collections."[7] A mission statement can prove useful not only in defining a museum but also in guiding marketing, publicity, and fundraising. The statement may be printed on museum publications—from letterhead and business cards to brochures and catalogues—or it may become part of advertising such as appearing as a bottom line on publicity materials.[8] A museum's mission becomes its words to live by, benefiting the organization by focusing and inspiring employees, board, and visitors.

As Gail Anderson correctly observes, a museum must create a well-written statement that conveys the primary purpose of the institution not only to the staff and board, but also to the public.[9] "The mission of a nonprofit organization is more difficult to define than that of a for-profit entity." The mission of a for-profit organization is centered on "profitability, thus the criteria for success includes the bottom line, return on investment, sales, profit margins, and market share," and these easily are calculated. In a nonprofit institution the mission is focused on education and public service, which are more difficult to define and more challenging to measure.[10] For example, how can a museum, which educates the public through exhibits, evaluate its success? A museum may count its number of visitors, but the amount or quality of learning is not so easily quantified.

Development of an effective mission statement depends on creating text that is broad enough to cover the many possible activities in which a museum may wish to engage. This is crucial because laws obligate the board of the museum to limit its activities to those in the mission statement. The mission should be both a broad statement of purpose and a guide for the museum in regard to programs, services, and activities. Although it is necessary to file the statement of purpose with the museum's incorporation papers, this document can be amended by the appropriate legal procedure. Thus, a museum's mission statement is not etched in stone and can be reviewed and revised if necessary.[11]

The responsibility for developing a museum's mission statement resides with the board and the director or executive officer. These leaders may choose to inform staff members of the intent to create or revise the mission statement and invite their input.[12] While the board ultimately has final approval of the mission statement, it is valuable to include input from staff to help clarify the assumptions and desires of those most involved in the museum.

There is no "proper" length for a mission statement, but it should be clear and concise. In some institutions, the mission statements are contained in a single sentence or phrase, for example:

> The mission of The National Center for Civil and Human Rights is to empower people to take the protection of every human's rights personally.[13]
> The Shiloh Museum of Ozark History serves the public by providing resources for finding meaning, enjoyment, and inspiration in the exploration of the Arkansas Ozarks.[14]

Often a mission statement will be accompanied by a vision statement that offers "a snapshot of the organization at a future point, perhaps two to eight years hence."[15] It can be measurable, directed to a specific audience, and/or focused on a specific goal, for example, accreditation. An example of how these two statements relate comes from the Abbe Museum in Bar Harbor, Maine:

> MISSION—To inspire new learning about the Wabanaki Nations with every visit.
> VISION—The Abbe Museum will reflect and realize the values of decolonization in all of its practices, working with the Wabanaki Nations to share their stories, history, and culture with a broader audience.[16]

In some instances, a museum chooses to meld the two into one, making a guiding purpose statement that reflects the museum's identity, but more importantly specifies the type of work it does and what they hope to do. An example of this can be seen at the Homestead Museum in the City of Industry, California:

> Creating advocates for history through the stories of greater Los Angeles. To do this, we concentrate on:
> - the period of 1830 to 1930, mainly the 1840s, 1870s, and 1920s.
> - aspects of everyday life including home, work, and play.
> - the Workman and Temple families in relation to their contemporaries.[17]

While length and format may differ from museum to museum, it is imperative that the contents of the statement follow several guidelines. First, the mission statement must be free of jargon or verbosity, as it will be read not only by the museum's personnel but also by the general public.[18] If the public cannot fully understand and relate to the museum's mission, the mission statement has failed. According to Skramstad and Skramstad, the mission must also include three key elements:[19]

- Action: What does the museum do that is distinctive?
- Outcome: What is the result of this action?
- Value: Why does the action and outcome matter?

And as a matter of operation, the American Alliance of Museums' core document verification process requires that a mission statement must: be educational in scope, describe the institution's unique purpose/focus/role, and be approved by the governing authority.[20]

In the end, the mission should be capable of being realized. A museum is guaranteed to fail if its mission statement cannot be understood, followed, or fulfilled. The mission statement also directly affects how the institution is managed. By setting the priorities for the museum, the mission statement can put the organization on the track for success. The mission statement becomes the most important starting point for a museum, and must be made visible and obvious through public programs. The statement drives a museum by directly spelling out its purpose and serving as the guide for how it will realize those goals. Any given museum *could* do a myriad of things. The mission statement serves to inform board, staff, and the public of what the museum *should* do. Only through careful creation and constant evaluation of its mission statement can a museum not only survive, but thrive.

Text Box 2.1 Case Study: We Are on a Mission

You have just been appointed the assistant director for operations and programs of the International Museum of Indigenous Art in Bettendorf, Iowa. The museum was founded in 1989 with a major donation of African art from Niger, Nigeria, and Benin and an endowment of $10 million bequeathed to the City of Bettendorf. The anonymous donors were presumably from the Quad Cities area, but gave no guidance for the direction of their generous gift. The city has set up the museum as a separate nonprofit organization with a board composed of the mayor, two city council members, four private citizens appointed by the mayor and serving four-year alternating terms, and the mayor of Moline, Illinois as an ex officio member. The staff of the museum is now fifteen people and is anticipated to grow to twenty-five by the year 2018.

On your first day at work the director presents you with a stack of documents including budgets, acquisition policy, collection policy, strategic

(continued)

plan, exhibit schedule, annual schedule of educational programs, and code of professional conduct. On the top of the stack was the museum's mission statement adopted by the board in 2003. You pick up the statement and read:

Mission

The mission of the International Museum of Indigenous Art is to collect, exhibit, and present programming concerning art from around the world, with special emphasis on West Africa, Mexico, and Thailand. The Museum will promote interest and knowledge of Indigenous art through traveling major exhibits throughout the U.S., Canada, and Mexico, loaning of art to private citizens and businesses in the Quad Cities area, and the production of films about Indigenous art and artists. The Museum will further promote Indigenous art by holding at least one event annually that brings artists to the Museum.

You spend the remainder of the week reading the other documents. Finally on Friday you read through the budget. You are shocked to see that the museum has had a budget deficit of over $150,000 the past three years and that money was withdrawn from the principal of the endowment to cover the deficit. The board has capitalized the collections to cover the funds withdrawn from the endowment.

On Friday afternoon, you are meeting with Director Andy Smiley and Assistant Director for Collections and Traveling Exhibits Joe Kool. You aren't five minutes into the meeting when you blurt out, "Do you know that we have been running a budget deficit for the past three years?" Director Smiley replies calmly: "Oh, yes, but that will take care of itself when we get things really rolling around here." "But we are using up the principal of our endowment," you respond in a slightly elevated voice. "We will be putting it back as the money starts to roll in," responds Director Smiley with a knowing nod to Joe Kool. "I have reviewed the budgets and clearly our largest expenses have been for travel and purchase of collections. In fact, they have far exceeded the amount of our deficit each year. Can't we cut back in those areas?"

Mr. Smiley replies with a slightly irritated tone in his voice: "Well, we must collect to carry out our mission. Joe and his wife Reel, our curator of collections, have been traveling to West Africa each year to collect.

They usually spend only about eight weeks. That is all they can handle. It is difficult work, you know. It is clear that our donor expected us to continue to build and fill out our West African collection so we have made that a prime goal of our mission and strategic plan. Board member Councilwoman Mary Mutton has business interests in Thailand and elsewhere in Southeast Asia. She has been willing to collect for us so it seemed only appropriate that we pay her expenses. You know Southeast Asians are one of the fastest growing segment of tourists coming to the United States, so the board decided that it was important to include collecting folk art from Thailand in our scope of collections. We wanted to get started collecting this art before some large metropolitan art museum beats us. And of course we had to send two-person film crews with each of these parties to fulfill part of our educational mission." Finally, totally losing your cool, you shout out, "To hell with the mission statement, mission statements can always be changed, but you can never get back endowment funds that you have spent."

Director Smiley showing his keen insight into staff management, responds: "Well, why don't you rewrite our mission statement so that it better suits our resources? Bring it in at 10 a.m. on Tuesday so that we can review it. We have a board meeting on Thursday. I will introduce you and you can present your ideas for revising our mission statement." Smiley and Kool give each other knowing smiles and slight nods.

1. Revise the mission statement.
2. How will your new mission statement better serve the International Museum of Indigenous Art?
3. How will your new mission statement help cut the budget deficit that your museum is experiencing?
4. What other museum documents and policies should be examined in light of museum's budget deficit?
5. What resistance to changing the mission statement do you expect to have from the staff? Director? Board?
6. How will you defend your belief that the museum's mission statement must be changed?

BYLAWS

"Bylaws are the significant written rules by which a museum is governed."[21] The bylaws define, in procedural detail, the roles and responsibilities of the board of trustees, officers, members, and staff. This document must cover all aspects of the museum's activities in the broadest sense. A museum's tax-exempt status may depend on the bylaws to satisfy legal requirements related to the museum's internal management.

Bylaws take on an added importance during disputes about the way a museum is carrying out its mission or when board members disagree about proper governance procedure. Conflicts, such as dissatisfied board members who attempt to gain control of the board, or a group from outside the organization mounting a legal challenge to the museum, may be resolved by consulting the formal procedures and the rights and powers of trustees and members outlined in the bylaws. Well-written bylaws, when adhered to, will ensure board decisions are fair and will provide protection against legal challenges.

The bylaws document begins with a title and the sections of bylaws are typically titled "Articles," and numbered with Roman numerals.[22]

Article I should include the official name of the museum and its location including city, county, and state. If there is a governing or parent organization, its name should also be listed.

Article II should include the purpose of the museum, expressed in terms of its mission, including mandates, goals, and objectives.

Article III should outline the composition of the board of trustees, board of directors, or other governing authority for the museum, including number and qualifications for membership. Size of board membership will depend on the museum's size and nature. The bylaws also should define terms of office for board members and nomination and selection or election procedures. The board may be self-perpetuating, appointed by the parent organization, elected from the membership of the organization, or consist of both appointed and elected members. Museums often stagger terms of office by grouping board members together in classes. The bylaws also should account for the first few years of the museum's existence, when, for example, one-third of the board would be elected for a one-year term and one-third for a two-year term and one-third for a three-year term. Some bylaws may also limit the number of terms any single trustee can serve, whereas others will not let board members serve consecutive terms.

Article III may also detail the responsibilities of board members. According to Lord and Lord in the *Manual of Museum Management*, boards are expected:

1. To ensure the continuity of the museum's mission, mandate, and purposes;
2. To act as an advocate in the community for public involvement in the museum;
3. To provide for the present and long-term security and preservation of the collection, and the safety of staff and visitors, at a level consistent with the museum's mission and mandate;
4. To ensure that the museum serves as wide a public as possible;
5. To ensure that the museum undertakes research to create and disseminate accurate and objective knowledge relevant to its collection;
6. To review and approve policies consistent with the museum's mission and mandate, and to monitor staff implementation of these policies;
7. To plan for the future of the museum, including reviewing and approving a corporate plan (or strategic plan or business plan) that identifies the museum's goals and ways to attain them, and monitoring implementation of the plan;
8. To assure the financial stability of the museum, through reviewing, approving and monitoring budgets and financial reports, arranging for regular audits, investing the museum's financial assets wisely and raising funds as required to allow the museum to meet it current and future financial responsibilities;
9. To recruit and negotiate a contract with the museum's director, to evaluate his or her performance, and to terminate his or her employment if necessary; and
10. To ensure that the museum has adequate staff to undertake all museum functions.[23]

Article III also should specify the number of board meetings per year. It may specify the time, day, and place where they will be held, and the number of members necessary to constitute a quorum for the transaction of business. A provision concerning filling vacancies on the board also is necessary. Whether appointed by the board president or elected by the board, persons filling vacancies usually serve until the original term expires.

Most boards appoint their members to committees so that the board can work on a wide range of issues simultaneously. Standing committees address ongoing activities fundamental to the purpose and programs of the museum. Chairpersons of standing committees are appointed by the president and should be a member of the board of trustees. Committee members are often recruited from among the museum membership and are not necessarily board members. Standing committees may include:

- Executive
- Governance (includes nominating roles)
- Finance
- Development and Membership
- Personnel
- Planning
- Public Programming
- Public and Media Relations
- Diversity and/or Community Advisory

If a standing committee is created, it is important for it to have substantive work all year long. If not, a less formal structure may be used.[24] In this article, you may include a statement that ad hoc committees will be formed as needed.[25] If the officer and committee sections are extensive, they may be separated into a separate article for ease of reference.[26]

Article IV should include a description of the general responsibilities of professional staff, especially the executive director's functions, duties, and limitations. The executive director should be in charge of the museum's management and administration, subject only to direction from the board of trustees and state laws. Care should be exercised to ensure that a change in job description for staff does not require a change of bylaws.

Article V should define the power and duties of officers of the board. The president is the chief executive officer and presides at all meetings of the museum membership, the board of trustees, and the executive committee. The president also is responsible for making an annual report to the secretary of state as required by law. The president usually appoints all committee chairpersons and committee members authorized by the board of trustees. The president is also a nonvoting member of all committees. In the absence of the president, the vice president performs the duties of the president. The vice president should assist the president in the general supervision of the museum and the future planning by the museum. The secretary attends and keeps minutes of all meetings and should conduct routine correspondence for the board. The treasurer is responsible for all funds of the museum and/or membership organization. The treasurer collects membership fees or other dues of the museum membership organization, keeps a full and accurate account of receipts and expenditures, and makes disbursements as directed by the board of trustees. In larger museums, the treasurer's duties in most cases will relate primarily to the membership organization, and the museum's operations will be handled by paid staff, such as a business manager. In smaller museums, the treasurer may handle the finances of the membership organization as well as those from museum operations. The treasurer annually arranges for, and presents to the board, an audit of all funds.

Article VI may describe the various classifications for membership. Because a museum is a public institution, its membership should be open to all persons, businesses, and organizations that support the mission of the museum and are willing to pay the prescribed dues. Typical membership categories may include individual, family, patron, affiliate organization, corporate, benefactor, and honorary life. Some museums offer their members voting rights as long as they are in good standing. The bylaws should not be so specific that they list the actual amount of dues, because any raise in rates would require a change in bylaws. Instead, the bylaws should state that the board will determine the scale and amount of membership dues at the annual meeting of the museum.

Article VII describes any financial provisions for the museum. It defines the fiscal year and may also assign authority to sign checks, transfer funds, enter contracts, and accept gifts and donations. It should furthermore detail financial reporting requirements and budget preparations.

Article VIII determines the parliamentary authority by which the board meetings will be governed. In most cases, the authority used for governing meetings is the most current edition of Robert's Rules of Order.[27] These rules should be used in all cases in which they are applicable and in which they are not inconsistent with state statutes, the bylaws, or any special rules the museum may adopt. An alternative meeting style may also be engaged if it is better suited for your board culture and organizational values. Consensus decision making is an excellent alternative that allows for a variety of responses to a presented idea. Group leadership facilitates the conversation until everyone is in agreement, knowing there will be adjustments to the idea along the way.[28]

Article IX provides for the amendment of the bylaws. It determines the number of members needed to amend the bylaws. Proposed changes in the bylaws are typically approved by the board of trustees and distributed to the membership in writing at least twenty-one days prior to the meeting at which the amendments will be considered.

Article X should provide for the potential dissolution of the museum. The bylaws may determine the number of members necessary to dissolve the museum and usually at least two-thirds of the membership would be needed to cease operations. Article X also needs to state where any remaining property, whether real or personal, should be donated. The museum, after donating its collections, would be considered dissolved and its corporate status terminated.

ARTICLES OF INCORPORATION

The articles of incorporation and the bylaws are the museum's two governing documents. The bylaws define a system of internal law and government, and the articles of incorporation establish the relationship between the museum as a nonprofit corporation and the state in which it operates. The articles of incorporation also establish the museum's legal existence as a nonprofit organization, authorize its perpetual operation, specify its 501(c) (3) Federal tax status (although this must be applied for and granted by the Internal Revenue Service) or other tax status, declare its right to hold property and receive gifts, and make provisions for the museum's assets in the event of dissolution. Regulations regarding articles of incorporation are different from state to state. Nonprofit corporations must be founded on, and adhere strictly to, the prescribed legal regulations or statutes in their state of incorporation.

All states have laws governing incorporation. Check for online resources from the secretary of state's office. Many require steps similar to those followed in Nebraska:

1. Choose who will be the initial directors [board members] for your nonprofit;
2. Choose a name for your nonprofit corporation;
3. Prepare and file your nonprofit articles of incorporation;
4. Prepare bylaws for your nonprofit corporation;
5. Hold an organizational meeting of your board to approve the bylaws, appoint officers, set an accounting period and tax year, and approve initial transactions of the board such as opening a corporate bank account;
6. Obtain a federal ID number from the Internal Revenue Service (Form 1023);
7. Obtain a state tax exemption; and
8. Follow other reporting and registration requirements, such as registering with the attorney general before doing any fundraising activities.[29]

Many states have standard "certificate of incorporation" or "articles of incorporation" forms, but in Nebraska, the incorporators of an organization must draft their own legal documents. These articles of incorporation must be filed with the secretary of state by incorporators who are the chief organizers or promoters of the museum. An attorney could be helpful when preparing and filing the articles of incorporation, drafting bylaws, and disbursing and filing fees. If a lawyer helps substantially, he or she may be listed as an incorporator.

State statutes will outline the information required in the articles of incorporation, which will be similar to those in the State of Nebraska where the essential items required are:[30]

1. Title or heading of document (e.g., "Articles of Incorporation");
2. A corporate name for the organization (name of the museum);
3. Statement of the nonprofit nature of the organization. It should include one of the following statements:
     i.   This corporation is a public benefit corporation.
     ii. This corporation is a mutual benefit corporation.
     iii. This corporation is a religious corporation.
4. The street address for the corporate office or principal place of activity, and the name of its initial registered agent at that office for service of processes;
5. The name and street address of each incorporator;
6. Whether or not the corporation will have members;
7. Provisions not inconsistent with law regarding the distribution of assets on dissolution;
8. Signatures of each incorporator and every board of trustee member listed in the articles; and
9. Consent or approval from the secretary of state's office.

The most common organizational structure for museums is the nonprofit corporation. Not all museum organizations go to the trouble to incorporate and obtain a federal ID number, despite the benefits. The corporate structure not only establishes a framework within which the museum operates, but it also offers financial stability and limited tax liability.

IRS STATUS

As an incorporated entity, a museum can apply for nonprofit status and thereby obtain certain benefits. The organization must complete the appropriate paperwork and be granted 501(c)(3) status by the IRS. Museums that are a unit of state or local government, including educational institution such as a college or university, will derive similar benefits from the IRS status 170(c)(1) possessed by their parent institution.[31]

To receive 501(c)(3) status, a museum is recognized as a charitable institution. The term "charitable" is used in its generally accepted legal sense by the IRS and includes the advancement of education or science and the erection or maintenance of public buildings or monuments, under which museums qualify. The articles of incorporation of an institution must limit the organization's purposes to one or more of the exempt purposes set forth by the IRS in section 501(c)(3).[32]

In addition, the assets of the organization must be permanently dedicated to an exempt purpose. Thus should the institution dissolve, its assets must be distributed for an exempt purpose or to the federal, state, or local government for a public purpose. While state law may dictate that the assets must be distributed to an exempt entity, the IRS recommends writing the provision into the articles of incorporation because the organization's application for nonprofit status will be processed more rapidly.

The governing structures of an institution must preclude self-interest or private financial gain to achieve nonprofit status. The IRS states that for an organization to qualify for 501(c)(3) status, "No part of the net earnings will inure to the benefit of organization's private shareholders or individuals."[33]

A museum granted section 501(c)(3) status also must not produce propaganda or otherwise attempt to influence legislation as a substantial part of its activities. The museum is barred from any political activities and may not participate in or intervene in any political campaign on behalf of, or in opposition to, any candidate for public office.[34] This does not exclude museums staff from engaging in museum advocacy work or in their personal political activity.

Museums with a 501(c)(3) status are eligible to receive tax-deductible contributions. These contributions benefit not only the institution but also the donor who receives a tax deduction. The rules governing tax-deductible contributions apply most specifically to the donor, and an organization is not responsible for reporting contribution information to the IRS on behalf of a donor. Except in the case of a quid pro quo contribution, the donor must request and obtain written acknowledgment of the donation from the organization. Although there is no prescribed format for written acknowledgment, the museum must provide sufficient information to substantiate the amount of the contribution. In the case of donation of objects or artifacts, museums must encourage donors to secure an independent third party appraisal of the fair market value of the object or artifact. This value may then be submitted by the donor to the IRS to substantiate the tax deduction. The IRS requires a receipt for gifts valued over $250.[35]

A written disclosure statement to donors of a quid pro quo contribution in excess of $75 is required of the organization. For example, if a donor gives a museum $100 and receives tickets for a special exhibition valued at $40, the donor has made a quid pro quo contribution. The charitable contribution portion of the payment is $60. Even though the part of the payment available for deduction does not exceed $75, a disclosure statement must be filed because the donor's payment (quid pro quo contribution) exceeds $75. According to the IRS, the required written statement must:

1. Inform the donor that the amount of the contribution that is deductible for federal income tax purposes is limited to the excess of any money (and the value of any property other than money) contributed by the donor over the value of goods or services provided by the organization; and
2. Provide the donor with a good faith estimate of the value of the goods or service that the donor received.

In order to retain its 501(c)(3) status, a museum organization will be required to file annually IRS forms 990, 990EZ, or 990-PF and pay any unrelated business income tax.[36]

Text Box 2.2 Case Study: The Case of the "Purloined" Documents

Susie Jay has just completed her degree in museum studies and has accepted the position as the first paid director of the Moose Antler City Historical Society. Moose Antler is a town of 25,000 located in the northern United States, near the Canadian border. The Moose Antler City Historical Society was founded in 1959, has a collection of 30,000 objects, and has just built a new museum building. Susie is expected to catalog the collection, prepare exhibits, and plan and present educational programs. The collections have accumulated primarily through donations from members of the local community. The building was paid for with contributions from local citizens, fundraising activities, and grants from two private foundations, resulting in a total amount of $230,000. The board has done amazing work in planning and executing the fund drive, recording donations, and sending letters confirming all donations.

(continued)

Text Box 2.2 Case Study: The Case of the "Purloined" Documents (continued)

Ms. Jay attacks her new job with all the energy of a recent graduate hop-ing to make an impression and do her best for the future of the museum. A letter arrives from the Forest Foundation, one of the donors to the fundraising effort. The foundation staff is completing its annual report and needs a copy of the historical society's IRS status statement. Ms. Jay, know-ing the importance of the request and wanting to respond in a timely man-ner, goes to the files to make a copy of the IRS document, but it is not there.

Susie calls Jack Pine, long-time treasurer of the historical society, believing that he will have the document in question, but Jack is vague. When Susie mentions IRS 990 annual report forms and quid pro quo contribution letters for the members, Jack seems even vaguer. Susie closes this conversation. Guessing that Jack may be suffering a bit of old age memory loss, Susie calls the society's new president, Fannie Foxx. Mrs. Foxx is wife of the Moose Antler bank president and is the immedi-ate past president of the Moose Antler Junior League. Susie's conversa-tion with Fannie is even more confusing and ends with Fannie saying "Well Susie, just leave this to Jack and me and we will take care of it." With relief Susie goes back to planning the museum's opening exhibit.

Two weeks later Susie receives a call from Mary Mink at the Forest Foundation. She seems a little irritated and firmly requests the IRS sta-tus document, making the point that the foundation auditor is coming in a week and this document is needed. Susie makes a lame excuse and promises to have it in tomorrow's mail. Susie is now in a panic. She calls her closest ally on the board, Sugar Maples, who served as the chair of the fundraising campaign. Sugar has been very open and supportive of Susie. Sugar is puzzled by Susie's request and professes no knowledge of an IRS status form, has never heard of a 990 form or a quid pro quo let-ter, and asks a lot of questions about the importance of these documents. Sugar calls Fannie and the conversation lasts about fifteen minutes. Sugar returns to report that Fannie has confessed that no one has ever seen an IRS status form and that Jack has never filed a 990 form. Fannie suspects that the historical society has not been incorporated or received IRS 501(c)(3) status.

1. What are Susie's responsibilities in this situation?
2. What are the board's responsibilities?
3. How can Susie determine if the historical society has been incorpo-rated or received IRS 501(c)(3) status?

4. If the museum is not incorporated, what documents will Susie need to work with the board to write?
5. What procedures should Susie and the board follow to get the 501(c)(3) IRS status?

MUSEUM STANDARD AND BEST PRACTICES

Once the legal processes are in place, it's equally important to take care of the collections, the people, the volunteers, and the facilities in the best way possible. The museum board and staff need to be mindful of museum standards and best practices, established by the museum field for the betterment and sustainability of museum organizations. There is a wealth of resources available; it is important to know that the standards exist and that your organization will make a plan to adhere to them to the best of its ability.

Museum decision makers come from all walks of life—board members have diverse backgrounds, volunteers bring their own experiences, and staff may come from museum and nonmuseum backgrounds. Knowledge of museum standards offers a common language that all stakeholders and committed parties may use to achieve their collective goals. Sharing and discussing the standards during board meetings, staff meetings, strategic planning sessions, and other points of discussion will help the museum move toward excellence.[37]

There are numerous standards and best practices that inform the museum field and AAM offers a comprehensive program that outlines, researches, and refines the standards, offers resources to achieve them through peer assessment (Museum Assessment Program is discussed in chapter 5), and accreditation. As such, they offer these useful definitions:

> Standards are generally accepted levels of attainment that all museum are expected to achieve. Best practices are commendable actions and philosophies that demonstrate an awareness of standards, successfully solve problems, can be replicated, and that museums may choose to emulate if appropriate to their circumstances.[38]

AAM refers to a core set of standards as the Characteristics for Excellence and offers, via their website aam-us.org, a list of other sources for standards that compliement this core list or are in addition to this core list. The standards are organized in seven categories:

1. Public trust and accountability
2. Mission and planning
3. Leadership and organizational structure
4. Collections stewardship
5. Education and interpretation
6. Financial stability
7. Facilities and risk management[39]

For museums that are looking to adopt and comply with the standards at all times, accreditation offers museums a "mark of distinction" and heightens their visibility in the community, the museum field, and to their donors. In operation since 1971, this program relies on a process of self-study and peer review over the course of eight to sixteen months and once awarded, a museum is accredited for ten years. It can apply for reaccreditation. The benefits of accreditation are significant: credibility and accountability, clearer sense of purpose, leverage, and support, and sustainability and a stronger institution.[40] Of the 35,000 museums in the United States, 779 are accredited.[41]

Accreditation is an excellent milestone for any museum, it is more realistic to consider core standards and work through the process as time and resources allow. Some small and mid-sized museums might find the accreditation process difficult to tackle when there is a pressure to secure resources. Those same museums are pursuing or are interested in pursuing best practices and would benefit from a structured achievement process. In 2009, AASLH introduced the Standards and Excellence Program for History Organizations. Known as StEPS, this self-study program is aligned with the same standards AAM outlines with the addition of preservation standards for historic structures and landscapes. An incremental assessment process, StEPs offers an accessible tool for any budget size. With completion of the seven standards areas at the gold level, museums will be ready to pursue accreditation. The same can be said for AAM's Museum Assessment Program discussed in chapter 5.[42]

CONCLUSION

More common than starting a museum from scratch is reforming and reorganizing an existing museum that has lacked administrative leadership. A museum professional rarely will be faced with the challenging task of building a museum from its beginning. No matter the circumstance, anyone seeking a professional museum position must expect a certain amount of her time will be devoted to administrative duties and, therefore, should understand the mechanisms and significance of the mission statement, bylaws, articles of incorporation, IRS nonprofit status, and standards and best practices.

Following the steps outlined in this chapter can be a complicated and tedious process; however, each new museum does not need to reinvent the wheel. There are numerous resources available to guide a museum professional through the process. The references cited in the bibliography are useful and are available from professional organizations such as the AAM and AASLH.

By taking the steps outlined in this chapter, a museum is at the end of its beginning. With this solid organizational foundation, the museum can move forward to build the programs, collections, and facilities that fulfill its mission. It is ready to get to work.

Text Box 2.3 Guiding Questions

1. Amy Lent thinks there are enough museums and that new ones should be formed only after careful consideration. What is your response to her perspective?
2. Are there other considerations for a museum starting up? What are they?
3. In your first thirty, sixty, and one hundred days as a museum director, what are your priorities?

NOTES

1. George and Maryan-George, *Starting Right*, 21.
2. Lent, interview.
3. Bailey, interview.
4. Silberman, interview.
5. Lynch-McWhite, interview.
6. Stroh, interview.
7. American Alliance of Museums.
8. Hoagland, *Guidelines*.
9. Anderson, *Museum Mission Statements*.
10. Wolf, *Managing a Nonprofit*.
11. Ibid.
12. Hoagland, *Guidelines*.

13. Bailey, interview.

14. Lord, interview.

15. Skramstad and Skramstad, "Mission and Vision . . .," 73.

16. Abbe Museum.

17. Rasic, interview.

18. Anderson, *Museum Mission Statements*.

19. Skramstad and Skramstad, "Mission and Vision . . .," 69.

20. American Alliance of Museums.

21. Zeitlan and Dorn, *Nonprofit Board's Guide*, 1.

22. Robert, *Robert's Rules*, 559–92.

23. Lord and Lord, *The Manual of Museum Management*, 19.

24. Robinson, *Great Boards for Small Groups*, 62.

25. Ad hoc committees are temporary committees that exist to address a particular question or issue.

26. George and Maryan-George, *Starting Right*, 128–30.

27. Robert, *Robert's Rules*.

28. Robinson, "Going for Consensus . . ."

29. NOLO Law for All, "How to Form . . ."

30. Nebraska Revised Statute 21-1921, *Nebraska Legislature*.

31. Internal Revenue Service, "Tax Exempt Status . . ."

32. Ibid.

33. Ibid.

34. Ibid.

35. Malaro and DeAngelis, *A Legal Primer*.

36. Internal Revenue Service, "Tax Exempt Status . . ."

37. Merritt, *National Standards*.

38. Ibid., 6.

39. American Alliance of Museums.

40. Ibid.

41. Institute for Museum and Library Services; American Alliance of Museums.

42. American Association for State and Local History.

❸

STRATEGIC PLANNING

Museums over the last three decades have experienced incredible change, due mostly to their success but also because of societal and governmental expectations and pressures.[1] "Organizations that want to survive, prosper, and do good and important work must respond to the challenges the world presents."[2] To do this, museums need to adopt an organized approach to mission fulfillment and organizational excellence. Time and resources are far too scarce to squander them on a lack of vision and planning. There are a number of plans that will find a home in museum administration—collections, interpretation, facilities, development, marketing—but all should align with the comprehensive museum strategic plan.[3]

Text Box 3.1 Forces of Change in Museums

EXTERNAL FACTORS

1. The number of museums in many areas have more than doubled, providing greater access but also increasing competition among museums.
2. The dramatic increase in educational attainment levels has resulted in higher museum attendance overall.

(continued)

3. New government and foundation policies link museum funding to fulfillment of educational and social objectives.
4. Cultural tourism is a major industry highly reliant on museums.
5. Security threats, gasoline price increases, and other unforeseen changes can produce sudden negative impacts on attendance and increase costs such as insurance.
6. Steady decline in government funding.
7. Rise of cities (where the majority of museums are located) as centers of economic power.
8. Accessibility of electronic and digital technologies through the Web.
9. Public demand for "blockbuster" exhibitions.

INTERNAL FACTORS

1. Increasing professionalism of museum staff leading to new ideas and higher performance standards.
2. Positive enthusiasm among museum staff for improving services for visitors.
3. More museum board members from the corporate sector with expectations that museums should operate "like businesses."
4. Rising operating costs.
5. Collections growth in new fields and materials.
6. Expansion of museum buildings.
7. Growth in administrative personnel needed to increase revenue streams.
8. Development of national and global museum systems and "brands."
9. Dependence on "blockbuster" exhibitions.

Source: Adapted from Lord and Markert, *The Manual of Strategic Planning.*

WHAT IS STRATEGIC PLANNING?

John Bryson considers strategic planning "a deliberative, disciplined approach to producing fundamental decisions and actions that shape and guide what an organization . . . is, what it does, and why."[4] Lord and Markert define strategic planning as "determining the optimal future for an organization and the changes required to achieve it."[5] The result of this process is a written strategic plan that is a "map or chart that an organization agrees to follow for three or five years in order to reach its goals."[6]

Creating this unified, shared, and comprehensive plan requires the board and staff to work jointly—and the director is poised in the middle, communicating between both groups and balancing interests. And many times, the strategic planning process will involve input from outside stakeholders and will often rely on an outside consultant who facilitates conversation and ideas while guiding the museum into a clear strategy and plan.[7]

Strategic plans are different from long-range or operational plans. Plans are strategic when the goals respond to the museum's environment, seek a competitive edge, effectively serve stakeholders, and identify the keys to long-term sustainability. Long range or operational plans do not redefine the organization and are not concerned about positioning the museum in the community. These plans are more focused on laying out immediate and future goals and are less concerned with organizational change. Strategic plans should be living documents, reviewed and revised, if necessary. During the life of a strategic plan, the museum team and board will take the time to evaluate the success of the plan and consider next steps and adjustments. If at the end of the plan's timeline, all efforts were successful and there's more work to do on that same path, changing course may not be necessary. The organization may simply need to plan the next five years along the same course. This next type of plan would be considered a long-range or operational plan.[8]

The strategic plan is a critical lens through which activities can be focused, leading to the museum's success. A successful organization is one that has a clear understanding of mandates and an established, well-communicated, and inspiring mission. Additionally the museum effectively manages resources to fulfill its mission, provides a clear communication network, develops a strategic organization, and produces effective and competent leadership.[9] Hassan Najjar, executive director of the Museum Center at 5ive Points in Cleveland, Tennessee, shares how strategic planning has served him and his team. "Strategic planning serves as a road map for me and my staff. It is a clear set of goals that not only gives us direction but also serves as protection against ideas that don't fit our mission. Our donors like to see that we are meeting our goals and as the director I like to tell them that we are 75% of the way in meeting our goals with two years left in a three-year plan."[10]

Ultimately, strategic planning provides a focus and alignment of resources in the museum. This creates more effective board and staff teams and operations. The process and plan will solve major problems and boost the museum's image to donors, grant makers and other constituents. The museum will appear to be organized and well-focused.[11] Museum size does not matter; even volunteer-operated museums need to focus on success. Facilitators and books can help inexperienced museums with strategic planning, and although strategic planning is theoretical at times, it includes action plans to make the theories reality. Strategic planning sometimes is opposed by key stakeholders who fear a favorite program will be eliminated. This may happen, but strategic planning will also help stakeholders to see that certain programs offer the best advantage to further the museum's mission, and ensure that these programs, and the museum itself, succeed.[12]

Bryson and Alston argue in their book *Creating and Implementing Your Strategic Plan* that a museum in crisis or major transition (that is, the building just burned down or a new director is being sought) needs to deal with the issues at hand and postpone strategic planning until a later date. This does not eliminate the need for planning; it only affects its timing. Even crises will require planning.[13] A museum experiencing a major financial crisis, for example, might want to consider a modified version of strategic planning and develop a plan focused on that situation. Finally, if the board and management of a museum will not commit to developing a strategic plan, the planning process should not be initiated. A lack of commitment raises concern about the feasibility of a plan, and may signal the time to replace board members and/or staff.

A museum experiencing any of these symptoms is operating below optimal level and the timing for strategic planning must be considered. And sometimes, an organization is inexperienced in institutional planning and is not ready to take the first step. To optimize for success, it is wise to consider how ready your museum is for strategic planning by answering the questions in table 3.1.[14]

The process of strategic planning can be simple or complex. Authors have defined it variously with a few simple steps, or multiple steps or phases. Text box 3.2 offers five ways of viewing the strategic planning process.

Although they use different terminology, all of these strategic planning processes are virtually the same. They direct museum strategic planners to clarify their mission and values, identify the external and internal forces that

Table 3.1 Is Your Museum Ready for Strategic Planning?

Readiness Issues	Yes. You are ready!	No. You need to fix/review a few things first.	Considerations (if not ready)
The museum has enough money to pay bills over the next six months.			How can your museum get enough money? By when? Start strategic planning when?
The museum has a history of being able to plan and implement its plans.			What can be done to address this issue? Leadership development? Other ideas? Start strategic planning when?
Board members work well together. Staff members get along.			Problem in board? Problem with staff? What can be done? Start strategic planning when?
Board members willing to be involved in top-level planning.			What can be done? Start strategic planning when?
Board members and staff will find the time to do the planning.			What can be done to free up more time? Start strategic planning when?
No major changes are expected in the next one to two months.			What changes? What can be done to get ready for strategic planning? By when?
There is extensive support for planning in your museum (internally and externally).			What can you do to address any cynicism? Start strategic planning when?
Strategic planning efforts are underway because the museum is ready for change and not just because a grant-maker or funder is asking for it.			What should you do about this? Start strategic planning when?

Source: Adapted from McNamara, *Field Guide.*

influence their activities, identify specifics to fulfill their mission, formulate action plans and responsibility centered on achieving goal objectives, and evaluate their success in achieving these goals. Here is a modified version of Bryson and Alston's ten-step process, incorporating elements from other authors.[15]

Text Box 3.2 Phases of Strategic Planning

Creating and Implementing Your Strategic Plan
by J. M. Bryson and F. K. Alston

1. Initiate and agree on strategic planning process
2. Clarify organizational mandates
3. Identify and understand stakeholders, develop and refine mission and values, and consider developing a vision sketch
4. Assess the environment to identify strengths, weaknesses, opportunities, and challenges
5. Identify and frame strategic issues
6. Formulate strategies to manage strategic issues
7. Review and adopt the strategic plan
8. Establish an effective organizational vision for the future
9. Develop an effective implementation process
10. Reassess strategies and strategic planning process

The Manual of Strategic Planning for Museums
by G. D. Lord and K. Markert

1. Internal and external assessment
2. Identify critical issues
3. Comparison and benchmarking
4. Board and staff retreats
5. Write the plan
6. Implement the plan
7. Evaluate the plan

DIY Strategic Planning
by Cinnamon Catlin-Legutko

1. Preparation
2. Facilitation
3. Formatting
4. Measuring

A *Guide to Strategic Planning*
by The Kresge Foundation

1. Involve stakeholders
2. Start from the value proposition
3. Perform a competitive analysis of the operation environment
4. Isolate your competitive advantage
5. Consider resources needed to achieve value proposition
6. Design the overall capitalization strategy
7. Assess and articulate potential risks

Field Guide to Nonprofit Strategic Planning and Facilitation
by Carter McNamara

1. Conduct a situational analysis
2. Establish mission, vision, and values
3. Identify issues and goals
4. Develop strategies
5. Create action plans and documents
6. Implement, monitor, and adjust

Step 1: Initiate and Agree on Process

Some basic agreements are needed prior to beginning the strategic planning process. First, the museum board, staff, and volunteers need to be supportive and ready to participate. This broad sponsorship keeps the process from becoming one person's or group's project. Lack of inclusion is a common reason planning fails.[16] Anita Durel of Durel Consulting Partners believes that the board should always be involved in the planning process, and if it's a large organization, the department heads are key members in the planning process as well.[17] In a smaller museum, it may be the entire board and the sole employee (or key volunteers) who participate in strategic planning.

At the Brooklyn Historical Society in Brooklyn, New York, President Deborah Schwartz shares that her "strategic planning efforts involve senior staff and trustees." With a committed and involved process for the museum, "the president and the development director lead the process with an outside facilitator. In our relatively small shop (total staff of 27), this is largely because the Development Director knows and works with the Trustees very closely on a regular basis, and so the strategic planning effort is a natural extension of her work. We also hire a facilitator to help us organize the process: keep us on a schedule, facilitate a retreat, and to draft the plan."[18]

Once broad support is achieved, a strategic planning committee of effective policy makers is formed. It is imperative that staff, the "doers," be involved in all aspects of strategic planning to ensure their commitment to accomplishing the goals outlined by the plan. It also is wise to include representatives of constituent groups (stakeholders) to ensure that the strategic planning process is not overly internalized, and outside factors are always represented. This will help the museum develop new stakeholders and enhance the commitment of existing stakeholders. It can be interesting to have a representative or two from groups that do not use the museum or that the museum wishes to gain as a future audience. Using an outside facilitator is a good idea for an organization's first attempt at strategic planning, or for a museum with a limited number of staff. Even if strategic planning is a common event for a museum, an outside facilitator may still make the process unbiased, nonthreatening, and nonjudgmental.[19] A gifted facilitator will certainly push the group toward imaginative thinking and help participants think broadly about the museum's future, beyond the normal "we've always done it this way" approach.

Once the strategic planning committee is formed it will establish why the strategic planning effort is needed now, what steps will be included in the process, who will be responsible for carrying out the steps, and deadlines and guidelines for reports. The committee will also determine what resources are needed for the process, if they are available, and where they can be obtained.[20] At this point, the committee will determine how long the planning process should take, and plan the time and place for periodic retreats. Periodic retreats are advised as they allow the committee to refocus and regroup away from the museum and daily pressures. The strategic planning effort should take place over six to twelve months, to allow time for adequate information-gathering and to avoid rushing the process.

The Abbe Museum in Bar Harbor, Maine, completed a new strategic plan in 2015. Discussions, stakeholder interviews, research, and writing took place over a twelve-month period. The goals identified in the plan are the result of three board member retreats—one of these retreats included all staff and two of them included the leadership team only—a staff-only retreat, and a meeting of the Native Advisory Council. Additionally, over thirty stakeholder interviews were conducted, resulting in a well-informed and feasible strategic plan that will guide the next five years.[21]

Step 2: Identify Organizational Mandates

Organizational mandates are the "musts" a museum faces, usually dictated by external forces. These mandates may be laws, guidelines imposed by funders, budgets, or societal expectations. In the process of strategic planning and possible mission restructuring, the museum must have a clear understanding of what it is expected and required to do. After the mandates have been compiled, they should be clearly listed and distributed to all committee members and regularly referenced to ensure compliance.[22]

Step 3: Identify and Understand Stakeholders and Develop Mission

A museum should identify its stakeholders and understand what they want or expect from the museum. A stakeholder is any person or group that can place a claim on the museum's resources and products. This may include members, employees, board members, teachers, civic leaders, granting or funding organizations, cooperating organizations, competing organizations, the media, visitors, and others. Each museum will have a different set of stakeholders depending on its mission and situation.

Once stakeholders are identified, it is important to understand their needs and the criteria they use to assess the museum's performance. This is vital because the success of the museum depends on the support of stakeholders. The strategic planning committee can identify internal stakeholder needs and criteria, and it also can brainstorm criteria it believes external stakeholders are using; however, direct stakeholder surveys provide much more detailed, accurate, and worthwhile information. If external stakeholder (constituent) representatives have been included on the strategic planning committee, they could be surveyed, or could assist with survey development. This analysis will ascertain stakeholder needs and criteria as well as stakeholder perceptions of current operations and suggestions for future changes.

Addressing the mission is an especially important part of strategic planning. As the museum's statement of purpose (see chapter 2), the mission guides the direction and activities of the museum. It is important to develop or revise the mission statement early in the strategic planning process, as it serves as the "compass" for the museum's operations. Its clarity will offer strong, ongoing focus for the board and staff.[23] You may also choose not to revise the mission statement because it is serving the organization well; do not overlook the opportunity to review it and assess its relevancy during the planning process. Values and purpose, not projects or campaigns, drive the museum to success over time.[24]

Step 4: External and Internal Assessments

Strategic planning often fails because it was based on incomplete information. This fourth step in the strategic planning process is commonly called a SWOT analysis. A SWOT is a situational analysis that evaluates Strengths and Weaknesses and Opportunities and Threats. The objective of any museum should be to take advantage of strengths and opportunities and minimize weaknesses and threats.[25]

An external review of the museum includes consideration of the Opportunities and Threats in the SWOT analysis. Opportunities are "usually some seemingly positive situation in the current or future environment" for the museum.[26] For example, a museum opportunity could be audience interests, a potential partnership or collaboration, or the development of a new community service. A threat is the opposite, "a seemingly negative situation in the current or future environment."[27] A museum may be threatened by decreasing donations or diminishing tax support, competitors for time (sports, movie theaters, etc.), or changing audience expectations.

Looking internally, the SWOT analysis focuses on Strengths and Weaknesses, which may be defined in the same way as Opportunities and Threats, but with an internal eye. A strength may be a wildly popular educational program series that attracts target audiences, an outstanding staff team, community respect, or a large volunteer corps. A weakness would identify insufficient funding, disengaged board members, a lack of staff expertise, or undersized facilities.[28]

Step 5: Identify Strategic Issues

A strategic issue is a fundamental policy choice determined by a museum's mandates, mission, values, product, audience, financing, and management. Look to internal and external stakeholder perceptions and suggestions for common themes and relate these to the museum's mandates and mission, and to the SWOT analysis. This will help identify the issues that the museum needs to address.[29] To determine if an issue is strategic, define the consequences if the issue is not addressed; if there are no consequences, the issue is not strategic. There are three kinds of strategic issues: (1) those where no action is required but the issue must be monitored, (2) those that can be handled as part of the regular strategic planning cycle, and (3) those that require immediate response.[30]

Once they are identified, list the strategic issues in priority order. This list should contain a description of the issue, a discussion of the factors that make the issue strategic, and a discussion of the consequences if the issue is not addressed. Turn the issues into opportunities, compare these opportunities to the mission, and, if consistent, prepare to work on them. Ranking the issues enables the museum to focus on the most critical issues.

Step 6: Review and Adopt Strategic Issues

Before starting the next step in the strategic planning process, review again what strategic issues should be pursued. Involvement of many people in the planning process can create a hodgepodge of inconsistent and contradictory ideas.[31]

In the previous section, three criteria are offered that help determine what makes an issue strategic. Building on this, McNamara offers additional ways to determine if an issue is strategic:

1. New information is revealed during the assessments and analysis.
2. The topic is important rather than urgent.
3. This is something that the organization can do something about.
4. There is a major problem if the organization does nothing about it.
5. The issue is focused on the organization, in total, or at least on a key program.[32]

The final list of strategic issues must be agreed upon and formally adopted by the strategic planning committee.

To select the most important or priority topics, or to help respond to a "Big Question" that arises during the planning process, David La Piana offers a clever tool. Developing a strategy screen ahead of time, before any difficult questions or challenges arise in the planning process, will help an organization "focus on picking the best strategy, consistent with the [organization's] identity." The specific criteria selected for screening depends up on the museum's "mission, identity, and competitive advantages, and your assessment of the your current market position. The criteria will: (1) be different for each organization, (2) evolve over time as the organization adapts to the changes in the environment, and (3) usually include five to eight elements." [33] Weighing a new strategy against a museum's mission is certainly the first screening criterion followed by criteria related to finances and competition. La Piana also recommends that the strategy screen is developed by a group of strategic thinkers and then vetted widely before adoption. [34]

Step 7: Formulate Strategies (Action or Work Plans) to Manage Strategic Issues

Strategic issues can be converted into goals, or strategic directives, for the museum to pursue. It has been suggested that the number of goals be limited to three or five, because more will inhibit a shared vision. [35] The timeframe for the plan is contingent on the size of the museum as well. The plan should cover "a period long enough to make major shifts in your organization's direction but not so long to seem absurd." [36] If it is an all-volunteer museum, or a small museum with part-time paid staff, reducing the time frame to three years is suggested. A larger museum is advised to map out at least five years, but it's advisable to not extend past ten years. Volunteer organizations can experience a greater need for focused planning to keep everyone moving in the same direction with complete buy-in.

Once the time frame is agreed upon, the next step is to formulate goals that make the mission and vision reality. "While missions and visions are essential to inspiring commitment to [the museum], they may be seen as hollow unless accompanied by an organized description of activities needed to fulfill desired aims." [37] Working together with a facilitator, the planning committee will sift through the strategic issues and begin to formulate prioritized goals. This is also the time to check for what is missing and consider how urgent those issues are. The facilitator's job is to make sure the sifting process isn't overwhelming, goals are measurable, and the group builds consensus. [38]

Flowing out of these goals are action plans that outline objects and tasks, detailing what must be accomplished, who is responsible for achievement, what is the timing (start and stop dates), what resources are needed, how it will be monitored, and what is the outcome, or performance target, of the goal. [39] The format for the action plan varies, but it's typically a table or chart that board and staff members, donors, and stakeholders can easily read.

When the actions are agreed upon, it may signal a significant organizational change that demands a reallocation of resources. Will it be necessary to add, redistribute, or reduce resources? This realization may require an additional ranking process that prioritizes goals and aligns them with available resources, especially in smaller museums.

Step 8: Establish a Vision for the Future of the Museum

Crafting a vision statement is an integral step to the strategic planning process. It may be articulated earlier in the process, possibly at the same time the mission is drafted. It may also be an activity for later in the planning process. Skramstad and Skramstad describe the statement of vision as a "snapshot of the organization at a future point." As such, the vision cannot be realized without a supporting strategic plan. A vision statement is not a lofty statement, but rather a measurable future reality.[40] The vision may be very specific and focused on budget size, audience, staffing, or programming, but it can also focus outwardly and articulate the museum's societal impact.[41] Board and staff will know when the vision is realized as there are indicators articulated in the plan. The Boston Children's Museum offers an inspiring vision statement that engages board members, staff, and visitors alike:

> Boston Children's Museum's vision is to be a welcoming, imaginative, child-centered learning environment that supports diverse families in nurturing their children's creativity and curiosity. We promote the healthy development of all children so that they will fulfill their potential and contribute to our collective wellbeing and future prosperity.[42]

For a small museum in a small or rural community, sharing the museum's vision with the broader community can be quite newsworthy and will help attract new volunteers and donors. During an annual meeting, the director can make a presentation about the plan or create a poster highlighting the goals. Make the plan *the* topic of conversation and share the vision with everyone who will listen. Creating an informed local public will help the museum achieve goals in a timely manner because of the enthusiasm created in donors and volunteers.

Step 9: Evaluation and Reassessment

If a detailed work plan has been established, it should be relatively easy to evaluate whether the strategic plan is working successfully. Evaluations should be done on a regular basis, approximately every year to establish which goals have been met, if new ones should be undertaken, if some should be scrapped, or if plans should be reworked.

Each year, at the very least, the board needs to review the plan and the status of each goal. Any timeline adjustments can be disclosed and discussed, for example, due to funding changes, unexpected opportunities, or other issues. To keep the plan in the minds all year long, designing the board meeting agenda around strategic topics and discussion points is wise. No one should think of the museum's strategic plan simply as a notebook sitting on a shelf gathering dust. Instead, it is a living document—a means to an end—that energizes and motivates the museum toward successful results. Throughout the course of the plan, budgets and opportunities will flex and the museum will need to respond in the best interest of the organization. So long as the end goal is still in sight, taking an alternate path to get there is acceptable.[43]

Step 10: Finalizing the Plan

With agreement ensured, communicate the plan in a clear, easy to read format. A well-designed strategic plan document can be a key tool in making the case for your museum to individuals and groups whose support you seek. [44]

Include these sections to offer a clear picture of the museum's intent and direction:

- Introduction—An introductory section that briefly indicates organizational commitment to pursue these strategies and may be combined with the executive summary. This section may also provide a brief description of the methodology used.
- Executive Summary—Only one to three pages long, the summary will reference the mission and vision and paint a broad picture of the museum's priorities.
- Mission and Vision Statements—This section of the written plan offers a simple, clear statement of mission and vision.
- History—Ever-so-briefly, highlight the museum's founding and milestones, bringing the story up to the present.
- Summary of Strategies/Goals—The heart of the plan, this section makes explicit the strategic thinking and organizational commitments that will guide the museum for the next three to five years.
- Action Plans—Usually designed as a table, this section delineates the projects and tasks that will make the strategic goals reality. It will also list responsibilities, timelines, and required resources. There may be additional information in the plan that may not be included in public versions, but are for internal reference only, for example, priorities, metrics.
- Evaluation—Present how the board and staff will monitor the plan and provide updates.[45]

It is critically important to not lose site of the plan's goals and commitments. Evaluation must be an ongoing process that connects the board and staff to the larger purpose of the museum by checking in regularly to see if all of the moving parts on still on course. Burt Logan, executive director and CEO of the Ohio History Connection in Columbus, Ohio, believes that a museum must be self-aware to ensure its relevance and necessity to its communities:

> At times an organization can fall prey to believing in its own relevance and importance, when in fact the opposite is true. Work that the organization itself finds engaging and compelling may in reality be of little or no consequence.
>
> The most important question every organization must continually ask itself, as well as obtaining verification of from those it serves, is: "Are we having a positive, lasting impact, and are we making a difference?" The converse may be: "If we went out of business tomorrow, would anyone notice or care?"[46]

Asking these questions regularly and with open eyes and minds will help museum leadership craft an effective strategic plan that keeps the museum on a sustainable path.

IMPLEMENTATION

When the strategic planning committee has completed its work, the plan is submitted to the museum staff members for their approval. This is a critical step because staff—the "doers"—involvement is key to implementation of the plan. Finally, the plan must be approved by the board—the "deciders."[47] The board, as the governing body for the museum, must fully support the document because it will direct the museum for the next three to five years. The goal of the strategic plan is to translate vision into specific, annual operational plans. Lauren Silberman, deputy director of Historic London Town and Gardens in Edgewater, Maryland, shared that on her staff team, "there is a clamor for a plan so that we can know which items are being focused on in which years and so that we can begin setting up annual work plans for our departments. A real strategic plan would allow us to say "yes" to some ideas and "no" to others, break goals down into annual steps, and determine when what would be happening."[48]

When the plan has been accepted by the board—the goals, action plan, and work plan have been set—whose responsibility is it to see that the strategic plan is successfully implemented? The director! More strategic plans fail at this point than at any other time in this long and time-consuming process. The director of the museum must be the person who is responsible for implementing the strategic plan. The director sits in a pivotal position between the board and the staff. The director must work with the board to obtain the resources necessary for implementation. The board must approve the annual budgets that allocate resources. The director needs to report progress on the plan to the board on a regular basis and keep the board's focus on this document.

The director has the responsibility to see that appropriate portions of the plan are placed in the performance expectations of direct report managers for the coming year. These managers must incorporate portions of the plan in the expectations for staff members reporting to them. The fulfillment of these expectations must become a major portion of the annual evaluation of all of the museum's staff. In subsequent years, as the staff sets expectations for the coming year, appropriate portions of the plan must be incorporated. It is the director who must be certain that staff members who fulfill their expectations are rewarded and that the evaluation process is occurring at least on an annual basis.

Janet Gallimore, executive director of the Idaho State Historical Society, infuses the organization with the strategic plan. "We use our strategic plan to form an annual work plan that connects to staff accountabilities through goals that cascade from the annual plan. This document is on our intranet and 'shows up' at staff and board meetings; in guiding documents on the intranet; and is used as the cornerstone in all agency planning."[49]

Text Box 3.3 Exercise: Strategic Plan Review

Grab a copy of your museum's strategic plan or the plan for a museum with which you are familiar. Some museums make their plans available in print or electronic format. Be certain that you have permission to obtain a copy of the document if it's not publicly distributed. Study the strategic plan carefully and consider these questions:

1. Does the strategic plan follow one of the models discussed above? Is it a combination of several of these models?
2. Does the plan have an executive summary? Does the summary effectively present the overall plan?
3. Is the museum's mission statement a guiding principle for the strategic plan? Is there a vision articulated?

4. Are the museum's mandates identified?
5. Were internal and external assessments conducted? Are the results included in the strategic plan?
6. Are strategic issues identified? Are the strategic issues put in priority order?
7. Are stakeholders identified? Are stakeholders involved in the planning process?
8. Is there an action plan? Is it appropriately detailed? If not, what details should be added?
9. Is there a plan in place for the implementation of the strategic plan?
10. Is there a process in place to evaluate progress on the implementation of the strategic plan?
11. Is the director's role in implementing the strategic plan well defined? The remaining staff's? The trustees'?
12. Is there a process in place to update the strategic plan on a regular basis?
13. What is the strongest section of the plan?
14. What is the weakest section of the plan? Rewrite this section to bring it to the level of the stronger sections.
15. Was the plan prepared through a bottom up or top down process?
16. Review another museum's strategic plan. To what do you attribute the differences between the plans?

Well-implemented plans achieve the desired results on time, and with few unintended side effects. The secret of good implementation is simple—it requires commitment from all who are needed to do the work and acquire the resources needed to carry out the plan.

CONCLUSION

The strategic planning process is, at the most basic level, focused on establishing "first things first" for a museum. There is a universe of planning strategies, facilitator styles, and formats. This may seem like an extraordinary amount of effort and planning, but those museums that engage in strategic planning and follow through with implementation will be better managed museums—museums that attract and keep dedicated staff, obtain necessary resources, and provide recognized value to their constituents. The museum's mission statement is its most important document, but it is the strategic plan that outlines the actions through which that mission is brought to life and realized.

Text Box 3.4 Guiding Questions

1. Have you ever been involved in strategic planning, as a staff member, volunteer, board member, or stakeholder? If so, what was the experience like and how did the plan impact the organization? Your experience need not pertain to a museum example.
2. Considering the phases of a strategic plan outlined in text box 3.2, are there other approaches or phases to strategic planning that you are aware of or would develop?
3. How would you integrate the strategic plan into work flow, board discussions, public relations, and other activities? Where does the plan "show up" in a museum?

NOTES

1. Lord and Markert, *The Manual of . . .*
2. Bryson, *Strategic Planning*, 5.
3. Durel, interview.
4. Bryson, *Strategic Planning*, 7–8.
5. Lord and Markert, *The Manual of . . .*, 4.
6. Catlin-Legutko, *DIY Strategic Planning*, 77.
7. Lord and Markert, *The Manual of . . .*
8. Catlin-Legutko, *DIY Strategic Planning*.
9. Bryson and Alston, *Creating and Implementing*.
10. Najjar, interview.
11. McNamara *Field Guide*.
12. Bryson and Alston, *Creating and Implementing*.
13. Ibid.
14. McNamara, *Field Guide*.
15. Bryson and Alston, *Creating and Implementing*.
16. Phillips, *Why Plans Fail*.
17. Durel, interview.
18. Schwartz, interview.

19. Bryson, *Strategic Planning*; Bryson and Alston, *Creating and Implementing*.

20. Bryson and Alston, *Creating and Implementing*.

21. Catlin-Legutko, interview.

22. Bryson, *Strategic Planning*; Bryson and Alston, *Creating and Implementing*.

23. McNamara, *Field Guide*.

24. Phillips, *Why Plans Fail*.

25. Bryson and Alston, *Creating and Implementing*.

26. McNamara, *Field Guide*, 60.

27. Ibid.

28. Ibid., 66–67.

29. Bryson, *Strategic Planning*.

30. Bryson and Alston, *Creating and Implementing*.

31. Phillips, *Why Plans Fail*, 10.

32. McNamara, *Field Guide*, 71.

33. LaPiana, *The Nonprofit Strategy Revolution*, 63.

34. Ibid., 63–64.

35. Lord and Lord, *The Manual of . . .*

36. Barry, *Strategic Planning*, 6.

37. Mittenthal, "Ten Keys," 7.

38. McNamara, *Field Guide*; Mittenthal, "Ten Keys."

39. McNamara, *Field Guide*.

40. Skramstad and Skramstad, "Mission and Vision . . .," 73.

41. Mittenthal, "Ten Keys."

42. "Mission, Vision, and Values."

43. Catlin-Legutko, *DIY Strategic Planning*; McNamara, *Field Guide*.

44. Pakroo, "Create a Strategic Plan . . ."

45. Allison and Kaye, *Strategic Planning for Nonprofit*; Catlin-Legutko *DIY Strategic Planning*.

46. Logan, interview.

47. Phillips, *Why Plans Fail*.

48. Silberman, interview.

49. Gallimore, interview.

4

FINANCE

In the changing nonprofit world of shrinking budgets and the search for new revenue streams, it's critical for staff to understand museum finances. Staff understanding of how the museum is funded and its primary funding sources is crucial to know. It's also important for staff to have a handle on how money is spent as this helps them make effective decisions with significant financial impact. But so often, when you mention the word "budget" to museum staff members, a resounding sigh of resignation echoes through the halls.

For most, number crunching does not rank high on the list of exciting museum duties. Although they may not look forward to this fiscal activity, most museum staff will admit that the budgeting and accounting process is crucial to fulfilling the museum's mission. Without the proper allocation of resources, museums cannot operate in the present, much less preserve their collections in perpetuity. Donor and grant maker confidence is built on sound accounting practices. Serving the needs of stakeholders and fulfilling the mission is ultimately a question of the bottom line; if the financial wherewithal is missing, the museum cannot succeed, regardless of how brilliant its intent.

DEVELOPING A BUDGET

Budget Terminology

Ensuring the financial well-being of the museum has become a growing concern for museum administrators and staff. Familiarity with some budget and accounting terminology is key to understanding financial management. A budget is the "translation of strategic plans into measurable quantities that express the expected resources required and anticipated returns over a certain period."[1] The annual budget looks at the fiscal year's monetary goals, often driven by the strategic plan, and provides an informed estimate of the money that will come into the organization and what money will go out during the fiscal year.

The annual budget is often made of two principal parts: the operating budget and the capital budget. The operating budget includes the revenues and expenses for the museum's day-to-day collections care, public programming, and basic operation (salaries, utilities, maintenance, and other ongoing expenses) of the museum building and site. The capital budget contains the amount retained for planned big-ticket investment in equipment and systems, as well as development of the museum's site or buildings via renovation, relocation, new construction, or renewal of exhibits.[2]

To keep budget numbers straight and to ensure that reporting is clear and consistent, accounting systems need be integrated into the museum's operations. Finance staff typically use accounting software to track income and expense, review monthly performance, and report results. Budget performance is understood by comparing the cumulative income and expenses to the budgeted figures. Reviewing these numbers through the years provides indicators of future budget performance, but keep in mind that annual budgets are a target, not a performance forecast.

Types of Funds

Many museums base their budgeting and accounting systems on the principles of fund accounting. A variety of funds exist in nonprofits and are often governed by restrictions set up by the organization, donors, and other outside parties.[3] An easy way of visualizing funds is as separate "pots" or "piggy banks" of money.

The general fund (which may also be called the "current" or "operating" fund) holds the money used, at the museum's discretion, to provide activities related to the organization's primary mission. Capital funds support long-lived and/or nonoperating needs, also known as fixed assets or physical plant needs.[4]

A restricted fund designates revenue or investment income earned from revenue that must be spent according to stipulations placed on the income by a donor or a governing body.[5] A sinking fund may be established to hold money set aside to retire debts, such as bond issues or mortgages.[6]

Acquisition funds refer to the amount reserved for the purchase of objects for the collection, or for expenses associated with acquisitions.

Endowment funds are donated monies that are invested; the income generated from returns on unrestricted endowment funds may be used for operations or other legitimate purposes, whereas earnings from restricted endowment funds are earmarked for specific aims, such as acquisitions, exhibits, or seminars.[7] The endowment principal is that portion of the fund that remains invested and untouched and continues to earn income. Only the interest or other income earned from the principal should be expended for appropriate purposes.

Accounting Terms

Assets are items of monetary value, which are owned or controlled by the museum. Assets can include cash, buildings, land, permanent equipment, accounts receivable (money owed to the museum), endowments, and

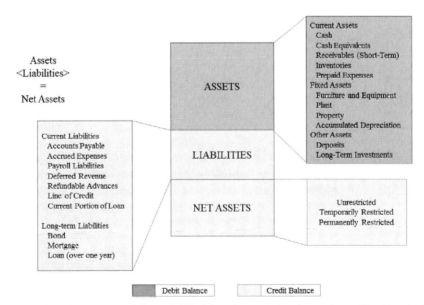

Figure 4.1 Statement of Financial Position. *Source*: Coley, "Accounting and Bookkeeping"

inventory. Because museums hold their collections in perpetuity, they have staunchly refused to consider the collections "assets."

Liabilities are any monies owed to other parties, and would include accounts and notes payable, salaries, and benefits. To determine a fund balance liabilities are subtracted from assets.

Museum budgets may also rely on grant projects supported by government or foundation funds that often require separate accounting.[8] Direct costs are the actual expenses incurred in carrying out the activities proposed under the grant. Salaries, benefits, equipment, rentals, travel, expendable supplies, and contracted faculty are examples of direct costs. Indirect costs, or overhead, reflect the costs involved in carrying out the activity or production. Heating and lighting of the building where the activities will be conducted, Internet, copier usage, management staff time, maintenance of the building, and housekeeping are examples.[9]

A myriad of resources, including the works cited, offer more extensive definitions of budget and accounting terminology. Familiarization with the terms used in your particular museum is essential.

The Fiscal Year

The fiscal year serves to place all financial transactions within typically a twelve-month time frame. The beginning and ending for the fiscal year should be determined in consideration of: (1) the museum's program year so that activities are reflected in one fiscal year rather than being split between two; (2) the museum's more inactive period within the year so that financial reckoning and audits put less strain on staff; and (3) the fiscal year of the primary funding source for the organization.[10] Many states and universities have fiscal years that run from July 1 to June 30. The fiscal year for the federal government is October 1 to September 30. Some organizations choose a fiscal year that corresponds to the calendar year—January 1 to December 31, while others consider the seasonality of their operations. Carl Nold, president and CEO of Historic New England, shared that its fiscal year ends March 31 "so that the bulk of our income from our seasonal museums falls in the first half of the fiscal year, allowing us to adjust budgets in the second half if we have a poor revenue year."[11] The fiscal year is set in the bylaws of the organization; any changes in the calendar will necessitate bylaws amendments as well.

Once the fiscal year is in place, budget preparation can begin. As a financial plan for the museum, the budget estimates the revenues and expenses

Table 4.1   Example of Line-Item Museum Budget

Revenue	
Admissions and memberships	$135,000
Gift shop	$ 43,800
Corporate sponsors	$ 70,000
Grants	$ 52,000
Contributions	$ 91,500
TOTAL	$392,300
Expenses	
Salaries	$232,000
Facilities	$ 65,000
Promotions	$ 24,500
Program costs	$ 11,800
Exhibit supplies	$ 4,500
Office and other	$ 54,500
TOTAL	$392,300

This budget shows expenses by type. It lists operating expenses, but does not tie them to specific programs or outcomes. The majority of the budget will support staff salaries, but information on what those staff will do will have to be communicated via other written material, for example.

for the coming year. Revenues and expenses are subdivided into specific categories, with each containing dollar estimates.

The Budget Cycle

Brenda Granger, executive director of the Oklahoma Museums Association, creates and monitors a healthy balanced budget each year. While we can probably all agree that budgets are simply a plan, Brenda adds that to achieve a balanced budget you need a crystal ball as well as regular review of past financial activity to project future growth and projects.[12] Nold further adds that to achieve a balanced budget requires "discipline at all levels—board of trustees, leadership staff, all staff—and excellent financial information systems that allow for informed decision making."[13] Museum leadership dictates how a budget will be built each cycle and most leaders include staff at all levels of budget planning to ensure accuracy and accountability.

Budget cycles begin with budget development, which flows out of planning. Here is where the museum's strategic plan serves as an invaluable budget tool, outlining the institution's highest priorities. Needs assessments and feasibility studies can help staff determine what it is the museum will do; costs are then estimated for those programs and exhibits. Fixed costs are projected in the budget by reviewing the past three to five years of activity, combined with expectations of the future, for example, rising fuel costs projected for the next three quarters. The challenge comes as proposed costs are then matched to funds available. It's a rare museum where there are sufficient funds to go around. Budget cycles for publicly funded museums may be dictated by governmental or parent organization requirements.

The simple allocation of money is not effective budgeting; a clear understanding of the museum's mission, organizational goals, and available resources is essential in the budget-development process. The strategic plan will make sure that financial decisions align with the mission and keep the organization on target to reach its goals. The budget in many ways activates the strategic plan—it shows the board and staff how programs, exhibits, and initiatives are possible in a fiscal year and into the future. It also connects fundraising to the mission-driven activity and realistic financial goals. A budget and regular reporting and analysis demonstrate how departments are performing, spur conversation about budget performance, and hold staff accountable for spending and fundraising. Including staff in budget development can generate enthusiasm for museum goals, as well as an increased understanding of the costs of doing business.

At the Indiana Historical Society, the budget cycle begins with department heads when they receive income and expense reports for the previous year and review them with the finance director. Working with the president and CEO, department heads develop work plans for the coming year. Once approved by the president and chief executive officer, department budgets are submitted to the finance director who compiles them into an institutional budget. This comprehensive budget is reviewed by the finance committee and submitted to the board of trustees for review and adoption.[14]

Similar to this process but even more inclusive, George Mason's Gunston Hall uses a process prescribed by Durel Consulting Partners that involves all staff teams, at all levels.[15] The teams identify priorities, then they review current finances and fixed costs, followed by departments projecting revenue and expenses. With these data, the teams collaborate on the decision-making that results in a balanced budget. Once complete, the budget is

Table 4.2   Example of a Program Budget

Revenue	
Admissions and memberships	$135,000
Gift shop	$ 43,800
Corporate sponsors	$ 70,000
Grants	$ 52,000
Contributions	$ 91,500
TOTAL	$392,300
Expenses	
Traveling exhibit	$ 50,000
Outreach kits	$ 25,500
Degas exhibit	$ 80,800
Imperial China exhibit	$120,000
Permanent collection	$ 70,000
Docent training	$ 5,000
Security training	$ 2,000
Lecture series	$ 9,000
General admission	$ 10,000
Membership	$ 20,000
TOTAL	$ 392,300

This budget outlines expenses by program. It lists expenses for particular activities, but does not break down the amount of staff time, facilities costs, and materials that go into a particular program.

submitted to the finance and executive committees prior to review and adoption by the full board.[16] For public museums, this internal procedure is only the first step; the budget is then submitted to a city council, county board, or state legislature for consideration. The director and board members will often formally present the budget request, respond to questions, and then advocate to ensure that needed funding is appropriated.

After the board approves the budget or funding is approved by governmental or parental organization authority, the budget cycle turns to the fiscal management stage, during which internal funds are allocated, restricted accounts are established, financial transactions are recorded, and operations are monitored. The planned budget can be used as a control device and as a measuring stick by which the museum's performance can be assessed and its course set for succeeding years.

The last stage of the budget cycle involves end-of-the-year financial statements, a financial audit, and cost and program analyses. This year-long activity is managed by the executive director, working closely with the board, to ensure transparency and accountability. A finance policy and procedure manual is an excellent way to ensure compliance and sound fiscal management.[17]

Preparing the Budget

Who is responsible for the budgetary process? Ultimately, the board of trustees has final financial responsibility for the museum, and for setting long-range goals and program priorities.[18] Budgeting should include staff involvement, which ensures that they will "perform in a way that is consistent with the organization's financial goals and constraints."[19] In other words, involving people at all levels of leadership, management, and operations will lead to a greater awareness of the budget's goals, which leads to greater responsibility for performance.

Typically, the museum director will work with a finance committee established by the board to develop and monitor the budget. The finance committee may include staff and resource people with fiduciary expertise who may not be board members. A well-built budget is possible when you consider these steps, whether using traditional top down strategies or inclusive budgeting:

Create a Plan

Take time to look at a calendar of activities to see funding needs and the approximate timing of cash flow needs. Also review your strategic plan to see what is intended for that year and how it may fit into the budget. Be sure to do an organizational scan to identify everything that needs to be in the budget and then use past and current actual income and expense to estimate the budget numbers. Keep in mind that there are fluctuations from year to year because of special project and gifts, so be sure to account for those to see trends.[20]

Once the numbers are better understood, take time to strategize and understand where the money/income is coming from and make a plan to achieve those targets. Lastly, know that the internal workings of the budget are flexible, avoiding significant variances whenever possible. The budget, like a strategic plan, can be a means to an end. Change happens during the course of a fiscal year and the budget needs to be flexible enough to respond to the changes.[21]

Approximate Cost

"A budget is a plan with dollar signs attached." The planned activities identified should be assigned an approximated cost. In order not to under-budget for the coming year, costs should be estimated on the high side or a ten percent contingency fund should be established. Budget planners must factor in administrative costs for programs and activities; adding new programs adds costs for staff, office space, and equipment. One approach is to review the museum's budgets from previous years and add a percent-age increment for inflation and other factors to create a new figure for the coming year. "Zero-based budgeting," by contrast, assumes nothing and starts from zero, adding on expenses for programs identified in the strategic plan. In such a scenario every facet of the museum program is reconsidered. Regardless the approach used, to place the budget plan within a strategic future scenario, planners must consider changes in sala-ries and workload, possible efficiencies and economies, and the needs of the museum's audience as well as the future social, political, economic, and cultural environments.[22]

Allocate Resources

The income expected from the program activities should be considered along with the museum's other revenue sources. In nonprofit museums as a general rule, all income should be underestimated by at least five percent; however, the museum's past history should be reviewed as a reference in generating these figures. Consideration has to be given to whether future revenue generation will be in the form of unrestricted funds (such as admis-sions, memberships, museum store sales, general donations, and board-designated funds) or as restricted funds (grants and other income given with special conditions for its use).[23]

Unrestricted income can be allocated to cover salaries, utilities, and other administrative costs, as well as exhibits and program costs. Income restricted by the donor or grant-maker must be spent on the intended activity or project.[24] Previously set-aside board designated funds may be allocated for special projects.[25]

Compare and Set Priorities

In order to balance the budget, museum program activities must be evalu-ated and compared to determine their cost-effectiveness. At this stage in the process, some activities may have to be delayed or sacrificed if revenues are not meeting expenses. To help in determining which activities must be delayed or sacrificed and which will be implemented, the administrative staff and board return to the mission and strategic plan to ensure that the budget will meet the organization's goals and continue to fulfill its purpose.[26]

Adjust and Balance

Once priorities have been set, the budget is adjusted and balanced by real-locating estimated revenue. This balanced budget, however, will become unbalanced if unexpected expenses in the future cause revenues to fall short. Overstating expenses and underestimating revenues during the budget planning process in theory will make up for minor discrepancies and a balance can be maintained as the budget is implemented.[27] Public museums may be required to substantiate projected expenses so this "over/under" tactic may not be possible.

Board Approval

Once the budget figures have been developed, the board will review and approve the budget. At this time, the board will officially set the financial limitations for the museum staff. By approving the budget, the board has stated its commitment to finding the means to meet the expenses; therefore, the budget must be feasible and not based on the wishful thinking of board members or museum staff.[28]

Evaluate and Amend

The final stage of the budget process involves the continual monitoring and amending of the budget to fit the revenues and expenses as they develop during the year. It is almost certain the budget will be changed during the fiscal year; a degree of flexibility must be allowed by the board and the director to tailor the budget to financial situations as they arise.

This process is not limited to one-year budget development; it can be applied to future budgets planned several years in advance. Some public museums operate on a biennial budget system that anticipates expenses and revenues over a two-year period. Museum exhibitions often take several years to develop; therefore, long-term budgeting allows for their cost to be spread over a longer period of time in order to raise and commit funds to the project. This form of long-range budget planning is critical to successful strategic planning for museums. It involves the use of historical budgetary figures, the current year's budget, and the projected budget. With these data, trends are analyzed and projections are made for future budgets. Typically, projections are made for the next three to four years and both conservative and optimistic figures are generated. Public museum staff must be aware of funding projections of governmental entities and priorities that may change as elected officials take or leave office. Visualizing future budgets serves as an ongoing management tool that allows the board and staff to evaluate the budget in new or changing circumstances.[29] Budget development, management, and planning assure that the museum is fulfilling its mission and strategic plans and its obligation to serve the public.

BUDGET MANAGEMENT

What happens when everything goes wrong? Multiple years of deficits, accounts payable backed up, cash flow is negative, and donor confidence is low, or depressed tax revenues prompt a 10 percent across-the-board funding cut for all governmental agencies—what do you do? These possibilities strike real fear into the hearts of museum directors and trustees. Financial shortfalls and other organizational decisions at the Corcoran Gallery of Art (see text box 4.1) affected staff, directors, and trustees as well the community, creating years of tension and fear since the 1970s. In 2014, the board made the excruciating decision to close the Corcoran and give the art collection to the National Gallery of Art and merge its College of Art and Design with George Washington University.[30] Optimism and expansion fueled by economic boom times look imprudent once the bubble bursts. What can a museum do to protect itself? The creation and maintenance of a budgeting system, in addition to a mature and effective development program, are key to carrying out museum programs in the present and to ensuring the likelihood of operating into the future. Some public museums are required to develop a "95 percent" budget that identifies cuts that will be made if 5 percent or more cuts are required by the governmental funder.

Monitoring the Budget

Making sure there are organization-wide systems in place to monitor budget performance is critical to keeping financial plans on track and your

Text Box 4.1 Case Review: Corcoran Gallery of Art

The Corcoran Gallery of Art, a venerable Washington, DC museum, traces its origins to 1869 when financier William Wilson Corcoran donated its original building, a collection of American art, and over $1 million in cash gifts. In 1890, it opened the College of Art and Design. Through the ensuing decades, the museum continue to grow and stabilize until, in what many consider its first death knell, American millionaire Andrew Mellon and Congress funded the formation of the National Gallery of Art in 1937, "a well-endowed, taxpayer-subsidized model."" The Corcoran didn't effectively respond to this new marketplace and was plagued with funding challenges exacerbated by "erratic leadership, poor timing, and bad luck" beginning in the 1980s. Its final signs of failure were confused and dissident donors and patrons who, when asked, would have given to the Corcoran but were never asked, or if they had given to the museum, they were never cultivated for future gifts. Interests and philanthropy moved to other museums.

After internally reviewing solutions beginning in 2009, concerns regarding the future sustainability came to a head in 2012 as the board began to publicly seek funding alternatives. The *Washington Post* tracked the Corcoran's demise closely and reported in 2012 these telling metrics:

- "Total fundraising for the last two fiscal years available ($3.2 million in the year ending June 2011; $4.4 million, June 2010) is the lowest since before 1995, the earliest year for which the gallery's tax filings are readily accessible.
- The Corcoran has had budget deficits in seven of the last ten years.
- The endowment has dwindled from $28 four years ago to $19 million because of investment losses during the recession, deficit spending and recalculating some lost pledges tied to the Gehry campaign [a failed building campaign].
- Membership is down to 3,800, after topping 9,000 late in the Gehry campaign.
- The number of visitors to the gallery has sunk below 100,000 for the first time in memory, dropping to 69,442 for the year ending June 30.""

That year, during a public forum, the museum director shared that it was about to post a second $7 million deficit in a row. The need for bold action was evident. Fast forward to 2014, and millions of opinions and comments later, a solution was hatched, but not without more controversy. Approved by a DC Superior Court judge, the decision was made to move the College to George Washington University, with a slow transition to GWU curriculum and tuition prices. The National Gallery of Art will have first right of refusal of 17,000 artworks, and what they don't acquire will go to other museums and universities in DC. During the seven-day evidentiary hearing, the board chair testified that "the Corcoran was in default to creditors, on the verge of missing a payroll . . . over the past six years to cover the $26 million in losses, the Corcoran cannibalized $9 million from its endowment and 'borrowed' millions more from restricted accounts, promising to pay back the money from sales of real estate and other one-time windfalls."°°° With this court action, the Corcoran had a way forward.

As there is much more complexity to the story than can be presented here and it continues to unfold, take some time to research this case online. Then, consider these questions:

1. Was the merger financially prudent?
2. Consider the donor perspective. Was it possible to recover their support?
3. What is preserved when the collection is transferred to another Washington, DC museum?
4. If the Corcoran didn't enter this three-way merger, what financial options did it have?

°Montgomery, "Corcoran Gallery."
°°Ibid.
°°°Montgomery and Judkis, "Judge Approves . . ."; McGlone, "Secrecy Breeds Anxiety . . ."

targets in sight. Empowering staff members to understand the budget structure and decision-making process is the best first step to take. Selecting readings and training, sharing financial histories of the museum, and scheduling budget work sessions with open and transparent discussions are great ways to get everyone on the same page.

Budget Management Involves Everyone

The budget management process relies on both the museum's governing body and its staff. The roles they play depend on the size, structure, and income sources of the nonprofit. Those who plan the museum's finances should spell out roles and responsibilities through written policies and procedures, which should be kept up to date and be completely understood by those involved.

The trustees are crucial to the budget process. As Larry Yerdon, president and CEO at Strawbery Banke, rightly observes, "there is no secret to ensuring a balanced budget. The staff and board simply must adopt the discipline of balanced budgets."[31] It is the trustees' responsibility to not only ensure that the organization has the resources it needs to operate and meet strategic goals, but it is also their responsibility to ensure "that the museum's operating budget is developed in a way that reflects its priorities; formatted in a way that is clear and understandable to the board; and monitored by the board to make sure that funds are used to advance the mission and goals of the museum in an accurate, efficient, and effective way."[32]

Long-range planning and other financial planning, initiated by the board, serves as a means of balancing anticipated resources against future financial needs. The creation of a detailed five-year plan, with revisions each year based on current fiscal numbers, is essential to a museum's financial future. Trustees also have a vested interest in the museum's annual budget, because the board is ultimately responsible for the allocation of the museum's resources. Trustees cannot abdicate this responsibility by simply accepting the director's proposed budget without a critical evaluation. The board, in addition to its role of authorizing and overseeing expenditures, needs to provide policies and guidelines to help measure the impact of the budget, positive or negative.[33] The board's finance committee is often charged to work with the director and to evaluate changes during the fiscal year and adjust when making new projections to avoid potentially dangerous errors.

The executive director also figures into the equation of budget management. In a sustained, year-round effort, the director typically arranges any early strategic planning sessions with the trustees. The director prepares recommendations to guide budget development, ensures that the budget schedule deadlines are met, reviews the draft budgets, and makes resource allocation decisions. Once the budget receives board approval, the director moves to the monitoring stage with the assistance of the chief financial officer (CFO), provided one is on staff. The director works to communicate the results of financial observations and corrective actions to the trustees and also seeks the board's input and approval for the necessary fiscal or program changes. The CFO, who bears the day-to-day responsibilities of coordinating budget development, implementation, and monitoring, prepares and analyzes reports on budgeted versus actual income and expenses for the museum's fiscal management and for board use. The CFO must also oversee any corrective actions, such as reallocations or cuts, undertaken.[34]

The museum's program or division managers (curators, collection managers, educators, and so forth) provide specialized knowledge of the current program needs and costs and the impacts caused by any reduction or expansion of their program's operations. Managers develop draft budgets for their programs and divisions. As the budget is carried out, the managers are best qualified to participate in monitoring and to submit to the director resource allocation decisions or recommended changes in activities to meet the budgeted expense or income targets. Once the board, the director, and the CFO approve the budget, the program or division managers inform the staff about any budget or operational changes. Managers review regular financial reports created by the CFO, scrutinize income and expenses, and help determine and carry out corrective changes.[35]

Other possible participants in the process include the office support staff, whose responsibilities may include preparing documents and materials throughout the budgeting process. In small museums, one or two people may perform all the tasks associated with budget management; the director and support staff may divide the functions of the CFO.[36]

Consultants and outside specialists, such as independent auditors and accountants, architects, engineers, bond counsel, and program area specialists, also figure into the budget development and monitoring. Selected clients and volunteers may be needed to provide ideas for improving the budget. Specialized analysis may require the assistance of the information technology department, if there is one, or the museum's computer specialist.[37]

Management of the budget never ends with the approval by the board. Instead, the budgeting process is yearlong, involving people at every level in the institution, from the board to the director and chief financial officer to the department level. Each employee, by virtue of the paycheck received and the materials consumed in performance of the job, is a direct participant in the museum's budget management.

Tools of Measurement for Budget Management

Internal controls are a critical system to ensure the integrity and the financial well-being of the museum. To be sure, internal controls are not just occasional reviews but a whole system affecting day to day financial transactions, involving separation of duties, review and compliance, and more. These reviews, conducted by the treasurer or the whole finance committee may be conducted at periodic intervals and take a random look at the museum's accounting forms, payment authorization policies, inventory records, financial statements, or petty cash receipts. For example, at the American Association for State and Local History (AASLH), a small operation, the board treasurer reviews monthly reconciliation reports and bank and credit card statements and has the option to take a closer look at one or two additional reports at the same time. While the entire AASLH team has a role in budget performance, only the president, CEO, and business manager have direct responsibility for monitoring transactions.[38] Adding review by the treasurer offers an extra layer of oversight that can catch misstatements, incomplete documentation, and the worst, internal fraud. The same practice has been adopted by the Abbe Museum in Bar Harbor, Maine, as well as other small museum operations across the United States.

Sadly, fraud is common in nonprofits and museums are taking great steps to segregate duties. An example of this practice with limited finance staff is to have the administrative associate pick up the mail, while another like the director opens the mail and sorts it into the appropriate mailboxes, with the finance manager receiving all incoming donations, grants, and other payables. Some government systems require two people to open mail together to ensure logging of incoming receipts. The finance manager processes the transactions, prepares the bank deposit, and makes the deposit. The director reviews all of the income and expense documentation when signing checks and thank you letters. (Sometimes, museum policy requires two signatures on a check for them to be valid.) When reviewing incoming mail, the director takes a closer look at bank and credit statements and then reviews them again when reconciled. Once a month, the board treasurer reviews the finance manager's files and reviews reconciliation reports. And each month, the finance committee meets to report the past month's performance. The process can be tailored to each museum's culture, but ultimately, "no one individual should be responsible for all of the duties, whether dealing with revenues or expenses."[39]

Timing is a critical element to watch when monitoring the budget. You can have a great plan for the year, but cash will vary due to seasonality, planned investment disbursements (endowment draws), delayed receivables, and more. In government or public museums, budget allotments may be made only on a quarterly basis. A helpful tool is a cash flow projection.[40] The term "cash flow" designates the relationship between the amount of cash a museum actually has available in the bank during a given period and the amount it requires to pay the bills during the same period. Effective cash flow management requires ongoing attention, rather than a reactive response once cash flow problems develop. Cash flow projections predict when cash will be received by the museum each month and then compare cash expected with anticipated cash expenditures. The board and top management must then identify any projected periods of negative cash flow and plan specific actions to avoid such shortfalls so that programs and services may continue without interruption.[41]

Negative cash flow problems typically occur when the museum receives its income later than it is needed. A negative situation would occur, for example, in the case of "after-the-fact funding," in which some grants or contracts reimburse the museum only after specific services have been rendered. Nevertheless, the nonprofit has to pay for staff, office space, equipment and supplies, and other needed resources in advance. Similarly, in a seasonal museum the bulk of earned income may happen in the summer but there remains a year-round staff and other overhead costs to support. Monthly cash flow projections that focus on the anticipated timing of cash receipts and disbursements, supplemented by regular financial reports, help highlight times when cash flow problems are likely to occur or when cash would be available for investment or public funding source. The board and the museum's financial managers and director must plan far enough in advance of potential problems to allow for action to offset the risky negative cash flow. Possible solutions include the postponement of major purchases, hiring of new staff, or instituting wage increases.[42]

Another solution for budget managers in private nonprofit museums is short-term borrowing. Incurring debt should be considered with great caution; this seductive short-term solution can have long-term repercussions. More than one museum has found itself barely able to generate sufficient income to pay heavy debt interest, much less the principal owed.[43] The best scenario is one where there is a sizeable board-designated fund that can cover cash fluctuations and will replenish naturally at the end of the fiscal year. Most public museums are not allowed to incur debt.

An audit of a museum's finances by a neutral third party is a critical tool in museum financial management. For many museums, it's mandated by policy or a governing body, or the museum needs one to apply for certain grants. In some states, audits are required if the museum plans to fundraise.

Further, if a museum receives more than $750,000 in federal money during a single fiscal year, it is subject to an audit for that year and there are additional reviews and reports for that audit.[44]

To conduct an audit, a museum will engage a certified public accountant (CPA) who follows protocols that provide assurances, in written form, that the museum's financial records are "free from material misstatements and are fairly presented based on the application of generally accepted accounting principles (GAAP)."[45] A less in depth examination is called a review and even lesser is the compilation, but all often have an external audience—funders, public agencies, donors—as well as an internal audience—trustees and staff.[46] An audit boosts confidence in an organization's performance when the auditor's management letter offers no material weaknesses; and when the financial statements are reported with an unqualified opinion (or clean). This means that the statements are fairly presented. A qualified opinion is used when the statements are not in accordance with GAAP.[47]

Budget Management in Practice

Museums, whether nonprofit organizations or government entities, walk a delicate balance in budget management. As part of their mission of public service, museums can and do make money. It is advisable to have a surplus each year so that you can build funds to take care of facilities, launch mission-driven initiatives, retire debt, plan for the future, and more.[48] If circumstances make a large surplus unavoidable, the nonprofit board may designate such surpluses as "funds functioning as endowment."[49] But it's important to note that many museums, specifically those that are publicly owned and/or government funded, operate under a "balanced budget constraint" in which future funding may be jeopardized if there is a surplus at the end of the fiscal year. Elected officials may also look at revenues the museum earns as evidence the museum "can earn its own way." Some public museums are faced with a "use it or lose it" conundrum; unspent amounts revert back to the parent organization or governmental entity at the end of the fiscal year. Any "cushion" or contingency must be quickly spent, usually on equipment. Alert managers in such systems will prepare a list of potential expenditures to implement if circumstances allow/demand.

Financial Statements and Reports

A variety of internal reports may be used by museums to monitor their budgets, but the Federal Accounting Standards Board (FASB) has

Text Box 4.2 Internal Controls for the Smallest Museum

While this checklist speaks directly to small museums, larger institutions should have an internal control plan. Larger museums have the advantage of more people who can separate duties, but they have the same need to prevent fraud:

1. Set the control environment. Inform museum staff and board that there are policies in place to protect the assets of the museum and each person is expected to follow them.
2. Define clearly who is responsible for what. Who opens the mail? Who prepares checks for payment? Who signs checks?
3. Ensure physical controls. Be sure to lock up checks in drawers and secure assets.
4. After a big fundraising or income event, have two people count the cash together.
5. Reconcile the bank statements each month. Make sure someone other than the bookkeeper is reviewing the statements monthly.
6. Monitor payroll. Approve timesheets to prevent fraud.
7. Monitor credit card statements. Just like with bank statements, be sure to have someone other than the bookkeeper review monthly transactions.
8. Have two signatures on checks over a certain amount. While banks don't often enforce this policy, it is a good practice so for setting the right tone about internal controls.
9. The person handling the money should not sign checks. Avoid having the bookkeeper sign checks. In the smallest of museums, there may only be one staff person. In that case, have the board president or treasurer sign checks.

Source: Adapted from Ho, "Five Internal Controls for the Very Small Nonprofit."

designated standardized formal financial statements for nonprofits. These include:

1. Statement of Financial Position (Balance Sheet) offers an overall picture of the museum by reporting how much it has (assets like cash, investments, and property), how much it owes (liabilities like accounts

Text Box 4.3 Factors for Determining Reserve Levels*

1. Mission and long-term plans or strategies
2. Type of organization—higher education, religious, social services, museum, cultural, association, foundation, or other
3. Corporate structure—sole entity, parent/subsidiary entities, brother/sister entities, loosely affiliated groups, or others.
4. Investment in the physical plant—the facilities owned and/or leased
5. Complexities of the debt structure
6. Current and future commitments
7. Funding sources, including fundraising activities
8. Types of programs provided
9. Self-insurance
10. Workforce compensation and benefits issues

*When allowed by law and/or institutional policy.
Source: Adapted from Kennerley, "Maintaining Sufficient Reserves . . ."

payable, mortgage, bond debt), and how much it is owed (accounts receivable).[50]
2. Income Statement (Statement of Revenues and Expenses), a report of the amount of change in net assets for the period.
3. Statement of Cash Flows, which provides information about cash receipts and cash payments during a period.[51]

These statements may not apply to public/government funded entities but that they will have specific financial reports that board and staff should reference.

The information provided on these statements is important for external audits and for filing the tax-exempt nonprofit's annual return (Form 990) with the Internal Revenue Service (IRS). The financial statements help trustees and the director to determine whether the organization has a surplus, a deficit, or has made any unusually large expenditures or revenues.[52] This information is crucial in order for the nonprofit to engage in useful long- and short-term financial and strategic planning. Large deficits, of course, signify an institution in substantial trouble, with closure and dispersal of the collections a looming threat.

Text Box 4.4 Financial Reports Inventory

1. Monthly reports to all board and senior staff
   a. Dashboard—one-page; four to six boxes for very basic financial data and selected indicators
   a. Summary SOP (Statement of Financial Position/Balance Sheet)—one-page; year-to-date; disaggregated per undesignated, board designated, temporarily restricted, and permanently restricted; prior year comparison
   b. Summary SOA (Statement of Activities/P&L)—one-page; prior year comparison; year-to-date; annual budget; percentage of budget to date; year-end projection; variance budget vs. year-end; narrative re: variances
   c. Summary SFE (Statement of Functional Expenses)—one-page; year-to-date; summarized by major expense category; columns for aggregate total plus major activity classes; graph showing percentage of expenses per activity class
   d. Trend Graphs—one-page; several graphs or charts showing trend for selected indicators
   e. Development Summary—one-page; listed by source category with separate goals for restricted funds; budget; year-to-date; percentage of year-to-date; comparison to two prior years; chart of endowment fund balances to date
2. As needed and relevant, reports to all board and senior staff
   a. Ticket sales report
   b. Cash flow
   c. Special event report
3. Monthly reports to board committees, senior staff, and any board member by request
   a. Finance Committee
      i. Detail SOA
      ii. Net Assets History
      iii. Detail Line Item P&L
      iv. Detail Program P&L
   b. Development Committee
      i. Detail Development Report
      ii. Detail Gala/Special Event P&L
      iii. Restricted Grants Report

(continued)

Text Box 4.4 Financial Reports Inventory (continued)

   c. Marketing Committee
     i. Comprehensive (Ticket/Tuition) Sales Report / Detail P&L
     ii. Subscription/Package Sales Report (as relevant)
   d. Investments Committee
     i. Investments Analysis—endowment fund balances as a per-
       centage of long-term investments; updated with additions,
       withdrawals, transfers, income and adjustments to market
       value

Source: Adapted from Foley, "Internal Reports."

Cutting the Budget

What happens when the team misses the target and the budget has a
25 percent deficit or when a budget cut is mandated by the governmental
entity that provides substantial support? If the prior three years were at
least balanced or had a surplus, the team might not make a change for
next year's budget. But if there's no surplus allowable, such as with many
public entities, what can be done? Prudent practice depends on the nature
of the deficit. Did a major foundation shift its funding priorities and the
museum can no longer receive operational funds? There may not need to
be a cut because another foundation is lined up for next year. Are all of the
museum's income categories trending down? If so, it may be time to cut
because there's a pattern and it's time to retrench.

Increasing revenue is a logical way to combat the deficit but it's often the
steeper hill to climb. More revenue can often mean more costs—organizations have to spend money to make money. Cutting the budget is easier, but
it is difficult to climb out of the hole and regain donors.

Looking for warning signs will help. Is the local community experiencing
an economic downturn (mass layoffs nearby?). Are visitation numbers on
a steep decline (people aren't visiting as much)? Multiple bad quarters for
your investments may foreshadow a market correction that could hit your
endowment funds (is another recession on the horizon?). These indicators
do not necessarily signal impending disaster, but they are reasons to examine finances very closely and make course corrections.

Budget cutting is as complex as budget building and similarly should
involve participation of both board and staff in an honest assessment of
circumstances and options. Political and marketing skills are needed just as

much as financial expertise in order to preserve organizational morale and create mechanisms not only for survival but future growth. The Corcoran Gallery of Art example shows how mistakes of the past, ongoing missteps, and revolving doors of leadership can spell the end (see text box 4.1). A solid budget plan, matched with a "fundraising board" and mature development office, can fuel the sustainability of a museum.

ACCOUNTING

Budget management requires both a day-to-day approach and a long view. The critical data for this management are provided by the accounting system. Accounting is essentially an information system, which records, classifies, and summarizes business activity. The rules that govern how accountants measure, process, and communicate financial information are called Generally Accepted Accounting Principles (GAAP) and are sanctioned by the Financial Accounting Standards Board (FASB). This conformity provides assurances to interested parties—donors, lenders, trustees, and staff.[53]

Accounting Methods

Adequate accounting procedures and records are essential for the museum to manage monies received wisely and in accordance with its charitable purposes. There are two basic types of accounting systems—accrual and cash.

The accrual accounting system details revenues when they are received and expenses when they are committed. In the accrual system funds that have been committed are encumbered, and show on the books as having been spent, even if the money has not been paid out. The benefit of this system is that it gives you a clear view of the balance available for operating at any one point in time.

Cash accounting records transactions at the time they occur; revenue is noted when it is received and expenses are recorded when they are paid out. Dollars that have been committed to ordered materials or services not yet received are not reflected, nor is income owed but not yet received. The administrator must keep in mind that X dollars have been promised to Y, and therefore are not available to pay for Z. The benefit of this system is that it is simple, much like a personal checking account, and it reflects funds that are on hand at any one time. Many public/governmental museums operate on a modified cash basis, which allows for encumbrance of certain types of expenditures.

Text Box 4.5 Case Review: Chart of Accounts

A clearly articulated chart of accounts helps differentiate and track expenses. Excerpts from a private nonprofit museum's chart of accounts illustrate the range of expenditures incorporated under each account name:

50000   Cost of Goods Sold—describes the direct costs attributable to goods produced and sold in the museum shops

60000   Payroll—Wages and Salaries—expenses related to permanent and temporary employees

60200   Employee Benefits—expenses related to insurance, long-term disability, and retirement

60800   Payroll Taxes—staff and federal tax expenses

61000   Professional Fees—expenses related to legal, accounting, and payroll processing

61200   Recruitment Expense—costs associated with hiring employees

61400   Acquisition Expense—collections acquisitions expensed at the time of acquisition rather than added to Fixed Assets

61500   Management Fees—Endowment—any costs associated with investment funds

62000   Outside Personnel—consultants, presenters, fabricators, and other contractors hired for special projects

62100   Materials and Supplies—typically expenses related to educational programs and exhibits

62200   Shipping and Handling—shipping costs related to exhibit projects; shipping expenses from shop purchases are included in cost of goods sold

62300   Programs and Activities—program related expenses including membership

62400   Travel, Meals, and Lodging—expenses related to staff and presenter travel

62500   Conference and Professional Development—conference registration costs and other training expenses

62600   Dues and Memberships—organizational membership costs

62800   Marketing—advertising and promotion costs

62900   Events—goods and services purchases for events

65000   Office—costs associated with office supplies, postage, technology (hardware and software), and printing

66000   Organizational Expense—state and federal filing fees

66900   Reconciliation Discrepancies—any discrepancies during the monthly reconciliation process may be parked here until resolved

67000   Interest—fees associated with lines of credit and other credit and monthly banking fees

68000   Insurance—costs associated with fine arts coverage, the facilities, liability, and directors and officers insurance

80000   Occupancy Expenses—overhead costs of operating the museum including utilities, repairs and maintenance, telephone and data costs, and alarm systems

82000   In Kind Expense—when goods and services are donated, there must be a record on both the income and expense side

83000   Miscellaneous Other Expense—used sparingly, this line records unattributed expenses

84000   Depreciation and Amortization—transactions that record the loss in value of long-term assets

Source: Abbe Museum, 2015.

Regardless of the basis of accounting, museums will use a double entry process based on the algebraic formula, Assets = Liabilities + Net Assets. (Some of us find this equation easier to grasp if it is stated Assets – Liabilities = Net Assets.) Simply put, this means what the museum owns (assets) is equal to what it owes (liabilities) plus the net assets. Debits and credits are used to record changes in revenue, income, and expenses. For ease in recording and tracking information about specific transactions, specific account numbers are assigned to designate types of expenditures or income. A chart of accounts is the master list of all of the budget categories and typically contains the same categories seen on an income statement.[54]

The accounting system provides managers with critical monthly activity, rather than income statements, so that managers have information about outgoing funds as well as income. This information allows managers to make adjustments in implementing the planned budget, such as initiating or deferring purchases, delaying hiring of temporary staff, and so on, depending on the fiscal picture.

Monthly income status reports compare budgeted amounts to monthly expenditures and year-to-date totals. Many accounting software systems also calculate percentage of time elapsed and percentage of budget expended, a useful measure for tracking expenditures, like permanent salaries, that vary little from month to month.[55] Not all museum expenditures or income are regular; extra staff may be required during high visitation seasons, and admissions income may fluctuate due to weather or time of year. In such cases, data from prior fiscal years also may be included on these reports for comparative purposes, so that managers can see patterns over time. (See table 4.3 for an excerpt of a sample budget status report.)

The general ledger itemizes specific expenditures paid out and revenue generated. Access to this level of detail allows the manager to ascertain whether a particular vendor has been paid, how much income a given program has been generating, whether a grant payment has been received, and so on. (See table 4.4 for an excerpt of a sample general ledger.)

Table 4.3   Excerpt of a Monthly Budget Status Report

Budget Status Report as of 08/31/2015 Pct. of Time Elapsed = 17.26					
Expenditures	Budgeted Amount	Current Month	Year-to-Date	Pct. of Budget	Variance
4111 Permanent Salaries-Wages	$467,485.00	52,673.88	87,445.56	18.71	380,039.44
4131 Retirement Plans Expense	32,353.00	3,758.27	6,185.18	19.12	26,167.82
4132 OASDI Expense	33,899.00	3,893.66	6,427.02	18.96	27,471.98
4134 Life and Accident Insurance Expense	325.00	26.46	52.92	16.28	272.08
4135 Health Insurance Expense	61,464.00	4,636.02	9,047.45	14.72	52,416.55
4144 Employee Assistance Program	201.00				201.00
4211 Postage Expense	8,500.00	434.39	856.83	10.08	7,643.17
4212 Communication Expense	7,000.00	559.56	1,114.95	15.93	5,885.05
4215 Publication and Printing Expense	12,010.00	205.57	1,569.82	13.07	10,440.18

4311 Office Supplies Expense	7,795.00	646.45	1,940.63	24.90	5,854.37
4483 Workers Comp Premiums	1,100.00	2469.48	1,459.27	132.66	(359.27)
4100 Personal Services	$595,727.00	64,988.29	109,158.13	18.32	486,568.87
4200 Operating Account Total	93,727.00	6,107.40	12,214.46	13.03	81,512.54
4700 Travel Account Total	10,300.00	1,689.16	2,436.09	23.65	7,863.91
4800 Capital Outlay Account Total	7,700.00				7,700.00
Expenditures Total	707,454.00	691,46.93	123,808.68	17.5	561,767.60

Summary of Expenditures by Fund Type	Budgeted Amount	Current Month	Year-to-Date	Pct. of Budget	Variance
1000 General Fund	606,394.00	69,146.93	120,901.04	19.94	463,615.24
2000 Cash Fund	101,060.00		2,907.64	2.88	98,152.36
Expenditures Total	707,454.00	69,146.93	123,808.68	17.5	561,767.60

Clues to Deciphering Budget Status Report

Note date of report and percent of time elapsed. This will tell you when the fiscal year began, in this case, July 1.

Read column headers to ascertain what column numbers designate, and whether numbers indicate dollars, percentages, or other measures.

Comparing percentages of budget expended year-to-date with percentage of time elapsed is one way of tracking expenditures. Be aware that not all expenses occur on a regular basis; seasonal spending decreases or increases can cause a false sense of security or panic. Ideally your budget report would include the previous year's history, providing a ready comparison for determining whether increased or decreased expenditures are typical.

Parentheses ( ) indicate negative numbers, indicating overspent accounts where actual expenses exceeded budgeted amounts.

Most reports include summary lines that group related accounts together—in this case, all accounts related to employee salaries and benefits are lumped together for easy reference under "Personal Services Account Total."

Blanks indicate no activity in the particular account. In some reports this lack of activity might be reflected by zeros or dashes (---).

In fund accounting systems, reports may indicate which fund or "pot" expenditures have been made from. Revenue sources and amounts will be included in most reports, although they are not excerpted here.

Source: Adapted from Nebraska State Historical Society, 2015.

Accounting Software

Good budget management relies on the accurate and complete analysis of as much fiscal data as possible. While nothing is technically wrong with using traditional paper and pencil ledger books, it's really only effective for small museums with very few transactions or with an absence of able

Table 4.4   Excerpts from Monthly General Ledger Report

General Ledger as of 8/31/2015

Account	Trans Date	Payee/Explanation	Current Month	Year-to-Date
4111	8/11/2000	Payroll B16	64,988.29	109,158.13
4211	8/17/2000	All Needs Computer and Mailing	434.39	856.83
4212	8/28/2000	DAS Communications	559.56	1,114.95
4215	8/23/2000	Snapper's Camera	205.57	801.21
4311	8/14/2000	Information Technology Solutions	404.80	
4311	8/18/2000	WF Office Equipment		
4311	8/23/2000	Laser Blazers, Inc.	178.00	
		Detail account 4311 total	646.65	1058.58
4483		Balance Forward		1459.27
		Revenue		
7111	8/03/2000	Admissions for week of 7/26	693.75	35,782.00
7211	8/09/2000	MF Producer Services	93.27	
	8/17/2000	Educational Telecommunications	475.69	
	8/21/2000	Houghton Mifflin	1000.00	
		Detail account 7211 total	1568.96	11,152.64

Clues to Deciphering General Ledger Reports
General ledgers function somewhat like a "checkbook," and show the date an amount was paid, the payee, and the amount paid from that account to date. The report breaks down the lump sums listed as paid out of particular accounts in the monthly status report. (Compare the three transactions paid from account 4311 on this general ledger report to the amount listed under that account on the budget status report in table 4.3.)
"Balance Forward" denotes accounts in which there was no activity in the reporting period.
General ledger reports also list specific amounts of revenue and their sources (income from museum admissions, sales of photographs, or other reproductions of collections materials).
Source: Adapted from Nebraska State Historical Society, 2015.

volunteers or board members. Many software packages are available for museum use that link the database functions essential for budgeting and the accounting function of the spreadsheet. These software solutions lead to efficiency and accuracy, and many, like QuickBooks™, are easy to learn. The most popular solution for smaller nonprofits, QuickBooks™ also simplifies Internal Revenue Service reporting requirements and payroll services. The skill is in making sure data entry is consistent, accurate, and logical so that reports are clear and replicable so that review and analysis can be accomplished.[56]

The Necessity of Number Crunching

Accounting is a critical means of accomplishing financial record keeping for museums. Accounting practices and procedures may be slightly more casual or formal depending on the size and complexity of the organization and on whether most accounting is done internally or externally. Regardless of the size of the nonprofit, accounting practices are valuable aids in decision making and for communicating fiscal information.

While financial statements deliver considerable information about the health of an organization, its level of fitness can be better understood through ratio analysis. Ratios will tell how efficient and "profitable" the museum is and they will help an analyst predict the financial future. To gather the most meaning, it's helpful to compare this ratio to other like organizations and industry standards. Ratios are most informative when comparing organizations of similar size and age, geographic area, and missions and programs. And they are most appropriate when tracking progress over time. A snapshot, out of context, can be misleading.[57] The key is to pick three or four ratios that relate the most to your mission and inform your fundraising practices. Table 4.5 offers a selection of ratios.

Table 4.5   Exercise: Nonprofit Financial Ratios

To gain a better understanding of the museum financial management, reach out to a local museum director or museum chief financial officer and ask for a six-month and twelve-month profit and loss statement and balance sheet. Using the ratio formula below, make the calculations and assess the financial health of the museum. Obtain permission from the director or financial officer of the museum before sharing with colleagues or classmates.

Income Ratio: Reliance Ratio	Largest type of income ÷ total income	Reliance on type of income. Awareness of the risk of a major reduction in income if this type is reduced or stopped. May be helpful for more than one type of income, including special events.
Expense Ratio: Personnel Costs Ratio	Total wages, taxes, and benefits ÷ total expenses	Since staff cost is usually the largest part of the budget, any changes in the percentage of budget used for staff is notable.
Balance Sheet Ratio: Current Ratio	Current assets ÷ current liabilities	An indication of the organization's ability to pay obligations in a timely way (within twelve months). It is also a useful indicator of cash flow in the near future.

(continued)

Balance Sheet Ratio: Days Cash on Hand	**Step 1:** (Annual expense budget − depreciation − in-kind expense − pass-through funds − unusual, one-time expenses) ÷ annual cash requirement	A quick test of the operating cash or adequacy of the operating reserve. Include all unrestricted cash accounts such as savings and money market accounts.
	Annual cash requirement ÷ 365 = Daily cash requirement **Step 2:** Cash and current investments ÷ daily cash requirement	Setting a target for case accounts should take several factors into consideration, including reliability of income.
Balance Sheet Ratio: Debt Ratio	Total liabilities ÷ total unrestricted next assets	How much the organization is relying on funding from others, such as loans, payables, and obligated funds. Indication of how much of a cushion there is.

Source: Excerpted from "Analyzing Financial Information Using Ratios."

CONCLUSION

The easiest way to become familiar with budgeting and accounting systems is to jump in and start dealing with numbers. While the terms and steps involved in the budgetary process are many and complex, it is worth the time it takes to fully understand the flow of money and how it is accounted for in a museum, whether it's a nonprofit or publicly funded. Understanding how the money works gives a museum staff member knowledge and power, even if the staff member isn't directly involved in day-to-day financial management. By looking at consistent reports and addressing real situations, the process becomes clearer.

All museums, large and small, need to have policies and procedures in place that guarantee the budget, once prepared, is followed. The board is ultimately responsible for ensuring that the budget produced is realistic and that it is carried out. But it's the staff who actually expend funds, generate and receive income. Budgeting affects every department and every program in every museum. In an environment where funding is less than abundant, responsible staff will stick to the budget developed through the museum's process. While most staff did not join the museum profession purely for the joy of budgeting and accounting, it will be to their and the museum's benefit to spend time and energy attending to financial processes. Without sound fiscal practices, the museum's future (as well as the staff member's) is endangered.

Budget management provides one of the major keys to an institution's failure or success. Museums face a world of increased competition for public and private funds. Developing and monitoring an annual budget in support of the organization's "mission-driven" focus bolsters the museum's chances for financial stability and security. Budget failure or success determines the future for the museum director, as well. Budget management requires sufficient planning and development, staff involvement, and continual monitoring aided by tools of monthly reports and annual audits to ensure that the doors will remain open and services will be provided to the community.

Financial mismanagement, as some museums have learned, is a very possible precursor to institutional closure. The finest collections, best-designed facilities and programs, and most talented staff in the world cannot ensure the financial stability of the museum. Without a solid economic foundation, maintained by careful budget planning and accurate accounting, the museum's physical and human assets are in jeopardy. Understanding the museum's financial processes empowers staff to actively participate in wise use of museum resources and its ultimate survival and success. Whether you serve on the board or staff of a museum, it is your duty to understand the organization's finances.

Text Box 4.6 Guiding Questions

1. Consider the many ways museums attract income. What ideas for finding new income do you have?
2. If you work in a museum, consider your involvement in finances. Is it adequate?
3. What is the secret to building a balanced budget?

NOTES

1. Harvard Business School, *Finance for Managers*, 111.
2. Lord and Lord, *The Manual of . . .*, 215.
3. AccountingEdu.org, "Fund Accountancy."
4. Foley, "Internal Reports."

5. Miller, "Donor Imposed Restrictions."

6. Kennerley, "Maintaining Sufficient . . .," 5.

7. Lord and Lord, *The Manual of . . .*, 214.

8. Ibid., 215.

9. Foley, "Budgeting Terms . . ."

10. Wolf, *Managing a Nonprofit*, 174–75.

11. Nold, interview.

12. Granger, interview.

13. Nold, interview.

14. Batic, interview.

15. Durel and Phillips, *Strategic and Inclusive*.

16. Stroh, interview.

17. Granger, "The Good, the Best . . .," 10, 18.

18. Skramstad and Skramstad, *Handbook*, 51.

19. Durel and Phillips, *Strategic and Inclusive*, 1.

20. Klingler and Roberts, "Building Better Budgets," 2.

21. Ibid.

22. Wolf, *Managing a Nonprofit*, 188–89.

23. Ibid., 189–91.

24. Miller, "Donor Imposed . . ."

25. Boland, "The Importance . . ."

26. Wolf, *Managing a Nonprofit*, 191–93.

27. Ibid., 194–95.

28. Ibid,. 195.

29. Ibid., 196–97.

30. Montgomery, "Corcoran Gallery"; Montgomery and Judkis, "Judge Approves . . ."

31. Yerdon, interview.

32. Skramstad and Skramstad, *Handbook*, 51.

33. Granger, "The Good, the Best . . .," 10.

34. Dropkin et al., *The Budget-Building Book*, 14.

35. Ibid., 15–16.

36. Ibid., 15.

37. Ibid., 16

38. AASLH, *Financial Policies*.

39. Granger, "The Good, the Best . . ."

40. Klingler and Roberts, "Improving Financial . . .," 6.

41. Dropkin et al., *The Budget-Building Book*, 9.

42. Ibid., 88–89.

43. Ibid., 102–3.

44. National Council of Nonprofits, "Does Your Nonprofit Need . . .," and "Federal Law Audit Requirements."

45. Washington, "Audit vs Review."

46. Klingler and Roberts, "Improving Financial . . .;" Washington, "Audit vs Review."

47. Washington, "Audit vs Review."

48. Kennerley, "Maintaining Sufficient . . .," 5.

49. Wolf, *Managing a Nonprofit*, 185–86.

50. Klinger and Roberts, "Improving Financial . . .," 2.

51. Phelan, *Museum Law*, 40.

52. Wolf, *Managing a Nonprofit*, 215.

53. Harvard Business School, *Finance for Managers*, 38.

54. Wolf, *Managing a Nonprofit*, 176, 216.

55. Ibid., 221–22.

56. Klingler and Roberts, "Building Better Budgets," 6–7.

57. McLean and Coffman, "Why Ratios . . ."

❺

SUSTAINABILITY

As predominantly nonprofit organizations or governmental entities, museums' financial stability and future rely on effective fundraising and revenue-generating practices that provide for present operational needs and generate income for future capital and operational needs. The sustainability of any museum requires this present and future mindset. And to be sustainable, the museum must also be able to weather leadership and economic change, and other unexpected transitions or impacts.[1] Nothing compromises a museum's operational ability more than a lack of funding. Luckily, there are legions of articles, books, blog posts, and professional training that share how to attract resources to the museum's mission and retain annual support. This chapter aims to distill for administrators the key information about development and earned income that will create a financially viable museum.

DEVELOPMENT

Development is an ongoing effort that relies on a variety of strategies and it considers a long-term view. Fundraising is one part of the development, or advancement, process. While the end result of development is money, development is really about building relationships with people.[2] It is individual people who make the decision to become a member, attend a special event, contribute to a campaign, or write a will. And it is groups of people who decide which grants to fund. So successful development activity requires the involvement of individuals (e.g., the director, development officer, or board members) who are as personable as they are financially savvy.

When asked what the characteristics of a good fundraiser are, Fruitlands Executive Director Wyona Lynch-McWhite shared, "Effective fundraisers are good at listening, connecting with folks, and following through with the process. They are museum ambassadors who help connect people with gifts they want to share to the projects and activities that are meaningful to them. And when this is a development officer, he should also be an organized multi-tasker who has a master plan for how potential donors are being stewarded and solicited."[3]

It's also helpful to remember that fundraising, while focused on asking for money, is really about sharing a story you are passionate about with someone with similar interests. That's all. If you believe in the mission, and have a little training in fundraising techniques, you can transform yourself from a hesitant participant to a dynamic fundraiser.

Successful fundraising organizations also know that development is everyone's job—the staff member, the volunteer, the trustee—and each is expected to participate in appropriate ways. Anita Durel, museum consultant and fundraising expert, explains it this way, "It's about creating a culture of philanthropy in your organization by building a welcoming museum that manifests care for the visitor and focuses on bringing the mission to as many people as possible. This may not sound like development, but development is based on every relationship that everyone on the board and staff and front line folks encounter. This must be taught and staff must be trained to understand that this is an institutional value."[4]

Development can be broken down into three principal monetary areas:

- Annual Needs—the funding required for a museum's yearly programming and daily operations;
- Capital Needs—new buildings, renovations, and repairs a museum anticipates it will require in the next ten to fifteen years to continue to develop its programming and to serve its constituency; and
- Endowment Needs—Interest earned from endowment funds ensures a steady source of operating support to offset fluctuations in donations and grants. An endowment provides a secondary source of income.

Table 5.1 Exercise: Are You Ready to Raise Money?

Take a moment and review the following questions. If the answer is yes to all of them, then the museum has an outstanding development program underway. If there are one or two "no" answers, no problem. Not every program is fully functional, but awareness of the issues is helpful. If the museum has six or more "no" answers, a serious review of development functions is recommended.

If this exercise is being reviewed for a class, reach out to a development professional in a local museum and interview him or her about these questions. If this exercise is being used in a museum setting, please use it as a quick way to assess the readiness of the museum's development program.

	Yes	No
1. We have a clearly defined, fully understood, and completely accepted mission statement that addresses the difference our organization will make for those it serves, rather than merely describing what it does.		
2. We know exactly what our operational budget numbers are. When it comes to raising money, we know our expenses, and we can set fundraising goals and let prospective donors know our needs.		
3. We have a board of trustees committed to leading our organization and raising funds, and all fundraising campaigns begin with those trustees.		
4. We always present compelling cases for support that not only state the amounts we need, but present the reasons our organization merits support.		
5. We always follow the steps of major prospect cultivation—identification, information, interest, and involvement—because successful fundraising is based upon relationships, relationships, and more relationships.		
6. We prioritize individuals, corporations, and foundations for best funding potential, understanding that real wealth lies in the hands of individuals and that corporations and foundations are not usually the best source or first-choice for our organization's needs.		
7. We never assume our fundraisers know our organization, the purpose of the campaign, or how to ask for money, and we always equip them with easy-to-use solicitation kits that provide needed information and instill confidence.		
8. We always suggest a specific gift amount to every prospect, and while we know the dollar amount we want, we suggest donors contribute it, rather than tell them they should give it.		
9. We always record gifts and collect money in a timely fashion following required practices of our finance department and auditors. This can greatly relieve problems with disputed or canceled pledges. And we promptly send out thank you messages.		
10. We promptly deposit checks, acknowledge gifts, and apprise fundraisers of receipts of those gifts. We never want to hear from our donors, "I sent my check in two months ago, but still don't know if you received it."		
11. We cultivate donors and prospects by inviting them to events, annual meetings, and site visits and issuing newsletters and other communications, making sure that they hear from us at times other than when we are asking for money.		
12. We announce results, give recognition, and thank donors and volunteers, giving credit where it's due and oft times where it's not, so that as many volunteers as possible feel a sense of accomplishment for our success.		

Source: Adapted from Poderis, "Check Out Your Organization's Fund-Raising."

Every museum could argue that it deserves charitable donations and grants, but is the museum ready to accept donations and steward donors? If the museum isn't ready, the development cycle will be frustrating and ultimately unsuccessful. A thorough internal assessment should be done by board and staff to determine readiness (see text box 5.1).

MAKING A PLAN

There are a few well-proven facts and best practices that board members and staff need to understand as they establish fundraising goals and make plans to achieve them:

- In 2014, a total of $358.31 billion was contributed to nonprofit organizations, according to Giving USA 2015.[5]
- Individual giving is the cornerstone of nonprofit annual and major giving. In 2014, 72 percent of the charitable gifts to nonprofit organizations came from individual donors, with only 15 percent coming from foundations, another 8 percent from bequests, and 5 percent from corporations.[6]
- Of the total giving in 2014, just under 5 percent went to arts, culture, and humanities (this is the sector where museums and history organization show up). The largest sector, religion, received 33 percent of the contributions. Of particular note, education is second at 17 percent. The more connected you are with K-12 education, the more eligible you are for a bigger piece of the funding pie.[7]
- There is often an 80/20 rule in fundraising. On average, 80 percent of the dollars comes from 20 percent of your donor base. And 80 percent of the dollars raised annually occur within 20 percent of the annual calendar (year-end giving).[8]
- It's a very rare gift that is a large first gift. With caring stewardship combined with appropriate solicitation methods, identifiable segments of the membership base will move up the donor ladder toward larger and larger gifts. This process is a natural progression—a continuum—for our solicitation efforts and our donors.
- Donors must be an involved constituency and care about the service you provide.
- The board must be the vanguard of those supporting the museum. They must have 100 percent participation in the giving program at the highest level they can each support. Major gifts usually come in large part from the board and their relationships.

Text Box 5.1 Development Plan Structure

It is an excellent idea to develop a plan that annually guides a museum's fundraising activity. At the core of the plan are strategies for membership acquisition and renewal, annual fund donations, major gifts program details, planned giving strategies, and if the timing is right, a capital campaign. The audience for the plan is the staff team and the board of trustees and it should align closely with the strategic plan.

Each gift strategy will identify the financial goal, the objective for that pursuit, actions to be taken, and a timeline for completion. The following checklist offers a template for drafting a development plan:

1. Introduction—Offer a brief introduction about philanthropy in general and how it is evident locally. A description of the plan's purpose is valuable as well. Include the mission and vision of the museum to remind readers what these strategies will make possible. This section may also include a situational analysis that shares what the museum does well and where the museum needs to improve.

2. Annual Membership Drives—Establish the time of year and number of mailings for acquiring new members (acquisition mailing). The nature of the membership program can be identified here, including benefits offered and the renewal cycle (frequency and type of mailings). Identify the source(s) of acquisition names— board members turn in names, exchange lists with collaborators, purchase a list, etc. Renewal mailing frequency should be established as well, preferably monthly and on the anniversary of the member's last renewal.

3. Annual Fund—At least twice per year, request for annual fund donations will be made through direct mail. To alleviate donor confusion, it's best to make sure the membership program has taken root (one to two renewal cycles) before asking for donations above the membership level. It is also advisable to segment the mailing list so that membership renewal letter and an annual appeal letter are not going to the same house at the same time. In addition to direct mail, face-to-face requests may be planned as well.

4. Major Gifts Program—In addition to a well-established annual fund appeal process, a major gift program is advisable. How a major gift is defined depends on the museum ($500 and above?

(continued)

Text Box 5.1 Development Plan Structure (continued)

$1,000 and above? $2,500 and above?). This section will also outline the approach to donor prospect research; for example, paying for database access, relying on internal database, and sharing
information among board members.

5. Stewardship—Intrinsic to the fundraising process is the expression of gratitude. The number and type of thank you letter(s)
should be identified here as well as the signatory. Other ways to
keep members and donors close is to host annual events or parties
to show gratitude in addition to standard museum discounts.

6. Grant Development—Identify the frequency and annual goals of
grant writing projects; keeping in mind the balance between staff
time and the amount of money requested. It's helpful to back up
this section with a spreadsheet that identifies likely and past grant
makers matched to specific projects, listed with deadlines.

7. Capital Campaign—Capital campaigns can be time-consuming
and costly, but they tend to be the easier to fulfill. They represent
tangible results, such as restoration project, expansion of a wing,
etc. However, board members and staff always know that steady
funding is needed for operating expenses and that it's more difficult to secure it. With an established membership and annual
fund campaign, adding a capital campaign to the mix should
minimally impact operating income. The key is in proper timing,
an established donor base, and suitable prospect research—asking
the right people at the right time. If a capital campaign is on the
horizon, identify it here along with the timeline.

8. Endowment Campaign—The proper timing for an endowment
campaign is contingent upon capital campaign timing and its success. For an endowment campaign, a feasibility study is essential
and its timing can be identified here. Once an endowment campaign is launched, the strategies will be included in this plan.

9. Fundraising Events—Identify each year's planned events and
the goals for each. This can include a major fundraising event as
well as small cultivation parties. It's easy to fall into the special
event trap where board members are comfortable throwing an
event together, but the development goals for the event are an
afterthought. Special events are the mother of all time eaters for
museum staff—if there's no logical, clear reason for the event,
don't do it.

10. Planned Giving—An easily overlooked piece of fundraising, this section can identify how information about the museum can be disseminated to wealth planners and attorneys. Many museums don't have a planned giving expert on staff, but they can connect with knowledgeable people in the community. This section can also identify what steps will be taken upon notification of a bequest or charitable trust gift and planned visits to make requests.

11. Communications—Similar to the stewardship strategies, this section will call attention to the ways in which the museum keeps its donors informed. Strategies may include newsletters, individualized letters, annual report, greeting cards, public relations, and marketing.

12. Evaluation—The most apparent measure of a plan's success is increased contributions and improvement in the organization's "bottom line." It can also be measured through anecdotal examples and surveys. This information should be regularly reported in board meetings and communicated to the community through the newsletter and press releases. In addition, if funds are not flowing in as projected, course corrections are needed. Plans to evaluate the fundraising progress should be spelled out here. A great way to visually demonstrate the impact of the museum's fundraising efforts is with a dashboard that tracks the goals compared to actual results. This dashboard is regularly shared with board and staff to encourage fundraising activity and to celebrate successes.

Sources: Adapted from Catlin-Legutko, "Fearless Fundraising"; Anderson, *2015 Abbe Museum Development Plan*; Andrews, *Children's Museum of Tacoma FY16 Development Team Plan*.

Diversified income streams are critical to the sustainability of any organization. If one revenue source is negatively impacted by external or internal forces, then the other sources of income can pick up the slack in a given budget cycle.

To be effective, a museum's development plan needs to identify all potential sources of income that the museum will pursue, taking special care to target individual giving. A development plan should also be consistent with the goals of a museum's strategic plan, and starts where the strategic plan ends by mapping out how the museum will raise funds in each

Text Box 5.2 A Word about Development Committees

Typically, development committees are part of a museum's governance structure and many consultants and peer assessors will recommend forming one to support the fundraising actions of the board. However, it's very easy for board members to shunt their fundraising role to the committee and forget that bringing resources to the organization is a primary responsibility for board members. And it's very easy for a committee to get stuck or overstep boundaries without clear purpose.

Unless your board has a proven track record of universal participation in fundraising activities, you need a development committee with a chair or chairs who are focused on engaging their board peers. How that committee operates depends on the museum's staffing structure. If you're a small museum with one employee, you need all the help you can get and a properly functioning committee will help. If you have someone on staff, in addition to the director, responsible for fundraising, a committee may not be needed as much. Instead, that staff member, or director of development, will work with specific board members as fundraising visits are made. This structure is possible with only one employee as well.

If you decide that a development committee is what you need, a clear job description is required at the outset. Here is a sample committee overview:

> The development committee leads the fundraising efforts of the organization. Although fundraising is the responsibility of all board members, the committee is responsible for setting the policies and expectations, planning the donor approach, coordinating leads, facilitating and implementing direct asks, and making a case to the community. Committee members may include board members, members of the executive committee, and other individuals not yet engaged on the board, such as members or volunteers.

As you develop the description it would be a good idea to fully outline what roles the committee will fulfill in the development plan. Whatever you do, be very clear about what everyone's roles and responsibilities are and give them deadlines. Museums can be easily shackled by a lack of action in the development arena.

Source: Adapted from Catlin-Legutko, "Fearless Fundraising."

of the identified areas. The scope of the development plan depends on the needs of the museum and the scope of the fundraising campaign. Together the strategic plan and the development plan help a museum determine and achieve its fundraising priorities.[9]

Regardless of the goal amount or the funding source being pursued, the benefits of creating a development plan outweigh the costs. Generating funds has become more sophisticated and requires careful planning and analysis. Understanding fundraising principles enables a museum to target different funding sources (donations, grants, and earned income) effectively. Many efforts have failed because of inadequate understanding or planning. The planning process allows the people involved to examine all the factors from different perspectives and gain full knowledge of the goal of the fundraising effort, their responsibilities, how the campaign will be operated, and the schedule.

With the plan in place, "the institution has clear priorities for development officers to follow," shared Jill Rudnitski, chief development officer at the Minnesota Historical Society. "It is less successful to send development staff out to meet with donors without this, and can lead to some funky, overly-restricted gifts that may not be useful to the organization, but follow a donor's passion instead." An organized development office is also critical. "It's important to have a smoothly functioning back-office that can generate annual gifts and memberships, freeing development officers to be out the door. If the back office functions don't work, donor receipts get lost, or thank you notes are not prompt and personal, a lot of positive initiative can be lost fixing relationships with disappointed donors."[10] Of course, in smaller museums where there is limited development staff, board members and volunteers can help with these functions.

RAISING FUNDS

The dynamics of giving follow three paths to your organization: linkage, ability, and interest.[11] A linkage can happen through membership, a regular program participation, or a donation to the collection. Ability is simply having the resources to make a gift. Research will determine how able the individual is. An interest or inclination toward the organization makes "the ask" more "warm." Linkage and interest can be influenced by museum board and staff.

To change and improve linkages and interests, the development staff, committee, and trustees work in the community spreading the message for the museum and building confidence in the organization. Inviting people to the museum for a personal tour with the director or curator is a great way to orient a potential donor to the mission. Follow-up can include inviting them back to see an educational program in action. The strategic plan, case statement, direct mailings, member parties, and personal interaction all provide the contact and discussion points for this effort.

Keeping in mind that development is about building relationships, it is also wise to learn individual and corporate giving motivations. Understanding these motivations is critical to the fundraising cycle and you can use a donor's interest to develop connections.

A great story about an exciting gift illustrates how linkage, interest, and capacity can come together. At the Golden History Museums in Golden, Colorado, museum director Nathan Richie offered how a lead gift came unexpectedly. "We are in the midst of a rehabilitation of one of our historic sites which received a state historical fund grant, which was a great catalyst. But we are also working on a whole new reinterpretation of the site. I put together a presentation and used the Friends (our auxiliary group) as my test audience. One of my board members was so excited by the idea that she asked immediately if it would be helpful to have some seed money to get things rolling—to which of course I said yes. Less than an hour later she called me to pledge $5,000 towards the project. As a small museum, this is one of our largest individual contributions ever. It feels so exhilarating to know that people are jazzed by our ideas and want to help them come to reality."[12]

Individuals

Individual donors give from the heart. While their donations may be advantageous to their pocketbooks by lessening their tax burdens, most donors give to what they believe in and their motivations vary. Possibly the best research into why people contribute large gifts is the 1994 landmark social study, *Seven Faces of Philanthropy*. Understanding these "faces" helps the fundraiser make a case for giving, prepare the appropriate ask, and steward the donor in the best way possible:

1. Repayer: Doing Good in Return—a donor who has benefitted from the mission in some way.
2. Investor: Doing Good Is Good Business—a donor who invests in the mission for tax benefits and an appreciation for the organizational strategy.

3. Socialite: Doing Good Is Fun—these donors believe they can make a difference by giving but also believe in having a good time doing it.
4. Communitarian: Doing Good Makes Sense—they believe in active community involvement and by giving they make the community a better place.
5. Devout: Doing Good Is a Moral Obligation—the donor is motivated by belief, and sometimes by faith.
6. Altruist: Doing Good Feels Right—a donor who gives out of empathy and generosity and typically chooses to be anonymous.
7. Dynast: Doing Good Is a Family Tradition—this is a donor who gives because it is part of their family and personal identity to give.[13]

These categories have mostly held true through the years and will manifest in a fundraiser's portfolio of prospects. In 2011, Guidestar and Hope Consulting published *Money for Good II*, and in it they proposed six new donor segments that over some overlap with the *Seven Faces* construct:

1. Casual Giver: "I give to well-known nonprofits because it isn't very complicated" (18 percent of donors).
2. Repayer: "I give to my alma mater" or "I support organizations that have had an impact on me or a loved one" (23 percent of donors).
3. High Impact: "I support causes that seem overlooked" or "I give to nonprofits I feel are doing the most good" (16 percent of donors)
4. Faith Based: "We give to our church" or "We only give to organizations that fit with our religious beliefs" (16 percent of donors).
5. See the Difference: "I think its important to support local charities" or "I give to small organizations where I feel I can make a difference" (13 percent of donors).
6. Personal Ties: "I give when I am familiar with the people who run an organization" (14 percent of donors).[14]

As with any fundraising strategy or program, it's critical to know as much as possible about the prospective donors. Of particular note are the millennial donors, born between the 1980s and late 1990s, who see themselves as investors when they donate. They make up 25 percent of the U.S. population. Millennials are giving in dramatically different ways than their older colleagues, family members, and friends. They appreciate a sense of belonging and they are very interested in impact and tangible results of their giving. And they are concerned about many social issues, not just one or two. They perceive that many social problems are interrelated and complex.

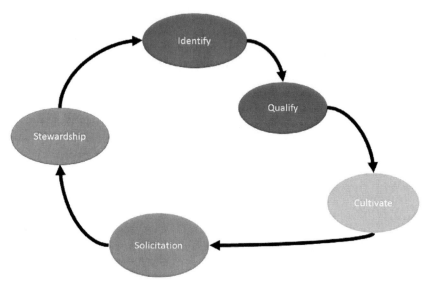

Figure 5.1 Moves Management Cycle. *Source*: Cinnamon Catlin-Legutko

They are not the type of donor who gives because her family always gave in a specific way. She gives to a cause. And millennial donors are happy to give micro-gifts as to a nonprofit that they may not be familiar with, but are motivated by the cause. A recent study found that 60 percent of adult millennials give, which accounts for 11 percent of total giving each year. While not fully on par with the other generations, millennials are a sizeable donor group that will only grow in giving amounts and individual gifts as millennials age.[15]

In addition to knowing what motivates a prospective donor, it's also smart to have a plan for moving a donor toward a first gift and then toward bigger gifts. Popularized by David Dunlop at Cornell University, moves management is the process of developing individuals into major donors. These strategies offer a tool for measuring the progress of fundraisers and keeps the process focused until success. They can also be used to develop and steward grant funders and other donor types.[16] Moves are defined as cultivation opportunities that can nurture linkage and interest for the museum, such as special curator-led tours, behind-the-scenes experiences, dining opportunities with the CEO, and opportunities to provide feedback on programs and initiatives. These "moves" are tailored for the individual and her motivations and seek to engage the donor in the mission so that gift solicitation is appropriate and more successful. In short, moves management can be seen in four steps:

1. Identify and qualify the donor—Are they a match? Are they able to give?
2. Cultivate the individual into becoming a donor—Get to know the person and confirm his area of interest.
3. Solicit the gift—Make a well-prepared formal request for a gift.
4. Stewardship—Thank the donor and keep her apprised of the gift's impact.[17]

When it's time to make the next request for funds, the cycle starts all over again. Ideally you've maintained a solid relationship with the donor through savvy stewardship, but don't assume status quo when you return for an additional ask.

Corporations

Corporations give for several reasons: good corporate citizenship, enlightened self-interest, individual leadership, location, and *quid pro quo* interests. In this "cause-related" or "strategic" philanthropy, corporations give to help themselves. Corporations are conservative in their giving patterns because they are accountable to stockholders, customers, unions, and executives. They usually do not support projects that are controversial or antibusiness, so as to prevent potential conflict of interest with their shareholders.

The current trend of corporate donations to museums is through corporate sponsorship. Sponsorship of museums and their programs allows profit-making companies to reach a specific group of consumers and get a bargain for corporate marketing dollars. In a deal with Hyundai Capital America, for example, the Museum of Modern Art (MoMA) secured a two-year sponsorship in support of their collection exhibitions produced by their Architecture and Design Department. The company gains significant exposure for its car brand in New York City, while showcasing their support for architecture and design "as allied and interdependent arts." In return, MoMA is offering free admission to all of Hyundai's employees so they may inspired by the exhibitions.[18]

Corporate sponsorship can come in many forms depending on the needs of the museum and the corporation. And the gifts can be large and small. In Greeley, Colorado, Guaranty Bank sponsored free admission for Greeley History Museum's 2015 Halloween programming. For several years, Machias Savings Bank has underwritten free admission for the Abbe Museum (Bar Harbor, Maine) visitors in the off season (November through April).

As is typical practice, corporations, as well as many individuals, like to have their name attached to their support. These opportunities range from a program series, to an endowed position, or the naming of a building. Corporations appreciate the strengthened image and goodwill that goes along with substantial financial underwriting; nonprofits benefit from the big bucks associated with big corporations. But what to some looks like a match made in heaven is causing others grave concern.

Careful consideration must be given to public perception of the supporting corporation and its products and the appearance of potential conflicts of interest. Museums have traditionally been a refuge from commercialism and some visitors are not happy about having yet another place for their children to be imprinted with the Golden Arches, or being confronted with corporate logos themselves. Other people raise questions about a tobacco company's underwriting of the national tour of the U.S. Constitution. Should profits earned by an industry from sales of harmful products be used, even for a good purpose? If a museum is committed to reducing its carbon footprint, should it accept sponsorship dollars from oil companies?

This level of branding can influence consumerism. For example, the Children's Museum of Houston benefits from a gift from Bank of America, which underwrote the "Kidtropolis" exhibit. Inside, children deposit pretend earnings in Bank of America-branded ATMs and corporate sponsors are threaded throughout in the pretend grocery store, hospital, and restaurant.[19] Should children be subjected to this level of commercialism in a learning landscape? Many parents and physicians say no in the face of shrinking funds to support museums and their educational missions.

In addition to public relations issues, corporate sponsorship may subject the museum to tax scrutiny. The Internal Revenue Service has closely examined corporate sponsorships and issued final regulations in 2002, which clarified the appropriate exposure (logo placement, benefits, exclusivity) corporations should receive in return for a tax-deductible sponsorship.[20] These regulations draw the line between taxable advertising and nontaxable charitable contribution. While controversies come and go, the 1999 "Sensation" traveling exhibition was remarkable. The U.S. venue was at the Brooklyn Museum of Art and it caused controversy not only because some artwork was decried as obscene, but also because all the pieces were owned by one individual, London advertising executive Charles Saatchi, and the exhibition's principal corporate sponsor, Christie's, stood to gain financially when it auctioned the work after the exhibition closed.

Guarding museums' valuable status as institutions the public can trust, the American Alliance of Museums developed peer-reviewed standards to guide museums in their relationships with business. AAM offers, "Museums should create policies regarding business and individual donor support either as separate documents or as part of other museum policies. A museum should be consistent in following its policy; any changes should be driven by evolving standards and best practices and the institution's mission and strategic direction. A museum should not change policy solely in response to a specific situation."[21]

Museums that can adapt and work in creative ways to meet the changing concerns of corporations will find an unfailing source of funding for many years. Careful consultation in advance will ensure both parties benefit from the relationship.

CONTRIBUTED INCOME

Membership

Every nonprofit concentrates on building its donor base—from the $5 donor to the $100 donor, there is typically a large contingent of supporters who give fairly regularly at modest levels. In the museum world, memberships constitute the base of support—a pool of individuals who have the potential for making larger gifts to the annual fund and beyond. This is not to say that all donors are members; often the membership program doesn't appeal to a major donor. For the regular museumgoer, membership programs are well known and are a great way for people to engage with an institution and receive benefits.

While memberships are not the most lucrative way to attract income they provide the first connection to an individual and an opening for sharing the museum's story and goals. Paid membership is a vote of support for the ideas and programs a museum represents and serves as a bond between the member and the museum. Paid dues give the museum access to valuable information about the people who really care about the museum's focus, programs, and services. Beyond the dollars they bring, members are a source of potential volunteers, contacts, and donors.

Most museums complete a membership drive periodically, but promote memberships at the door and through the mail year-round. In selling memberships, museums should consider carefully the benefits offered to members and calculate their cost to ensure that it does not cost more to service the membership than the basic membership brings in. If the benefits of a fifteen-dollar membership (for example, four issues of a museum magazine, twelve monthly newsletters, and regular mailings for special events and free admission) cost the museum twenty dollars to produce, the membership program operates at a loss. Generally the lowest-cost memberships are offered by history museums; art museums and planetariums are usually highest. Typical fees are around $30 for individuals and $50 for families. Additional membership categories that identify special member needs and interests have been used by museums with success; these categories feature benefits supplemental to the free admission and museum store discount that are widely standard.

Clear, straightforward communication with members about what they are getting for their money, and what it costs the museum to produce those benefits is important. Not only will members feel a sense of satisfaction about the "good deal" that they are getting, they also will start to develop an understanding of why the museum needs to approach them for help with annual, capital, or endowment funds. At some public museums, members also elect members of the governing body, which gives them an additional connection to the museum and its future. Member lists are usually the starting point for annual fund solicitations.[22]

Annual Giving

Building an annual fund is essential for building a budget. Recall that memberships often have a higher cost associated, making the gift not fully tax deductible (in some organizations, the cost of benefits equal the membership price). As the organization grows and fulfills its mission, the need for operating income will increase. Asking for an annual gift helps balance the budget and provide for a sustainable future. Annual giving includes annual fund drives and major gifts solicitation.

The annual fund provides critical support to every aspect of the museum's programs and operations. It bridges the gap between admissions, museum store sales, special event revenues, and the actual cost of running the museum and its programs. Funds provided through the annual fund are typically unrestricted and can be requested by direct mail and by face-to-face meetings. In addition, special events can raise money for the annual fund. Be careful not to "accidentally" restrict donations to the annual fund by being too specific about how you will use the money.

Annual fund donors are usually identified from the existing membership, but are also in the larger community and visiting populace. Major gift acquisition may be a part of the annual giving cycle and/or part of project-specific fundraising. A major gift is a donation at a specifically higher level

($1,000, $5,000, $25,000 and so forth) that requires cultivation and a face-to-face meeting to ask for the gift. That amount depends on the organization and your community.

A good rule of thumb is this—pick the number that has the most meaning to your organization and it should be the gift amount that prompts exceptional donor treatment. For example, at the Abbe Museum in Bar Harbor, Maine, major donors are donors who give $1,000 or more annually and they receive frequent communication from the development team. Whenever possible, special meetings are scheduled to personally share with the donor the impact their giving has on the organization. This higher level of stewardship leads to greater donor satisfaction and retention.

Sponsorships

Sponsorships can support your organization's programs, exhibits, and events; individuals as well as businesses can serve as sponsors by donating to your specific request. In return the sponsor receives recognition and an association with a particular product the museum delivers. For many businesses, this is valuable advertising.

As reported earlier, only 4 percent of annual contributions are from corporate gifts. This indicates that a minimal amount of time should be spent on securing sponsorships; however, depending where the museum is in the United States, sponsorships offer unique marketing opportunities for businesses. Sometimes this makes it worth the time investment. Many businesses don't classify their sponsorships as a charitable contribution, but rather as a marketing expense. And corporations can be good sources of in-kind support or volunteers. Even if a business declines to write a check, they can do a great deal of good by putting the event poster or membership information in their employee lunch room or newsletter.

Corporate giving can be a sticky wicket. In order to attract a diverse pool of corporate sponsors, the museum may have to produce high profile projects and/or events. But sometimes, the local bank, large employer, or supermarket may have an affinity for a special children's program the museum produces each year and there's value in having a business's name attached.

It's a good idea to ask a business to become a sponsor only once a year, but some businesses may really like your organization and the association. This may reveal interest in a number of sponsorship opportunities, which you can bundle together into one proposal.

In the end, if you treat the sponsorship development process the same way you treat the major gift development process, you will streamline efforts with the same degree of success. The key difference is that with a corporate sponsor, you need to outline in your proposal how you will promote their business (for example, on a donor wall, in print media, on the website, and/or create a special marquee). Get creative and think of as many places you feel comfortable inserting a corporate logo. Remember, the business owner may be thinking philanthropically when she says yes to a sponsorship, but she is also thinking about how to market her business to the community at large.

Fundraising Events

Special events are an especially effective method that help museums reach a broad range of contributors, but at the same time, beware the special event designed to raise money for an organization. By the time you calculate staff time, volunteer time, and cash investment for a gala, festival, or event, you usually reach astronomical expense costs in proportion to the event's revenue and the annual budget. Before embarking, analyze the cost/benefit ratio to ensure the event will be profitable. But if you can create an event that raises a significant amount of money and is meaningful to your community, then it may be worth the risk.

If you have a great idea for an event, and you're not sure how much you can invest to make it a go, try smaller scaled events and measure the results. For example, at the General Lew Wallace Study and Museum in Crawfordsville, Indiana, the Taste of Montgomery County is held as an annual fundraiser for the museum that includes live music and food samples from county-based restauranteurs and caterers. Before launching the first event, the staff held a series of small concerts two years beforehand and a smattering of related activities. In year three, the time came to either take a leap and go big with an event, or decide not to do it. The board and staff, along with numerous community volunteers, decided to make the leap and produced the first Taste in 2007. Continuing today, the Taste is a profitable fundraising model that also brings new audiences to the museum grounds each year.

The variety of special events a museum can offer is limitless; receptions, dinners, exhibit openings, lectures, performances, tours, and gala auctions are common. Different events may attract different participants. Some individuals unlikely to buy memberships or make donations to the museum may be attracted by the nature, location, or subject of the special event. The tax deductibility of the difference between the ticket price and the actual value of the benefit received is icing on the cake, but it is not the principal motivating factor for these participants.

More pressure is being placed on museums to compromise traditional rules in order to accommodate special events. The good news is that more people are viewing museums as great places to hold parties, and they're willing to pay for the privilege of doing so. The bad news is that as revenue sources become tight, it becomes tempting to let the potential of special event income dictate exhibition decisions or alter museum policies.

Special events are a multifaceted tool. Besides raising funds, they have the potential to attract and identify new donors and members, enhance public recognition, promote favorable news coverage, provide a service to the constituency, and recognize community leadership. They also can lose money, take time away from core programs, distract from more difficult (but often more lucrative) personal solicitations, and exclude certain audience segments. Museums need to develop special events policies that take into consideration their mission, ethics, and role in their communities. A realistic appreciation of the resources required, coupled with the creativity and enthusiasm necessary for success, can produce special events which make both friends and money for the museum.

Campaigns

There are basically two types of large-scale fundraising campaigns museums engage in—capital and endowment. Capital tends to be the less difficult cause to raise money for because it supports very tangible items—building renovation, construction or expansion, historic preservation work, storage furniture, office computers, repairs, a new climate control system. Donors really like to see the object(s) that represents their gift. Endowment campaigns, conversely, have a challenge because giving money to a savings account is far less sexy, even through the income produces highly tangible things, such as programs, exhibits, staff labor, utility costs, and so on.

For both campaign types, if resources permit, a feasibility study is wise. Led by an outside, impartial consultant, this process includes interviewing key individuals and community leaders about the importance of the museum, determines their willingness to give, and establishes how much money would be given. This helps to determine realistic campaign goals. Such a study can also indicate steps a museum must take to build relationships if the consultant deems a campaign unlikely to succeed.

With any campaign launch, adequate staff time must be applied to the project—someone has to stay on top of it and manage the volunteers and staff engaged in the effort. A strong, engaged board of trustees must also be ready to help with the fundraising. Otherwise, the fundraising goal will likely be unmet and the campaign will fail.

Large campaigns benefit from a quiet and a public phase. At the outset, the board members decide how much has to be raised quietly, face-to-face in board rooms and meetings rooms, before issuing a public campaign challenge to realize the total goal. One word of caution: it's a rare successful campaign that achieves its total goal without a preexisting donor base. The combination of a broad donor base, ample staff time, and an engaged board of trustees will lead to a successful campaign result.

PLANNED GIVING

There are many options for individuals to direct their wealth during their lifetime and upon their death: charitable remainder trusts, bequests, and other financial instruments. It is important to remind individuals that the museum is a viable recipient of their generosity and that their legacy will be held in capable hands. This information can be transmitted in newsletters, through a direct mail effort, and with key professionals in your community. For example, trust officers, CPAs, estate planning attorneys, and wealth managers often are the most likely professionals to have discussions with community members who are actively looking to make a bequest or charitable gift. Make sure these professionals have the museum's information close at hand.

The development committee may designate a planned giving "expert" who will cultivate planned gifts within the community or you may contract with a wealth planner to help guide this process. Another option is to hire a development staff member with this role. In the process of giving, make sure that the donor is advised by a financial professional or attorney during the process.

GOVERNMENT SUPPORT

Many museums are city, county, or state-owned and funded and rely primarily on public dollars. Other public museums may have a nonprofit friends group funding special projects and/or the operating budget (quasi-governmental). If either is true, then it is wise to enact safeguards to protect

Text Box 5.3 Instruments for Planned Giving

A variety of options exist for donors and museums, including:

- *Charitable Lead Trust*—The income from the trust property is directed to the museum for a predetermined period of years. At the end of the predetermined period the trust reverts back to the donor or his/her designee.
- *Expectancies: Bequests, Retirement Plans and IRAs, and Life Insurance*—The donors make provisions in their wills for the museum to receive a gift of money or assets upon their deaths. The gift can be small or large and may or may not be designated for certain uses. This may include cash, stock, and real estate. Alternatively, the museum may be named a partial or full beneficiary of a retirement plan, IRA, or life insurance policy. All of these may be revoked at any time prior to the donors' death.
- *Charitable Gift Annuity*—This is a contract between the donor and the museum. The museum promises to pay the donor a predetermined amount annually, in exchange for the gift.
- *Charitable Remainder Annuity Trust*—The donor irrevocably transfers a principal sum of money that is invested by the museum. The donor or her designee receives annual payment of a fixed-dollar amount. The annual payments must be at least five percent of the initial net market value of the contributed principal. Upon the death of the donor or her designee the asset belongs to the museum.
- *Charitable Remainder Unitrust*—The donor irrevocably transfers money, stock certificates, or property to the museum. The trustee pays the donor or his designee an income for life or for a period of years determined when the assets are transferred. The donor or his designee receives an annual income in payments based on a fixed percentage (not less than five percent) of the fair market value of the trust assets. This means the income will vary each year. Upon the death of the donor, the asset belongs to the museum.

Source: Excerpted from Tempel, Seiler, and Aldrich, *Achieving Excellence in Fundraising*.

funding levels. Through recent years, public funds for museums have dwindled significantly leaving a funding void that jeopardizes the important work museums do. Before arriving at budget season, there are a few steps that can be done to improve the odds for continued funding or budget increases.

During the months interceding budget months, museum leadership and trustees should spend quality time with elected officials—talking about the museum, showing them around the facility, sending event invitations, providing written status updates—and helping them become informed leaders. Measuring the museum's impact and posting quantifiable results is a great strategy. When they enter the budget cycle, there shouldn't be any question about the importance of the museum to the community.

While there's very little that can be done if political leaders decide to defund the organization, you may be able to control the timing a bit. Have an attorney draft a formal agreement that determines the fiduciary responsibilities of the nonprofit friends group and the governmental agency. The agreement should identify how much notice each party requires should there be funding cuts. It will also describe how each entity funds the organization, who is responsible for governance, and who has signatory authority over any future agreements or addenda. Through impact measurements, advocacy, and formal agreements, government support can become less uncertain.

GRANTS

A grant is a gift of money from an established organization designated for a specific purpose. Grants are obtained through an application or proposal process, depending on the organization. Grant seeking is a complex kind of matchmaking; museums need to find organizations that have grant, programming, size, and location requirements complimentary to their particular museum's project.

Grants are part of the museum's fundraising effort, but should not be the focus as they are too variable.[23] While large grant awards can be transformational for an institution, they should never be the primary source of a museum's funding. In developing a grant-writing program, Sarah Brophy offers a good metric. For a museum that is new at writing grant applications she believes that a 50 percent yes/no success rate is very acceptable, however, with an established grant writing program 75 percent to 90 percent is realistic.[24]

Two basic types of funding organizations—government agencies and private foundations—award grants. Each of these funding entities has its own unique characteristics and objectives, often determined by law. Researching the particular focus and requirements of funding sources is the critical first step in the grant-seeking process. A basic understanding of these types of entities and their general emphases is a good place to start.

Government Agencies

Government grants usually involve long and complex proposals and applications, and are highly competitive. Grants from government agencies require careful record keeping because the agencies are accountable to taxpayers. Recipients will be required to conform to federal, state, or reporting and accounting standards outlined by the funding entity. The application and review process may take from eight to eighteen months to complete. Government grants are distributed through federal and state agencies.

Federal Agencies

A few federal agencies specifically target museums, while others support the subject matter or audience objective of museum projects. Common sources of federal funding used by museums are the Institute of Museum and Library Services, the National Endowment for the Arts, the National Endowment for the Humanities, and the National Science Foundation.

Institute of Museum and Library Services (IMLS): Created as a joint museum and library funding agency in 1996 with the Museum and Library Services Act, the mission of the IMLS is to inspire libraries and museums to advance innovation, lifelong learning, and cultural and civic engagement. Providing leadership through research, policy development, and grant making, IMLS has a number of different programs that provide funding, matching grants, or professional services to improve museums:[25]

- Museums for America (MFA): This matching grant program supports projects that strengthen the ability of an individual museum to serve its public. Proposed projects must focus on providing learning experiences, the museum as a community anchor, or promote collections stewardship.
- Museum Assessment Programs (MAP): The MAP is a noncompetitive grant program designed to help smaller museums identify strengths, weaknesses, and future courses of action. (MAP assessments can help museums develop and put in place the systems and programs

necessary for national museum accreditation offered by the American Alliance of Museums.) The museum engages in a rigorous self-study that is complemented by the assessment of one or more museum professionals serving as outside evaluators, who interview the museum staff and board on site. A report is then produced offering observations and recommendations. This assessment process is available for three different areas:

1. Organizational Assessment: Reviews all areas of operations.
2. Collections Stewardship Assessment: Focuses on collections policies, planning access, documentation, and collections care within the context of the museum's total operations.
3. Community Engagement Assessment: Assesses the museum's understanding of and relationship with its communities as well as its communities' perceptions of and experiences with the museum.

This program is funded by IMLS and is administered by the American Alliance of Museums.[26]

- Conservation Assessment Program (CAP): CAP supports a noncompetitive grant for general assessment of a museum's entire conservation program. CAP funds a two-day assessment by one or two conservation professionals and preparation of a written report. ReCAPs are also offered for institutions who have experienced significant organizational change since its first CAP. This program is funded by IMLS and is administered by the Foundation of the American Institute for Conservation of Historic and Artistic Works.[27]

- National Leadership Grants for Museums: These grants support projects that address critical needs of the museum field and that have the potential to advance practice in the profession so that museums can improve services for the American public. A variable matching-grant program, it has the same focused categories of the MFA program.

- Museum Grants for African American History and Culture: Another variable matching-grant program, these grants support projects that improve the operations, care of collections, and development of professional management at African American museums.

- Native American/Native Hawaiian Museum Services Grants: These grants support projects and initiatives in Native communities that are designed to sustain heritage, culture, and knowledge through strengthened activities in areas such as exhibitions, educational services and programming, professional development, and collections stewardship.

- Spark! Ignition Grants: As one of the newer IMLS grant programs, funding encourages museums to prototype and evaluate specific innovations in the ways they operate and the services they provide. Project results—be they success, failure, or a combination thereof—should offer valuable information to the museum field and the potential for improvement in the ways museums serve their communities.[28]

National Endowment for the Arts (NEA): Established by Congress in 1965, the NEA is the independent federal agency whose funding and support gives Americans the opportunity to participate in the arts, exercise their imaginations, and develop their creative capacities. Through partnerships with state arts agencies, local leaders, other federal agencies, and the philanthropic sector, the NEA supports arts learning, affirms and celebrates America's rich and diverse cultural heritage, and extends its work to promote equal access to the arts in every community across America. The NEA awards grants to individuals and to organizations, and funds partnership agreements and leadership initiatives.[29]

National Endowment for the Humanities (NEH): Also founded by Congress in 1965, NEH's mission is to serves and strengthen the United States by promoting excellence in the humanities and conveying the lessons of history to all Americans. NEH grants typically go to cultural institutions, such as museums, archives, libraries, colleges, universities, public television and radio stations, and to individual scholars. Examples of fundable projects are the research and preservation of texts and materials, translation of an important work, public programming through exhibits, public discussion, television, and radio. NEH projects can be funded through fellowships, grants, and matching grants.[30]

National Science Foundation (NSF): The primary area in which NSF provides grants of interest to museums is informal science education. These are major grants to support science exhibits and other types of public programming in science education that support STEM learning. Some NSF programs provide funding to assist in the preservation of systematic and scientific collections and may help underwrite collections storage materials or equipment.[31]

The IMLS is the only government agency set up to address the specific needs of museums. The NEA and NEH are examples of government agencies museums can access. Museums can also access NEA and NEH funding through state and regional sources; these endowments distribute a portion of their funding to state or regional agencies so it can be distributed within a specific geographic area.

State Agencies

State agencies are another funding source for museums. Some state entities are funded by the state tax dollars, but others receive funds through federal agencies, on the premise that the state can better evaluate and set priorities regarding projects and areas of need on the statewide level.

State-distributed grants are mainly for projects that are strongly supported by the community. Grants from state agencies are easier to access because the state agency is physically closer; this proximity encourages good working relationships and makes assistance in the grant process simpler to obtain. Be aware that grants from state agencies may be even more closely scrutinized because they must adhere to both state and federal guidelines.

Each state has a state humanities and state arts agency, but the specific names of these organizations and their configuration varies from state to state. In Maine, the agencies are the Maine Arts Commission and the Maine Humanities Council; in Indiana, the agencies are Indiana Humanities and the Indiana Arts Commission; and in Nebraska, the agencies are the Nebraska Arts Council and Humanities Nebraska. The mission of these state agencies is similar to their respective national counterparts, the NEA and the NEH, and part of the state-based programs' funding is appropriated to them by their national equivalents. Partial funding is often allocated from state budgets as well.

Other Sources

In addition to these traditional sources, museums can tap into other federal and state agencies that may not be obvious matches. A little research and creativity may be needed to find a fit within the unorthodox museum partner agencies such as the Department of Energy, Environmental Protection Agency, National Institutes of Health, or the Department of Labor. Museums are defined as "educational organizations," therefore they are eligible to apply under many different federally funded programs. Initially, the Department of Agriculture or the Department of Education may not appear to be an accessible source of funding, yet both have been sources of funding for museums.

An example of a seemingly incongruous match is a twenty-minute documentary produced by the Wing Luke Asian Museum (WLAM) in Seattle with funding from the USDA Forest Service. The film documents a five-day Chinese Heritage tour of the American West through historical sites in Washington, Oregon, and Idaho. These sites, many of which are on public land, tell the stories of the Chinese pioneers whose labors were instrumental in the development of the West. The film increased public awareness of the national forests and educated about Asian heritages in these national forest lands. In this way it fulfilled both the USDA Forest Service's objective of increasing awareness of the national forest and the WLAM's mission to document and exhibit Asian-American history.

Private Foundations

Foundations are nonprofit entities that have been established to provide support to charitable organizations through grants. Foundations generally favor giving support to capital funds, demonstration projects, and educational programs. They rarely support requests for operating expenses.

Foundations give according to the foundation's charter or mission statement, and sometimes by the guidelines and/or geographic area set forth by the governing board. Foundations can be categorized according to size, purpose, and the chartering entity.

The following foundation types are descriptive, not legal names. They have much in common and are typically established to aid social, educational, religious, or other charitable needs. Sometimes they have staff but generally, there is a board of directors that makes discretionary giving decisions.[32]

Family Foundations

Family foundations have dramatically grown in number since 2001, when there were just over 3,000, to the over 40,000 reported in in 2012.[33] The fund was created by a family and grant decisions are often made directly by the donor or members of the donor's family.[34]

This dramatic growth in family foundations has a variety of causes. Friendly tax breaks and charitable giving has been part of the reason, but also, baby boomers are interested in instilling values in their children about giving and compassion.[35] For example, the parents will set up the foundation and empower their children to govern the fund and make grant making decisions align with their family's values. The Quimby Family Foundation in Maine is a great example of this. Founded in 2004 after Roxanne Quimby sold Burt's Bees, the foundation leads with the vision "to advance wilderness values and to increase access to the arts throughout Maine."[36] It is primarily Roxanne's children along with other family and close friends who continue to make funding decisions that are transformative to Maine communities and arts organizations. Warren Buffett's family members administer foundations, including the Susan Thompson Buffett Foundation named for his late wife, the Sherwood Foundation, and the Howard G. Buffett Foundation. Making impact in Nebraska and across the globe, these groups focus on urban and rural community efforts, early childhood education and environmental issues and malnourished populations in the developing world.

Independent Foundations

Independent foundations are not governed by the benefactor, or the benefactor's family or corporation. Rather, an individual or group of individuals may endow funds to create the foundation.[37]

Community Foundations

Community foundations are created to address the problems and the interests of a community. The community can be a predetermined geographical area such as the city limits or state boundaries. Community foundations are derived through the funds of numerous community sources. The Lincoln Community Foundation, for example, operates to provide grants to enrich the quality of life in Lincoln and Lancaster County, Nebraska. The Nebraska Community Foundation has a wider emphasis as it acquires and manages resources and provides support for numerous communities around the state. Community foundations tend to fund projects that work and can be replicated.

Corporate Foundations

Corporate foundations are extensions of private corporations. Grants are awarded with business objectives in mind; support favors local community projects and educational activities. Corporate foundations such as the Intel Foundation and The Coca-Cola Foundation are numerous. Understanding the foundation's philanthropic goals and how its support of your project will further the corporate good name is key to success with this funding source.

National Foundations

National foundations are large and take a national or international scope. The Ford Foundation, the Johnson Foundation, the W. K. Kellogg Foundation, the Fidelity Foundation, and The Rockefeller Foundation are well-known examples. Foundations in this classification are prone to support highly visible, pilot, or demonstration programs and programs with national applicability.

Foundations in each of these categories not only fund different types of proposals, they also look for different characteristics. As a result, it is important to research the foundation to understand its giving pattern before ever considering submission of a grant proposal. Calling and talking with foundation staff about your proposal is always a good idea. Foundation proposal turn-around time is anywhere from three to eighteen months; formats may vary from a one-page letter to completion of more extensive application forms.

The Grant Process

Each government agency and foundation has its own set of guidelines and preferred charitable causes. Yet the steps to finding, applying for, and receiving a grant from these funding sources are essentially similar. Finding a funding organization with guidelines that match a museum's proposed project requires research.

Numerous books, periodicals, and Internet sites provide information about government agencies and foundations. The Internet is a gateway to abundant information on all government agencies and foundations. Two excellent sites to start with are those of The NonProfit Gateway and the Foundation Center. The NonProfit Gateway is the first place to go to find information on government agencies and departments. This site provides links to many federal departments and agencies.[38] There is also a link to an electronic version of *Catalog of Federal Domestic Assistance*. This site provides a search engine that can be used to find grants that may be applicable to a museum's potential project. There are numerous ways to research foundations, but a great starting point is the Foundation Center's web site which provides information and tips on applying for and writing grants, grant sources, and trends. The site also lists available courses and links to public, private, and community foundations.[39]

Another useful source of information about specific foundations can be found via the website GuideStar which lists information on 1.8 million IRS-recognized tax-exempt organizations. These listings include Form 990PFs, which detail private nonoperating foundation activity including grants awarded, how to apply, deadlines, and contact person(s) with address.[40]

Ultimately, people are a great source of information about government agencies and foundations. A museum staff interacts daily with board members, staff members, constituents, and countless public and private organizations. Insights into a government agency or foundation, suggestions on where to search, leads on grant requirements the museum may meet, and introductions to funding sources can come out of these museum relationships.

When pursuing *any* grants from *any* source, it is important to do your homework. Check the website or call the funding entity before applying to obtain the most up-to-date information about emphases and application requirements, guidelines, and deadlines. Some funding sources are very hands-on and will guide an applicant from the beginning to the end of the grant process. Other funding sources prefer minimal or no advance contact. Do not hesitate to find out the level of interaction the funding source prefers and utilize the staff's generosity to the fullest.

It is advisable to set an informational meeting with representatives of funding organizations that welcome advance contact and that includes governmental grants-givers. This meeting will: (1) provide the opportunity to initiate and establish a relationship with the funding organization; (2) help determine if the nonprofit organization meets the funding organization's criteria; and (3) offer the museum an opportunity to understand what will be most appealing to the representative in the position to accept or reject the proposal (ideally the same representative with whom the museum staff meets). It is through this rapport that the museum will be able to present the project to the funding organization in the best possible light. If, based on this initial conversation, the museum project is found to be eligible, the funding organization may request a letter of inquiry outlining the proposal or project before it sends out an application or guidelines.

After the grant is submitted, a review board will either reject or accept the grant proposal. Governmental entities involve professional peers in the grants review process, and specialists are likely to examine proposals in more technical categories (e.g., conservation); foundation applications are likely to be reviewed by the same review committee, regardless the subject matter or emphasis of the grant proposal. There may be circumstances in which the review board will request changes before approving a grant proposal, or opt to fund only part of the request.

Not all grant agencies will provide a form for their application processes. Form or not, there are six basic elements a grant proposal should present (see text box 5.4).

Who will write the grant? Some museums have a grant writer on staff, but in many cases grant proposal preparation will fall to senior administrative staff with input from the director. If the grant has a particular focus

Text Box 5.4 Elements of Grant Proposals

- *Introduction/Abstract*—A brief or condensed summary of the pro-posed project.
- *Problem/Needs Statement*—A description of the problem or need the museum will be addressing. Documented facts and statistics are commonly used in this section. Devote considerable effort to this statement because it is your initial opportunity to get the interest of the reviewer.
- *Goals/Objectives*—The description of project goals should be made in quantitative terms to provide a gauge for measuring the success of the project.
- *Methods/Approaches/Program Description*—How the goals and objectives will be accomplished. It is wise to include a timeline or task schedule.
- *Evaluation Strategy*—Identify the methods and benchmarks used to evaluate the success of the project.
- *Program Budget*—The budget will justify the amount requested by showing how it will be spent. It is important to show three figures: (1) the amount requested for the project; (2) the costs associated with the project such as materials, staff time, use of facilities, and honoraria; and (3) additional funding sources, in-kind services, and the amount contributed by the museum. Check and then double check all numbers and calculations. You cannot afford a mistake here.

Source: Excerpted from Wolf, *Managing a Nonprofit,* 270–74.

(for example, collections preservation or education programming), then the staff members responsible for those areas may shoulder the major respon-sibility for the proposal. Broad-based applications such as those for IMLS Museums for America grant will necessarily involve input from a variety of museum staff. Most proposals will require good communication with and input from the budget accounting office to ensure financial information is accurate and clearly expressed.

Grant proposals are essentially high stakes marketing tools. The goal is sell-ing the museum's good idea in such a convincing way that the funding entity commits financial resources to make it happen. The museum's financial need should be made clear, but the appeal should most strongly articulate the vigor of the proposed project and how well it fulfills the museum's mission

Text Box 5.5 Exercise: Grant Writing

In this exercise, you will prepare a grant application to a state-based humanities council. You will design a project of your own choosing that fits within the funding guidelines of the council, complete a cover sheet, write a one-hundred-word abstract, respond to questions in a project narrative, prepare a budget, and complete scholar participation sheets for humanities resource persons working on the project. We recommend state humanities grant forms for this exercise because these tend to be very general types of proposals and can be used for a wide variety of projects. We are aware of natural science and art museums that have received funding from these agencies as well as history museums that may be thought to be the traditional organizations receiving funding. Your success depends on your ability to write a coherent and convincing grant proposal.

A second part of this exercise will have you working with your classmates or peers as the reviewers for the proposals. This part of the exercise is discussed in text box 5.6. The reader may wish to look at that portion of the exercise before beginning to write a proposal because the criteria by which the proposal will be evaluated are listed there. Readers may find it useful to work on this effort as a group and recruit colleagues, friends, or volunteers to serve as a review panel.

Acquire the current proposal guidelines and forms from the state humanities council in your location. (Many are available on state council websites.) Your state humanities council may also share the materials used by reviewers to evaluate proposals.

SAMPLE GUIDELINES

Eligibility

Any nonprofit group is eligible to apply for grants. Examples of eligible organizations include libraries, museums, civic groups, service clubs, tribal organizations, professional associations, historical societies, educational institutions, archives, botanical gardens, zoos, and community organizations.

Applications must demonstrate that the humanities are central to the project. The National Endowment for the Humanities has defined the humanities as including, but not limited to, history, literature, languages, jurisprudence, philosophy, comparative religion, archaeology, ethnography, anthropology, ethics, the social sciences when they employ humanistic perspectives, history of science and technology, and the history, theory, and criticism of the arts.

All projects must include humanities resource people. Typically, the humanist is a college or university professor in a humanities discipline. If a nonacademic humanist is chosen for a project, the applicant must provide sufficient background information on the individual to demonstrate that he/she will capably represent the humanities. An example of such an individual would be someone whose life experience makes them an expert on a humanistic topic such as a tribal elder or a long-time member of an ethnic community. In place of the résumé or biographical sketch, please complete a scholar participation sheet, for each humanities resource person involved in the project.

Any age group may be served. Projects need a creative publicity plan and a means of evaluation by audience participants or an outside reviewer. At least one half of the total project costs must be provided by the applicant in local cost-share, either in cash or in-kind services. At least 20 percent of this local cost share must be cash.

and goals. Regardless of the source of their funds, all grant-giving entities want to help underwrite successful programs that have significant effects.

Crafting successful grant proposals takes practice. We encourage you to take the time to complete the grant writing and review exercises outlined in text boxes 5.5 and 5.6.

Ben Hruska reminds us in the *Small Museum Toolkit* that when developing a grant program, being mindful of ethical concerns is critical. The museum's bedrock is its public trust status and receiving a grant is a legally binding contract between the grant maker and the museum. Once a grant is awarded there are often compliance requirements—reporting, bookkeeping, matching funds, timelines—that must be fulfilled. These time commitments and any matching resources must be well understood before applying for a grant.[41]

Grants will continue to play a substantial role in creating the museum's financial package. Staff must be constantly alert to the missions, philosophies, and agendas of these funding entities in order to tap effectively their resources for the benefit of the museum and its constituents.

Text Box 5.6 Exercise: Grant Reviewing

Divide the group into two grant review panels. Exchange grant proposals between the groups so that each member has a full compliment of the proposals from the other group. We do this "blind" so that no one knows whose proposals they are reviewing. Individuals have two weeks to review their group of proposals using the following grant review instructions.

GRANT REVIEW INSTRUCTIONS

1. Keep your review of grants strictly confidential. You will discuss them with no one outside of class.
2. Using a separate grant evaluation form for each grant, you will evaluate each aspect of the grant as instructed. At the bottom of the sheet you will give an overall evaluation for the grant.
3. You will rank all grants in decreasing order from number 1, the most fundable, to the last number, the least fundable.
4. Grant panels will meet for the first forty-five minutes of the class period when grant decisions are made. You will establish a joint ranking of your grants from number 1 through the last.
5. The last thirty minutes of class we will come together to decide which grants will receive funding. We will have $25,000 to award. The funded proposals will receive five bonus points.
6. You should remember throughout this entire process that your grading and review will be affecting the lives and careers of your classmates.

GRANT EVALUATION FORM

Proposal Tile _____ Proposal No. _____

Scoring should be from 1 to 10, with 1 the lowest and 10 the best.

1. Humanities contents: Are humanities disciplines and methodology central?

Score _____

2. Staff and consultants: Are humanities scholars involved in the planning, implementation, and evaluation of the project? Do the participants have the necessary qualifications?

Score _____

3. Value for the audience: Will the project increase the intended audience's knowledge of the humanities? Is the audience clearly defined?

Score _____

4. Plan of work: Are the project's activities clearly defined and stated? Are the project's goals realistic? Is the timeline reasonable?

Score _____

5. Budget: Is the budget appropriate in scope and in terms of the anticipated results? Is the budget cost effective?

Score _____

6. Publicity: Are the planned publicity methods appropriate for reaching the intended audience?

Score _____

7. Evaluation: Are adequate provisions made for evaluation of the project?

Score _____

8. Other issues: Does the project reach audiences from across the state or that are underserved by the agency? Is this the first grant to the organization from the agency? Is there a co-sponsor? Is the project innovative?

Score _____

9. Overall impression: How important is it that this project be accomplished? Would it be important to have this project associated with the agency? Reviewer's overall impression of the proposal and project?

Score _____

Total Score_____
Rank: _____
Recommendation (circle one):

REJECT   RESUBMIT   FUND (low priority)   FUND (high priority)

Comments and Conditions:

EARNED INCOME

Museums are looking inward as well as outward for ways to generate income. Facilities use, services, and programming are among typical sources of earned income. The nonprofit arts and culture industry (museums) generates over $135 billion every year through admissions, memberships, gifts shops, restaurants, parking, publications, and services to other museums every year.[42] Typically earned income accounted for one-third of total operating income of museums. These statistics send a signal to museums in need of increased revenue—there are numerous income opportunities within their walls.

Assessing the feasibility, tax implications, and income-generating potential of ventures is a critical first step in developing new earned income possibilities. Published guides to business development for nonprofit organizations, as well as board members with business planning experience, can assist in this important evaluation.

The most consistent way to earn income is through museum admissions, museum store sales, program fees, and rentals. A business plan is the best way to strategically develop this area, but as you can imagine, developing a business plan requires an in depth discussion, which is beyond the scope of this chapter. In short, in a business plan you will: share the need and idea for revenue, identify the market around the museum, and the desired audience, describe what it will cost to invest in your strategy, offer income and expense projections, outline how to get the word out, such as advertising, and monitor and report the results. Sharing this information with the board and seeking their input is a great way to get board members engaged in attracting revenue for the museum. Convening a revenue task force may also be a good idea—they can analyze these income streams and local competition and then brainstorm opportunities.

Admission Fees

At present, nearly 40 percent of U.S. museums are free or have only suggested fees, whereas the remainder charge a fee but offer discounts or free admission days.[43] Clearly charging admission is a common, but sometimes controversial, earned income opportunity. Admission fees provide a source of revenue (between 1 and 4 percent of art museums' annual income),[44] but there is concern that they affect the museum's constituents and other museum programming. There are arguments that donations and volunteers will decrease because donors feel they are already contributing to the museum through the admission fees. Others argue that museums are educational institutions. Admission can create a financial barrier, leaving certain socioeconomic levels outside of the museum.

Admission fees also may discourage visitors from spending on other services offered by a museum, thereby reducing the total amount earned from a group of visitors. However, charging admission may be advantageous in the overall scheme to generate income. Admission fees can be a marketing and membership tool, and can provide valuable information on visitor demographics, and peak attendance times and days. When a museum charges admission, it also has the power to waive it. Marketing opportunities can be created between businesses and the museum in which businesses can sponsor a free admissions day in exchange for advertisement at the museum. Free admissions can also be part of a membership package. This could encourage visitors to become members, thus increasing membership revenues. Nina Simon posits in her popular blog, *Museum 2.0*, that maybe there is a formula for free admission:

1. Secure a philanthropic gift equivalent to three to seven years of the lost revenue from daytime admissions.
2. Aggressively market the philanthropic benefits of a free museum. Create a new value proposition for giving that is rooted in the idea that the museum is free and open to all. Recruit new members and donors who are invested in supporting public access.[45]

Charging admission fees is a difficult decision because of the uncertain impact on the museum's viability. Many museums have found a balance by offering a variety of admission options in order to make the museum affordable and accessible. All eyes are watching the bold experiment at the Dallas Museum of Art for clues. In 2013, the DMA switched to free admission and attendance is consistently growing. To offset the membership expectation of free admission, individuals can select to become a DMA Friend, which is a membership at the base level.[46] Between 12,000 and 14,000 individuals voluntarily pay $100 for partner memberships each year. An exciting by-product of this change was a $9 million anonymous gift given because of this program.[47] While it is still too early to tell if this experiment will be successful, the early indications are inspiring.

One element that is clear is that art museums have a more difficult time with admissions seen as barriers than peer museums, such as history and science. It is important for each museum to examine what its constituency will support and the impact of admission fees on other museum revenue sources like the museum store, dining facility, the planetarium, or IMAX theater.

Museum Store

Operating a museum store offers many advantages. A store can generate income for a museum, provide additional information about the collection, offer a point of personal contact with the staff, and feature merchandise that reflects the museum's mission and exhibits. Visitors may take home a souvenir of their experience or gain additional educational materials about an exhibit or collection. Ideally the store should be located near an exit or entrance; most people tend to buy goods at the end of their visit. Some newer museums, like the San Francisco Museum of Modern Art, have street-side museum stores accessible through a separate entrance, so that the store can serve customers whether or not the museum itself is open.[48] At a small museum, staff can service incoming and outgoing visitors while operating a well-situated museum store.

Museum merchandise is now offered off the museum premises through print and electronic catalogs and other retail outlets. The Metropolitan Museum of Art, Boston Museum of Fine Arts, and the Art Institute of Chicago are among museums with stores located off-site. In fact, the Met has five different shops operating around the country and another ten overseas.[49] (It should be noted that the Met had a greater store presence prior to the Great Recession of 2007. By 2009, the Met closed eight stores around the country.)[50] Museums are also offering their merchandise through both printed and online catalogs and on television in order to reach more consumers.

Several museums—the Boston Museum of Fine Arts, Metropolitan Museum of Art, Smithsonian Institution, Winterthur Museum, and Colonial Williamsburg, among others—partnered with the home shopping network QVC. During the "two-hour tour" of each museum QVC broadcast, merchandise related to the museum's collections was marketed. Although these mass marketing campaigns help museums reach more consumers, they have generated controversy about preserving the integrity of both the museums and their collections, particularly in the case of works of art. Do adaptations of artistic motifs in the form of puzzles, mugs, scarves, and prints, demean the significance of the art and its creator? Some argue that nontraditional partnerships with entities like QVC draw nonvisitors, make art less threatening and more comfortable, and ultimately attract the nonvisitor to the museum.[51]

A more practical concern is attracting the attention of the Internal Revenue Service and engendering unrelated business income tax (UBIT). Museums maintain their tax-exempt status on the basis of their educational purposes. Increasingly the IRS is questioning the educational value of some museum store merchandise, such as tee-shirts or coffee mugs that merely feature the name or logo of the institution. Items that feature reproductions of materials in the museum collections are less subject to scrutiny (and to the charging of income tax on the profits from their sales). Museum shop merchandise currently generates nearly $1 billion annually, so it is reasonable to expect increased IRS attention to this substantial revenue generator.[52] Advice on protecting tax-exempt status while offering attractive merchandise to visitors is available from the Museum Store Association.

The proliferation of online shopping is prompting many museums to allow "virtual visitors" to purchase store merchandise via the museum website. Frequent analysis of both print and online catalogs will help determine the benefits and costs of such visitor services. There may be some advantage to an online presence even if sales are not immediately significant, since every indicator predicts expansion of this type of commerce.

Dining Facilities

Museums with cafes, restaurants, or refreshment areas can attract and comfort visitors and become community resources. Since the Metropolitan Museum of Art installed a public restaurant in 1954 and others followed suit, visitors have come to anticipate opportunities for refreshment and rest in a pleasant atmosphere. Having a spot to relax and refuel makes visitors more willing to spend several hours at the museum.

A small museum with numerous visitors and limited space may find a "refreshment stand" approach useful. While the primary goal of operating an eating facility is to earn additional income, a well-run food service can help create the ambiance that builds a return audience. The number of visitors, their visiting pattern, and the space available will help determine what the museum can offer. A good dining experience can have a strong impact on the visitor's overall museum visit; bad food or service can create negative word-of-mouth.

Some museums, aquariums, and zoos contract with known national or regional brand-name restaurants to provide food service. McDonald's, Taco Bell, Pizza Hut, Wendy's, Burger King, and Starbucks work particularly well in institutions that attract families and children, while "art museums . . . tend to be good partners for well-known local or regional restaurant operators who are interested in lending their names, talent, creativity, and resources to the museum environment."[53] The same visitors who seek a refuge from commercialism in museums and therefore criticize promotion of corporate financial partners may complain about museum food service that encourages brand recognition and purchases.

Museums of any size can maximize their facilities' usage and exposure to the public by offering facilities for after-hour events. Depending on the size and food preparation facilities available, a museum can offer catering service or permit an outside caterer to serve the function. Beware: each of these catering methods has its downside. In-house catering service may be convenient to the renter and safer for the museum. The catering staff familiar with the museum will have established procedures on service, setup, and cleanup. However, users may find their options limited with an in-house caterer.

Some renters will want to use an outside catering service to provide specific foods and drinks. Allowing outside caterers to serve means a museum does not need to provide cooking facilities, but outside caterers may present security problems and it's important to maintain a staff presence when any outside vendor is present and during rental events. Well-vetted rental policies and procedures are helpful in managing vendor expectations. Additional information may be found in chapter 9.

Regardless of catering particulars, these details and all other procedures, guidelines, and expectations should be communicated in writing to outside groups using the museum. Acknowledgment of the renters' receipt and acceptance of the requirements should also be received in writing prior to the special event. Effective communication within the museum is also essential to ensure that the special use of the museum facility is a positive experience for all involved and that neither the museum nor its collections are placed at risk.

Planetariums and Theaters

Planetariums and IMAX or other large screen theaters expand a museum's offering to visitors through intense multimedia experiences. These entertaining and educational shows can attract additional dollars because visitors are willing to pay extra for something out of the ordinary. Some visitors may be lured solely by the planetarium or IMAX presentation.

These features can provide a comfortable transition to the museum world and the shows can be seen as a form of temporary exhibit. They can be easily changed, making them effective tools to provide new materials to the public and encouraging a return visit. Museums need to be alert to the income stream large format theater companies expect to see and ensure that their projected attendance figures are realistic and allow them to meet their contractual obligations. More than one museum has been left with extremely expensive projection equipment when its large screen film provider cancelled its contract.

The Mueller Planetarium of the University of Nebraska State Museum offers "laser shows" (laser light displays set to music shown on the dome) and other movie experiences. The shows are an excellent source of income for the museum and also help hold and expand its audience. High school and college students on weekend dates make up the majority of the audience. This group was difficult to attract to the museum for other events; the laser shows helped bridge the gap between the children's programs and the museum's adult events.

Educational Programming

Museum education departments normally offer tours, lectures, hands-on activities, workshops, and other educational activities for children and adults. These entertaining and educational offerings can be another source of earned income. The Frye Art Museum in Seattle offers workshops ranging from oil painting to meditation for people of different ages, interests, and backgrounds.

The Children's Museum of Tacoma produces a preschool "powered by play" that supports parental engagement and focuses on a child's ability to learn through playful discovery. The museum is their classroom.

Programming possibilities are limited only by staff and facilities. Educational activities provide opportunities for the community and museum staff to interact. While the museum's educators are primarily teachers, curators can oversee content or serve as guest experts. Teaching a workshop or facilitating a lecture gives museum staff direct feedback from the community. Well-organized and effective educational programs not only add to the museum's potential for earned income, but help humanize the institution in the eyes of its constituents.

Special Exhibits

Changing an exhibit is a common way to offer a new subject for current members to explore and to attract new members who are interested in the subject. They can also be an important mechanism for diversifying the museum's audiences and allowing focus on contemporary issues and change in the community or region. Special exhibits may have a brief run or be extended a year or more. In addition to changing exhibits produced for the museum's in-house use, traveling exhibits and blockbuster exhibits are effective at bringing the museum to a larger audience and generating new income. Additional information may be found in chapter 12.

Traveling Exhibits

Traveling exhibits can maximize a museum's research and design efforts and provide a medium for communicating its message to a wider audience. The potential programming opportunities and audience contact traveling exhibits offer are both exciting and unlimited. Some museums travel their exhibits around the nation while others focus on their immediate state. Some traveling exhibits may require professional movers, while others can fit in one minivan. They can be comprised of two-dimensional or three-dimensional objects or a combination of these two elements. Entities like the Smithsonian Institution Traveling Exhibition Service (SITES) and Exhibits USA provide a broad range of temporary exhibitions to museums nationwide from the high-cost, high security to the inexpensive, low-security. The Indiana Historical Society's traveling exhibits primarily stay in the state and are designed to travel to small venues and fit into one minivan.

The income potential for these exhibits is usually enough to supplement some of the costs to produce the actual exhibit. The primary benefits to traveling exhibits are outreach and exposure. The glimpse of a museum's collection may prompt people to visit the museum to see its other holdings.

Blockbuster Exhibits and Other Partnerships

The blockbuster exhibit is a temporary exhibition designed to attract record museum audiences coming to see once-in-a-lifetime artifacts and stories. Over the past ten years, blockbuster exhibits have become a losing proposition, especially with the Great Recession of 2007. Financing continues to be challenging and loan negotiations can often prove difficult.[54] The first American museum blockbuster dates to 1976 when the Metropolitan Museum of Art and the National Gallery of Art produced the *Treasures of Tutankhamun* traveling exhibition.[55]

Millions of visitors have attended dozens of blockbusters (primarily art exhibitions) since then. Related revenue generated by tourism-related facilities during these exhibitions was in the hundreds of millions of dollars. Many memberships are sold during blockbuster exhibitions, particularly if membership provides a discount on or preferred time for admission.[56] Retaining those members becomes a subsequent challenge.

Blockbuster exhibits are marketed as projects that are mutually beneficial for corporations, museums, and the communities, but they require huge amounts of time, effort, and money. Governments, foundations, and corporate sponsorships are needed to generate the funds to organize or accommodate these types of exhibits.

Small- and medium-sized museums may not have adequate staff resources or space to hold a blockbuster exhibit, but the overall development concept of blockbuster exhibits is available to all museums. Forming relationships and partnerships with the city, businesses, and other private and public community organizations results in many benefits for museums.

Partnerships with a related community event can mean joint public relations and marketing efforts. Partnerships can lead to artifact loans, sponsorship, or donations of services or expertise in addition to directly increasing the museum's earned income.

CONCLUSION

The most obvious determinant of how the museum's fundraising efforts are doing is an increase in donations and an improvement in the organization's "bottom line." It can also be measured through anecdotal examples and surveys—how do people feel about giving to the museum?

To keep the board members informed and energized, this information should be regularly reported in board meetings and communicated to the community through the newsletter and press releases. In addition, if funds are not flowing in as projected, course corrections are needed. Finding the organization deep into a new initiative and learning that there are not enough funds to complete the task will not only imperil the initiative, but will also promote negative feelings about management and affect board morale. And heaven forbid that the information gets out into the community—donors might start questioning whether a gift to the museum is a good investment.

Remember, fundraising is about sharing a story. And who better to tell the story than the staff who takes great care of the museum and the board members who volunteer their time and expertise in service? If you believe in what you're doing, it's easy to make the next person believe too. Being strategic about whom that next person might be is the secret to fundraising.

Text Box 5.7 Guiding Questions

1. What are the characteristics of an effective fundraising professional? Do you see yourself in that role? Why or why not?
2. What's the role of the executive director in fundraising?
3. Should museums charge admission? Consider both sides of the argument.

NOTES

1. Durel, *Building a Sustainable*, 2.
2. Independent School Management, "Fund Raising . . ."
3. Lynch-McWhite, interview.
4. Durel, interview.
5. Indiana University Lilly Family School of Philanthropy, *Giving USA*.
6. Ibid.
7. Ibid.
8. Love, "Should the Pareto . . .?"
9. Public museums with governmental funding support can still be engaged in development and fundraising, but may need to work with a cooperating or supporting foundation or other entity in order to build funds like endowments for the long term.
10. Rudnitski, interview.
11. Seiler, "Plan to Succeed," 15.
12. Richie, interview.
13. Prince and File, *Seven Faces*.
14. Hope Consulting, *Money for Good II*, 34–35.
15. Janus, "Three Ways to Engage . . ."; Schorr, "What Makes Millennials . . .?"; Sharpe Group, "Millennial Donors Rising?"
16. deLearie, "Who Moved My Funder?"
17. Wellen, "Moves Management . . ."
18. "Hyundai Capital America . . ."
19. Smith, "Children's Museums Brand . . ."
20. Tenebaum and Constantine, "Corporate Sponsorship."
21. American Alliance of Museums, "Standards Regarding . . ."

22. For an in depth discussion of the membership renewal and acquisition cycle, read "Fearless Fundraising" in *Small Museum Toolkit* by Cinnamon Catlin-Legutko.

23. Brophy, "Is Your Site . . .," 8.

24. Ibid.

25. Institute of Museum and Library Services.

26. Ibid.

27. Ibid.

28. Ibid.

29. National Endowment for the Arts.

30. National Endowment for the Humanities.

31. National Science Foundation.

32. Council on Federations.

33. Foundation Center.

34. Council on Federations.

35. Hannon, "Family Foundations . . ."

36. Quimby Family Foundation.

37. Council on Federations.

38. NonProfit Gateway.

39. Foundation Center.

40. Phelan, *Museum Law*.

41. Hruska, "Oh, Just Write a Grant . . .," 63.

42. American Alliance of Museums.

43. Ibid.

44. Simon, "Is There a Formula . . .?"

45. Ibid.

46. "DMA Friends."

47. Johnson, "More Museums . . ."

48. Schwarzer, "Schizophrenic Agora," 45.

49. Metropolitan Museum of Art Store.

50. Knight, "Metropolitan Museum . . ."

51. Gregg, "From Bathers . . .," 120.

52. Schwarzer, "Schizophrenic Agora," 45.

53. Ibid., 44–45.

54. Adams, "What Happened . . .?"

55. Kamp, "The King . . ."

56. Kotler et al., *Museum Marketing*.

6

THE WORKING MUSEUM

At the heart of every museum are the people who make the gears turn—inspiring visitors to smile and engage, caring for precious collections on behalf of the public, managing teams, committees, and boards of directors. Although museums exist to collect, preserve, and interpret objects, staff (whether paid or volunteer) are the museum's most valuable asset. Its disparate group of talents will fulfill the museum's mission and produce programs and exhibits. Administrators, accountants, artisans, exhibit designers, discipline-area experts, curators, conservators, collection managers, educators, housekeepers, administrative assistants, salespersons, groundskeepers, maintenance staff, secretaries, docents, and many others must be integrated into a functional unit that is capable of accomplishing complex tasks.

Museum administrators will find working with their staff members to be the most challenging, frustrating, and rewarding part of their jobs. This chapter explores how the staff of a museum interacts and how that interaction can be managed to keep the museum working smoothly.

ORGANIZATION

Organizational charts offer staff, board members, and volunteers a quick visual reference as to where they fit in relationship to everyone else in the museum. These are especially helpful to new people joining the organization. The organizational chart is a road map that outlines routes and connections; the system it describes can be an impediment or an enhancement to the flow of museum work, depending on how that operational structure was designed.[1]

Most frequently, organizational charts are hierarchical in design and practice. Through vertical lines and horizontal levels, authority, or a chain of command, is established. Allyn Lord, director of the Shiloh Museum of Ozark History in Springdale, Arkansas, offers her thoughts on the effectiveness of hierarchical structure: "When it works well, authority and responsibilities are understood, opportunities exist for promotion, and staff members become experts in their areas. But sometimes it doesn't work well when there are rivalries between departments, a lack of effective communication at all levels, a bureaucracy making it slower to change, and salary disparities. But for small and mid-sized museums like ours, with a small and relatively small staff (we have 12), the hierarchy is less rigid, there's more teamwork across departments (mostly departments of one), and change isn't that slow."[2]

Organizational charts may vary from the hierarchical format in an effort to express a different kind of work structure or culture. A web or wheel chart depicts departments of staff members in circles that surround the director or the board. This structure is used "to avoid suggestions of subserviency and encourage motivation." A matrix chart is meant to reveal

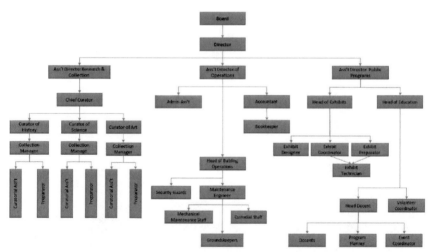

Figure 6.1   Hierarchical Organizational Chart. *Source:* Cinnamon Catlin-Legutko

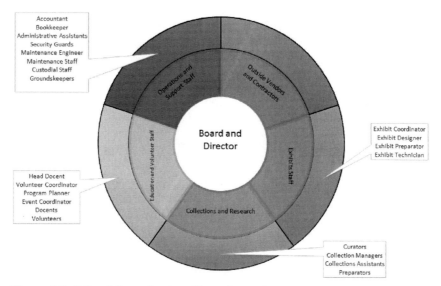

Accountant
Bookkeeper
Administrative Assistants
Security Guards
Maintenance Engineer
Maintenance Staff
Custodial Staff
Groundskeepers

Operations and Support Staff

Outside Vendors and Contractors

Board and Director

Exhibits Staff

Exhibit Coordinator
Exhibit Designer
Exhibit Preparator
Exhibit Technician

Education and Volunteer Staff

Collections and Research

Head Docent
Volunteer Coordinator
Program Planner
Event Coordinator
Docents
Volunteers

Curators
Collection Managers
Collections Assistants
Preparators

Figure 6.2 Wheel Organization Chart. *Source*: Cinnamon Catlin-Legutko

working relationships and focuses on the subject of the department, for example, collections or education.[3] In each of these examples, in larger museums there is typically an executive or leadership staff group that works closely with the chief executive.

Volunteers, also known as unpaid staff, are often represented in organizational charts and their location is indicative of how they are used in the museum. Susan Ellis argues in *The Non-Profit Times* that when volunteers are buried deep in the organizational structure it "sends a message as to their importance." She recommends either placing volunteers in the executive offices, reporting directly to the executive director, or with a separate volunteer department whose leader is seen as a department head.[4]

A clear and well-communicated organizational structure will serve any museum well. But it is equally critical to recognize who or what is at the top or center of the chart. Placing the mission at the top or center of the organizational chart reminds everyone that the work matters and it guides museum activity with purpose.[5]

THE MUSEUM EMPLOYEE

Museum activity is often divided into departments and the smaller the museum, the fewer number of departments or there even may be a

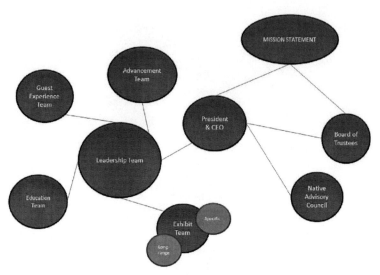

Figure 6.3 Web Organizational Chart. *Source*: Created by Cinnamon Catlin-Legutko

complete absence of departments. Functionally divided, these departments and job duties tend to coalesce into three categories: administration, collections, and programs.[6] Staff working in each category, in a
well-managed museum, will often work cross-functionally to produce
exhibits, programs, or fundraising events. At the Abbe Museum in Bar
Harbor, Maine, the staff of nine includes educators, fundraisers, a graphic
designer, a collections manager, and a president and CEO. Seven of them
work together on the exhibits team to successfully produce a changing
exhibits program. Alternately, all nine staff members work together to produce the annual fundraiser. Whether it's an all-hands-on-deck situation or
a single employee project, clear job expectations, team training and development, and sound personnel management will create a high-achieving
work environment.

Job Descriptions

In a large, fully staffed museum, job titles range from curator to webmaster,
from CEO to adult education manager. In an all-volunteer or a staff-of-
one museum setting, the duties of the job persist, but are collapsed into
a shorter list of titles. A small museum may have a paid director and she
depends on hard-working committees of volunteers made up of board

members and community members. And if there are only three personnel, it is likely that one will focus on collections, another on education, and a third on administration (likely the director).[7]

Written job descriptions for all employees, volunteers, and board members will make clear working relationships, decision-making power, and expectations. Certainly sample job descriptions can be found on museum job sites hosted by national, regional, and state museum associations, but in general, job descriptions will include:

- Title of the position
- To whom the employee reports
- Position summary
- Listing of major specific duties
- Knowledge, skills, training and experience (minimal requirements)
- Salary range for the position[8]

Once the job description is in place, it is equally important to regularly review and revise, if needed. An annual cycle of review is recommended, if nothing significant happens during the year. Updating job expectations during the course of the year is also wise. For employees already in positions, it is ideal to include them in the review process to make sure what they are doing aligns with what is stated in the description.[9]

Job descriptions for volunteers, including board members, will only vary in the salary category. Such descriptions are helpful in the recruiting process and will attract committed volunteers and board members. They will begin their engagement with the museum with a clear understanding of authority, decision-making powers, and what is expected of them. Job descriptions are also helpful when a volunteer or board member isn't acting appropriately or doing his or her job. Written documentation will be useful when and if the volunteer or board member is relieved of his or her duties.[10]

Personnel Policy

Every museum can and should have a set of written personnel policies. A written policy manual ensures uniformity in response and enhances the employees' faith in that uniformity. Personnel policies guide all levels of staff, establishing consistency in operations and enhancing the integrity and credibility of important operational decisions. This type of organizational consistency serves to protect both the museum and its staff.

Personnel matters present the greatest legal exposure for museum boards. In the 1990s, employment practice complaints began to rise and while they've leveled off, the severity of claims has increased. The majority of allegations are around race discrimination and/or harassment, followed by sexual harassment, discrimination due to disability, and age discrimination.[11] As such, it is advisable to have an attorney review the personnel policy before the board takes action to approve it. As labor laws change, periodic reviews and updates are also recommended.

Deciding exactly what information should be included in the personnel policy can be a daunting task. A personnel policy should be comprehensive enough to address typical policy questions without attempting to answer *all* possible policy questions, many of which are more effectively handled on an individual basis. Any potential problem areas should be included in the policy. The museum's code of professional conduct should be screened for any items that should be included in the personnel policy as well. Existing or desired day-to-day practices, such as work hours, vacation time, and sick leave, should be addressed. Background information on the museum, general advice and information associated with the workings of the facility itself also may be addressed. A personnel policy will, at minimum, include the following sections:

- Employment and pay procedures—This section outlines how employees are hired and compensated; training and probationary periods, affirmative action policy (if there is one), and the payroll and promotion process.
- Performance planning and evaluation—How a staff person will be evaluated for her performance is critical to staff morale and establishing clear expectations is helpful for both employee and supervisor. The policy will outline these procedures and how they are tied to compensation and it identifies who has the authority to evaluate. This section may also reference progressive disciplinary processes.
- Conflict-of-interest policies—Just like boards, staff members are to disclose conflicts-of-interest and the personnel policy will outline how these are handled.
- Termination and grievance procedures—This section should clearly outline the activities that will prompt immediate dismissal, such as drug use and violence in the work place. A more likely situation is a growing concern for an employee's deteriorating performance. Clear steps that outline the supervisor and employee's roles and responsibilities are needed.

- Sexual harassment policies—Many states require a policy statement that denounces this practice. Developing procedures for dealing with complaints is advisable as well as preventive staff training.
- General office practices and procedures—This last section outlines the day-to-day expectations for staff, such as work hours and conditions, authorization to purchase, intellectual property and confidentiality issues, guidelines for travel, rules regarding use and care of office equipment, and so on.[12]

Diversity and Inclusion

The United States is a mix of cultures and races and this diversity is increasing in the third millennium. Further, diversity sensitivity extends beyond cultural concerns when gender, sexual orientation, and range of ability and age are included. Museums will need to design culturally and linguistically appropriate programs and strategies targeted to the particular needs of their heterogeneous workforce and audiences. Museums must be prepared and willing to serve their diverse audiences if they wish to continue to have the support of the community. A critical step in meeting the diverse needs of the community is a diverse staff that reflects its community and understands the larger societal realities.

The Pew Research Center (2014) published telling statistics about the changing U.S. demographics and The Andrew W. Mellon Foundation (2015) reported on U.S. art museums' changing demographics. By 2060, the racial majority (white) will become the minority at 43 percent and in the interceding years, the slow change will become increasingly apparent in ads and political campaigns. Millennials (born in the early 1980s to the late 1990s) are the most "racially and ethnically diverse generation ever," and more than "four-in-ten are non-white, many the U.S.-born children of Hispanic and Asian immigrants who began arriving a half a century ago."[13]

But will the arts and culture sector be as responsive to the changing demographic? The Mellon research reveals that in art museums, African Americans comprise only 4 percent of the curators, conservators, educators, and leaders (the positions most associated with the intellectual and educational mission of museums); and Latinos are represented at 3 percent. In these jobs, 84 percent are white, which is significantly out of step with the diversity of American culture (62 percent white). Interestingly, women make up 60 percent of art museum staff nationwide and are increasingly leaders in their institutions, demonstrating a swifter path to leadership for gender equality than minority representation. Another finding of the

Text Box 6.1 Exercise: Write a Diversity and Inclusion Policy

Individually or as a member of a group, prepare a one-paragraph diversity and inclusion policy for a museum of your choosing. Try to avoid generalizations and words with indefinite meanings, such as "appropriate" and "professional." What areas and programs of the museum will your statement cover? What is the diversity and inclusion mission of your museum? Who is responsible for the implementation and "enforcement" of your policy?

Share your or your group's policy with other members of the class. What weaknesses and strengths do you see in the other policy statements? How would you revise your policy after seeing the other statements? Feel free to reference the American Alliance of Museum's Diversity and Inclusion policy on their website, www.aam-us.org.

If you are working on this policy statement on your own, share your policy with other staff members. Ask for their feedback on your statement. After receiving this feedback, how would you revise your policy?

Mellon report is that promotion protocols will not diversify museum leadership until there is diversity in the educational pipeline. While this study focused on art museums, more studies will likely present similar results; having this baseline of research will only help the field change policy and opportunity to attract diversity.[14]

A first step for any museum administrator is to be part of the development of a diversity and inclusion policy (may also be known as a statement). Drawing from examples in academia and the corporate world, this kind of policy is written by a diverse team of staff members, trustees, and stakeholders. Reviewing other policies is helpful to the process, and be sure to include in the policy the museum's values and goals for diversity. The final policy will need to be vetted by the organization and board to ensure awareness and compliance.[15]

Volunteers

Because volunteers are such an integral part of a museum's survival and daily operations, it is vital to consider them whenever personnel policy issues are addressed. Volunteers are essentially unpaid staff and should be treated as formally as paid staff members. Outstanding volunteer contributions can result from a program based on the same level of expected commitment and respect accorded paid employees. Because certain personnel policy issues (such as paid holidays and salary benefits) do not apply to volunteers, create a separate volunteer manual that is distributed during volunteer training. This might include a welcoming statement, museum mission statement, museum overview, fact sheet, description of rewards and benefits, calendar of volunteer activities, job descriptions, grievance procedures, and a code of professional conduct (see chapter 7).[16]

It is equally important to remember that while volunteers are a wonderful asset to a museum, they can also be a hindrance, just as an employee can when not well managed or trained. "The old adage that a volunteer is someone who works for no pay and therefore can't be fired is not true. What is true is that the situation has to be handled with finesse." If a volunteer is not performing well, it is important to investigate, determine what level of training is needed, and/or re-assign the volunteer until the situation is remedied. In some instances the volunteer may be told that his services are no longer needed.[17] While it's a terribly unpleasant position to be in, an underperforming volunteer can impact visitor experience and staff morale. Museums have important work to do and it is unrealistic to think that just because someone isn't paid to be doing the work, he can be allowed to derail progress.

Team Work

Researchers have concluded that humans evolved larger brains because they needed to work together to survive. Cooperation may be a natural tendency of humans, and there is speculation that we cooperate because it activates the reward regions of the brain, making us feel good. And social norms around sharing help us perpetuate this tendency.[18] If this is true, why is it often so challenging to work in teams?

Management consultant Patrick Lencioni tells us that it is difficult to measure and achieve team work. Nevertheless, "teamwork remains the one sustainable competitive advantage that has been largely untapped."[19] Trevor Jones, director of Historical Resources at the Kentucky Historical Society (KHS) in Frankfort, Kentucky, has great success in building teams and frequently shares ideas and strategies at national museum conferences. When asked how he built his team at KHS he shared, "I think you build a team by creating a common purpose that people believe in, setting goals to get there, getting agreement on how the work will get done, and then having the team hold each other accountable to reach those goals. I work really hard at this with my team. When I got (to KHS) they were seen as difficult and unproductive (the team), but the truth is that no one had really told them what they were here to do and why that mattered to the mission. Once I communicated the common purpose, things got better from there!"[20]

In the past twenty years, Lencioni's work has lead the way to a deeper understanding of how teams work and don't work and what managers and team mates can do to become high performers. Other strategies for team building include using assessment tools that identify personality traits, thinking styles, and generational studies.

Developing a Team

Lencioni's book, *The Five Dysfunctions of a Team*, demonstrates how a simple framework for developing a team can help the biggest and smallest of museums. In choosing the best people to be on the team, it is equally important to nurture their development, communicate the shared purpose, and consider the whole person (who they are at work and when they are not) when working with colleagues.

Lencioni identifies the first dysfunction as absence of trust, "No quality of characteristic is more important than trust."[21] Securing this in the team is the first task and it forms the base of a functional team. Trust is not an expectation of behavior, it is about vulnerability. People have a tough time admitting weaknesses and mistakes; in a team that values trust, members can be vulnerable. They can, instead, focus on solutions and strategy and not waste time on figuring out how to protect themselves. When trust is secured and maintained, morale is very high and staff turnover is less prevalent.[22]

When trust has a chance, teams develop the ability to engage in productive conflict. Fear of conflict is the second dysfunction. There is a sharp difference between productive conflict and destructive fighting. Focusing on concepts and ideas and not personal attacks can help a team get to a solution faster. Issues are resolved quickly and egos are not bruised; team members are willing to tackle the next issue. Avoiding the conflict allows the issue at hand to worsen, and individuals become tense and resort to gossip and back-channel personal attacks. This second dysfunction is uncomfortable and damaging to a team's progress. Operating at the midpoint between artificial harmony and personal attacks is ideal, and the team must push itself to stay in that zone, no matter how uncomfortable it can get. It's in that zone where the best organizational decisions are made.[23]

The third dysfunction, lack of commitment, can be overcome once trust and productive conflict are present. Teams need not agree on every decision through consensus, but buy-in is desirable. If the team environment has allowed all of the issues and concerns to be aired, team members may continue to disagree with a course of action, but they will understand that it was the best course having considered all of the options in a safe and protected environment. And most people will feel supportive of the decision so long as they were heard in the decision-making process. Certainty helps to unite the team as well; a decision is better than no decision. And the team is comfortable with a change in direction if they learn the direction they chose isn't the best.[24]

Moving up the Lencioni pyramid (see figure 6.4), the team has trust, no fear of conflict, and commitment. With this in place, it's time to focus on accountability, the lack of which is the fourth dysfunction. "Peer pressure and the distaste for letting down a colleague will motivate a team player more than any fear of authoritative punishment or rebuke."[25] Reminding each other about the group's performance standard is a tough job. When a team is working closely together, personal relationships develop which can stand in the way of holding each other accountable. This is where the leader has a starring role. Seeing the CEO step in and call someone on their behavior builds confidence in the team to do the same peer-to-peer. This critical feedback will only strengthen the team and clear roadblocks and land mines, focusing the team on results.[26]

Finally, at the top of the dysfunction pyramid is inattention to results. The team has already achieved so much at this point, but losing sight of the results is all too common. Using a type of scoreboard helps the team establish agreed upon goals and focus on the end result as a measure of their success. It is human nature to focus on personal goals and forgo the collective goals. But it's in these collective goals where a team will see how well it is doing and focus on the win.[27] "When players on a team stop caring about the scoreboard, they inevitably start caring about something else."[28] These results aren't always financial either; a strategic plan often holds metrics for success around students reached, teachers trained, publications produced, and the learning outcomes these produce. These are results.

While there are numerous trade publications that can guide how a team works and develops, Lencioni's work resonates in the museum world because it is sensitive to the personal traits humans possess and demonstrates a logical progression of development that any museum can tackle, despite financial resources. Museum workers are passionate people who

Figure 6.4   The Five Dysfunctions of a Team. *Source:* Cinnamon Catlin-Legutko

stay in the game because of commitment to mission and purpose. Turning Lencioni's model into a positive list of characteristics describes the perfect team for any museum:

1. They trust one another.
2. They engage in unfiltered conflict around ideas.
3. They commit to decisions and plans for action.
4. They hold one another accountable for delivering against those plans.
5. They focus on the achievement of collective results.[29]

Helping the team to gel and embrace functionality is an excellent strategy for any administrator.

Assessing Ourselves and the Team

As teams form and begin working together regularly, and as staff members get to know each other in break rooms, conference rooms, offices, and elsewhere, a picture of each of them as whole individuals begins to emerge. While the performance each individual brings into the workplace is guided by job duties and expectations as well as work place culture, personality types, and nonwork challenges and opportunities will influence how an employee presents in the workplace. When the whole person is not understood, the team, deadlines, and outcomes can be impacted.

One way to better understand employees is a formal assessment. Choosing which of these to administer can be a daunting task; there are heaps of employee assessments available and most are fee-based. And they all measure different things, thinking style, personality traits, work style preference. When thinking about building a team, it is important to remember that whatever assessment tool you choose, only use it used for general coaching and job placement analysis. Text box 6.2 offers thirteen criteria for choosing the best assessment product.[30]

Text Box 6.2 Exercise: Disc Behavioral Assessment

Circle all the words that you think describe you, as many or as few as you like. When you're done, tally the number of words/phrases you've circled under each letter, D, I, S, and C. Everyone has a different combination of these descriptors. The letters under which you circled the most and the second-most number of words or phrases probably are your preferred behaviors. These preferences are interpreted on page 154.

C		D
Careful	Urgent	
Objective, Clear	Pioneering	
Has high standards	Innovative	
Good analyst	Driven	
Detailed	Likes a challenge	
Picky	Demanding	
Aloof	Quick	
Fearful		
Steady and sincere	Optimist	
Patient	Motivator	
Empathetic	Team Player	
Logical	Problem solver	
Service-oriented	Emotionally needy	
Apathetic under stress	Inattentive	
Passive	Trusting	
S Resistant to change	Poor with details	I

Source: Adapted from Russell, *10 Steps*, 102.

Pigeonholing people because of their assessment results isn't advisable; many people can rise to the challenge of any job despite what make them comfortable. Some behaviors are easier to manage, some are not. For some this just means at the end of the work day, their energy may be depleted, thus negatively affecting their work/life balance. While the latter is out of a museum administrator's scope of control, it is important to recognize what employees need from a workplace and to provide it for them when you can.

A quick and easy workplace assessment is known as the DISC. Once managers and team members understand its basics, it becomes a handy tool for understanding ourselves and each other, and the four quadrants are easy to remember. William Moulton Marston posited a theory in 1920 about how people emotionally respond to stimuli. The twenty-first century DISC assessment is based on his initial research and is based on four personality quadrants: dominance, influence, steadiness, and compliance. Each person has a combination of two of these, with one stronger than the other. Everyone has traits from all four quadrants and the results measure how individuals behave and how others would describe that individual's behavior:

> Dominance (D)—This individual is driven and task-oriented. A measurement of her success is how many tasks were checked off her list in one day. When tasks are left open and unfinished, it causes stress and can manifest as anger when others are preventing the completion.
>
> Influence (I)—A strong "I" individual is eager to sway people quickly in a direction. And he needs regular positive reinforcement to know he is successful. He is stressed when he thinks his team is upset with him and may not like him; he will appear hurt.
>
> Steadiness (S)—This individual is most common in the workplace and is one of the best team players to have. She works behind the scenes and wants everything and everyone on an even keel. Stress comes for her when she isn't able to take care of people; the stress manifests as passive-aggressive behavior.
>
> Compliance (C)—A "C" will typically be called a perfectionist. He is systematic and likes to take his time to complete the task perfectly. Anything less is stressful to him. This shows up in redirection—distracting others so he can finish the task perfectly.

Understanding these characteristics helps administrators choose team members for a project or activity. A team full of strong "D"s will butt heads as will a team of all "C"s. A team of just "I"s and "S"s will have a fabulous time together but may be unable to move the project forward without strong

Text Box 6.3 Guidelines for Choosing an Assessment

1. Use assessment tools in a purposeful manner.
2. Use the "whole-person" approach to assessment.
3. Use only assessment instruments that are unbiased and fair to all groups.
4. Use only reliable assessment instruments and procedures.
5. Use only assessment procedures and instruments that have been demonstrated to be valid for the specific purpose for which they are being used.
6. Use assessment tools that are appropriate for the target population.
7. Use assessment instruments for which understandable and comprehensive documentation is available.
8. Ensure that administrative staff is properly trained.
9. Ensure that testing conditions are suitable for all test takers.
10. Provide reasonable accommodation in the assessment process for people with disabilities.
11. Maintain security of assessment instruments.
12. Maintain confidentiality of assessment results.
13. Ensure that scores are interpreted properly and consistently.

Source: U.S. Department of Labor, *Testing and Assessment*.

leadership. A good team leader will understand that team members can help each other when they know their gaps.[31] Jackie Hoff, director of collections services at the Science Museum of Minnesota in St. Paul, Minnesota, finds that the best group is one where "folks … actually enjoy the job at hand (and) can express the work they are doing in a positive light." They also "strive to learn more and enjoy the process while all along they know where the finish line is."[32] A team mix of DISCers will help achieve this ideal.

Generations in the Workplace

In addition to employee assessments, it is advisable to build a team with generational differences in mind. And if you can't build a team because of budget restrictions or personnel policies, understanding generational difference can create harmony and increase productivity in the work place. "Understanding generational differences is critical to making them work for the organization and not against it."[33] The work of William Strauss and

Neil Howe tells us that generational styles change fairly predictably in history.[34] They define a generation as "people moving through time, each group or generation of people possessing a distinctive sense of self." They "look at history just as an individual looks at his own life, and a generation is shaped by its 'age location'—that is, by its age-determined participation in epochal event that occur during its lifecycle. The age location produces a 'peer personality'—a set of collective behavioral traits and attitudes that later expresses itself throughout a generation's lifecycle trajectory."[35] One generation, the Boomers, have a shared memory of President Kennedy's assassination and it shaped their worldview at an impressionable age. The Millennials all experienced 9/11, which forever shaped their worldview. Other factors like how they were taught in school (teaching styles and tools) will also influence generations and their values in the workplace.

There are a variety of publications that define the generational groups in the workplace. For simple reference, they can be clustered as such:

- Veterans were born between 1922 and 1943 and have World War II as a life defining event. There are approximately 52 million veterans in the United States, and the majority are retired from paid work. In a museum setting, they frequently appear as volunteers.
- Boomers were born post–World War II (1943–1960) and they were raised in an era of optimism, opportunity, and progress. There are over 73 million in the United States, the largest percentage of the workforce, and they started retiring in the early part of the twenty-first century.
- Gen X grew up in the shadow of Boomers and were born between 1960 and 1980. They reject all labels and categories (they really don't like assessments and chapters like this!) and number just over 70 million in the United States.
- Millenials, also known as Gen Y, are just entering the workplace. Born between 1980 and 2000, their work style is still being defined but they are typically high-tech, neo-optimistic. There are close to 70 million of them as well.[36]

Just as with employee assessments, these generational groupings should not be used to define an individual or used as stereotypes. Instead assessment results and generational studies help the team leader manage and help team members understand each other, using their strengths to complement each other and achieve excellence.

Table 6.1   **Generational Core Values**

Veterans	Boomers	Generation X	Millennials
Dedication/Sacrifice	Optimism	Diversity	Optimism
Hard work	Term orientation	Thinking globally	Civic duty
Law and order	Health and wellness	Technoliteracy	Achievement
Respect for authority	Personal growth	Fun	Sociability
Patience	Youth	Informality	Morality
Delayed reward	Work	Self-reliance	Street smarts
Duty before pleasure	Involvement	Pragmatism	Diversity
Adherence to rules			
Honor			

Source: Adapted from Zempke et al., Generations at Work.

LEADERSHIP

When the following leaders were asked why they lead, their responses were quick and clear.

I was never satisfied with the status quo.

—Ellen Rosenthal, president and CEO (retired),
Conner Prairie, Fishers, Indiana

I'm so passionate about museums that I chose to lead.

—Trevor Jones, director of Historical Resources,
Kentucky Historical Society, Frankfort, Kentucky

Leadership is a calling.

—Bob Beatty, chief of engagement, American Association for State
and Local History, Nashville, Tennessee

These comments reflect the signature, the hallmark, of a leader. Leaders are able to see the future clearly and act decisively. Nurturing and developing a leadership style will ensure that a leader has followers. A leader must prioritize self-care so that she is able to lead. The museum field needs and deserves strong, well-trained, and passionate leaders, but so often, training in nonprofit graduate and post-graduate programs is focused on training managers and not leaders. Coursework needs to focus on developing strategic thinking and other leadership skills like "learning to live with ambiguity, taking risk, and moving out of one's comfort zone."[37] The following section offers a snapshot of what museum leadership is about—developing your leadership abilities, emotional intelligence, and work-life balance.

Five Practices of Exemplary Leaders

Thousands of books and articles have been written about leadership, with more published each day. Beginning their research in the 1980s and continuing into the present, James Kouzes and Barry Posner developed a clear understanding of what leaders are doing when they are at their best. They describe leadership as a relationship. The book, *The Leadership Challenge*, and training tools and programs offer an excellent place for any leader to begin developing his style and toolkit.[38]

Model the Way

The first practice is modeling the way. Leaders will clarify values by finding their voice and affirming shared ideals. They set the example by aligning actions with shared values. Words often used to describe leaders like this include confidence, integrity, guidance, direction, inspiration, honesty, forward-looking, competence, and a track record of getting things done. The leader who models the way is truly demonstrating "do what you say you will do" or DWYSYWD. Credibility is the foundation of leadership and people will not believe the message unless they believe in the messenger.

Leaders must stand for something, believe in something, and care about something. They must find their voices by clarifying their personal values and then express those values in their own style. But good leaders don't force their views on others. Instead, they work tirelessly to build consensus on a set of common principles. Then they set the example by aligning their personal actions with shared values. When constituents know that leaders have the courage of their convictions, they become willingly engaged in following that example.[39]

Inspire a Shared Vision

Leaders envision the future by imagining exciting and ennobling possibilities and it's their challenge to enlist others in a common vision by appealing to shared aspirations. Leaders passionately believe they can make a difference. They "envision the future by imagining exciting and ennobling possibilities."[40] But visions seen only by the leader are insufficient to mobilize and energize. Leaders enlist others in their dreams by appealing to shared aspirations. The second practice, inspiring a shared vision, sees leaders breathing life into ideal and unique images of the future. People will see how their own dreams can be realized through a common vision.

Challenge the Process

With the practice of challenging the process, leaders search for opportunities by seizing the initiative and by looking outward for innovative ways to improve. They experiment and take risks by constantly generating small wins and learning from experience (forces for status quo are more organized than the forces for change).

The work of leaders is change. The status quo is unacceptable to them. Leaders search for opportunities by seeking innovative ways to change, grow, innovate, and improve. Through experimentation and risk taking, leaders constantly generate small wins and learn from mistakes. Extraordinary things don't get done in huge leaps forward; they get done one step at a time. Leaders demonstrate the courage to continue the quest despite opposition and setbacks.[41]

Enable Others to Act

Leadership is a team effort, and effective leaders can be gauged by how often they say "we." With the practice of enabling others to act, leaders foster collaboration by building trust and facilitating relationships. They strengthen others by increasing self-determination and developing competence.

Leaders know they can't do it alone and they foster collaboration by promoting cooperative goals and building trust. Leaders promote a sense of reciprocity and a feeling of "We're all in this together." They understand that mutual is what sustains extraordinary efforts. Leaders also strengthen others by sharing power and providing choice, making each person feel competent and confident.

Encourage the Heart

The fifth practice, encouraging the heart, finds leaders recognizing contributions by showing appreciation for individual excellence. Leaders celebrate the values and victories by creating a spirit of community.

Achieving a museum's mission is not easy. People become exhausted, frustrated, and disenchanted, and they're tempted to give up. Leaders encourage the heart of their constituents to carry on. To keep hope and determination alive, leaders recognize contributions by showing appreciation for individual excellence. Genuine acts of caring uplift spirits and strengthen courage. In every winning team, the members need to share in the rewards of their efforts, so leaders celebrate the values and the victories by creating a sense of community.[42]

Leaders who are cognizant of these five exemplary practices and work to develop their behavior around them are frequently seen as:

- More effective in meeting job-related demands;
- More successful in representing their department to management;
- Creating higher performing teams;
- Fostering loyalty and commitment;
- Increasing motivational levels and willingness to work; and
- Possessing high degrees of personal credibility.[43]

According to research conducted by the global firm, Right Management, the number one reason leaders fail is their inability to "build relationships and a team environment."[44] Leaders are successful because of their relationship with constituents. And article after article states that the main reason people leave their job is because of their boss. Leadership is a continual professional development process to stay ahead of the norm and lead a team and an organization to success.

Emotional Intelligence

As leaders build their toolkits and develop themselves and others, focusing on emotional intelligence may be the key to their effectiveness. Emotional intelligence (EI) is defined by the "ability to understand and manage our emotions and those around us."[45] Cultivating a leader's EI is possible, especially by tapping into the primal nature of emotions. Sensitivity, careful thought and language, and empathy are the core of EI, but there are four competency areas that a leader may focus on, that when mastered, she becomes the best leader she can be:

- Self-Awareness—Leaders with high EI are emotionally self-aware and are able to speak candidly and openly about their emotions and convictions. They are also able to self-assess and know their limitation and strengths, and with this they are perceived as self-assured and will stand out in a group.

- Self-Management—Emotional self-control is an indicator of EI; these leaders are calm and clear-headed during a crisis. They are also transparent about their mistakes, adaptable and nimble with change and task management, and focused on high achievement, able to set attainable and measurable goals. These leaders also possesses initiative and maintain optimism even with punches are rolling one after another.

- Social Awareness—Emotional signals are highly visible to leaders with EI and this makes them able to work easily with diverse constituents. A sense of service and organizational awareness is also evident. This makes leaders politically astute, networking masters, and available when needed.

- Relationship Management—This category of EI aligns nicely with the leadership practices identified by Kouzes and Posner earlier in this chapter. Leaders with a high EI will be able to inspire people to make their vision possible. Influence follows this closely as does the ability to develop others. These leaders are seen as change agents—they can advocate for change even when the odds are stacked against them. And they're not afraid of the natural conflicts that develop and can easily draw out all of the parties involved and create safe space for dialogue and resolution.[46] Ultimately these leaders can manage teamwork and collaboration and "forge and cement close relationships beyond mere work obligations."[47]

Managing the Work-Life Balance

By far, striking a work-life balance is the biggest challenge museum workers have. The list of pressures and expectations is endless. But balance is within reach and with a strong personal commitment to self-care, museum leaders can make it possible. Museum professionals can easily demonstrate the challenge when asked. Robert Trio, museum consultant, observes, "It is a difficult balance because, (especially) in a small organization, you want to help out whenever you can. But when someone begins to pull back on going the extra mile, it is perceived that that person no longer cares even though they are doing what is expected."[48]

Allyn Lord, has difficulty separating the demands of her job and her personal interests, which reveals the typical passion museum leaders bring to the job. "I pay attention to (work-life balance) but I don't do it very well.

Text Box 6.4 Tips for Becoming a Better Leader

- Be Self-Aware—The best leaders are highly attuned to what's going on inside of them as they are leading; they're also very aware of the impact they're having on others. This awareness helps you receive clues about what's going on inside you and in your environment; your emotions are messages. Learn to listen to them. Keep a journal to help you manage self-awareness.
- Manage Your Emotions—Leaders exercise self-control. There will be times when you're frustrated and you want to yell or break something—don't do it. Instead, walk around the block first. Be aware of your emotions but manage them, and if you can't, seek help.
- Seek Feedback—Ask colleagues and supervisors for feedback about what you're doing well and not doing well. Be sure to keep your emotions in check and thank people for the feedback. It's also important to act on the feedback when necessary.
- Take the Initiative—The best leaders are proactive. Take the initiative to find and solve problems and to meet and create challenges. Leaders seek the developmental opportunities they need and if resources aren't available, they find a way. "It's your learning. It's your career. It's your life. Take charge of it."
- Engage a Coach—Leadership is a performing art and a coach may be from inside or outside of the organization: a peer, a manager, a trainer, or someone with expertise. Coaches can help with feedback, but more importantly they can offer social support, which is essential to resilience and persistence. It's lonely at the top and having someone to lean on is crucial.
- Set Goals and Make a Plan—Leaders make sure their work is purposeful action. Set high expectations for yourself and for your constituents. Make your goals public to ensure commitment and once goals are set, make a plan and focus on a few things at a time.
- Practice, Practice, Practice—People who practice are more likely to become experts. Practice could be through role-playing a negotiation, rehearsing a speech, or a one-on-one dialogue with a coach or staff member. This is a great way to try unfamiliar methods, behaviors, and tools in a safer environment than on-the-job.
- Measure Progress—Measuring progress is crucial to improvement, no matter what the activity. Knowing how well you've done is crucial to motivation and achievement. Create a system to monitor and

measure progress on a regular basis and keep a log that records your accomplishments.

- Reward Yourself—"If new behavior is not rewarded, it will be quickly forgotten." Connect performance to rewards and put it in your goal plan—take yourself to lunch with a friend, mark the achievement on your calendar, brag to a colleague, or whatever makes you happy. It's ok to toot your horn at times.
- Be Honest with Yourself and Humble with Others—"Credibility is the foundation of leadership and honesty is at the top of the list of what constituents look for in a leader." We all can improve and the first step is understanding what most needs improving. By being intellectually and emotionally honest, it will produce a level of humility that earns credibility. People don't respect know-it-alls. People like people who show they are human by admitting mistakes and being open to accepting new ideas and new learning communicates that you are willing to grow. Plus it promotes a culture of honesty and openness. "Hubris is the killer disease in leadership." It's easy to be seduced by power and importance—you can avoid excessive pride only if you recognize that you're human and need the help of others.

Source: Adapted from Kouzes and Posner, *Leadership Practices Inventory*, 37–44.

I tend to go through periods of making myself take personal time, resulting in a little more even balance. But, in general, because I love what I do and have personal interests related to my work (genealogy, museum visiting, history in general), it's hard sometimes to even define what's work and what's life."[49]

Trevor Jones offers his perspective:

The big thing with a work-life balance is that you need to think about it in the aggregate and not on a day-to-day balance. I recognize that sometimes my life will always be imbalanced and that's ok. However, I strive for balance—and that's the important part. When I look back over the year I want it to more or less balance out, while realizing that even on a month-to-month basis, it won't be balanced. I think a lot of nonprofit workers fail to recognize that there is always going to be more work than you can possibly do. Come to terms with that, and then prioritize your most important tasks and do those. We are incredibly passionate people and we want to do it all—but there's nothing in that direction but madness. I love what I do, but I think it's really important to remember that work does not love you back, but your family does. So, go spend time with them and be fully present when you're at home![50]

Time away from the office with family and friends, unplugged from the job, truly does the body, mind, and soul good. Concentrating energy into something not work related like exercise or a hobby will also help strike a balance. If a leader is unable to find the time, burnout is inevitable and the message he is transmitting to his team is harmful. Seeking help through a life coach or a licensed therapist is certainly a smart move. A mindful leader will make sure that she is taking care of his "whole person" and will develop an effective toolkit full of smart practices and emotional intelligence that is peppered with personal interests, family, and friends.

BOARD-DIRECTOR-STAFF INTERACTIONS

No matter what its internal structure, every corporation operates under a board of directors or trustees. In the nonprofit and governmental sector these board members are volunteers. Expectations placed on them will vary depending on the size and nature of the organization they govern, and may change with time and the development of the organization they serve. One thing remains constant: trustees are expected to conduct the business of the organization in such a way as to uphold the public trust. Nonprofit organizations are allowed special legal status predicated on their operation for the public good.[51] Board members are ultimately responsible for ensuring this trust is uncompromised, which is one reason many nonprofits refer to their board members as "trustees" rather than "directors." This serves as a constant, subtle reminder of the nature of the service with which board members are entrusted.

The framework within which the organization governs and manages itself is usually three-legged; the board delegates some of its authority and responsibility to an executive director, who in turn shares this power and obligation with the museum staff. All three legs must move in coordination to fulfill the museum's mission and meet the needs of its constituencies. If the organization is a public institution, subject to control by municipal, county, state, or federal entities, another leg may exist—a government body of elected and/or appointed officials.

Text Box 6.5 Responsibilities of Board Members

1. Ensure the continuity of the museum's mission, mandate, and purposes.
2. Act as an advocate in the community for public involvement in the museum.
3. Provide for the present and long-term security and preservation of the collection.
4. Ensure that the museum serves a broad public audience.
5. Ensure that the museum undertakes research to create and disseminate accurate and objective knowledge relevant to its collection.
6. Review and approve policies consistent with the museum's mission and mandate, and to monitor staff implementation of these policies.
7. Plan for the future of the museum, including review and approval of a strategic plan that identifies the museum's goals and ways to attain them, and monitoring implementation of the plan.
8. Assure the financial stability of the museum through approval and monitoring of budgets and financial reports, arranging for regular audits, wisely investing, and raising funds as required to meet its current and future financial responsibilities.
9. Recruit and negotiate a contract with the museum's director, to evaluate her performance, and to terminate her employment if necessary.
10. Ensure that the museum has adequate staff to fulfill its mission.

Source: Lord and Lord, *The Manual of Museum Management*, 21–22.

Discussion here is limited to the interaction of board members, the executive director, and the museum staff. Many of the same dynamics and strategies are applicable to organizations where governmental officials may exercise some control.

A clear definition of roles and responsibilities of board members, the executive director, and staff is critical in the creation and maintenance of an effectively run museum. Misunderstanding of or refusal to observe these necessarily different roles are at the root of many internal museum conflicts. Fortunately, good advice abounds outlining the duties trustees, executive directors, and staff must fulfill, and there's plenty of work to go around!

"Board-staff relationships" usually refers to the interaction between the board and the executive director, because the staff generally has limited direct contact and lesser influence with board members. The executive director of a museum or nonprofit occupies a unique role vis-à-vis the board, which functions as "the boss." Although the director serves at the pleasure of and is answerable to the board, she can exercise considerable influence over it. The trustees' information about and understanding of the organization and its operations will largely come from the director, who also will set agendas, lead the strategic planning process, and participate in most committee work. The director is ethically and legally obliged to provide accurate and concise information about the museum's programs in a form accessible to the board. Information must be timely and relevant to decision making.

In highly functioning museums, the relationship between the board and the director is a partnership, not a top-down or parent-child relationship. Museum leadership responsibility is shared by the CEO and the board, which means that both parties are in the room when discussing recruiting trustees and establishing criteria for trustees, plus all other aspects of governance that impact the CEO's work.[52]

The extent to which the board and the director achieve this balance will vary from museum to museum and will depend on the size and life cycle of the organization, or the size of the museum. When a museum is forming, the board is more likely to be involved in the museum work because the resources the trustees bring to the organization are extremely critical. Early on the executive director may be the only paid staff member, requiring board members to assume active roles. In the midlife of an organization, the board may again be pushed into dominance to deal with events such as an identity crisis, a consolidation, merger, or major expansion.

Despite the changing roles that trustees, the executive director, or staff members may play during times of organizational change, respect for communication channels and the hierarchy of the structure must be maintained. The more effective and accurate the communication among the three "legs," the more likely whatever changes unfold will be accommodated smoothly. In a small museum, the working board may persist to supplement the work of paid staff or work in the absence of paid staff (all volunteer). In either case, a clear chain of command is required so that museum leadership is ensured and the organization continues to move forward.[53]

Table 6.2   Trustees Are Volunteers, Where Is the Fine Line?

Governance Role	Volunteer Role
Voting at board meeting	Helping to install an exhibit
Recruiting new board members	Working in the store
Evaluating the director	Setting up for an event
Reading and analyzing operational and financial reports	Selling raffle tickets or participating in a phone bank
Sitting on a Collections Committee that determines what to accession	Working with staff to process accessions to the collection

Source: Excerpted from Anderson, "Marry Me!" 124.

Board Composition

Board members bring a variety of values with them to their service; these differing economic, technological, social, political, legal, religious, ethical, aesthetic, and cultural outlooks will be determined, in part, by their respective backgrounds and experiences. A director's success is directly related to his understanding of the board and its values. Becoming acquainted with board members as individuals and learning more about their particular beliefs will help both the director and the board president develop strategies for minimizing potential conflicts of values and help board members stay on the same page.[54]

A variety of backgrounds makes a board diverse, but the board is also constructed to meet the needs of the organization. Maybe a museum is planning a big construction project in the next three to five years—recruiting fundraisers and construction-knowledgeable people will be a priority. Perhaps the organization is preparing for a strategic planning effort—recruiting trustees who can help the board expand its vision and work closely with the director is a priority. At the same time, all boards and directors are looking for people with the same type of expertise:

- Nonprofit trusteeship
- Organizational planning
- Financial/accounting
- Fund raising (including business/corporate, individual, public agency, and foundation)
- Personnel management
- Legal matters especially relating to nonprofit corporations, contracts, and personnel
- Public relations[55]

Lastly, but more importantly, a board's composition needs to be reflective of the community it serves. A diversity of cultural and ethnic backgrounds is crucial in building trust and support from the community and this diversity provides the appropriate range of perspectives needed to effectively govern and plan for the future of the museum. Even if the board is not directly self-perpetuating, the board nominating committee can help ensure that a slate of candidates presented to the membership for election possess a variety of skills and backgrounds to help create the diversity required.

Committees

The vast majority of nonprofit boards organize their work with committees and task forces. Some of these groups are standing, meaning they exist so long as the board exists. Others committees are shorter lived and they end when a project or task is complete. These are known as task forces or ad hoc committees. Standing committees and their duties are typically specified in the bylaws.[56] The director as well as additional staff members are often members of each committee. For example, the director of development will attend development meetings and the director of finance will attend the finance meetings.

While there may be a variety committees because of a museum's particular mission, common committees include:

- Executive—Comprised of board officers, this committee works closely with the director. It typically has the authority to work on behalf of the board between meetings and in case of emergency.
- Finance—Empowered to review the museum's finances and make recommendations to staff and the board, this committee is absolutely critical for nurturing the board's fiduciary responsibility. In some museums, there will also be an investment committee and a separate audit committee.
- Development—This committee works closely with development staff to plan and support the museum's fundraising activities. While it is the responsibility of the entire board to be involved in fundraising, this committee will help the board reach its fundraising potential.[57]
- Governance—Primarily responsible for recruiting and nominating new trustees, the committee also works on a year round cycle of board development—orientation, self-assessments, training, and more.
- Program—This committee is concerned with the delivery of high quality programs and exhibits and works very closely with staff. As such,

this committee focuses on planning, evaluation, and community outreach, if needed.[58]

The board's additional committees may include personnel, building and grounds, planning, marketing/public relations, and events. Because boards are all volunteer and staff can be easily over-taxed, it is important to keep committee numbers to the absolute minimum and reflective of the real work of the museum.

Officers

To meet legal requirements in most states, boards must have at least three officers—president (or chair), treasurer, and clerk (secretary). It is just as common to see additional officers—vice presidents and assistant treasurer. The types and duties of officers are indicated in the bylaws and the election process is specified.[59]

The president has the closest working relationship with the director and should be someone who is experienced and respected by the board, staff, and community. A wise director will nurture this relationship and develop the president as her chief ally, and vice versa. The president is the one who will keep the board moving forward and focused on their responsibilities. When the president is not working in lockstep with the director, she can inadvertently cause confusion among trustees and the delegation of authority can be muddled and compromised.[60]

The treasurer must understand nonprofit finance and be comfortable with accounting measures and can serve as a resource for the board. The secretary is typically a well-organized individual who maintains the records of the board and ensures that the agenda and minutes are shared with the board in a timely fashion. He is responsible for the "official and binding record of board decisions."[61]

Museum staff members are accountable not only to the director and the board but also to the professional community, of which each is a part. The professional communities of curators, historians, archivists, and other professionals each have their own standards and ideology, and these professional guidelines may conflict with the standards and ideologies that board members bring to the organization. To lessen or alleviate conflict, everyone should help foster an atmosphere of mutual respect for each person's qualifications and contributions. The board of directors must set the tone and share it with the staff via the executive director.

Text Box 6.6 How Boards Make Decisions*

MAJORITY VOTE GROUP DECISIONS

- Votes are often based on *Robert's Rules of Order* and monitored by a chair.
- Members make proposals in the form of motions. The motions are discussed. Votes are taken. If four out of seven members agree, the vote is carried.
- Members try to convince the majority of the value of their proposals.
- All remarks are addressed to the chair (not directly to other group members).
- The chair does not argue for or against any motion. His or her task is to ensure orderly discussion procedures.
- The secretary records the majority decisions as they are made.

CONSENSUS GROUP DECISIONS

- Members express opinions on the issue. Issues are discussed until solutions are found which incorporate all points of view or are satisfying to all members.
- Members try to formulate solutions, which will achieve consensus (all agree).
- All remarks are addressed to the group as a whole with the permission of the coordinator (not directly to other group members).
- The coordinator does not argue for or against any solution. He or she helps the group reach consensus by formulating proposals which may be acceptable to all members. (The sense of the meeting.)
- The recorder records proposals, which appear to represent consensus, and reads them to the group so that group members can confirm agreement or modify the proposals.

VOTE COUNTING

- Similar to majority vote procedures, this process relies on polling strategies—vote by speaking, raising hands, writing on ballots or electronic voting.

- Voting happens secretly or simultaneously to avoid sequential voting (if you're the fifth person after a run of yes votes, you will likely
  vote yes).
- Polls can be structured with more than two choices, to uncover
  complexities and nuances in the voting body and to be more sensitive to the full diversity of views.
- Abstentions are counted as absent votes.

Source: Adapted from Gastil, *Democracy in Small Groups.*
°Ultimately, board decision-making is determined by the organization's bylaws.

Text Box 6.7 Case Review: A Tiger Escaped Today . . . and I'm on the Zoo Board*

Near closing time on the Christmas Day in 2007, a female Siberian tiger
escaped its enclosure in the San Francisco Zoo and killed one visitor and
mauled two others before it was killed by the police. There were various accusations that the three young men had been provoking the tiger
prior to the escape. The reports varied from throwing objects at the tiger,
yelling at the animal, and standing on the edge of the enclosure. The
Dhaliwal brothers received deep bites and claw wounds on their heads,
necks, arms, and hands. Their companion, Carlos Sousa, was killed by
the tiger when he reportedly came to the rescue of one of the brothers
being mauled in the initial attack. He had a large gash across his neck
and throat and probably died of blood loss. The tiger then pursued the
brothers for several hundred yards to near one of the zoo's dining areas,
where the attack continued until the arrival of the police.

The zoo initially claimed that the moat wall of the tiger's grotto was
18 feet (5.5 m) tall, but after officials measured it they found it was actually 12.5 feet (3.8 m) tall. The Association of Zoos and Aquariums recommendation for big cat enclosures is a moat wall of 16.5 feet (5.0 m).
The tiger's paws were found to carry concrete chips, suggesting that she
climbed out of the moat using her claws on the wall. On February 16,
2008, the zoo reopened the exterior tiger exhibit, which was extensively
renovated so that the concrete moat wall reached a minimum height of
16 feet 4 inches from the bottom of the moat, addition of a glass fencing
on the top of the wall to extend the height to 19 feet, and installation of
electrified "hotwire." The legal issues were subsequently settled with the

(continued)

brothers receiving $900,000 compensation for their injuries and emotional harm. The Sousa family suit sought damages for wrongful death, negligence, and reckless conduct. The suit was settled in February 2009; terms of the settlement were not disclosed.

In 2015, in an article in the *Blue Avocado*, an anonymous member of the zoo's board gave a glimpse behind the scenes of this tragic incident. The board member stated: "One good thing that happened was that it rallied the board. It's a big board—nearly sixty members—and everybody threw themselves into the crisis. We were eager to help out. I was intensely sad, it also felt good to be standing shoulder-to-shoulder with the other board members." It is not always obvious how board members can help in a situation like this, but in this case: "one thing was legal. We had lawyers on the board who assisted on a variety of legal issues raised by the incident. Board members also worked closely with Zoo management in meetings with City officials and other constituencies. The board reached out to major donors with phone calls and face-to-face meetings. We sought feedback from various groups, particularly Zoo employees . . . Admissions and membership dropped. Events were canceled. There were massive expenses that were out of the ordinary. The Zoo had to pay the crisis management team, legal fees, and the like. But donors stepped up, too. One friend who had not been a donor gave us a large check because he knew we would have challenges. Similarly, another friend and regular donor, doubled his family's support since he recognized the Zoo needed extra operating funds."

Asked about the biggest takeaways for the Zoo's board, this member responded as follows:

> In a crisis, people get energized and can put in extraordinary efforts such as late night meetings . . . It's like a surgeon coming in and cutting out the cancer: a lot of energy, a lot of drama, a lot of acclaim. But being a good board member or executive is more like preventive medicine. Doing the long-term stuff that prevents problems. Making sure the infrastructure is funded. Looking for the slow time bombs that aren't visible.
>
> For example, for budgetary reasons, the Zoo had largely stopped participating in the Association of Zoos and Aquariums breeding programs. As a result, we had an aging animal population. This problem was recognized, and the Zoo again became active in these programs. And as a result the animal age profile improved, and the Zoo was better able to promote its conservation mission."

One hopes that such terrible events do not happen to a nonprofit institution for which she serves as a board member, but experience shows that the San Francisco Zoo is an organization that can survive such a tragedy. With strong board participation, an institution can strengthen it programs and community involvement and emerge as a better organization.

*Case review contributed by Hugh H. Genoways, 2016.
**Anonymous, "A Tiger Escaped . . ."; Batey, "Taunting Allegations . . ."; Fagan et al., "Tiger Grotto . . ."

Although it is not uncommon for trustees to experience confusion regarding the boundaries between their responsibilities and those of the staff, a board that insists on participation in operational matters signals an underlying problem. Regular involvement by board members in personnel matters reflects a management deficiency, such as a lack of internal policies and practices for staff. Constant trustee involvement in administrative issues also indicates weak or ineffective administration, or a loss of confidence in the executive director's leadership. However, such actions also could be motivated by the misguided zeal of individual members of the board who interpret their responsibility as running the organization rather than ensuring that the organization is well run. Emphasizing the structure that exists for board involvement, and recognizing appropriate board accomplishments and productivity may help curb excessive board involvement.

The varied and complex relationships that exist in the administration and management of a nonprofit museum can potentially lead to conflict, and ultimately jeopardize the purpose or programs of the museum. All persons involved with the museum should be given a detailed description of their responsibilities and duties and understand the roles and obligations of board, director, and staff branches. At every turn, it is important for each to respect the authority, abilities, and contributions of the others. This essential mutual respect builds trust, and without trust communication lines break down. Communication—honest, efficient, and accurate—is at the crux of this complex interaction.

Tools to assist in creating and nurturing effective boards are available and useful. Guides to board relations for nonprofit organizations in general may be helpful, but the resources of the Museum Trustee Association (MTA) are particularly aimed at the unique dynamics of museum leadership. This nonprofit organization, founded in 1986, addresses major issues such as strategy, policy, ethics, inclusion, sustainability, and stewardship faced by the over 75,000 museum trustees in the United States. The Baltimore-based association can be reached at www.museumtrustee.org.

CONCLUSION

It is people who make a museum work, and people who work together in a productive manner to create the most effective museum. The multifaceted talents of the staff members are the museum's most valuable assets. Each person on the staff is a unique individual with distinct needs, emotions, and personality traits. Today's museum administrators need to possess sensitivity to individuals and identify the resources and challenges they will bring to the larger group.

Working effectively with groups and within groups is critical to the success of any museum professional and to the success of any museum. The board members, director, and staff can work together to create mechanisms through which the museum's mission can be fulfilled, to the benefit not only the museum's constituents, but to those directly involved in making it happen. Organizational structures can help or hinder the museum at work, but more telling are the factors of shared vision, clear, open, honest communication, cooperative spirit, and trust. These elements have a far greater impact on what the museum, through its governing body and workers, is able to accomplish than any organizational method.

A working museum is made up of team players. Each person will work as part of many groups, and the dynamics of group interaction are important to understand in order to maximize productivity. Museum professionals

Text Box 6.8 Guiding Questions

1. How would you describe yourself as a leader? As a team member?
2. How do you manage a work-life balance, or do you?
3. Describe the characteristics of the best employer, employee, and coworker you have experienced in the work place. What characteristics or behaviors cause you to describe them as the best? Are these attributes you can or will incorporate into your own practice as a team member and/or leader?

will face some of their most difficult challenges as members of the small groups that will be responsible for making many of the decisions and implementing policies within the museum. An effective organizational structure, well-defined roles for board, director, and staff, and capable teams, when combined in an atmosphere of communication, cooperation, diversity, inclusion, and trust, can create a museum that really works.

NOTES

1. Martin, "Organisation Charts."
2. Lord, interview.
3. Martin, "Organisation Charts."
4. Ellis, "The Organizational Chart."
5. Skramstad and Skramstad, *Handbook*.
6. Lord and Lord, *The Manual of . . .*
7. Ibid.
8. Murphy, "Human Resources . . ."
9. Tyler, "Job Worth Doing."
10. Miller, "Are You Being Served?"
11. Schall, "Liability Trends . . ."
12. Wolf, *Managing a Nonprofit*.
13. Taylor, *The Next America*.
14. Schonfeld and Westermann, *The Andrew W. Mellon Foundation . . .*
15. Wolfenden, "How to Write a Diversity . . ."
16. Condrey, *Handbook of Human Resource*.
17. Wolf, *Managing a Nonprofit*, 94–95.
18. Karlgaard and Malone, *Team Genius*.
19. Lencioni, *The Five Dysfunctions*, 3–4.
20. Jones, interview.
21. Lencioni, *The Five Dysfunctions*, 13.
22. Lencioni, *Overcoming the Five Dysfunctions*; Lencioni, *The Five Dysfunctions*.
23. Ibid.
24. Ibid.
25. Lencioni, *The Five Dysfunctions*, 61.
26. Lencioni, *Overcoming the Five Dysfunctions*; Lencioni, *The Five Dysfunctions*.
27. Ibid.
28. Lencioni, *The Five Dysfunctions*, 72.
29. Lencioni, *Overcoming the Five Dysfunctions*, 189–90.
30. U.S. Department of Labor, *Testing and Assessment*.

31. Russell, *10 Steps*.
32. Hoff, interview.
33. Zemke et al., *Generations at Work*, 17.
34. Strauss and Howe, *The Fourth Turning*.
35. Strauss and Howe, *Generations*, 32.
36. Zemke et al., *Generations at Work*, 3.
37. Male, "Nonprofit Weaknesses . . ."
38. Kouzes and Posner, *The Leadership Challenge*.
39. Ibid.
40. Kouzes and Posner, *The Leadership Challenge*, 17.
41. Ibid.
42. Ibid.
43. Ibid., 343.
44. Right Management, *Why Global Leaders*, 12.
45. Fletcher, *5 Reasons Why*.
46. Fletcher, *5 Reasons Why*; Goleman et al., *Primal Leadership*.
47. Goleman et al., *Primal Leadership*, 256.
48. Trio, interview.
49. Lord, interview.
50. Jones, interview.
51. Lord and Lord, "*The Manual of . . .*"; George and Maryan-George, *Starting Right*.
52. Skramstad and Skramstad, *Handbook*.
53. Goforth, "Thousands of Small . . ."
54. Anderson, "Marry Me!"
55. Wolf, *Managing a Nonprofit*, 52.
56. Renz, "Leadership . . ."
57. See Text Box 5.2.
58. Renz, "Leadership . . ."; Wolf, *Managing a Nonprofit*.
59. Wolf, *Managing a Nonprofit*.
60. Anderson, "Marry Me!"; Wolf, *Managing a Nonprofit*.
61. Wolf, *Managing a Nonprofit*, 62.

7

ETHICS AND PROFESSIONAL CONDUCT

There is almost universal agreement that standards articulate a way to guide the thoughts and actions of museum professionals and provide some basis for judging the performance of institutions and individuals. Ethical principles are one of the cornerstones of the museum profession. But what those standards should entail and how they should be expressed and promoted has been the source of considerable conflict. The past twenty to thirty years have also presented significant change for museums—cultural diversity, educational initiatives, the environment, collections care, international exchange, and repatriation are just a few of the shifts. These changes have forced museum workers to keep a code of ethics close by and integral to decision making.[1]

When asked what the role of museum ethics has in her museum, Dina Bailey, director of educational strategies at the Center for Civil and Human Rights in Atlanta, Georgia, replied that discussions focusing on ethics are extremely important on a number of levels. "Because we discuss ethics as essential to the messaging of our institution's narrative (civil and human rights), we also acknowledge that ethics within our institution are paramount. We ensure that we sell fair trade products in our gift shops, we encourage the practice of high museum standards as set by the American Alliance of Museums, and we hold ourselves accountable because our volunteers, staff, and board want to practice what we preach."[2]

Ethics provide a base line of conduct—it's the floor. It's where decisionmaking begins. Hassan Najjar, executive director of the Museum Center at 5ive Points in Cleveland, Tennessee, states the importance of ethics for his institution: "Once you erode the public's trust, you might as well shut the doors. Ethics is all about public trust for us and we do everything we can to protect it."[3] When museums and museum staff are mindful of ethics and take measures to operate in ethical ways and follow a code of conduct, this is an indication of museum excellence. Museum ethics offer "an opportunity for growth rather than the burden of compliance."[4]

MUSEUM ETHICS

"Ethics" is derived from the Greek word ethos, meaning character, custom, a person's natural state. Aristotle, author of the first major systematic treatise on ethics in Western philosophy, conceived of ethics as the search for the highest good, for how one ought to act in the world. Ethics relies on rational thought as the means by which one chooses the highest good through open discourse about such universal values as virtue and justice. Ethical thought prompts us to ask questions about how to achieve excellence in both our private and public lives, thus promoting dialogue. This dialogue, coupled with practice and habit, enables individuals to make good choices, to do their work well. Rational thought enables us to make appropriate choices between right and wrong, or more often, "difficult choices between competing goods."[5] Ultimately, ethics is a "system of moral principles that govern the behavior of individuals and groups . . . It is about what is right, fair, truthful, honest, beautiful, or in one word, good."[6]

Developing a code of ethics for the museum field, the American Alliance of Museums (then known as the American Association of Museums) brought together professionals from all types of museums and charged them with creating a new code of ethics. The resulting 1991 *Code of Ethics for Museums* sparked a firestorm of controversy, which led to some revisions and a reissue of the code in 1994 (most recent addendum is 2000). Although many issues were debated, the most hotly contested were the use of funds from the sale of collections (direct care to be discussed below), adherence to the code as a requirement of institutional membership in AAM, and the threatened withdrawal of membership from institutions found to be in violation of the code.[7]

Since the time of Aristotle, ethics has been considered one of humankind's highest pursuits because it results in the elucidation of human good.

These discussions concerning museum ethics, then, were to be expected, but the tone and content of the dialogue were unanticipated. How could leaders in the museum profession, who espouse the highest professional ethical standards, disagree so strongly over what should be included in this code of ethics?

Part of the difficulty is semantic; there is great variation in the use and understanding of terms such as "ethics," "morals," "codes," and "regulations." Part of the problem is philosophical; there are widely disparate interpretations of what ethics should address and whether or how they can be enforced. The need for using correct, appropriate, and standardized terminology is well recognized within the museum profession. Another semantic note: throughout this chapter, the word "museums" is used in the broadest possible meaning and includes institutions and their staff, trustees, volunteers, contract employees, and anyone else associated with the institution.

Hugh Genoways and Mary Anne Andrei argue that more effective communication can result from precisely used language and the creation of a distinction between statements of ethics and codes of conduct.[8] Other points of view believe that these two parts make a whole when creating a code of ethics. Edson argues that the code of ethics targets aspects of the museum profession—the internal workings of the museum community and the acceptable conduct and practice of those working in the museum.[9] The structure of this chapter follows Genoways and Andrei's assertion that there is a difference between statements of ethics and codes of conducts, although readers will find that the majority of codes found in the museum field collapse the two into one.

The Ethics Task Force of the AAM, attempting to write the 1991 code, gave as its number one conclusion, "Ethics is not a list of commandments dictated from above but the traditional values drawn from experience on which standards and practices are based" and explained that the code was an attempt to reflect the traditional values of American museums.[10] Robin Lovin echoed this idea in stating, "ethics will not begin with a list of 'dos' and 'don'ts,' commands and prohibitions." What is required first is "some preliminary thinking about how museums and what they do relate to the human good that ethics seek. What does a museum contribute to the good lives of the people who visit it? How can the people who work for the museums enhance that contribution, and what are the characteristic ways that they might diminish it?"[11]

Robert Macdonald and Lovin both make a distinction in their writings between "values" and "rules," and Genoways and Andrei suggest that this is the difference that should separate statements of ethics from codes of

Text Box 7.1 Case Review: Museum Codes of Ethics

ACROSS THE GLOBE

American Alliance of Museums (AAM)
  Code of Ethics for Museums. Washington, DC: American Alliance
    of Museums, 2000. www.aam-us.org/resources/ethics-standards-
    and-best-practices/code-of-ethics.
Association of Art Museum Directors (AAMD)
  Code of Ethics. New York, NY: Association of Art Museum Directors,
    2011. https://aamd.org/about/code-of-ethics.
Canadian Museums Association (CMA)
  Ethics Guidelines. Ottawa, CA: Canadian Museums Association, 2006.
    www.museums.ca/site/ethics.
International Council of Museums (ICOM)
  Code of Ethics for Museums. Paris, France: International Council of
    Museums, 2006. http://archives.icom.museum/ethics.html.
Museum Association (MA)
  Code of Ethics for Museums. London, England: Museum Association,
    2015. www.museumsassociation.org/download?id=1151400.
Museums Aotearoa (MA)
  Code of Ethics and Professional Practice. Wellington, NZ: Museums
    Aotearoa, 2013. www.museumsaotearoa.org.nz/code-ethics.

PROFESSION SPECIFIC

Art History—*Code of Ethics for Art Historians*. College Art Association,
  2014. www.collegeart.org/guidelines/histethics.
Conservation—*Code of Ethics and Guidelines for Practice*. American
  Institute for Conservation of Historic and Artistic Works, 2008. www.
  conservation-us.org/about-us/core-documents/code-of-ethics-and-
  guidelines-for-practice/code-of-ethics-and-guidelines-for-practice#.
  VkQPnLerSiM.
Curation—*A Code of Ethics for Curators*. Curators Committee. American Alliance of Museums, 2009. www.aam-us.org/docs/continuum/
  curcomethics.pdf?sfvrsn=0.

History—*Statement of Professional Standards and Ethics*. American
   Association for State and Local History, 2012. http://resource.aaslh.
   org/view/aaslh-statement-of-professional-standards-and-ethics/.
Museum Stores—*Code of Ethics*, Museum Store Association, 2014.
   https://museumstoreassociation.org/code-of-ethics/.
Zoos and Aquariums—Association of Zoos and Aquariums.
   www.aza.org/ethics/.

All sites accessed November 14, 2015.

professional conduct. "The difference between a value and a rule is that
it makes sense to maximize a value—to increase it as much as possible—
whereas you can only comply with a rule."[12] Values (for example, honesty)
may spawn rules (tell the truth), but it's quite possible to behave in ways
contrary to the value (telling only part of the story) without actually breaking the rule (lying). Adherence to values is difficult to measure or enforce;
adherence to rules is more easily gauged, with compliance "encouraged" via
the negative consequences for rule breaking. In an ideal world, belief in and
acceptance of values would be universal; these values would guide conduct
so effectively that rules simply would not be necessary.

   But museums exist in the real world and are institutions composed of people; these individuals make ethical decisions that affect the museum community and our whole society. Through the development of museum ethics,
it's advisable to look beyond human frailties to consider how museums
contribute to the endeavor of human excellence and ultimately the highest
good. A statement or code of ethics should inspire ethical thought by raising
the awareness of museum professionals, ultimately creating an atmosphere
that encourages honesty, fairness, respect, excellence, and accountability.

   Museums are entrusted with the very objects—scientific, historic, cultural, and artistic—that represent our humanity. These objects embody
the entire spectrum of human behavior and the products of such behavior.
"What makes museum work morally risky is that those objects are often
fragile and sometimes irreplaceable, so that it is possible to deprive future
generations of an experience by exhibiting objects improperly or disposing
of them in ways that makes them unavailable to the public."[13] Museums
must then strive to develop ethical standards based on universal values that

are then translated into conduct in all matters. The root value must be a commitment to serve society as a whole, to serve the highest good.

Ethics Statements

A good statement of museum ethics will articulate the traditional values or morals and communal standards of the museum profession. These statements are essentially unenforceable, since no structure exists for the discovery or censure of violators, and the attempt to create such a system via the 1991 AAM code turned out to be both philosophically untenable and logistically impractical. It should be the shared professional expectation, however, that there will be observance of these ethical standards. Moral suasion more than legislation will govern professional attitudes and behavior. These traditional museum values are what define the museum profession. Acceptance of these values and embodiment of them in museum work marks the difference between simply being an employee of a museum and being a museum professional.[14]

Members of the museum profession will personify these values no matter where their institutions lie within the diversity of disciplines among museums or no matter what their range of duties may be. In a highly mobile work force, employees of one type of museum may be expected to move to a different type during their careers. Although their specific duties may change, the museum professionals' traditional values wouldn't change any more than the ethical behavior of a family practice doctor in a small rural clinic would to change once she sought further training and became a surgeon in an urban hospital.

The compilation of museum ethics in text box 7.1 is based on traditional museum values. Some of these are ideas expressed in earlier codes. Each of these statements is a "work in progress because members of the museum profession can only *attempt* to embody these aims; if an individual or institution attained these ends, they would exist in a utopia. These values will not change with place or time, but the mechanisms through which they are realized may evolve with new technologies, new pedagogical methods, and new understanding of social responsibilities. Museum professionals will be able to judge their ethical behavior by measuring the progress of their institution in terms of these values during their tenure. It should be kept in mind that a focus on progress toward one value that has a negative impact on progress toward other values may not be judged as ethical behavior. Balance in reflecting each of these values will always be the key goal."[15]

Text Box 7.2 Museum Ethics

- Museums will strive to maintain as their highest goal serving the public through the enhancement of the search for human knowledge, beauty, and understanding.
- Museums will strive to maintain their public trust responsibilities.
- Museums will strive to be guided by their missions in all activities, including collection acquisition and development of public programs.
- Museums will strive to conduct their business and programs in a legal and moral fashion and will strive to avoid even the appearance of impropriety.
- Museums will strive to identify actions that reveal all discriminatory behavior and will strive to overcome these behaviors by education and active diversification of their work forces.
- Museums will strive to maintain their nonprofit status.
- Museums will strive to ensure the expenses for their operations and programs do not exceed their revenues.
- Museums will strive to manage objects and artifacts placed in their care in such a manner as to assure the long-term preservation and conservation of the objects and artifacts.
- Museums will strive to maintain their collections and the associated records in an accurate and ordered manner.
- Museums will strive to work cooperatively with indigenous groups to provide patrimonial collections care that includes respect for the traditions of the cultural groups that produced them.
- Museums will strive to maintain the educational value of their pedagogical objects, but recognize that these objects will receive different use and treatment from those in the permanent collections.
- Museums will strive to create and disseminate new knowledge based on research with collections, informal education, preservation and conservation, and new technologies in exhibition and collection care.
- Museums will strive to make their public programs available for the education of a broad and diverse audience that is truly representative of the communities they serve.
- Museums will strive to involve the most knowledgeable experts available, including representatives of cultural groups when depicted and when planning and implementing exhibits and other public programs.

Sources: Adapted from Andrei and Genoways, "Museum Ethics," 10–11; Genoways, "To Members of . . .," 228–29.

CODES OF PROFESSIONAL MUSEUM CONDUCT

The Institute for Museum Ethics (IME), located at Seton Hall University, is actively generating conversations about museum ethics and responding to issues as they develop in the field. It is their position that "ethical issues underpin all aspects of work in museums—from governance to education, registration to exhibitions, finances to operations and visitor services." IME contends that museum ethics "are about an institution's relationship with people—individuals and groups in the communities a museum serves as well its staff and board members."[16] As such, these ethics influence codes of professional museum conduct.

Some scholars separate professional conduct into two types—those that are governance- and staff-related and those that are collections- or acquisitions-related. The governance type includes ethical considerations across the nonprofit world, with conflict-of-interest practices attracting the most concern. Governance issues rarely hit the front pages, unlike the collections type which focuses on how collection items were acquired or removed from collections.[17]

Governance

Conflicts of interest can be one of the most damaging challenges a board and staff can face. In essence, these conflicts are disabling and prevent the person with the conflict from being loyal to the museum. Loyalty is a key measure of performance. Further, a conflict of interest impairs judgment, compromising decisions that can have lasting impact on the museum.[18] The best way to manage these conflicts is to adopt a conflict of interest policy that includes a disclosure form that each board (and staff member) will complete at times deemed appropriate. Most often personal collecting practices raise the flag of concern; additionally, recusal from deliberations and maintenance of confidentiality are recommended actions to prevent and make transparent any conflicts.[19]

Collections

Ethics issues around the acquisition of the collections have developed out of historic, archaeological, art collection, paleontological, natural history, and living collections practices. Before the 1970s, museums did not actively produce codes of ethics or acquisitions policies. Even with the promulgation of the 1970 UNESCO Convention and its 1972 ratification by the United

Text Box 7.3 Exercise: Conflicts of Interest

At the core of all ethics issues are conflicts of interest. This is true for both staff and board members. For board members, their participation requires any conflicts are revealed and documented. Together the board and staff, as the museum professionals, set the expectations for ethical conduct. For many, what constitutes a conflict of interest may be challenging or confusing. "The potential for conflict of interest arises when members of the board or staff might find themselves in a position to benefit themselves, family members, or other organizations with which they associate by virtue of their position" within the museum.° In a nutshell, if you stand to financially gain from your participation you are entering a conflict of interest.

Conflicts may take many forms. Are you being paid by the museum for a service? Are you financially benefitting from your proximity to business transactions? These relationships may be for good and valid reasons. Documenting these conflicts through disclosure statements and regularly reviewing policy will prevent harmful situations from developing.

Examine the following real case examples presented in John Henry Merryman's article for Stanford Law School, "Museum Ethics":

Case 1: A prominent art dealer is invited to join the board of trustees of a major art museum that acquires and exhibits works of the kind that the dealer shows and sells.

Case 2: The director of art museum A is invited to become a trustee of museum B, which is active in the same fields as museum A.

Case 3: A distinguished art historian who is the leading expert on an important period of art history collects works from that period and occasionally bids at auction for herself. She also advises other collectors and bids for them at auction. She is employed as a senior curator at a major museum, which she advises on acquisitions and for which she bids at auction. She is also a trustee of another museum that actively collects in her field, which she advises and for which she also bids at auction.

Case 4: An active collector of works that the museum also acquires and shows who is invited to join the board of the museum.

Engage in discussion with your classmates or colleagues. Are conflicts of interest evident? Why? If so, what steps should be taken to mitigate the conflict?

Source: Excerpted from Merryman, "Museum Ethics."
°Wolf, *Managing a Nonprofit*, 40.

States, and subsequent legislation, the museum field was slow to publish policies in the spirit of UNESCO. There was a fear that curators buying in international markets would have their hands unduly tied. By 1973, the Association of Art Museum Directors (AAMD) began to push on this issue, taking a few decades of change and precedent to arrive at the 2008 revision to their guidelines which tightened the requirements and prompted AAM to do the same. Both organizations make clear, "no museum should acquire any archaeological or ancient work of art unless research indicates that work left the country of modern discovery legally after 1970."[20]

More recent pressures stemming from the economic crises of the early twenty-first century have created ethical issues that have grabbed news headlines. A handful of museums have tried, and some have succeeded, to sell collection items and use the proceeds to retire debt and make facility repairs, rather than using proceeds for the direct care and/or acquisition of collections. Others have sold collections to fund building renovations. The Philadelphia History Museum, formerly known as the Atwater Kent Museum, closed for three years (2009–2012) after an extensive renovation. To fund this, the museum sold 2,000 objects, arguing that the collections envelope, the building, contributes to direct care.[21] In 2013 the Petersen Automotive Museum in Los Angeles quietly began selling off a third of its car collection to fund building renovations along with new acquisitions.[22] Citing a new collecting and interpretation direction, which is a legitimate reason for deaccessioning, it was the use of proceeds to fund building renovations that caused concern in the museum community. Chicago's famed Field Museum, buried in crippling debt from bonds issued for construction, sold off its significant collection of George Catlin paintings, in two phases, to balance the annual budget. "In no event should those proceeds be used for anything other than the acquisitions or direct care of collections," said Burt Logan, chair of the AAM's accreditation commission, in an interview with National Public Radio.[23]

On the surface these decisions are contrary to museums' duty of care. But as endowments crumbled and bank notes came due from ambitious construction projects, trustees and staff were scrambling for cash and turned to the collections. Some examples were extreme cases, but there was enough concern and enough questions coming from the field that AAM's Accreditation Commission asked the AAM board of directors to create a Direct Care Task Force in 2014 to consider how proceeds are to be used from the sale of collections and to establish a definition of "direct care." Up to this point direct care has gone undefined. At the time of this writing, the final white paper is still to be released that will detail the results of the task force's survey. Preliminary findings are frustrating; they indicate that there are "1) a few areas of consensus from a statistical perspective and 2) a vast gray area." While respondents were glad to be asked, they couldn't offer a clear definition of "direct care." The work of the task force will focus on creating guiding principles, but this recent development provides evidence that museum professional conduct is ever evolving.[24]

Various groups of discipline-specific museums (art, history, natural science, children's, technology) through their umbrella organizations, such as the Association of Art Museum Directors, American Association for State and Local History, Natural Science Collections Alliance, Association of Youth Museums, and Association of Science and Technology Centers, will continue to promulgate codes of professional conduct that would apply to all of their affiliated institutions. For example, the federal laws covering the collection and holding of plants, animals, and cultural objects (Lacy Act, Endangered Species Act, Marine Mammal Protection Act, American Eagle Protection Act, Migratory Bird Treaty Act, and Antiquities Act) are of primary interest to museums of natural science. The Visual Artists Rights Act of 1990 will be most applicable to museums of fine art.

Institutional Codes of Professional Museum Conduct

Professional ethics influence the standards of conduct for any given occupation. These standards usually mandate more exacting expectations for behavior by members of the profession than that demanded of the general population. An individual citizen who collects, buys, and sells objects, for example, would be considered to be acting ethically so long as she was giving and asking fair value and was not dealing in stolen or otherwise illegal materials; a museum professional's behavior would be considerably more constrained. Some codes of conduct would prohibit the latter from accumulating or maintaining a personal collection; others would prohibit engaging in any trades or sales; others would limit the nature of materials collected; others would require disclosure of personal property. Similarly, corporations are regarded as ethically selling property they own so long as the transaction reflects a fair value and laws regulating commerce are observed. Museums, however, which are nonprofit corporations, are held to a higher standard when contemplating the sale of property in the form of museum collections.

Continuing with the argument that AAM and ICOM have written codes of professional conduct rather than codes of ethics, much of the material included in the current "codes of ethics" of AAM and ICOM can be used,

Text Box 7.4 Case Review: Repatriation Redux

DATELINE: THE NEAR FUTURE

In what can only be described as a stunning victory for the Egyptian culture, the United Nations has enacted the UN Egyptian Antiquities Protection and Repatriation Act (UNEAPRA). This act, in part, will repatriate "culturally significant artifacts" to Egypt from national museums around the world. Cultural significance will be determined by the Egyptian government and supervised by a specially commissioned, multinational task force, installed by the United Nations. Leading this special task force is a team of Egyptologists from the United States, Great Britain, France, and Russia.

It is expected that compliance with this act will be voluntary, or heavy UN sanctions (in the form of travel restrictions and export tariffs on certain commodities) will be placed upon nations refusing to comply. Implementation will begin within 180 days of the enactment of UNEAPRA, with total returns to be made or scheduled no more than five years from the date of enactment.

No details are yet forthcoming that outline fiscal responsibility of the returning nations. There are presently several bunkered warehouse locations in Egypt that will serve as the temporary repository of these artifacts, pending final approval of a $13 billion loan from the World Bank, which will be paid out in increments of $1.3 billion a year for the next ten years.

DATELINE: THE PRESENT

This parody news account may at first glance seem like something out of science fiction. But with the relative success of the Native American Graves Protection and Repatriation Act in the United States and the Greek government's demand that friezes from the Parthenon, long held by the British Museum, be repatriated, it may be possible that we will soon be entering a new era. Could there come a time when all the plundering from wars will have to be accounted for, and perhaps on a grand scale? We have in recent years seen numerous accounts of Holocaust survivors having their art collections returned to them, their family fortunes given back to their heirs, even receiving papal apologies made for not having the moral courage to stand up for what was right.

But how can we settle accounts with cultural groups and nations? Legal, ethical, and moral standards vary from country to country, region to region; even within a single town, there is no consensus about "the greater good."

Museums are public institutions; their holdings are intended to be exposed for all the world to see, and with this exposure comes claims to pieces within a museum's collection. These claims may be individual or family-based, but are increasingly being made in the name of the culture as a whole.

It has been said that the sins of the father migrate through his offspring, even to the fourth or fifth generation, but we now have a contemporary moral standard in which children disclaim responsibility for the wrongs committed by the father. This attitude is strongly evidenced in a statement by directors of leading European and U.S. museums opposing the wholesale repatriation of cultural artifacts seized during imperial rule or by means now considered unethical. They say the universal role played by objects in promoting culture outweighs the desire by individual countries or racial groups for their return. At issue are not only such "booty" as the Elgin Marbles, which the Greek government desperately wants back, the Benin bronzes in the British Museum, and thousands of Egyptian works in the Louvre, but Australian Aboriginal requests for the return of artifacts and human remains from Europe.

Is repatriation "a disservice to all visitors" as the directors declare? Although they are opposed to illegal trafficking in objects, they draw a distinction for material seized "decades or even centuries ago" and now held in museums. "We should recognise that objects acquired in earlier times must be viewed in the light of different sensitivities and values, reflective of that era."

Still, if subsequent generations are capable of righting what it perceives as wrongs, should they do so? Several European institutions have returned artifacts to countries of origin or traditional owners. Italy has agreed to repatriate an obelisk Mussolini seized from Ethiopia in 1937, and a Scottish museum returned a spiritually significant ghost-dance shirt, worn at the battle of Wounded Knee in 1890 to the Sioux.

We hold certain truths to be self-evident, that all men are created equal, but these words, a key tenet of Thomas Jefferson's Declaration of Independence, were written at a time when only some men (and no women) were created equal, and a large portion of the population—enslaved people—had no legal rights at all. Times have changed, and

(continued)

Text Box 7.4 Case Review: Repatriation Redux (Conitued)

we now consider slavery repugnant and indefensible, but the psycho-logical damage to our country continues into the twenty-first century. As a society we have attempted to acknowledge the great wrong, create compensatory programs that try to offer equal opportunity and teach our children that all people are truly created equal. So we have many moral and legal precedents (reparations for World War II–interred Japanese Americans, for example) for trying to make right the wrongs of the past.

But will returning artifacts to their place of origin right a past wrong? Opponents of object repatriation use the same justification—that collec-tions are universal—to deny attempts to return material culture as they use to deny requests to repatriate human remains.

In many cultures, the remains of deceased individuals are expected to stay within the care of the family or society, and their protection is a moral obligation. This is one reason the repatriation mandated under NAGPRA has been such an emotional issue. Claimants feel the graves of their ances-tors have been desecrated and used in a manner less than honorable. Orthodox Jews have similar feelings about Jewish remains that have been disturbed by archeological excavations. Almost two-thirds of European and British museums are believed to hold thousands of Aboriginal bones, hair and soft tissues, removed from Australia usually against the wishes of local people or without their knowledge. The Tasmanian Aboriginal Centre and the Foundation for Aboriginal and Island Research Action have campaigned for more than twenty years for the return of remains.

And what about the remains of those who are unclaimed? Is it any less wrong to possess human remains if there is no one to speak up for them? Can we claim, for example, Egyptian mummies may appropriately reside in museums because their ancient culture is no longer vital? Have we the right to claim their ceremonial goods, in the name of science, because there are no longer any practitioners of the ancient faith?

Do museums have the right to own the bodily remains or possessions of any individual, whether their culture is living or extinct? Should this fact influence museum practice? Do we retain or repatriate materials based on moral and ethical standards or political expediency? If it is ethi-cally and morally justifiable to return aboriginal remains and materials in North American and Australia, should non-Egyptian museums give Egyptian materials back?

Museums are not likely to give away their collections and close their doors. But how do they find the balance in these complex issues of who

has the legal, moral, and ethical right to what? How will you help your
museum make its choices and develop its policies?

Consider these questions and discuss with your peers or classmates.

with some reformatting and modification of emphasis, as standards for writing professional museum codes of conduct. These codes are also inspired
by federal laws and regulations. Some of the rules will be based primarily
on ethical issues—for example, all museums' obligation to serve the public,
to care for objects in their collections, and to avoid conflicts of interest—
whereas others will be included because of legal requirements.

Recent concerns about issues grouped under the terms "diversity and
inclusion," for example, are primarily of an ethical nature; desired staff
behavior in response should be set out in a code of conduct. The Native
American Graves Protection and Repatriation Act (NAGPRA), provisions of the Americans with Disabilities Act (ADA), and the IRS criteria
for exempt status and unrelated business income tax (UBIT) are among
the laws covering a broad range of museums (see chapter 8). Compliance
with these laws may be expressly addressed through codes of professional
museum conduct.

Individual museums should construct their codes of professional museum
conduct through an inclusive and public process that allows input from the
larger profession and members of the museum staff and board. The AAM
code concludes with a call to institutions "to regulate the ethical behavior of
members of their governing authority, employees, and volunteers," noting
that "formal adoption of an institutional code promotes higher and more
consistent ethical standards."[25]

Controversy is often the impetus for reexamination and reworking of
codes of conduct, and just as the repatriation issue flavored the AAM code
dialogues of the 1990s, so, too, may concerns about objects of cultural
patrimony instigate ethical debate among ICOM members in the early
twenty-first century.

Developing a professional code of conduct is complex and may contain
common elements for all museum workers. Because of this complexity,
each museum should employ the widest possible diversity of staff in creating this document. If this process is conducted openly and fairly, it should
result in all members of the staff, board, and support organizations becoming stakeholders in the document, which will make internal implementation far simpler.[26] In the final analysis, though, implementation will be a

Text Box 7.5 Case Study: The Scarf Dance

Constance Rader sighed as she inched her way to the back of the cluttered antique store. All the usual suspects were there—depression glass, crocks and stoneware bowls, bits and braces and crescent wrenches, tintypes and cabinet card portraits of people long dead, commemorative plates, horse collars, embroidered day-of-the-week tea towels—all stacked precariously in the dank cave. She breathed in the familiar smell of slow decay, and was turning to go when she saw it. There, draped over the back of a chair at the edge of a stack of feed sacks—a bright bit of silk. She carefully extricated the sheer square from the pile of muslin and burlap (she was a curator, after all, so she knew yanking on old fabric could shred it). Yes, it was a scarf, and yes, it was a souvenir scarf with pictures and words all over it, and as she moved into better light she saw, that yes, unbelievably, it was a souvenir scarf of Nebraska!

Now Connie had quite an extensive collection of souvenir headscarves from states and locations across the United States. She enjoyed wearing the scarves; their funky depictions of China Town and Yosemite and Mount Rushmore were an interesting contrast to her solid colored "curator suits." The scarves seemed like a safe thing to collect, because her museum wasn't interested in materials from California or Maine. In all her perusing of antique stores and junk shops and museum collections, she'd never seen a souvenir scarf of Nebraska. But here it was—goldenrod, the state flower, and field corn, and meadowlarks, and the towering State Capitol and herds of cattle and Boys Town—all depicted in yellow and green and black and fuchsia! She scanned the silk and saw something strange in the midst of all the familiar symbols—a little Victorian house. "Home of General Lew Wallace, author of Ben Hur," the black letters said. Now she'd studied history for almost two decades, but she'd never heard that General Wallace lived in Nebraska. Still, it was a souvenir scarf of Nebraska, and the price was right. She put down her money and left the store in a glow. What a find!

Once Connie got home, she spread out the scarf on the dining room table, and then looked up Wallace in the encyclopedia. She was right; he'd never lived in Nebraska. The house depicted on the scarf was in Indiana. A double find! Not only a Nebraska souvenir scarf, but one with a mistake! She imagined some overworked Japanese scarf designer sorting through piles of building sketches that all looked the same, and a postwar factory with few English readers to catch the error. She swooped up the scarf and draped it around her neck, admiring the "NEBRASKA" spelled out in green block letters. But as she caught her reflection in the curved glass front of her china cabinet, her smile faded.

"What am I thinking?" she said out loud. She was Constance Q. Rader, in charge of museum collections at the Nebraska Museum. She had signed a copy of the museum's code of professional conduct, agreeing to abide by its provisions, including offering the museum the right of first refusal on an item she might acquire that was within the museum's collecting scope. She *knew* the acquisitions committee would want the scarf the minute it was offered, even with the mistake printed on it, because there were no other such souvenir Nebraska scarves in the collection.

Still, she thought, the mistake made it a flawed piece. And since she'd never seen anything like it, what was the likelihood that her colleagues on the acquisition committee knew such an item even existed? And if she never wore it around work, who would know she had it? The museum often declined items without provenance, and the antique store owner, she was sure, would know nothing about who had owned or used the scarf or even where he had come across it.

It was only a twelve dollar scarf . . . it would probably just go into storage . . . she could always donate it later . . . if only she hadn't suggested just yesterday to her intern that a good guide to behavior was "the mom test"—if you couldn't tell your mother what you were going to do, you probably shouldn't do it.

1. What are Connie's obligations (legal, moral, ethical) in this case?
2. What would you do?
3. What should Connie's intern do if she sees Connie at a local restaurant wearing the scarf?

question of individual commitment. The most inspired and well-articulated code in the world will have meaning only if individuals use it as their personal guide in making choices and then acting on them.

Enforcement

Enforcing a code of ethics can be a tricky business, while enforcing a code of professional conduct is possible. When laws are broken, the ramifications are clear-cut, and with codes of professional conduct, they can be enforced

Text Box 7.6 Exercise: The Grand Bargain—Detroit Institute of Arts[1]

The Detroit Museum of Art was incorporated in 1885, and remained a private organization until 1919. The City of Detroit was doing well as the automobile industry boomed and a restructuring of the museum as a public-private partnership created the Detroit Institute of Arts (DIA).[2] The institution became a city department to cover operational costs; the nonprofit organization provided funds for art acquisition and other programming.[3] The partnership improved facilities—a new building was occupied in 1927 and major renovations and additions occurred in 1966, 1971, and 2007. But the DIA also experienced the financial fluctuations common to government agencies.

In 1975, a major crisis resulted in DIA staff layoffs and a brief closure. The State of Michigan stepped forward and aided the DIA with funding, which increased to over 70 percent of the annual operating budget by 1990. Again, financial troubles arrived when a new governor, in the face of a national recession, slashed DIA funding by 50 percent. A fundraising campaign sought to soften the loss of staff and programs, but it became clear fundraising would not succeed as long as the DIA was part of the City of Detroit government.

By 1998, the city signed an operating agreement with the non-profit organization under the new name of The Detroit Institute of Arts, Inc. This nonprofit group assumed control and operation of all functions of the DIA, running it as a 501(c)3. This led to fifteen years of relative financial stability, building expansion, and growth even with city's slow withdrawal of support. To regain some financial stability, the DIA submitted a millage levy to the voters in the three counties surrounding Detroit, and it was passed in all three counties in 2012.[4]

The DIA faced its greatest challenge in early 2013 when the state-appointed emergency manager for the City of Detroit filed for municipal bankruptcy and declared the DIA collection of art among the city's relative few assets. In preparation for potential sale of the art collection, three widely different estimates of its value were received—Art Capital suggested $8.5 billion, Artvest $4.6 billion, and Christie's $867 million (Christie's estimate was based only on the 2,800 pieces of art the City could prove it owned rather than the full collection of over 60,000 objects).[5] The DIA and its supporters presented a strong defense against the sale of art collection, raising such points as:

- "It is a national treasure and thus collectively owned by the people of the United States";[6]
- "The art is held in trust for the public";[7]
- "Arts and culture are important to Detroit's comeback and future";[8]
- "The donors of many of the pieces of art had imposed specific restrictions on them";[9]
- "Strong ethical guidelines promulgated by Association of Art Museum Directors declare that art may only be sold to buy more art and never to support operational costs or other basic needs";[10] and
- "Art collection of the DIA is held by the City of Detroit in charitable trust for the people of Michigan, and no piece in the collection may thus be sold, conveyed, or transferred to satisfy City debts or obligations."[11]

Although this was an extremely complex case, it was often presented as pitting the DIA resources tied up in the art collection versus the unfunded needs of the city employee pension funds.[12]

The situation was finally resolved on November 7, 2014, when bankruptcy judge Steven Rhodes issued his opinion. The resulting agreement, which became known as the "Grand Bargain," required contributions from all parties involved to solve Detroit's financial problems. The DIA portion of the settlement included:

- Resolving all of the disputes relating to the rights of all parties with respect to the DIA and the art;
- Paying $100 million into the general and police and fire retirement systems over twenty years;
- Various local and national charitable foundations contributing $366 million to these retirement systems over twenty years; and
- The City transferring the art to the DIA Corp., which will hold the art in perpetual charitable trust for the benefit of the people of Detroit and Michigan.[13]

Thus the DIA and its nonprofit corporation were able to retain all of the art collection and to gain title to it; however, this came at the cost of a major financial obligation to the two city retirement funds and the loss of any potential support from the City of Detroit.

As of October 2015, the DIA had met it $100 million fundraising obligation as part of the "Grand Bargain," but was expressing grave concerns

(continued)

Text Box 7.6 Exercise: The Grand Bargain—Detroit Institute of Arts¹ (continued)

about raising another $170 million in endowment for its operating budget by 2022 when the millage from the three surrounding counties will end.¹⁴

Exercises: This case study offers learning points related to collections, ethics, fundraising and development, and the challenges of public/private partnerships.

1. Take one of the points made by the DIA and its supporters against the sale of art collection and expand it into a one-page examination of the philosophical and legal basis of the argument.
2. You are the new director of the DIA faced with raising $170 million over a seven-year period. Write a two-page prospectus for donors reviewing the history of the DIA and why now is a critical time in the history of DIA for supporters to step forward.
3. What examples of public/private partnerships exist in your state? What laws govern bankruptcy of municipal and other governmental departments? How might these laws impact your museum, governmental museums, or public/private partnerships in your state?
4. Where do you believe the DIA made mistakes in documenting its acquisitions in the past leading to it becoming involved in the Grand Bargain? Write a new acquisition policy, in five pages or less, for the DIA including documentation of donor information.
5. What other ethical guidelines have been promulgated by Association of Art Museum Directors? How do they compare and contrast with guidelines of history, natural history.

NOTES

1. Exercise contributed by Hugh H. Genoways, 2015.
2. Austin, "Detroit Museum . . ."; Gallagher and Stryker, "Battle Brewing . . ."
3. Detroit Institute of Arts, *A Brief History*.
4. Ibid.
5. Heddaya, "11th-Hour . . ."; Stryker, "Detroit Rising . . ."
6. Kennicott, "Detroit Institute . . ."
7. Gallagher and Stryker, "Battle Brewing . . ."
8. Ibid.
9. Rhodes, *Oral Opinion*.
10. Kennicott, "Detroit Institute . . ."

11. Schuette, *Opinion No. 7272*.
12. Stryker, "Detroit Rising . . ."; Walsh, "Detroit Institute . . ."
13. Rhodes, *Oral Opinion*.
14. Stryker, "Detroit Rising . . ."

by the museum through hiring and continued employment. Codes of ethics cannot be enforced because they are the search for the greater good.

When the major 1991 revision to the AAM Code of Ethics was completed, an original draft specified stronger compliance: membership in AAM affirmed adherence to the Code, and if there were perceived violations of the code, an ethics commission would investigate and recommend action, including withdrawing the museum's membership. Pushback from the field and a rethinking of the process resulted in the present situation. Today, museums are able to be AAM members once they pay the dues. This more inclusive approach is a greater service for the field with the potential to unify over 30,000 U.S. museums.

Once a museum becomes a member, it is now part of the AAM community where museums are encouraged to work toward excellence. In 2012, AAM introduced a new approach to museum best practices when it renamed its middle "A" from association to alliance. The Continuum of Excellence outlines how museums can move up the slope to achieve accreditation. The Continuum includes assessment programs as well as the Pledge of Excellence, which museums make, indicating their adherence to AAM Codes of Ethics and museum best practices. While not the same as accreditation by any means, this self-regulation is how the museum field is managing ethical considerations. As of this writing, close to 3,000 museums have taken the pledge, which is considerably more than the 1,000 accredited museums.[27]

Museums in the United States that meet the highest professional standards while fulfilling their stated missions may be accredited by the AAM. Discussed in more detail in chapter 2, the accreditation process begins when a museum voluntarily applies for accreditation or is notified by the Accreditation Commission that it is time for a subsequent accreditation review. Ethical compliance is considered during these processes, and in the face of blatant disregard for museum ethics, the Commission can place a museum on probation and may take subsequent action to withdraw accreditation if the situation isn't remedied. Other sanctions may be considered.

Codes of professional conduct may be enforced, however, by the hiring museum and the governance nominating process. Board and staff members who adhere to these codes are desirable to the museum; violators can easily be dismissed when institutionally approved codes are not followed.

CONCLUSION

In a highly publicized ethics case, the Detroit Institute of Arts, a municipally owned museum, was targeted by the City of Detroit's federal bankruptcy court to sell its world-class art collection to settle the city's debts. Ultimately several foundations collaborated and secured an $800 million dollar deal to save the museum by transferring ownership of the museum from the city to a nonprofit.[28] The donors paid Detroit a ransom to liberate an art collection. While Detroit's financial troubles are significant, in this instance, the public trust status of the collection was compromised. How can museums strive to be ethical in governance decisions as well as collections concerns, when a municipal crisis can undermine the museum's commitments? There is no easy answer.

A statement of museum ethics outlining museum values and the principles for which the institution stands is an important moral compass that can guide board and staff in their fulfillment of the museum's mission. Just as the strategic plan outlines specific courses of action, a code of professional conduct should delineate specific expected behaviors. The strategic plan will specify what will be accomplished; the code of professional conduct will reveal how staff will go about doing that work in ways consistent with articulated museum values and that are protective of the public trust.

Active self-regulation by the museum profession will minimize the likelihood of outside regulation, but that should not be the principal motivation in writing statements and creating codes. The museum community will continue to explore both the philosophical and pragmatic issues of ethical thought and behavior because it is the right thing to do. And the museum community will continue to learn lessons from case study of the DIA, the Philadelphia History Museum, the Petersen, and the Field.

Text Box 7.7 Guiding Questions

1. When do ethics become laws?
2. How would you define direct care? Is it appropriate for museums to use proceeds from deaccessioning part of the collections for direct care?
3. Does your museum have a code of professional conduct? If yes, review for any necessary updating. If no, briefly outline such a code for the museum.

NOTES

1. Edson, *Museum Ethics*.
2. Bailey, interview.
3. Najjar, interview.
4. Marstine, "Introduction."
5. Lovin, "What Is Ethics?"
6. National Park Service, "Code of Ethics."
7. Macdonald, "Ethics."
8. Andrei and Genoways, "Museum Ethics," 6; Genoways, "To Members of . . ."
9. Edson, *Museum Ethics*.
10. Macdonald, "Ethics."
11. Lovin, "What Is Ethics?"
12. Andrei and Genoways, "Museum Ethics," 7.
13. Lovin, "What Is Ethics?"
14. Andrei and Genoways, "Museum Ethics," 9.
15. Genoways, "To Members of . . .," 229.
16. Institute of Museum Ethics.
17. Merryman, "Museum Ethics."
18. Ibid.
19. Lord and Lord, *The Manual of* . . .
20. DeAngelis, "Collections Ethics."
21. Rose, "Philadelphia Museum . . ."
22. Robinson, "A Furor over Sales . . ."
23. Corley, "Chicago's Famed Field Museum . . ."; Gillers and Grotto, "Hard Times at the Field."

24. American Alliance of Museums, "Updates."

25. American Alliance of Museums, *Code of Ethics*.

26. Andrei and Genoways, "Museum Ethics," 89–90.

27. American Alliance of Museums.

28. Kennedy, "Detroit Institute of Arts Meets . . ."; Kennedy, Davey, and Yaccino, "Foundations Aim . . ."

8

LEGAL ISSUES

A disclaimer: Nothing in this chapter should be considered legal advice. This material is presented solely to raise awareness of seven legal issues that commonly confront museum administrators and managers. The museum profession is indeed fortunate to have two excellent texts available concerning legal issues for museums—*Museum Law: A Guide for Officers, Director and Counsel*, by Marilyn E. Phelan, professor of law and museum science, Texas Tech University (2014), and the 2012 update of *A Legal Primer on Managing Museum Collections*, by Marie C. Malaro and Ildiko P. DeAngelis, both formerly the director of the Museum Studies program at George Washington University and legal counsel for the Smithsonian Institution. These two books offer a great start, and it is wise to seek legal counsel whenever necessary.

Depending on the type of museum, staff members may deal with one or two laws more than others. For example, in museums with archaeological collections, the Native American Graves Protection and Repatriation Act (NAGPRA) figures prominently in regular work (see more about NAGPRA below). For others, like Jenny Benjamin at the Museum of Vision[1] in San Francisco, California, "day to day my biggest legal issue is copyright. Licensing is a huge part of my job." And because of the nature of her museum and its holding of patient records in the archives, the Health Insurance Portability and Accountability Act (HIPAA) is important to know. "As a medical museum," Jenny shared, "I am dealing with health privacy all the time as my collections can reveal intimate information about former patients."[2] While HIPAA won't be discussed here, it is critical that you know what laws pertain to your museum operations and collections and that you reach out to legal professionals in a timely manner.

AMERICANS WITH DISABILITIES ACT (ADA)

Museums must work to enhance the experiences of their visitors with disabilities. Providing experiences for disabled visitors always has been the ethical thing to do, but with the passage of the Americans with Disabilities Act,[3] it is also the legal thing to do. To help you get started, visit the *Accessible Practices* pages of the Association of Science-Technology Centers website.[4]

What Is ADA?

President George H.W. Bush signed Public Law §101-336, the Americans with Disabilities Act (ADA), on July 26, 1990. ADA is a federal law that gives civil rights protection to individuals with disabilities and prohibits discrimination based on disability, and it guarantees equal opportunities for individuals with disabilities in employment, state and local government services, places of public accommodations, transportation, and telecommunications. ADA is modeled after the Civil Rights Act and Section 504 of the Rehabilitation Act of 1973.[5] Almost 13 percent of noninstitutionalized American citizens report a disability,[6] and 15 percent of the world's population lives with some form of disability and the number is growing as populations are aging.[7]

Contents of ADA

The following title review is adapted from the text of the ADA, approved in 1990 and amended in 2008, effective in 2009.[8] In 2010, final regulations were revised to include ADA Standards for Accessible Design.

Title I—Employment

Title I of ADA provides protection for qualified individuals with a disability against discrimination in employment and includes specific features related to reasonable accommodation, qualification standards, and other management issues. Employers, including museums, must reasonably accommodate the disabilities of qualified applicants or employees, including modifying workstations and equipment, unless undue hardship would result.

Title II—Public Services

The Public Services section of ADA consists of two subtitles, but only Subtitle A—Prohibition Against Discrimination and other Generally Applicable Provisions—has application for museums. This portion of Title II prohibits any public entity, defined as any part of state or local government, from discriminating against individuals based upon their disabilities in the provision of "services, programs, or activities." If a museum is a part of any branch of a state or local government, it will be covered by provisions of Title II.

Title III—Public Accommodations and Services Operated by Private Entities

If a museum is not covered by Title II, it will follow provisions of Title III, which prohibits discrimination on the basis of disability by private entities in places of public accommodation. This rule requires that all new places of public accommodation and commercial facilities be designed and constructed to be readily accessible to and usable by persons with disabilities. Those alterations must be to the maximum extent feasible.

Title IV—Telecommunications

Title IV of ADA sets forth two major requirements to expand telecommunication services for individuals with hearing impairments—telecommunications relay services and closed captioning of all federally funded television public service announcements. Both of these requirements may affect museums. Museums are expected to provide TDD "telephone" service, and any video used in exhibits or programs should be captioned.

Definitions of Terms

The definitions of the following terms for ADA must be understood in order to properly implement the law.

Disability

There are several general categories of disability that comprise most of the disabled population—mobility, visual, hearing, and cognitive. According to the Americans with Disabilities Act, a person with a disability is defined as: "a person with a physical or mental impairment that substantially limits one or more major life activities; or a person with a record of such a physical or mental impairment; or a person who is regarded as having such an impairment." Under ADA, the term "qualified individual with a disability" means an individual with a disability who is, with or without reasonable modifications to rules, policies, or practices, qualified for the removal of architectural, communication, or transportation barriers, or the participation in programs or activities provided by a public entity.

Accessibility

Under ADA, accessibility means compliance with the requirements of the American with Disabilities Act Standards for Accessible Design for new construction or alterations. To museums, accessibility means making the site's exhibits, programs, special events, publications and videos available to all visitors.[9] Different standards are defined for new construction as compared to alterations. ADA Accessibility Guidelines set standards that are applied during the design, construction, and alteration of buildings and facilities covered by Titles II and III.[10]

Universal Design

Valerie Fletcher with the Institute for Human Centered Design stated in a webinar that "one of the challenges of universal design is to get people to appreciate that we're talking about everybody. You have no idea who has heart disease. You can't guess who has less vision and you can't guess most people who have hearing loss" And she poses the question, "How do we create a sense of welcome for everyone?"[11] Universal design is the "design of products and environments to be usable by all people, to the greatest extent possible, without the need for adaptation or specialized design."[12]

Public Accommodation

Places of public accommodation are classified into twelve categories: places of lodging, establishments serving food or drink, places of exhibition or entertainment, places of public gathering, sales or rental establishments, service establishments, stations used for specified public transportation, places of public display or collection (museum), places of recreation, places of education, social service center establishments, and places of exercise or recreation.[13]

Accessibility for Museums

Accessibility is one of the most important factors for public places. Janice Majewski stated "accessibility is for the majority, not just for the largest minority in the country, and accessibility is for people who have different learning styles and communication problems as well as for people who use wheelchairs."[14] The American Alliance of Museums stated in *Everyone's Welcome,* "From museum guards to tour guides, curators to administrators, all of the public must be treated with dignity, courtesy, and human understanding. And accessibility for people with disabilities will make everyone's daily life easier."[15]

Barrier Removal

Barrier removal is the key to an accessible design and a universal design; it is an essential factor to Title II and III of ADA. ADA requires the removal of architectural barriers that are structural in nature from existing public accommodations where such removal is readily achievable. "Readily achievable" means easily accomplished and carried out without much difficulty or expense.[16] Because it is difficult to achieve all alterations at once, the ADA regulations suggest this order of priorities:

Priority 1: Providing access to your museum from public sidewalks, parking areas, and public transportation (that is, parking spaces, curb cuts, access ramps, wider entrances, thresholds, easy-open doors).
Priority 2: Providing access to the goods and services your museum offers (that is, door hardware, furniture arrangement, visual alarms, Braille and raised-character signs, ramps).
Priority 3: Providing access to public restrooms (that is, doors, ramps, signs, internal maneuvering room, fixture design and installation, grab bars).
Priority 4: Removing barriers to other amenities offered to the public (such as telephones and water fountains).[17]

Barrier removal is a challenge at historic properties. Federal laws may seem contradictory: the ADA mandates equal access, but the National Historic Preservation Act encourages preservation of the historic fabric and design of buildings. Working with the museum's community of mobility impaired people can help staff to provide alternative programming options for structures where some of the physical alterations cited here as required by ADA would affect the historic integrity of National Register–listed or other historic properties.

Text Box 8.1 ADA Barrier Removal Activities

The ADA National Network offers a checklist of activities that are readily achievable for most organizations right now, and all are readily achievable when funding is in place. Measures to be taken include:

1. Installing ramps
2. Making curb cuts in sidewalks and entrances
3. Lowering shelves
4. Rearranging tables, chairs, vending machines, display racks, and
   other features
5. Lowering telephones
6. Adding raised-letter markings on elevator control buttons
7. Installing flashing alarm lights
8. Widening doors
9. Installing hinges to widen doorways
10. Eliminating a turnstile or providing an alternate accessible path
11. Installing accessible door hardware
12. Installing grab bars in toilet stalls
13. Rearranging toilet partitions to increase maneuvering space
14. Installing lavatory pipes
15. Installing a raised toilet seat
16. Installing full length mirrors
17. Lowering the paper towel dispenser in a bathroom
18. Creating a designated accessible parking space
19. Installing an accessible paper cup dispenser at an existing inacces-
    sible water fountain
20. Removing high pile, low density carpeting
21. Installing vehicle hand controls

Source: Excerpted from New England ADA Center, *ADA Checklist for Existing
Facilities*.

Museum workers must study the ADA carefully. No museum administrator wants to find his/her museum in the news because of noncompliance
with ADA. Plus, the civil penalties are high and have recently grown. The
Department of Justice issued a final rule in 2014 that adjusts for inflation
and "increases the maximum civil penalty for a first violation under Title
III from $55,000 to $75,000; for a subsequent violation the new maximum

Text Box 8.2 Exercise: ADA Inspection

With someone knowledgeable about the Americans with Disabilities Act, such as an affirmative action officer, an architect, a volunteer from a local social services agency, a representative from an organization serving senior citizens, or a volunteer from a local agency for the disabled, visit your museum or another local museum. Make a list of physical barriers that detract from the museum experience of visitors.

1. Which of these physical barriers should be removed under ADA?
2. Which physical barriers would be good to remove, but their removal would not be required under ADA?
3. Make a list of barriers to be removed and put the items in priority order to determine which should be addressed immediately and which could be delayed until later.
4. If you were planning a new museum or renovating an existing building into a museum facility, what would be the most important physical barriers to avoid or eliminate from the future museum building?
5. How should the museum address accessibility for visually and hearing impaired visitors?

is $150,000."[18] Museums, rather than being driven by fear of legal actions, should be motivated to provide accessibility because it is the right thing to do.

NATIVE AMERICAN GRAVES PROTECTION AND REPATRIATION ACT (NAGPRA)

The history of museum representation of Indigenous peoples begins with the development of anthropology as an academic field in the 19th century. While there were museums that existed earlier, modern-day representation stems from the late 19th and early 20th centuries. Anthropologists were systematically collecting American Indian material culture. This was at a time Indians were thought to be vanishing from the landscape. So in the gap, in the academy, anthropologists were creating our understanding of Native people, not informed by the Indigenous perspective, but from the white, or colonizer perspective.[19] And often, the collecting of Native American material culture coincided with the collecting of human remains. Whether from burials or the battlefield, more than 300,000 sets of human remains could be found in American museums by the eve of NAGPRA's passing in 1990.[20] "Historically, Native Americans have found themselves disconnected from museums in this country; they were studied and interpreted from a distance, with little opportunity to speak for themselves. In addition, Native American artifacts and human remains that were part of museum collections seemed beyond their reach," according to Malaro.[21]

What Is NAGPRA?

President George H.W. Bush signed the Native American Graves Protection and Repatriation Act into law on November 16, 1990,[22] making the United States the first nation "to pass comprehensive repatriation legislation at the federal level."[23] According to Geoffrey Platt, "a guiding principal in crafting the final legislation was a desire to balance the need for respect of the human rights of Native Americans, with the value of scientific study and public education—all within a complex legal framework."[24] In trying to strike a balance between competing interests, NAGPRA only sets standards, conditions, and definitions under which certain Native American objects and remains can be repatriated, and encourages cooperation and consultation in its implementation.[25]

NAGPRA required all agencies and museums that receive federal funds (including state, local, and private institutions) to inventory all Native American ancestral remains and associated funerary objects, and to develop written summaries of all sacred objects, objects of cultural patrimony, and unassociated funerary objects within their collections. During this process, these institutions were to consult with Native American tribes, Native Alaskans, and Native Hawaiian organizations, to reach agreements on repatriation or other disposition of these remains and objects. NAGPRA not only affirms the right of individuals with lineal or culturally affiliated descent to decide on the disposition of or take possession of these items, but it also increases protection for unmarked Native American graves located on federal and tribal lands.[26] In addition, NAGPRA prohibits the trafficking of Native American human remains and cultural items.

Inventories

By November 16, 1993, museums and federal agencies were required to have a written summary for all sacred objects, objects of cultural patrimony, and unassociated funerary goods in their collection. During this process, museums and agencies were required to consult with tribal, Native Alaskan, and Native Hawaiian organizations, and traditional religious leaders identified as having a likely cultural affiliation with the items. The written summaries were to include information on the scope of these collections, kinds of objects included, information on the geographical location of origin, means and period of acquisition, and cultural affiliation. By 2015, over 42,000 written summaries had been submitted by 863 museums and federally funded institutions.[27] (However, numerous federal agencies have yet to comply, including the National Park Service and the Bureau of Land Management.)[28]

By November 16, 1995, museums were required to complete inventories of human remains and associated funerary objects and to prepare two documents based upon the inventories. One was a list of remains and objects that had been identified as affiliated with one or more Native American groups; the other was a list of remains and objects for which such affiliation could not be determined.[29] By 2015, 569 museums and federally funded institutions had submitted over 6,000 NAGPRA inventories of culturally affiliated remains and objects. There are a great many more inventories that identify culturally unidentifiable remains and objects, totaling over 18,000 records by 748 museums and federal agencies.[30]

Federal agencies and museums are to notify the appropriate tribes of inventory completion within six months of the date of compilation. This notification was to describe each set of human remains and associated funerary objects, including information on the acquisition of the objects. A copy of each notification is to be sent to the Secretary of the Interior, for eventual publication in the Federal Register. Under NAGPRA, all information discovered during the inventory process was to be made available to Native American tribes, Native Alaskans, or Native Hawaiian organizations.

Repatriation

NAGPRA provides a mechanism through which materials may be repatriated to lineal descendants, tribes that demonstrate ownership, or tribes with a cultural affiliation. Cultural affiliation is defined in the NAGPRA regulations "as a relationship of shared group identity which can be reasonably traced historically or prehistorically between a present day tribe, Native Alaskan, or Native Hawaiian organization and an identifiable earlier group." There are several different types of evidence that can be used to show cultural affiliation, including geographical, kinship, biological, archaeological, anthropological, linguistic, oral tradition, historical evidence, or other relevant information. Because it may be impossible for claimants to prove an absolute continuity of lineage from present-day tribes to older tribes, the evaluation of cultural affiliation is to be based on a preponderance of information pertaining to the relationship between the claimant and the claimed material. When cultural affiliation cannot be ascertained, NAGPRA provides criteria for placing the affiliated tribes in priority order.

The repatriation of cultural items involves a four-part process. First, Native peoples must show that the items being requested for return fall under the definition of objects of cultural patrimony, associated funerary objects, sacred objects, or unassociated funerary objects. Second, Native people must be able to prove a cultural affiliation with the object or show prior ownership. If these requirements are met, then Native people must prove that the federal agency or museum does not have right of possession to the object. The criteria for the right of possession are defined in NAGPRA "as possession obtained with the voluntary consent of an individual or group that had authority of alienation." The museum can choose to agree with the tribe's assessment or not.

Disputes concerning ownership can be resolved with the help of a review committee established by the Secretary of the Interior. If the review committee cannot come to a solution, disputes can be resolved in the federal courts. All objects meeting the four-part process requirements will be returned, following publication of a "notice of intent to repatriate" in the Federal Register by the museum or federal agency to the lineal descendant or tribe. NAGPRA states that lineal descendants or culturally affiliated Indian tribes, Native Alaskans, and Native Hawaiian organizations have the right to make final judgments on the treatment of their ancestral remains and cultural items. As of 2015, 50,518 individuals have been repatriated, along with 1,185,948 associated funerary objects, 219,956 unassociated funerary objects, 4,914 sacred objects, 8,118 objects of cultural patrimony, and 1,624 objects that are both sacred and patrimonial.[31]

Implementation

The implementation of NAGPRA was assigned to the Secretary of the Interior who is responsible for promulgating regulations to carry out the law. Under the direction of the Secretary of the Interior, a seven-member review committee was established to help monitor and review all inventories, identifications, and repatriation activities; to make recommendations for future care of repatriated cultural items; and to submit an annual report to Congress. NAGPRA provides the Secretary of the Interior with the right to assess civil penalties against museums and federal agencies that do not comply with the law. If a museum repatriates an item in good faith, however, it is not liable for claims against it predicated upon a claim of wrongful repatriation, breach of fiduciary duty, public trust, or violations of state law.

Unfinished Business

With the passage of NAGPRA centuries of human rights violations were on a path to recovery. Looking back twenty-five years since legislation, there is still significant work to be done. James Pepper Henry noted at the twenty-year mark, "The fact that the act even exists in definitely a plus." Pepper Henry is critical of the process as are other scholars for three key reasons. NAGPRA is managed by a federal agency, the National Park Service, which is not in compliance with NAGPRA, along with other agencies, and the federal government holds the most Native cultural materials. To mitigate this conflict of interest, Pepper Henry recommends that the Department of Justice manage the national NAGPRA office to ensure enforcement.[32]

Second, the larger more upsetting issue for tribal communities is the staggering number of culturally unaffiliated remains and objects still in American museums. With the number of inventories submitted, as of September 30, 2014, there are 122,736 individuals and 971,119 associated funerary objects that are considered culturally unidentifiable in museum and Federal agencies. This is 80 percent of the human remains reported held in museums and federal agencies. The high number is due to a lack of proper consultation with tribal communities, with the remaining numbers due to other failures.[33] It should also be noted that cultural affiliation is determined by the scientific community, not the tribal communities, which maintains power with the colonizer.[34]

Finally, NAGPRA does not address nonfederally recognized Indian nations, making the remains and objects culturally unidentifiable.[35] On May 14, 2010, Congress enacted a new rule that seeks to create a process for repatriating cultural unidentifiable material. Through consultation with tribal communities, museums and federal agencies now have a path to repatriation which impacts 120,000 sets of human remains.[36] This new provision is equally fraught with challenges and the resolution of which will chart the course for the next twenty-five years of NAGPRA.

The relationship between Native people and museums is complex and runs deep in American history. Museums are benefiting from NAGPRA because it has increased their communication with Native communities and has helped establish new partnerships with them. Native American people have begun to play a role in the planning of museum exhibits and

Text Box 8.3 Case Review: Maine and NAGPRA

While NAGPRA legislation may be murky at times, at other times its mandate is clear. Consultation with tribal representatives is a required process in NAGPRA. In the state of Maine, an alternative path was taken that continues to have a troubling impact on Wabanaki tribes in Maine.

As NAGPRA rolled out across the United States and museums began their inventories, a group of Maine archaeologists convened to decide a "cut-off" date for cultural affiliation. And their views differed from other archaeologists and certainly differed from the views of Wabanaki people. "Maine is a state that reflects 12,000 years of human occupation" which is a view shared by Wabanaki people and the Wabanaki Repatriation Committee (WRC).* "The WRC is a group formed by all four federally recognized tribes so that all claims in Maine could be made jointly. This action does not, however, negate the need to publish proposed repatriations in the national register, as all federally recognized tribes must be given the opportunity to review these decisions and make their own claim if they feel it is applicable."

Some Maine archaeologists believe there is a period of cultural discontinuity at the end of the Archaic Period (400 to 3,800 years ago) and because of this, contemporary Wabanaki people are not descended from Indigenous people prior to 3,800 BP. And many of these archaeologists believe that the last cultural affiliation in Maine can only be traced to 1,000 years ago. These views greatly diverge from the Wabanaki perspective and were formed without appropriate consultation. In the early 1990s, the archaeologists met, formed their official position and stance, then met with Wabanaki representatives who did not benefit from their conversations and/or witness the diversity of thought that led to the opinion (there were many dissenting opinions about the archaeological interpretation that prevail today). Complicating it further, and guided by experts, several institutions repatriated remains beyond 1,000 BP up to 3,000 BP.

NAGPRA is also clear in its legislation that there are multiple ways of tracing cultural affiliation in addition to archaeology—geography, kinship, biology, anthropology, linguistics, folklore, oral tradition, history, or other relevant information or expert opinion is to be considered when determining cultural affiliation."** Cultural affiliation in Maine was determined by a small group of archaeologists, without full consultative proceedings, and without regard to all the ways of knowing.

As one can imagine, this cut-off decision and additional meetings caused a contentious environment. This division remains today, festering since the early 1990s. Around 2011, the Wabanaki Repatriation Committee developed a new batch of claims that extend mostly beyond 3000 years. The Carnegie Museum in Pittsburgh, Pennsylvania, the R.S. Peabody Museum in Andover, Massachusetts, the Peabody Museum of Archeology and Ethnology at Harvard in Cambridge, Massachusetts, and the Maine State Museum in Augusta, Maine were all issued WRC claims. As of 2015, the Carnegie Museum has responded to the claims and repatriated and the R.S. Peabody Museum is considering it. The Peabody Museum at Harvard's position is not publicly known. The Maine State Museum turned over their repatriation claim directly to the attorney general's office and did not enter consultation. No response is forthcoming. The WRC is weighing options and not feeling encouraged. It must be noted that the majority of the human remains at the Peabody museums are from the Nevin site in Blue Hill, Maine. Harvard has the ancestors, the Andover museum holds the burial belongings.

Take a moment and consider what is presented in this chapter about NAGPRA and consider this case in Maine:

1. What are the implications when cultural affiliation is denied?
2. What does it mean when NAPGRA isn't followed to the letter of the law? What are the ramifications? How does compliance relate to the museum's ethics statement and/or code of conduct?
3. Are NAGPRA and its process complete? Or is it unfolding still? How?
4. What is the "good" that both archeologist/museum workers and tribal people see from their different perspectives. Which "good" has greater value? Is NAGPRA good legislation?

°Newsom, "Cultural Affiliation . . .," 2; Ranco and Clark, "The Abbe Museum."
°°25 U.S.C. 3005 Section a(4).

public programs. Creating these new partnerships allows museums to work together with Native Americans to increase the understanding of American Indian culture and history.[37] As changes in the law evolved, it is important for the museum administrator to understand how museums and federal agencies are instruments of colonization in the absence of transparency, consultation, and equitable solutions.

UNRELATED BUSINESS TAXABLE INCOME (UBIT)

Nonprofit organizations are subject to taxation on specific activities if these activities are unrelated to their exempt purposes. The source of the income, rather than how the proceeds are ultimately used, determines whether it is taxable or not. Those museums with more than $1,000 in income from unrelated business activities must file an IRS Form 990T. Phelan stated: "Unrelated business taxable income is defined as gross income derived from any unrelated trade or business, regularly carried on."[38] "Regularly carried on" is open to interpretation, but is generally determined by comparing the "sequence and continuity" of the activity carried on by the nonprofit organization with similar commercial activities of a taxable business. If they are similar, then the activity will most likely be judged to be "regularly carried on" and will be taxable. The purpose of this tax is to not give nonprofit organizations an unfair advantage in certain business activities over taxable organizations.[39]

Activities Excluded from Taxation

Three activities conducted by museums are specifically exempt from unrelated business income taxation. Activities conducted for a museum by volunteers are not subject to taxation. The receipts from the sale of donated merchandise are not subject to taxation. Any activity conducted primarily for the benefit of staff, volunteers, members, students, and visitors will not be taxed. It should also be noted that UBIT often does not apply to public museums run by governmental entities because those museums are exempt from *income* tax because of their governmental status, regardless of the source of the income generation. Because this differs by state, be sure to check applicable state laws.

Potentially Taxable Activities

Museum administrators should evaluate a variety of the museum's activities for the possibility of incurring unrelated business tax on its receipts. Among those activities that should be examined are museum stores, eating facilities, parking, travel tours, sale of collection objects, fundraising, advertising, income from investments, rentals, royalties, and certain programming.

Generally, eating facilities and parking lots that operate for the convenience of the staff, volunteers, members, and visitors will not be taxed. If used for other unrelated activities, the income from these facilities will be taxable. Fundraising activities are usually not regarded as unrelated business taxable income because they are not "regularly carried on" and these activities use a considerable number of volunteers. Income from investments should not be taxable, thus protecting the income from endowments that is vital to the operation of many museums. Royalties from licensing in most cases will not be taxed as unrelated business taxable income.

Receipts from the sale of items from the collection are usually taxed. This is an important issue for art museums and zoos that regularly sell items from their collections at moderate to extremely high prices. The theory is that if the item is being removed from the museum or zoo's collections the item can no longer support the mission of the organization. Generally, receipts from the sale of advertising in an organization's publication also are subject to taxes.

Rent from real property is not taxed as unrelated business income, whereas rent from personal property is generally taxed. Again, this can be seen as the museum being allowed to use its real property to the benefit of the museum and its programs. Some parts of a museum's programming also may need to be assessed for potential unrelated business taxable income. For example, a planetarium could use its theater for educational programs for school groups during weekdays, but use it for public entertainment programs on weekends. The former receipts would not be taxable, but the latter would be. Income from tours where a staff member is the leader of the tour and educational programs are offered as part of the tour should not be taxed, but if the museum works with a travel agency, which pays the museum a fee per person, this income is taxable.

The museum store will be the most difficult part of a museum's operation to assess for potential taxation of unrelated business income. The taxable status of merchandise to be sold in the gift shop must be determined on an item-by-item basis. Those items relating to the museum's exempt status will not be taxed, whereas those items not contributing to the museum's exempt status will be taxed. Although this sounds like a fairly straightforward issue, it has proven to be anything but, because the IRS continues to make new determinations. For example, items of apparel carrying the museum's logo were at one time exempt from taxation, but at this writing this determination is under review by the IRS.[40]

This is an important issue for museum administrators, especially directors, because an assessment of unrelated business income taxes could have a significant impact on the museum and its programs. Museums certainly can engage in unrelated business activities, but the resulting taxes must be taken into account as the financial benefit of the activity is calculated. The real challenge of unrelated business income tax is the constantly shifting determinations by the IRS on what will be taxed and what will be exempt. This means that the museum's director and business manager must monitor these changes at all times.

LEGAL LIABILITY

We live in an increasingly litigious society. Sometimes it seems as if just about everyone is either being sued or is busily suing someone else. As the tendency has grown to settle matters in the courtroom, there has been a corresponding decline in the traditional protection from legal peril afforded nonprofit organizations. The immunity that once was enjoyed by public service organizations has evaporated, and even museums are no longer safe from attack in courts as a result of their official activities.

Liability

Ultimate accountability and responsibility for ensuring the museum follows the law falls to the museum's board of trustees. The board is legally responsible to the state attorney general for all the museum does and is the entity against which any legal action will be directed. In some instances, trustees also can be individually sued and held liable for failing to carry out their fiduciary duties, although this action is relatively infrequent. More commonly, trustees become involved in threatened lawsuits that are settled before they get to court. These legal maneuverings require the diversion of valuable resources away from the museum's primary mission and may be just as damaging in the long run as a suit that runs its legal course. The museum also is indirectly liable for the acts of its officials, employees, docents, volunteers, and even outside contractors. This means the museum, as embodied by the board of trustees and as personified by the director, must be aware of the museum's legal obligations in a plethora of situations.

Tort and Contract Law

The museum may limit its liability by knowing in which activities to engage and which to avoid. Liability can stem from one of two branches of the law—either tort law or contract law. A tort is defined as any wrongful act, or failure to act, that does not involve a breach of contract; all other wrongs fall under contract law and are considered breaches of contract.

Loan agreements and work performed by outside contractors are examples of activities covered by contract law. The defining issue in tort law is the concept of "negligence," which Marilyn Phelan defines as "conduct that falls below a standard established by law for the protection of others." [41] In defining negligence, the legal system assumes that the museum director and the trustees are "prudent" people. That is, their standard of conduct will be measured against the conduct of a reasonable person under like circumstances. A museum director would thus be held to the care or skill that an ordinarily prudent museum director would exercise under similar circumstances. If his or her conduct does not meet this standard, the director would be negligent, and the museum is thus liable under tort law.

Governance

The documents, policies, papers, and contracts a museum uses in the operation of its business are called its governing documents. These may include the documents issued by a museum relating to the roles and responsibilities of trustees, the museum's bylaws, and its code of professional conduct, including its position on conflict of interest and personal collecting. The governing documents may also include warranties, contracts, sales policies, and licensing agreements—in other words, virtually everything a museum may publish relating to its methods of governance. From a legal standpoint, the position taken in each of these documents defines the museum's stated duties and responsibilities to the public; they form the basis of the museum's standards for meeting its obligations. For obvious reasons, most of the governance liability will relate to contract law and breaches of contract. A museum director should carefully examine and be familiar with all governing documents, as they form the foundation of any legal claim the museum may wish, or be forced, to make in the future.

A good safeguard for the board is to purchase directors and officers (D&O) insurance policy. These policies protect board members and the museum when actions are not covered by the museum's general liability policy.[42] Museums affiliated with governmental entities may be covered by that entities' risk management policies, so separate D&O insurance may not be required. Often, museum bylaws will include indemnification language, which commits the museum, when possible by law and availability of resources, to covering the costs of any legal action taken by and against the board.[43]

Personnel

Another area of potential liability relates to the policies that outline the responsibilities and privileges of the museum staff. If these policies are written in an employee handbook, they form a contract between the employees and the museum and thus are covered under contract law. The museum's lawyer or legal advisor should view all employee handbooks for their legal implications, just as he or she also should see all other contracts. The key here is equitable treatment in recruiting, hiring, evaluating, and terminating employees. Museums are not immune from legal actions brought by disgruntled employees or volunteers. Personnel problems, and the liability that may be incurred, would be subject to a breach of contract judgment. Tort law would come into effect over noncontractual issues involving negligence. For example, if a docent allows a group of children to play on a sculpture, and one child is subsequently injured when he falls, the museum is liable for negligence because the volunteer would legally be considered the museum's representative.

Risk Management

Risk management is a process whereby potential loss is evaluated and a program to decrease the possibility of loss is initiated and monitored on a regular basis. Most museum personnel think of risk management as fire safety, tornado drills, or shoveling snow off the museum's steps, but risk management extends much further than not locking the fire exits during business hours. Financial internal controls are also part of managing risk of fraud. There also are issues relating to the Occupational Safety and Health Act of 1970, the Americans with Disabilities Act (ADA) (see above), use of material safety data sheets (MSDS) (see chapter 9), and a host of others. Good risk management should reduce insurance costs by lessening the likelihood of litigation.

There are a variety of strategies that can be followed by a museum director or board of trustees to minimize the museum's liability:

- Avoid problems by being proactive instead of reactive.
- Include a lawyer or other qualified legal counsel on the board of trustees or at least have legal counsel available to the board.
- Carry insurance, including liability, comprehensive, and workers' compensation.
- Develop written policies to cover as many contingencies as possible. This includes having written employee's manuals (see chapter 6);

bylaws (see chapter 2); collections care policies (see chapter 11); and a code of professional conduct (see chapter 7).

When, despite the board's precautions, a situation does evolve into a legal issue, there are still a few options to pursue in the courtroom. Phelan outlines some legal defenses a museum may wish to investigate should it be sued for negligence. [44]

ARTISTS' RIGHTS

The Berne Convention Implementation Act of 1988 and the Visual Artists Rights Act of 1990 have expanded legal protection to recognize an artist's moral rights as well as his property rights to work he creates.[45]

Moral Rights

Phelan states that "an artwork is unique in that the artist's personality exists in the artist's creation. This special aspect of an artwork provides a distinct interest or private right for artists that warrant protection long after artists' works have passed to purchasers and collectors." Within moral rights, there are two elements—the right of paternity and the right of integrity. The right of paternity ensures that the public knows the creator of a work and prevents attribution to an artist of a work that he or she did not create. The right of integrity prevents any contortions of the work through distortion, mutilation, modification, or derogatory action. The right of integrity and right of paternity remain with the artist for life and are not transferred to subsequent copyright holders.[46]

Freedom of Expression

Artists are guaranteed the right of free expression by the First Amendment, but this right does have limits. The interests of others must be considered in this expression. Obscene materials as defined by community standards are not protected.

Property Rights

In the United States, the property of artists and writers is protected primarily by copyright laws. Property right affirms that the creator of a work has a temporary monopoly on its use.

COPYRIGHT

Copyright issues over the last twenty years are more complex and have grown because of the digital information revolution.[47] Copyright is a form of protection provided by the laws of the United States for "original works of authorship."[48] Museums and other institutions need to have a clear understanding of who owns the copyright for materials in their collections. Museums must honor and be aware of these copyrights not only to respect the artist or creator but also to protect themselves from illegal uses and subsequent litigation.[49]

Legal Basis

Congress passed two major copyright laws during the twentieth century. The first of these was the "1909 Act." This was Title 17 of the U.S. Code, which was amended on several occasions starting in 1947. Copyright law was modified significantly by the Copyright Act of 1976, which became effective on January 1, 1978.[50] This modification provided a single system of protection for works that can be copyrighted, instead of allowing regulation by the states.

Items Covered

Copyright covers tangible works of intellectual creation in the areas of literature, music, art, and science. Ideas, procedures, processes, systems, methods of operation, concepts, principles, or discoveries do not fall under the governance of copyright law, but they may be patented. Items that can be copyrighted are:

- Works of art
- Photographs
- Literary works
- Musical works (including any accompanying words)
- Dramatic works (including any accompanying music)
- Pantomimes and choreographic works
- Pictorial, graphic, and sculptural works
- Motion pictures and other audiovisual works
- Sound recordings
- Architectural works

The copyright owner has five rights in copyright material, including the right to reproduce their work, the right to make derivative works, the right to sell the work, the right of performance, and the right to publicly display the work. Singly or together, the copyright owner can transfer these rights. However, if no transfer occurs, the creator or copyright owner reserves all rights. The right to sell is terminated for the owner of copyright once the copyright holder sells the work. For this reason, a copyright owner cannot determine the subsequent sales of the work. Significantly for museums, the creator also loses the right to exhibit or display the sold work; however, the copyright owner can still reproduce the sold work. Museums need to exercise extreme care when accepting donations where copyrights may or may not be conveyed with the donation; a determination as to exactly who owns the copyright should be made in each instance upon acceptance of a new gift.

Work Made for Hire

In creating a new publication, work of art, or similar commodity, the museum will hold the copyright only if the individual creating the work does so under a contract that specifies that it is a "work made for hire." This contract should be written and the terms clearly stated. A work created by an employee of a museum will be considered a "work made for hire" if it is created by the employee within his or her scope of employment.

Protecting a Work

For a museum to protect the copyright of a work, the work should be marked, when possible, with © or "Copyright," the year of creation of the work, and the name of the museum. Two copies of a work bearing a copyright notice must be deposited with the Library of Congress within three months of publication. To assert the copyright protection, the museum, must some time during the term of the copyright, register the work with the Copyright Office.

Fair Use

"Fair use" of an item under copyright is not illegal. According to Phelan, it is the use "by reproduction of copyrighted works for criticism, comment, news reporting, teaching (including multiple copies for classroom use), scholarship, or research." To ensure that an item under copyright is utilized for "fair use" purposes only, four factors should be considered by the user: (1) whether the use of the work is for commercial gain or nonprofit educational purposes; (2) the nature of the copyrighted work; (3) the amount and substance of the portion used in relation to the complete work; and (4) the effect of the use of the copyrighted material upon the public and the market.[51]

Visual artist and copyright laws present museum administrators with a dual set of challenges. The museum must be careful to protect its interests when it has works created, either by regular staff or by contract. An explanation of "works for hire" should be included in the staff handbook to cover works created by the regular staff. The museum should be certain as it writes a contract for creation of a work that all copyrights are transferred to the museum.

The other challenge for museum administrators is researching the copyright status of created works donated to the museum for its collections and exhibition. Even more challenging can be determining the status of works that have been in the collection for a number of years. Does the museum own the work, the right to exhibit the work, the right to reproduce the work, or the right to create derivative works? Before making use of works in the collection, the museum must know which of these rights it owns. Also, the museum must know the creator of the work so that he or she can be acknowledged and the museum has the responsibility of protecting the work from damage or alteration. Because these issues carry the force of law, museum administrators must avoid their violation.

SARBANES-OXLEY

At the same time the first edition of this book was heading into production, the nonprofit field was bracing for the impact of the Sarbanes-Oxley Act (SOX) of 2002. The act was passed in response to the corporate and accounting scandals perpetrated by Enron, Arthur Anderson, and more in 2001 and 2002. The intent of the law was to rebuild public trust in the corporate sector. While all but two of the provisions of the bill apply to corporations, the nonprofit field was presented with new laws that helped to shine light on governance and organizational practices.[52]

Whistleblower Protection

Within the legislation, whistleblower protection was mandated for employees who speak out against their employer. Nonprofits cannot retaliate without facing criminal prosecution.[53] As recommended by Allyn Lord, "Your museum should have policies and procedures in place that encourage employees to come forward as soon as possible with credible information on workplace violations or illegal practices."[54] Government-affiliated museum employees may have protection via local, county, or state ombudsman or accountability provisions.

Document Retention Policy

This requirement was handed down by SOX to prevent nonprofits from destroying or tampering with administrative records and objects. If an investigation is underway, nonprofit leadership must protect these records from harm.[55] This isn't too far from the norm for museums as many have provisions in their collections management policies guiding how corporate records are managed and archived (see chapter 11 for more information on this policy). Using an established schedule, retaining documents is a best practice and it benefits the employer in many instances.[56]

While these two provision are seemingly small, they have led to greater nonprofit transparency via the revised Form 990, applicable with tax year 2008. This was the first revision of the form since 1979 and it primarily targeted governance with a series of thirty new questions. Questions such as "Does the organization have written policies on conflicts of interest, whistleblowers, and document retention?" and "What is the process for reviewing and approving executive compensation?" are now commonplace. For many museums, this transparency precipitated a cultural change that continues today and many of the corporate-specific provisions have been adopted by nonprofits for their betterment.[57] For example, increased use of outside auditors in the nonprofit sector has provided more ways for museums to demonstrate financial strength, accountability, and self-improvement.[58]

CONCLUSION

It must be reiterated that this chapter is designed to make the reader aware of relevant laws. The information expressed in this chapter should not be considered legal advice, but only as guideposts for navigating applicable laws for museum administration. It should be noted that there is a universe of legal issues related to collections management that have not been fully discussed in this chapter, but will be examined in chapter 11.

Text Box 8.4 Guiding Questions

1. Are there other laws that apply to museum work that are not cited in this chapter? If so, how do they apply?
2. How visible is ADA compliance in the museums and historic sites you visit or work in?
3. If you work in a museum, how is legal compliance monitored?

NOTES

1. The museum operates under the umbrella of the Foundation of the American Academy of Ophthalmology.
2. Benjamin, interview.
3. Americans with Disabilities Act.
4. Association of Science-Technology Centers, "Accessible Practices."
5. "Introduction to the ADA."
6. "Disability Statistics."
7. World Health Organization, *World Report.*
8. Americans with Disabilities Act of 1990.
9. U.S. Department of Justice, *Maintaining Accessibility in Museums.*
10. U.S. Department of Justice, *2010 ADA Standards.*
11. Fletcher et al., "Going Beyond."
12. "Principles of Universal Design."
13. Americans with Disabilities Act.
14. Majewski, "Accessibility for People . . ."
15. Salmen, *Everyone's Welcome.*
16. Malaro and DeAngelis, *A Legal Primer*, 485.
17. U. S. Department of Justice, *A Primer for . . .*
18. "Civil Penalties Increased . . ."
19. Lonetree, *Decolonizing Museums*, 9.
20. Daehnke and Lonetree, "Repatriation in the . . .," 88–91.
21. Malaro and DeAngelis, *A Legal Primer*, 128.
22. Native American Graves Protection and Repatriation Act.
23. Daehnke and Lonetree, "Repatriation in the . . .," 91.
24. Platt, "The Repatriation Law . . .," 91.
25. Dongoske, "The Native American Graves . . ."; Echo-Hawk, "The Native American Graves . . ."; Merrill et al., "The Return of the Ahayu:da"; Ferguson et al., "Repatration at the Pueblo . . ."; McManamon and Nordby, "Implementing the Native American . . ."
26. Rose et al., "NAGPRA Is Forever"; Killhefer and Guip, "Reburying the Past"; Tabah, "Native American Collections . . ."

27. National Park Service, National NAGPRA Online Database.

28. U.S. General Accounting Office, *Native American Graves.*

29. Public Law 101-601; 25 U.S.C.A. 3003(b)(1)(c).

30. National Park Service, National NAGPRA Online Database.

31. National Park Service, "Frequently Asked Questions."

32. Strand, "20 Years and Counting."

33. NAGPRA Review Committee, *Annual Report to Congress.*

34. Riding In, "Graves Protection . . ."

35. Daehnke and Lonetree, "Repatriation in the . . .," 94–95.

36. Birkhold, "Note."

37. Sackler, "Three Voices for . . ."; Thompson, "Dealing with the Past . . ."; Zimmerman, "Epilogue."

38. Phelan, *Museum Law*, 175.

39. Phelan, *Museum Law.*

40. Ibid.

41. Ibid., 70.

42. Lord, "Not Above the Law."

43. Nonprofit Risk Management Center, *Protecting Your Nonprofit.*

44. Phelan, *Museum Law.*

45. Ibid.

46. Ibid., 274–76.

47. Malaro and DeAngelis, *A Legal Primer*, 165.

48. U.S. Library of Congress, *Copyright Office.*

49. Phelan, *Museum Law.*

50. U.S. Library of Congress, *Copyright Office.*

51. Phelan, *Museum Law*, 319.

52. Cohen, "Sarbanes-Oxley"; Board Source and Independent Sector, "The Sarbanes-Oxley Act . . ."

53. Cohen, "Sarbanes-Oxley."

54. Lord, "Not Above the Law," 95.

55. Board Source and Independent Sector, "The Sarbanes-Oxley Act . . ."

56. Cohen, "Sarbanes-Oxley."

57. Green and Moskowitz, "Revised Form 990."

58. Cohen, "Sarbanes-Oxley."

9

FACILITIES MANAGEMENT

Museum buildings around the globe are some of the most iconic structures built. For many metropolitan art museums, the more innovative and inspirational the facility the better—it becomes a work of art (read: Frank Gehry, I.M.Pei, and Renzo Piano). Other museums are adaptively reusing space, sometimes in new and exciting ways, or are getting by with the facility made available to the organization.

Many of today's museums are built in response to societal interests and demands. As Gail Dexter Lord indicates, "New content, such as human rights, climate change, or worldwide migration, has stimulated the building of new museums based on *ideas* rather than collections."[1] As such, the drive to build, expand, or renovate museums varies. The twenty-first century museum, with an eye toward sustainability, will plan for change and evolution.[2]

MUSEUM FACILITIES

Sustainability is made possible with a facility that is well cared for and operations that are mindful of visitors and collections' needs. Proper management of these facilities includes the orchestration of people working to maintain and secure the day-to-day operations of the institution, its structure, grounds, and areas of special use. A good facilities management plan takes into account the needs of the people who work within the organization, the preservation and exhibition of objects in the museum's collection, and the people who visit the museum. U. Vincent Wilcox contends that these needs can be adequately met through the following six basic facility management actions:

1. Provide and maintain "the physical structure necessary to support the functions to be housed in the space";
2. Provide and maintain "the basic utility services necessary to support the functions of the space";
3. Provide housekeeping "services necessary to support the functions of the space";
4. Provide for the "health and safety of all persons using the space";
5. Provide "for the physical security of people and property in the space"; and
6. Provide "integrated pest management services for the space."[3]

Adherence to this basic outline provides a museum with the framework necessary to develop a facilities management program that should meet the diverse needs of the institution.

While planning is critical, the financial demands of the facility must be kept in mind as building or renovation decisions are made. Will the museum be able to afford the facility costs in five, ten, fifteen years? Deferred maintenance is a constant issue in the nonprofit and government sectors. Janet Gallimore, executive director of the Idaho State Historical Society, has responsibility for significant building and land holding on behalf of the state and is challenged by very little funding available to take care of these cultural assets. "We have 60 historic and modern building facilities in Boise and around the state; we manage 50 manicured acres and 100 plus acres of other land. The maintenance program is a huge challenge for us as we have only three maintenance employees and limited sources of funds to make programmatic or unanticipated repairs."[4]

A well-endowed building fund is an ideal way to keep up with preventive maintenance and building repairs. Finding ways to at least fund depreciation will help cover maintenance costs but it can be an elusive process. Dr. Tonya Matthews, president/CEO at the Michigan Science Center, shared that while it fully funds depreciation, deferred maintenance is the museum's biggest challenge. They "struggle to get these issues solved within our general operating budget, rather than through donor-based 'hail mary's' and creative capitalization strategies." To combat this challenge, her leadership team has made facilities management a key performance indicator (KPI), which makes the facility's care a mission critical activity and this care is measurable.[5]

Physical Structure

Each museum building has its own requirements for proper upkeep. A museum housed in a historic building requires extreme measures of care in order to retain the structure's historic value and, when appropriate, meet the Secretary of the Interior's Standards for the Treatment of Historic Properties.[6] Museums also can be installed within parts of other institutions, such as universities and libraries. Museums may exist in buildings designed exclusively for that purpose. Or, museums may occupy structures that were built entirely for other purposes, such as a fraternal lodge, a library, or a basketball gymnasium. For example, Phyllis Wahahrockah-Tasi, director of the Comanche National Museum and Cultural Center in Lawton, Oklahoma, operates the museum in a building leased from the city for approximately 100 years. As the building has needed improvements like a new storage facility, a new roof, and gallery renovations, they had to seek approval from the city. "With the support, first and foremost, of the Comanche people, museum board, and staff these improvements were made possible. And now, due to the overwhelming support of the Comanche people, we have outgrown the space."[7] Nurturing an equitable relationship between the city and the Comanche people has made these facility investments possible.

No matter what the type of structure, the administration and facilities staff of the museum needs to have a detailed knowledge of the infrastructure of the building; an assessment of the maintenance record of the building; a schedule of maintenance work to meet annual maintenance needs; and an appropriate budget that itemizes the expenses of the maintenance schedule.[8]

Those institutions that are able to design a museum must remember several considerations. The form a museum takes is dictated by its purpose and mission. A museum's unique nature dictates that form must follow function, and architects and designers need to be aware of this.[9] To ensure that preservation needs are met, curators, conservators, and facilities managers will be in direct consultation with the architect at all stages of planning and construction. In addition to the architectural design, a site for the new museum must be selected if one already has not been made available. If tourists are to be a principal focus group, a site may be chosen that is close to a primary tourist route, such as a major highway. Certainly, accessibility to the site is a consideration. A site in a metropolitan area may be near public transportation routes or selected on the basis of ample parking.

Finally, the neighborhood in which a site is selected also must be carefully considered. What impact will the museum have on the neighborhood and how will it be a good neighbor?

At the heart of the museum, whether it is a newly designed building or a 200-year-old Greek Revival mansion, is its collection storage area, which also includes those areas where objects are displayed. Preservation of the museum collections is a primary concern in any proper facilities management plan. Most museums have many times the number of objects in non-public storage as are on exhibit. As a rule of thumb, a planned museum will have twice as much collections storage space as exhibit space.

Planning for the next fifteen to twenty years of growth is wise.[10] As a general guideline, thirty percent of the building should be used for collections storage, thirty percent should be used for exhibits, and the remaining forty percent should be used for everything else (classrooms, offices, auditorium, lobby, bathrooms, libraries, mechanical units, and other areas).[11] In some instances, this ratio may vary. Niki Ciccotelli Stewart, chief engagement officer at Crystal Bridges Museum of American Art in Bentonville, Arkansas, shared that even in a new building, the biggest facility challenge is enough storage and office space because the museum's priority is to create public space.[12] So in some cases, the collections and office space may be much smaller than the average.

When allocating space for collection storage, Wilcox's recommendation is to "minimize the number of functions or activities designated for a given area."[13] The higher the number of activities conducted in an area, the greater chance that these activities will come into conflict with one another. The limitation of activities is especially important for security and conservation reasons. The storage area should support three basic functions: to maintain the "optimum environmental conditions necessary to ensure the preservation of the collections"; to provide "physical accessibility to the collections for the placement and retrieval of objects or specimens"; and to allow for the arrangement of "the collections in a manner that will optimize the efficiency of the space."[14]

Proper building materials are vital for storage construction. Many woods can harm a collection when they off-gas over time.[15] Raw concrete, plaster, and brick, common for walls and ceilings, generate dust. Surfaces should always be sealed and painted as a conservation measure. Vapor barriers (sheets of heavy-duty polyethylene) should be installed on the interior of all exterior walls to exclude water vapor and outside pollutants.[16]

The actual location of a collection area within a building is extremely important. The ideal storage area will be located away from exterior walls, because a controlled environment is easier to achieve within the central part of a building. Locate storage areas near a hallway for easy access to the loading dock and exhibit preparation areas. Keep the collection areas away from areas that house potentially harmful activities (food service, exhibit construction/fabrication, facilities maintenance). Passages in and out of collection storage are to be kept to a minimum. Many museums have only one access door into a storage area; building codes may require two for safety reasons. Entrances should be large enough to accommodate the largest objects in a collection, but small enough to be locked easily. Finally, storage areas should be kept out of basements and attics as much as possible. Attics tend toward high temperature and humidity fluctuations and basements may flood.[17]

Taking measures to secure the collections storage envelope is important, and establishing a stable climate is key. According to Scott Carrlee, curator of museum services at Alaska State Museums, conservators sought temperature and RH targets of fifty percent with a temperature of 70°F.[18] More recently, many conservators have updated these targets. Cooler and dryer conditions are best for collections, striving for an RH range between thirty to sixty percent. An excellent goal, especially for institutions with limited resources for facility improvements, avoiding extreme fluctuations of temperature and RH is desirable. Rapid changes can cause composite materials to expand and contract at different rates, causing serious harm to objects.[19] It should be noted that over the last decade the museum field has experienced a sea change in how we regard environmental conditions for collections. With pressing concerns for energy efficiency, the needs of the collections are being reexamined and a body of new data is growing. Instead of fixed set points for all collections storage areas, the model is moving toward monitoring conditions and aggregating the information to decide where best in the building to store each material type.[20] This will ultimately decrease the demand on electricity required for heating, cooling, and humidification.

Other important space considerations: the entrance should be easy to find and signs should direct visitors to it. The entrance to the museum should be easy for a visitor to find. If a building has multiple doors to the outside that are locked, it is helpful to post signs directing a visitor to the point of admission. The lobby should welcome visitors with sufficient space to ensure comfort with a clearly visible admission desk and easily accessible cloakroom. An admission desk needs to be clearly visible and easily accessible. A cloakroom for hats, coats, and umbrellas may be located just off of the lobby, near the entrance. Adequate signs will direct visitors to rest

Text Box 9.1 Case Review: Greening Museums

Museums have a specific role in society that must be taken into account when considering environmental impact and operational practices. Museums in general are a special case when it comes to environmental responsibility, mainly because of these four distinct characteristics:

1. Museums belong to humanity. They are often publicly funded and they have an ethical duty to be responsible stewards of their collections and serve the public.
2. Museums are educators. It is a place where friends and family of all ages learn together and as a single visitor.
3. Museums are forums of civic engagement. They can present complex, and often politicized issues in nonthreatening ways and be a location for dialogue and change.
4. Museums create and transmit culture. However, they are vulnerable when they do engage in controversial topics (funding is challenged, board support wanes, and more). Despite this, "they are institutions of authority that shape and transmit culture, giving meaning and value to people's personal and collective lives."[*]

With this charge and purpose, museums can lead by example and demonstrate their educational value. Making simple, visible steps has the opportunity to inspire hundreds and thousands of museum goers to take action.

There are a variety of steps museums can take to reduce their carbon footprint. Some institutions strive for and are built to be carbon neutral while others make incremental improvements as funding, technology, and time allows. Andrea Grover, Century Arts Foundation curator of special projects at the Parrish Art Museum in Water Mill, New York, describes her museum's greening efforts, "We have a geothermal system for climate control; the majority of light fixtures us CFLs; the majority of our fourteen-acre grounds are designed for low maintenance, chemical free, and low water usage."[**]

The Abbe Museum in Bar Harbor, Maine, launched its Greening the Abbe initiative in 2010 to reduce its impact on the environment while lowering the financial bottom line. As an organization working with Wabanaki people art, history, and culture, the museum strives to be consistent with the environmental stewardship values of Native people in Maine, while making a greater effort to improve efficiency and reduce its carbon footprint. Recent advances in the museum field have shown that it is possible to provide the necessary temperature, humidity, and light control while also being sustainable, and they have been taking advantage of improvements in LED lighting, more efficient humidity control technologies, and high efficiency heating options. This work was funded through National Endowment for the Humanities grant funding and a fundraising campaign. As of October 2015, the museum has invested over $250,000 in these improvements and they've realized a 10 percent reduction in oil consumption and a nearly 5 percent reduction in electrical demand. This is an annual cost savings of between $3,000 and $5,000 and the numbers will continue to improve as they convert their boilers away from oil to propane in late 2015.[***]

The Abbe has also taken additional steps by reusing and recycling exhibit materials, making more sustainable and environmentally friendly choices in office supplies and cleaning supplies, and adapting staff behavior by turning out overhead lights, keeping doors closed, and increased reuse and recycling. For example, materials from the 2011–2012 exhibit *Indians and Rusticators* were substantially repurposed or recycled to create the 2013 exhibit *Wabanaki Guides*. This information was turned into a museum-type label and was mounted prominently near the entrance to the exhibit:

- 80 percent repurposed: used in the fabrication of *Wabanaki Guides*.
- 10 percent repurposed: used to create or improve storage in exhibit prep space.
- 2 percent recycled: twelve pounds of metal recycled (screws, nails, etc.); scrap wood used for kindling.
- 8 percent discarded: to the landfill.[†]

To get started in greening efforts, refer to Sarah S. Brophy and Elizabeth Wylie's excellent publication, *The Green Museum: A Primer on Environmental Practice* (2013), and begin planning steps to reduce the museum's environmental impact. If a new museum building is order, consult with architects and choose an LEED-certified architect, preferably with museum experience, to guide the project.

[*]Byers, "Green Museums . . ."
[**]Grover, interview.
[***]Catlin-Legutko, interview.
[†]Ibid.

rooms, food service, museum store, and exhibit space. If possible, both the food area and gift shop should be located in a place that is visible to visitors when they first enter. Plenty of places to comfortably sit and rest should face areas of visual interest.[21] Finally, building facilities must be made accessible to people with disabilities. Whenever possible, elevators, gentle sloping stairways, and wheelchair ramps should be available.[22] Universal design concept is discussed in chapter 8, under ADA.

Utility Services

One of the challenging tasks for a facilities manager is to maintain an environment that does not harm the objects in the museum's collection but at the same time is pleasant for people. Air ventilation, temperature, and humidity are all factors that must be controlled in the modern museum.[23] These conditions are often controlled by systems known as heating, ventilating, and air-conditioning systems (HVAC). The mechanical systems that work together to provide HVAC control over a building's environment are often complicated and sophisticated. For this reason, computers that monitor the system for problems and provide a record of past performance often control HVACs. These systems require regular maintenance and should be located in areas that are easily accessible.

One of the most important functions of an HVAC system is movement of air throughout the building at a controlled temperature and humidity level. The input vent in the collection area should be located at one end of the room, with the air return at the opposite end. This layout helps to assure that clean, conditioned air is constantly being circulated throughout collection areas. The same manner of air circulation also is important in maintaining a healthy environment for the people that both work in and visit a museum. To ensure that the air circulating within the building is clean, intake ducts should be placed as far as possible from loading docks, laboratory exhaust hoods, and waste storage areas. The use of high-efficiency, particulate-air (HEPA) filters also helps to reduce the amount of pollutants within an HVAC system by as much as 99.9 percent. HEPA filters can be more expensive than lesser-quality filters and require more energy to circulate air. However, the HEPA filter greatly reduces the presence of dust particles within a building and will cut down on custodial work.[24]

The other major utility that must be closely monitored is the lighting of a museum. While exhibit installations depend on effective lighting techniques, lighting levels must be monitored closely because of their potential damaging effects on objects. Fluorescent lights emit ultraviolet (UV) rays that are as damaging to objects as is natural light. They are often the most popular choice because they are low maintenance, low power usage, and low heat generation. The problem of damaging light can be partly corrected through the use of UV filters on the fluorescent tubes. Some manufacturers have taken steps to reduce UV as well.[25]

When choosing a light fixture, a facilities manager should consult with the curator or a conservator as to the level of light that is safe for objects. Light levels can be measured using a light meter.[26] Proper light levels and limiting the time that objects are illuminated can greatly reduce the harmful effects of lighting on objects. The facilities management staff can ensure proper lighting by following a regular maintenance schedule for the replacement of bulbs. With improving technology and availability, light-emitting diode (LED) bulbs may fill many of the needs museums have for low UV lighting.[27]

FACILITY OPERATIONS

Housekeeping

A comprehensive cleaning program should be a top priority in the development of any facilities management plan for a museum. The maintenance of a clean work place is, according to Wilcox "part of the overall environmental requirements for the preservation of the collections as well as for the general health and safety of the people using the space."[28] Many times custodial work is contracted to outside companies or done by another part of a parent organization. While this standard is fine for the typical office setting, museums have unique custodial concerns that require a conservator to work closely with those who train the custodial staff—in-house or out. The conservator should train any member of the cleaning staff in proper techniques for cleaning around collection objects and exhibit cases. This is not to suggest that the cleaning staff should participate in the regular custodial maintenance of collection objects. Artifacts and specimens in the collections should be cleaned only by a professional conservator or someone working directly under the supervision of a conservator.[29]

A formal cleaning plan should include cleaning specifications for contract staff and state in writing the standards that must be achieved in every cleaning action. Because chemicals can often be harmful to objects in a collection, care must be taken to outline how and when products are to be used. This manual will indicate what areas of a museum need to be cleaned on a regular basis and how. For example, modern, carpeted floors may be vacuumed daily, while historic carpets should be carefully vacuumed, using a nozzle with a screen, every three to four months.[30]

Emergency Preparedness

An emergency preparedness plan is designed to provide safety and recovery for the public and staff and protect and recover all of the museum's assets. Responsibilities and procedures are also detailed in the plan and it is approved at the administrative level.[31] The emergency preparedness planning committee should include representatives from management, collections, security, facilities, administration, and a conservator.[32] In a small institution, there will be fewer people to choose from for this committee; all staff, key volunteers, and a board member will make a great committee as well.

After a list of possible emergencies has been established, the museum can prepare for or prevent them. Potential hazards like faulty plumbing, mold, overloaded electrical circuits, and storage of reactive chemicals and other materials in inappropriate areas can all be easily monitored and remedied before they become a disaster. Regular inspection of the facility should be done by maintenance staff and by the local fire marshal to insure the safety of the building. Listing the location of fire extinguishers (and their most recent inspection), first aid supplies, rolls of plastic, basic hand tools, and other resources will save valuable time because the staff will be able to easily find the resources. Emergency numbers, numbers of key staff members, and plans or diagrams of the facility should also be accessible.[33]

In deciding who is in charge when disaster strikes, one method that can be used is the "Incident Command System," a method developed for the California fire service in the 1970s. The organizational chart for emergencies is set forth by areas of responsibility, not by individual, so it does not matter which key personnel are present at the time. For each essential emergency assignment, a line of succession by title, as deep as the museum can support, is established. This system allows for the adjustment of the plan depending on the magnitude of the emergency. A checklist is a useful guideline giving step-by-step instructions for tasks such as shutting off natural gas, water, or electrical supply.[34] After developing an emergency preparedness plan, all personnel, paid and volunteer, must be trained to use the plan and drills should be used for testing the plan. The drill also allows the committee and staff to critique the plan before it is actually needed.

The most common factor to be dealt with after a disaster is water, whether it is caused by fire, earthquake, hurricane, tornado, or a broken

Text Box 9.2 Case Review: Flooding*

In the early morning hours of October 30, 1992, the staff of the bird and mammal collections of the Texas Cooperative Wildlife Collections at Texas A&M University received notice of an alarm in their research collection area housed in the basement of Sterling Evans Library on the main campus in College Station. They arrived to find a major portion of the collection storage and research areas filled with 3.5 feet of water and silt. A warm water line just outside of the library had broken and washed the mud and sand into basement rooms. About half of the scientific specimens in the ninety-six museum-grade storage cases had been standing in warm water for several hours. It was determined because of the amount of material to be cleaned and dried, the work could not be accomplished by the existing staff members before mold and rot would begin in the specimens. Volunteers, contractors, and other university staff were called in to help.

Freezer trucks were on campus by noon provided by an outside vender with emergency management experience hired by the university. All of the museum cases were emptied of water and transferred into the freezer trucks. Specimens were cleaned and dried using a variety of techniques, with a recovery of more than 90 percent of the total scientific value of the collections. The collections were moved to an off-campus building in 1994 into newly renovated space.

The cost for freeze-drying and the associated specimen recovery, moving the collections, and remodeling the off-campus space cost approximately $460,000 ($740,000 in 2015). Over the subsequent years, the storage cases began to warp and rust to the point that the cases were difficult to use and exposed the collection to insect damage. Finally, in 2010 the collections received support from the National Science Foundation to replace the cases and transfer the specimens into them. This four-year project was accomplished at a cost of $500,000.**

What does this case review teach us about emergency management? It is vital to assess all risks to the collection before a problem arises. Basements place collections at risk because sooner or later, they will flood. It is important to assess and keep records of the emergency management resources in your area—private companies, other museums, conservators, or conservation centers. In this way, staff will know whom to contact quickly when help is needed. Mitigating the results of an emergency can be an expensive and lengthy process.

*Case study contributed by Hugh H. Genoways, 2015.
**Texas A&M, "Biological Collections . . ."; Voelker, Light, and Marks, "A Conservation Imperative . . ."

pipe. Objects must be dried and cleaned as soon as possible. Some museums make arrangements in advance with meat plants and factories to use their freezers in case of emergencies. This allows for objects, especially papers, to be frozen in order to provide time for treatment. No matter what kind of damage a museum has endured, a conservator needs to be brought in to evaluate damage and determine methods of treatment as soon as possible.[35] A pocket- or wallet-sized emergency contact list is a great tool for all staff members to have.

The meaning of emergency preparedness was changed forever with the events of September 11, 2001. Among the many things impacted with the destruction of the World Trade Center and a portion of the Pentagon were cultural and historic resources. The Heritage Emergency National Task Force and Heritage Preservation studied and prepared a report on the impact of 9/11 and prepared recommendations for collecting institutions to mitigate future terrorist acts or major disasters:

- First, protect human life.
- Collecting institutions should integrate emergency management into all parts of their planning, budget, and operations.
- Emergency management plans should address both protection of collections and continuity of operations.
- Emergency management training should be provided to all staff of collecting institutions, not just those charged with specific responsibilities such as security or engineering.
- Priority should be given to maintaining complete and updated collection inventories and to placing such records in off-site storage. These efforts should be incorporated into emergency plans and should be considered essential to disaster mitigation.
- Emergency management agencies and collecting institutions should maintain an ongoing dialogue aimed at strengthening affiliations between the two communities.[36]

Health and Safety

Health and safety can include aspects of the emergency preparedness plan, but it also incorporates procedures for protection of staff and visitors through the prevention of fire, the use of safety data sheets (SDS),[37] the proper storage of hazardous materials, and the disposal of biological waste materials. Specific procedures and documentation that meet federal, state, and local regulations should be established for each of these issues.

Text Box 9.3 Exercise: Assessing Potential Disaster

Before writing an emergency preparedness plan, some quick assessments are needed of the museum.

RISK EVALUATION

A risk evaluation involves listing all of the potential types of emergency situations that could affect your collection. The list below illustrates a number of these types.

EMERGENCY TYPES

ANIMALS
AVALANCHE
CHEM/BIO ATTACK
CHEMICAL ACCIDENT
CHEMICAL SPILL
CIVIL DISORDER
COMPUTER FAILURE
DAM FAILURE
DROUGHT
EARTHQUAKE
EXPLOSION
FLOOD
FOREST OR GRASS FIRE
HIGH OR LOW RH
HURRICANE
HVAC INTERRUPTION
LANDSLIDE
METEOR IMPACT
MILITARY ATTACK
MISSILE ATTACK
PHYSICAL ASSAULT
POWER FAILURE
RADIOLOGIC ACCIDENT
RADIOLOGIC SPILL

(continued)

Text Box 9.3 Exercise: Assessing Potential Disaster (continued)

SEVERE WINTER STORM
SONIC BOOM
STRUCTURAL FIRE
SUBSIDENCE
TERRORISM
THEFT
TORNADO
TRANSPORT ACCIDENT
TROPICAL STORM
TSUNAMI
TUMBLEWEED DEPOSITION
VANDALISM
VISITOR/STAFF ACCIDENT
VOLCANO
WATER LEAK
WILDFIRE

CONTRIBUTING FACTORS IN EMERGENCIES

The following list indicates a number of contributing factors that can make an emergency much more serious than it might be otherwise. For example, a serious storm may not be a major threat to a collection housed in a new, purpose built facility, but it would be serious for a collection housed in a temporary location in a trailer or an unsound shed or barn. The following factors influence the relative risk of a potential emergency.

BUILDING LOCATION
BUILDING TYPE
CLIMATIC EXTREMES
CLIMATIC VARIABILITY
COLLECTION TYPES
SITE FEATURES
SITE LOCATION
SIZE OF STAFF
STATE OF MAINTENANCE OF THE BUILDING
STATE OF CONSERVATION OF COLLECTIONS
TRAINING AND PREPARATION OF STAFF

A vulnerability evaluation is a tool by which one can rank the list of emergency types for the actual potential for each type to affect your specific
institution and collection.

Type of Emergency	Probability	Impact			Resources		Total
	Occurence	Human	Property	Income	Internal	External	

Using these two lists, bank 5 as the highest and 1 as the lowest in this
table. The lower the score, the less vulnerability.

Source: Excerpted from Reilly, *Are You Prepared?*, 10–15.

The director must help establish a strong commitment to health and safety
through financial and programmatic support. A safety officer should be
appointed who has authority to require compliance with the health and
safety procedures of the museum. Semiannual inspections, investigation
of complaints, and evaluations of accidents, illnesses, and other incidents
should be made by the safety officer. The goal of all health and safety plans
is to improve working conditions and to eliminate as many dangers as possible to staff, visitors, and the collections.[38]

Fire Prevention

While there are numerous ways a collection can be destroyed, fire moves
quickly and without discretion. Prevention is critical. Museums are, by
nature, full of fuel for a fire—books, furniture, archives, records, and so
on. Once flames appear, this situation becomes a serious event requiring a
rapid, trained response.[39]

Fire protection includes preventing, detecting, controlling, and extinguishing a fire. In order to protect staff, visitors, and collections, a fire detection and suppression systems must be installed throughout the facility. Once a fire detection system is in place, the staff needs to be trained in fire prevention, which should include the use of a fire extinguisher. Safety features such as exit signs and emergency exits should be clearly marked and accessible throughout the museum. Regular inspections by the local fire department and maintenance of fire protection equipment and systems should be included in the fire safety policy. Smoking should be banned throughout the museum and all important records such as accession and catalog records are to be kept in fireproof cabinets, with copies kept off site. On a regular basis, drills and evaluations of evacuation procedures are conducted to insure the protection of visitors and staff. Specific measures in protecting the collection should be established by keeping storage and work areas clean and by not storing objects or materials too close to furnaces or water heaters.[40]

After fire extinguishers, the most common fire suppressant used by museums is a water-based sprinkler system. The sprinkler heads are governed by heat sensors that release water when enough heat is generated in a given area.[41] These heads can be set to go off individually, and not in concert, when the designated temperature is reached. Although wet-pipe sprinkler systems are the cheapest and statistically most efficient of fire suppressant systems, water also can cause significant damage to collections and libraries. For this reason, museums that can afford the more expensive CO_2 fire suppressant systems may invest in them for their collection storage areas. These systems suffocate the fire by quickly removing available oxygen in an area without the damaging effects of water. These systems also can suffocate any staff members caught within an area; therefore, oxygen masks must be provided in all areas where a CO_2 system is installed.[42]

A facilities manager, in conjunction with the collections staff, should form a disaster preparedness plan that distinguishes which objects in storage or on exhibit should receive the highest rescue priority. This plan will be implemented only if objects can be removed safely from a building without risk to staff members. In developing such a plan, it must be kept in mind that the most important resource to any institution is its human resources. A life should never be sacrificed to save any object, no matter its cultural or monetary value.

Safety Data Sheet

A safety data sheet (SDS) is provided by the manufacturer, in a consistent, user-friendly format. The SDS describes the properties of each chemical, any health hazards, protective measures, and safety precautions for handling, storing, and transporting.[43] The museum should have an individual sheet for each hazardous material or chemical used in the museum. The sheet must be available to all who use the chemical or material or work in the area where the chemicals or materials are used. There must be a designated place for these sheets in the work area and a master file should be kept with all SDS and other important information. This information can help the museum staff learn how to store, handle, dispose of, and prevent accidents when using hazardous products. A good practice is to have each person who will use the product read the SDS and initial it when he or she finishes reading it. Safety data sheets are also required for products (PSDS) and materials (MSDS) the museum uses. Staff and volunteers using products and materials should review this important information.

Hazardous Materials

Hazardous materials can lead to emergency situations if not stored properly. The museum's emergency response team should also have a chain of command for emergencies involving hazardous materials.[44] A file regarding all federal, state, and local regulations for the handling and disposal of hazardous chemical, biological, and radioactive waste on site should be assembled and an inventory of all chemicals, infectious agents, and other potential hazards at the museum should also be included.

Careful documentation of all purchases and disposals of hazardous materials should be kept on file, along with information about contaminated objects in the collection. Specific procedures for handling hazardous materials should be established and practiced by all staff members. Some common hazardous materials in museum collections are alcohol and formaldehyde—in wet-preserved specimens; lead—in paints; arsenic and mercury—in taxidermy specimens and other specimens and artifacts; gunpowder, ammunition, bombs, hand grenades, and artillery shells; most laboratory chemicals; copy machine toner; janitorial cleaning supplies; fumigants and pesticides.[45] All of these hazardous materials should be clearly labeled and documented and procedures for handling and using hazardous materials should be stated in the health and safety policy.

Special cabinets must be used for storing these materials and should be specifically labeled as such. Occupational and Safety Health Administration has specific regulations as to the type of cabinet to be used and which materials can be stored together. The cabinets need to be kept closed at all times.

The disposal of hazardous materials and anything that has come into contact with the hazardous material is important. Any containers, gloves, instruments, or other materials used in studying or using the hazardous material need to be disposed of in a specific sealed container or bag. These items, like the hazardous materials themselves, must be picked up by an authorized company or government agency to be disposed of properly. None of these materials should be thrown away in normal receptacles or poured down the drain. State and federal regulations for both the storage and disposal of hazardous materials need to be studied and included in the policy. When handling hazardous materials, precautions should be taken, including wearing rubber or latex gloves, rubber aprons, respirators, and goggles, and using a fume hood.[46]

Biological Waste Materials

Biological waste includes dead animals, animal parts, absorbents with body fluids, animal waste, food services organic wastes, and material coming in contact with the aforementioned material (for example, rubber gloves and scalpel blades). Each museum will need to develop its own disposal system for these materials in accordance with federal, state, and local regulations. The University of Nebraska State Museum has a specific method for the disposal of biological waste materials from its collection areas, which involves sealing the waste in a plastic bag that is then placed in a plastic-lined receptacle and held in a freezer. Once a week the bags are picked up by a special crew and taken for incineration. Any sharp materials must be placed in a crush-proof container that has a one-way opening. This container, when full, is then placed in a plastic bag and placed in normal housekeeping receptacles.

Integrated Pest Management

Pest damage can be one of the worst natural disasters to befall a museum; no geographical area or climatic region of the country is exempt from this possibility. Originally developed by the agriculture industry, integrated pest management (IPM) provides a system for preventing and controlling insects, while avoiding pesticides that are harmful to humans and to museum pieces.[47] It is also a very affordable approach to pest management.

Pests are a concern for collection preservation and a health risk, both of which must be addressed by a facilities management plan. Pest management starts with good housekeeping, so the museum's overall custodial staff must be considered part of the pest management team. A program should be established that looks for likely invasion routes of pests into a museum facility and takes steps to prevent use of these routes. Museums should be viewed as a series of boxes with the objects in the collection at the center. The outer box is the museum building itself. Efforts should be made to exclude pests at this level from points of entry into the building such as visitor entrances, service entrances, air intake points, food services, windows, and cracks and breaks in the building. Housekeeping should be concentrated at these points of entry. Outside the building certain types of flowers and other plantings can attract insects and, therefore, should be avoided.

The next box is the room in which the collections are stored or exhibited. Efforts must be made to keep these spaces as airtight and dust free as possible, especially at floor level, where creeping insects travel. Food should be excluded from these areas and trash removed on a daily basis. No shipping boxes or packing materials should enter the collection areas without fumigation or freezing and should not be stored in collection areas. Housekeeping must focus on removing all dust and other materials that accumulate on floors, in cracks in the floors and walls, on light fixtures, in corners, and between and under storage cases because this material makes excellent food for insects. Some museums have started elevating cases so that the dust and other particles can easily be accessed and removed.

The final box is the storage case or exhibit case that contains the objects. These must be acid free and airtight to exclude insects, dust, and other pollutants and to help maintain constant temperature and relative humidity.

Organic materials such as bone, horn, fur, textiles, wood, paper, and leather are the most vulnerable to pest infestation. Damage from pests can range from surface soiling and spotting to complete destruction of the object because some of the more common museum pests feed directly on the objects. Pests can be placed in three categories: microorganisms—molds and fungi; insects; or vertebrates—birds and mammals. Unfortunately, all three can support one another and each can contribute to the damage caused by the others. Cloth moths, wood borers (beetles), dermestid beetles (carpet beetles), silverfish, firebrats, cockroaches, rodents, and birds, such as pigeons and starlings, are commonly found affecting museum collections.[48]

Pests are a concern for collection preservation and a health risk, both of which must be addressed by a facilities management plan. The Northeast Document Conservation Center offers six IPM strategies that any museum could adopt:

- Make sure that all routes of entry are closed or sealed, including cracks, crevices, vents, and air ducts. And be careful to not plant shrubs, bushes, and other growing plants close to the building as it brings pests in closer proximity to the facility.
- Keep temperature and humidity within control. Some pests need moisture to survive and keeping it cool and less humid will keep insects away.
- Clean up damp areas and prevent any leaks.
- Remove food waste in kitchens and don't allow food in offices. Prevent potted plants from entering the museum and don't let cut flowers linger as the standing water attracts insects.
- Monitor and clean storage spaces as they are often quiet and dark, a desirable location for insects.[49]

Monitoring for pests by direct observation and sampling is critical. Direct observation includes looking through the collection for signs of insect infestation, such as frass, insect carcasses or remains, or damage to artifacts. Sampling can be done by setting and carefully monitoring insect traps throughout the facility. All pests found in and around the traps should be identified and documented so the museum can identify any present or potential problems. By knowing the type of pests that are invading the museum, the best method of dealing with the infestation can be determined.[50]

Museums also need to establish methods of stopping infestation once it has occurred. A special quarantine room is needed for infested objects and objects entering the museum.[51] All incoming objects should be placed in quarantine for approximately seven days and inspected in order to determine if the object is infested. If it is infested, various methods can be used to rid the object of pests. As an alternative to using chemical controls, many museums use freezing strategies. First, the object is isolated from the remainder of the collection and then sealed in clear polyethylene, using heat sealing or polyester tape. By sealing the bag completely, organic objects can control the environment inside the bag. The object is then placed in the freezer for a minimum of one week at a temperature below -20°C. The bag should then be removed and a twenty-four hour period allowed for the object to come to room temperature. If the bag was sealed correctly, condensation will occur only on the outside of the bag; therefore, there is no risk of mold. The object should again be quarantined for several days to check for surviving insects.[52] Once the object is freed of pests, it is to be carefully cleaned, removing all pest remains. This not only prevents attracting other pests, but also prevents false alarms of infestation by the

sight of the old infestation. There are other methods of stopping infestations. The Canadian Conservation Institute and the American Institute for
Conservation of Historic and Artistic Works are especially helpful in advis-
ing museums on the proper handling methods for infestation.

Pest management procedures need to be developed with the safety of
both collections and people in mind. It is important that all staff members
are educated on pest management because the key to any pest management
program is constant vigilance.

Security

Museums are repositories for items held in the public trust; therefore, collections must be secured. Museums are also public gathering places and are
highly visible in the community. Providing museum security means protection of the public, staff, and others while in the museum, and protection of
collections from all threats.[53]

Museum security can be developed by following a checklist that includes
assessment of security risks (such as neighborhood crime rates and traffic
patterns); reviewing roofs, walls, windows, and doors for strength and stability; checking locks for function and appropriateness, and reviewing staff and
visitor ingress and egress routes. Museum staff should survey the building
from the perspective of a thief or vandal; this type of observation may lead
to a more acute assessment of museum security and a better identification
of weaknesses.[54] It's also advisable to consult with local law enforcement.

The human factor is also important to consider in evaluating the security
of museum structures. Wilcox asserts that museum personnel "can be physically controlled by limiting their access to keys or devices that unlock the
physical barriers that control storage spaces."[55] All visitors should be monitored and their parcels inspected. Moreover, Steven Keller and Darrell
Wilson emphasize that internal security is essential: "hiring honest people
and impeding dishonest behavior" are keys to successful museum security.[56]
Although such actions are theoretically useful, these values are often difficult to assess because even the most thorough of background checks and
strictest of policies may not prevent human error or malfeasance.

Security Guard Staff

In most museums, the security staff will not be armed and will provide many services, such as providing visitor information, in addition
to security. It is, therefore, essential to clearly define the duties of the

security force and the priority for security of the collections, staff, and visitors. It also is essential that security staff be properly trained in all security issues such as prevention of theft, fire, and accidents. Many museum staff members should have certification in CPR. In smaller museums, staff and volunteers with other duties also will perform security responsibilities; the museum is responsible for having these personnel properly trained in security issues.

It is equally important to prepare staff to respond to acts of terrorism. Since 9/11 and other terror incidents in the United States and abroad, public places are increasingly targeted for acts of violence and the situation can develop very quickly. The Department of Homeland Security has an excellent publication on how to deal with an "active shooter."[57] At the very least, be sure to post emergency phone numbers in work areas and instruct staff to have them on their personal cell phones.

Alarm Systems

Museums should have alarm systems that monitor threats from fire, theft, and flood. The monitor for fire should always be connected to the local fire department. Security staff should work with the local fire department before any problems occur so that the emergency personnel are familiar with the museum's facilities and the needs of exhibits and collections.[58] Motion and infrared detectors are commonly used to secure areas from intrusion both during the open and closed hours. If the security staff is not on the premises twenty-four hours per day, then the security alarms are to be connected to the local police department. Panic alarms connected directly to security firms and local police should be installed in areas where significant amounts of cash are handled. Personal panic alarms can also provide security to personnel who work in remote areas. Flood alarms can be connected off the premises to appropriate staff members during those hours when the security staff is not on duty.

Surveillance

Museums with large facilities commonly use video monitoring to enhance security.[59] In smaller museums, security cameras enhance the staff's ability to monitor the building when a human presence isn't available. This is an affordable solution that deters thieves and vandals.[60]

VISITOR SERVICES

Museums provide a learning experience for their visitors, and this learning can be enhanced or undermined by the quality of other services provided. Some visitor services are mandated by law; others are not mandated but are still essential to customer satisfaction, while still others are "the icing on the cake." A visitor service is anything that adds value to the visitor's experience at the museum. As Tamara Hemmerlein writes, good visitor services should be a way of life in the museum setting. With training and awareness, it will become intuitive and automatic.[61] Providing a range of services can also enhance the visitor's experience, and make sure that they feel welcome and comfortable, assuring a return visit and recommendations.[62]

Previsit Information

Most museums solicit the patronage of "potential visitors" through the use of a website, brochures, posters, social media, and other promotions. It is critical for museum staff to take care that all of this information is current and correct.

When potential visitors call the museum, it is ideal to have a person answer the phone during operating hours and a voice mail service for after hours. During business hours there are many times when there are not enough staff members available to answer the phone. If voice mail is used, the museum should be careful that two things are done: keep the message short and updated, and be certain that early in the message a telephone number is given to reach a person at a later time.

Visitors develop their expectations from advertising, especially if they are visiting from out of town. Paid advertising can take the form of radio, television, and newspaper advertisements, billboards, and bus signs, among others. Sometimes, local radio and television stations will air public service announcements (PSAs) free of charge for nonprofit organizations.

Many museums have worked to get on- and off-right-of-way highway signs. Many cities are more than willing to work with museums that are significant tourist attractions in acquiring directional signs that help visitors in the last short distance to the facility. Museums should work to make their buildings, and especially the front entrance, highly visible and welcoming.

Parking

A museum ideally has a dedicated parking lot within easy walking distance of the front door. Unfortunately, many museums are presented with challenges in providing appropriate parking for their visitors. In cities, availability of a mass transit system will help resolve this issue. In other places, a shuttle bus or other dedicated transportation from parking areas to the museum will be helpful. Museums need to make every effort to mark the routes from remote parking to their front doors and include information on the availability of parking in their advertising brochures and press releases.

Accessibility

The Americans with Disabilities Act has mandated that all public facilities be made accessible to the disabled, although some exceptions are made for certain structures, such as historic buildings, in existence prior to the act's passage.[63] Once patrons are in the museum there are a variety of issues of accessibility, including rest rooms, drinking fountains, and, of course, the exhibits and programs offered by the museum. Making the exhibits accessible will involve placement of the exhibit labels, lighting levels, and height of cases and objects at an appropriate level. Braille labels or oversized letters can be useful for the visually disabled visitor. Those museums capable of doing so should make touchable objects available to all visitors. Because presentations in museums are primarily visual in nature, visually disabled visitors will continue to present museums with the greatest challenges. Those museum professionals who work to improve the museum experience for visually impaired constituents deserve the recognition of the entire museum profession. Museums may need to provide sign language interpretation for hearing disabled visitors, especially for some educational programs and special exhibits.

Orientation

Visitors have reported in numerous audience surveys that they find large museums difficult to navigate—orientation and way-finding information can improve their experience. Upon entering the museum and again throughout the visit, seeing a staff presence offers a sense of security by knowing that someone is present who can answer questions, provide

Text Box 9.4 Exercise: Visitor Services Survey

To gain a better understanding of the importance of visitor services, conduct a survey of these services at a local museum. Obtain permission from the director of the museum before doing a survey, using the chart below. It will be best if you make your visit unannounced so that you can come close to the real visitor experience. Try not to disrupt the museum experience of other persons visiting the museum during your survey.

In the chart below, use the rating of 1 for services that are as good as any that you have seen in a museum, 3 would be average service, and 5 would be for services as poor as any that you have seen in a museum. Use N/A if the service is not available or if the statement is not applicable.

VISITOR SURVEY CHART

Previsit Information

Quality of website (hours, admission cost, etc.)	N/A	1	2	3	4	5
Quality of listing in the local telephone book	N/A	1	2	3	4	5
White pages	N/A	1	2	3	4	5
Yellow pages	N/A	1	2	3	4	5
Brochures in local hotels and restaurants	N/A	1	2	3	4	5
Quality of museum contact						
Auto-attendant or voice mail information at museum's contact number	N/A	1	2	3	4	5
Ability to reach by telephone a person at the museum	N/A	1	2	3	4	5
Quality of directions received from person at the museum to find the museum and its parking facilities	N/A	1	2	3	4	5

Travel to Museum

	N/A	1	2	3	4	5
Quality of directional signs to museum	N/A	1	2	3	4	5
Quality of directional signs to public parking	N/A	1	2	3	4	5
Adequacy of parking area	N/A	1	2	3	4	5
Marked parking for disabled visitors	N/A	1	2	3	4	5
Quality of directional signs to guide visitors from parking to museum's entrance	N/A	1	2	3	4	5
Does the entrance meet ADA standards?	N/A	1	2	3	4	5
First impression of the museum's exterior and its grounds		1	2	3	4	5

(continued)

Text Box 9.4 Exercise: Visitor Services Survey (continued)

The Greeting

Greeting by a staff member	N/A	1	2	3	4	5
Amount of admission fee is obvious	N/A	1	2	3	4	5
Museum maps (floor plan)	N/A	1	2	3	4	5
Museum's mission obvious at this point	N/A	1	2	3	4	5
Quality of the front-line staff's knowledge and understanding of the museum's mission	N/A	1	2	3	4	5
Responses of front-line staff to questions about programs available on the day of your visit	N/A	1	2	3	4	5
Responses of front-line staff to questions about future educational and exhibit programs	N/A	1	2	3	4	5
Quality of other museum information available at front entrance	N/A	1	2	3	4	5
Quality of directional signs to rest rooms	N/A	1	2	3	4	5
Quality of directional signs to exhibits	N/A	1	2	3	4	5

Rest Rooms

Your first impression of the rest room		1	2	3	4	5
Rest room meets ADA standards		1	2	3	4	5
Cleanliness of rest room		1	2	3	4	5
Availability of toilet paper		1	2	3	4	5
Privacy within rest room		1	2	3	4	5
Availability of baby changing station (both in men's and women's)	N/A	1	2	3	4	5
Availability of all-gender restroom	N/A	1	2	3	4	5

Exhibitions

Overall impression of quality of exhibits		1	2	3	4	5
Impression of conservation measures for exhibits	N/A	1	2	3	4	5
Adequacy of lighting in exhibits	N/A	1	2	3	4	5
Accessibility of exhibit labels	N/A	1	2	3	4	5
Wheelchair accessibility of exhibits	N/A	1	2	3	4	5
Accessibility of exhibits for the visually disabled	N/A	1	2	3	4	5
Special accommodations for hearing disabled	N/A	1	2	3	4	5
Inclusive interpretation within exhibits apparent	N/A	1	2	3	4	5

Educational Programs

Quality of educational presentation	N/A	1	2	3	4	5
Appearance and demeanor of the staff or volunteer presenter	N/A	1	2	3	4	5
Accessibility of presentation space	N/A	1	2	3	4	5
Accommodations made for hearing or visually disabled	N/A	1	2	3	4	5
Quality of inclusive materials in presentation	N/A	1	2	3	4	5

Museum Store

General appearance of museum store	N/A	1	2	3	4	5
Greeting and appearance of store staff	N/A	1	2	3	4	5
Accessibility	N/A	1	2	3	4	5
Wheelchair	N/A	1	2	3	4	5
Visually disabled	N/A	1	2	3	4	5
Appropriateness of items for sale (any UBIT problems)	N/A	1	2	3	4	5

Food Service

General appearance of food service area	N/A	1	2	3	4	5
Greeting and appearance of food service staff	N/A	1	2	3	4	5
Accessibility	N/A	1	2	3	4	5
Wheelchair	N/A	1	2	3	4	5
Visually disabled	N/A	1	2	3	4	5
Hearing disabled	N/A	1	2	3	4	5
General quality of menu and food	N/A	1	2	3	4	5

General

Overall impression of facilities	N/A	1	2	3	4	5
Overall impression of staff	N/A	1	2	3	4	5
Overall impression of commitment to accessibility	N/A	1	2	3	4	5
Overall impression of commitment to diversity and inclusion	N/A	1	2	3	4	5
Overall impression of museum experience	N/A	1	2	3	4	5

(continued)

Text Box 9.4 Exercise: Visitor Services Survey (continued)

Following your museum visit, write a two-page evaluation of the museum's visitor services. Share the report with the museum director who gave you permission to assess the museum. Remember that this evaluation could contain sensitive material so be certain to keep it confidential.

When we have used this exercise in the classroom, we have invited representatives of the museums being surveyed to come and hear oral reports from the students. Even large museums may be surprised at what is missing. In some cases, you will get a demonstration of how sensitive issues raised by this visitor services survey can be. Try to avoid confrontation, which is best done by being professional and constructive in the evaluation. It is important to give equal coverage to services that are being done well as areas needing improvement, rather than just dwelling on the latter.

general information, or respond in case of an emergency. Clear, well-placed signs also improves the experience.

Museums, of course, want to have staff members on duty to provide security. Staff at all levels should be trained in greeting visitors and answering questions. This establishes a security presence, but more importantly it makes visitors feel welcome to the institution. Maps showing cloak rooms, rest rooms, and exhibits should be readily available.[64]

Museum Stores

Museums often rely on a retail shop to provide a source of revenue. Museum stores also meet visitor needs by providing publications for further learning as well as mementos they can take with them. In addition, many visitors derive some satisfaction from knowing that proceeds from sales help to fund the museum. Locating the shop near the museum exit is a wise decision as most visitors like to make purchase after the visit. Ideally the shop should be accessible whether someone is visiting the museum or not.[65] In recent years, museums wanting to maximize the receipts from their stores have turned over store management to volunteers from their support groups or have hired concessionaires that operate regional or national chains of museum stores.

Rest Rooms

Although not always a major topic of conversation, rest rooms are probably the one place that visitors will remember if they have a bad experience. Ideally rest rooms are located in "obvious" places such as adjacent to lobbies, are well marked, and are accessible to persons with disabilities. The rest rooms should be kept clean and well supplied with towels and toilet paper at all times, which should be a responsibility of *all* staff members. Changing stations for babies in both women and men's rest rooms and nursing stations are helpful to families. An all-gender restroom welcomes all kinds of visitors. Nursing stations are helpful to families as well. This does not seem like a critical issue for members of the museum profession, but rest room quality is high on the visitors' list of significant parts of their visit.

Food Service

Food service can be one of the most challenging services to offer to visitors. Because most museum staff members lack food service experience, providing it means evaluating and hiring staff with this expertise. Food service brings the museum under the purview of a variety of public health inspections and laws. Many museums have found it extremely difficult to generate profits from food services, because to do so requires specialized marketing and management knowledge. For these reasons, many museums have contracted or franchised this service. Food service also means more materials entering the museum and garbage to be removed. If not properly monitored, these functions can add to the museum's pest management problems; thus, extra effort in pest control and addition of rules, such as no food or drink outside the food service area, are required. Despite all of these considerations, many museums have found it profitable and good public relations to provide food service for their visitors. Plus, visitors will stay at the museum longer if they can eat on site.

Many small museums will not be able to consider providing food service because of a low number of visitors or a lack of space to provide the service. Or, the building has limitations and food service wasn't possible initially. For example, Dina Bailey, director of educational strategies at the National Center for Civil and Human Rights in Atlanta, Georgia, commented that they have a space challenge in their new facility: "While we wanted to open The Center as fiscally responsible agents (wanted to keep costs low), this led to The Center not having a cafe or basic back-of-house kitchen. Practically, we have found challenges in being able to offer catering options at a price that is reasonable for our target audiences."[66] They continue to work on solutions, using museum spaces in creative ways.

These institutions may consider cooperative agreements with one or more local food service businesses. The museum can provide display space with directions to these businesses and they, in turn, can prominently display posters and brochures from the museum. This can build good relations with the local business community, while providing more exposure for the museum.

Educational Services

The primary function of a museum is to educate the public in the field of the museum's mission. The number of educational programs a museum can offer depends upon such factors as museum size, resources, and demand for programs. Paying attention to how visitors will travel through the facility is critical for comfort and safety. It is advisable, especially with historic properties, to establish traffic routes to aid in preservation strategies. If a historic house is open to the public, the museum personnel should be concerned with the effects of foot traffic on surfaces such as steps and flooring.

CONCLUSION

People visit museums for varied reasons—to have a learning experience, to satisfy a curiosity, or simply for enjoyment. Without a stable building to house the exhibits, collections, and educational spaces, and office areas, it is a challenge to preserve collections for future generations and be part of the community's collective learning. It is incumbent on museums through their

Text Box 9.5 Guiding Questions

1. If you could design a museum, what would it look like and how would it operate?
2. Aside from water and fire, what is the biggest threat to a museum facility where you live? What steps need to be taken to be prepared and responsive?
3. Consider a time when you experienced great customer service. How might this standard be applied in a museum setting? If a public museum can't waive admission or offer refunds, what other options might be used to "make things right?"

services to provide for visitors an educational, safe, and enjoyable experience. A long-range facility management plan and endowment to support capital costs and preventive maintenance will do the trick.

NOTES

1. Lord, *The Manual of . . .*, 42.
2. Ibid.
3. Wilcox, "Facility Management," 31.
4. Gallimore, interview.
5. Matthews, interview.
6. While advisory, following these standards are often required if there is public funding assisting with the preservation, rehabilitation, restoration, and/or reconstruction of a historic property.
7. Wahahrockah-Tasi, interview.
8. Brown, *Facility Maintenance*; Wilcox, "Facility Management."
9. Ambrose and Paine, *Museum Basics*.
10. Herskovitz et al., *Building Museums*.
11. Hillberry, "Architectural Design . . ."
12. Stewart, interview.
13. Wilcox, "Facility Management," 30.
14. Ibid.
15. Hatchfield, "Wood . . ."
16. Ibid.; Sebor, "Heating . . ."
17. Hatchfield, "Wood . . ."; Hillberry, "Architectural Design . . ."; Sebor, "Heating . . ."; Wilcox, "Facility Management."
18. Carrlee, "Collections Care . . .," 5.
19. Ambrose and Paine, *Museum Basics*, 241; Ogden, "Temperature, Relative Humidity . . ."
20. Sutton, *Environmental Sustainability*, 68–69.
21. Ambrose and Paine, *Museum Basics*.
22. Hillberry, "Architectural Design . . ."; Wilcox, "Facility Management."
23. Ambrose and Paine, *Museum Basics*.
24. Wilcox, "Facility Management."
25. Conn, "Protection . . ."
26. Carrlee, "Collections Care . . ."
27. Ishii et al., "Color Degradation . . ."; Miller and Druzik, "Demonstration of . . ."
28. Wilcox, "Facility Management," 35.
29. Minnesota Historical Society, *Historic Housekeeping*; National Park Service, "Museum Housekeeping"; The National Trust, *The National Trust Manual*.

30. Minnesota Historical Society, *Historic Housekeeping*.
31. Reilly, *Are You Prepared?*
32. Tremain, "Developing an Emergency . . ."
33. Faulk, "Are You Ready . . .?"
34. Ibid.
35. Canadian Conservation Institute, "Emergency Preparedness . . ."
36. Hargraves, *Cataclysm and Challenge*.
37. In 2012, material safety data sheets became safety data sheets with the revision of the Hazard Communication Standard.
38. Liston, *Museum Security*.
39. Artim, "An Introduction to Fire . . ."
40. Wilson, "Fire Protection."
41. Ibid.
42. Wilcox, "Facility Management."
43. U.S. Department of Labor, "Hazard Communication . . ."
44. Makos and Dietrich, "Health and Environmental Safety."
45. Cockerline and Markell, "Handling and Exhibition . . ."; "Hazardous Materials."
46. Makos and Dietrich, "Health and Environmental Safety."
47. Carrlee, "Collections Care . . ."
48. National Park Service, "Identifying Museum Insect . . ."; Strang and Kigawa, "Agent of Deterioration."
49. Patkus, "Integrated Pest Management."
50. Strang and Kigawa, "Agent of Deterioration."
51. Linnie, "Integrated Pest . . ."
52. Strang, "Controlling Insect Pests . . ."
53. Lord and Lord, *The Manual of . . .*
54. Ambrose and Paine, *Museum Basics*; Liston, *Museum Security*.
55. Wilcox, "Facility Management," 40.
56. Keller and Wilson, "Security Systems," 55.
57. U.S. Department of Homeland Security, *Active Shooter*.
58. Wilson, "Fire Protection."
59. Liston, *Museum Security*.
60. Nicholson, "Can You Hand Me . . .?"
61. Hemmerlein, "Good Visitor Services . . ."
62. Ambrose and Paine, *Museum Basics*.
63. Phelan, *Museum Law*.
64. Kotler et al., *Museum Marketing*.
65. Ambrose and Paine, *Museum Basics*.
66. Bailey, interview.

10

MARKETING AND PUBLIC RELATIONS

Marketing and publics relations are married concepts. Both are concerned with communications and reaching the public. Some large museums have separate marketing and public relations departments, the majority of museums have these functions combined, if not represented in a single staff member. Because of this relationship, they are presented together in this chapter.

MARKETING

Historically a tension existed between curators and other content providers in the museum environment and the marketing world. This stems from concerns that content would be "dumbed down" to attract an audience.[1] As the pressure to secure funding sources and the need to be seen as relevant, museum administrators are welcoming marketing strategies that will connect the museum to the visitor.

Marketing is a process that helps people exchange something of value for something they need or want. Both museums and audiences are the beneficiaries of the marketing process "by which individuals and groups obtain what they need and want through creating, offering, and exchanging products of values with others."[2]

Marketing is akin to audience engagement in that both are looking to broaden the visitor base while deepening loyalty and relationships with the existing visitor core. Marketing is an administrative function, but in a highly functional team environment, a marketer will participate on project teams.[3]

In smaller organizations, the director or another staff member will wear the marketing hat, but will also have a host of other duties and responsibilities unrelated to marketing. It makes sense to acquire marketing skills, if needed, but also to think about how marketing tactics relate to fundraising and other development activities. There is a great deal of overlap; standardizing messages and communication channels can save time and results in a great connection with museum audiences.

"Marketing is a vital part of a museum's relationship with its audiences."[4] Remembering that all marketing activities, no matter what type of organization conducts them, are about linking to consumers (audience) and the product (museum). This may help museum staff view marketing in an appropriately positive light.

Motivations for Marketing

Why do organizations market themselves? Most people would say they do so in order to increase awareness of the organization and the goods it produces. "Marketing is necessary to help nonprofits promote their values, accomplish their missions, and develop increased resources to address a range of compelling concerns."[5] But marketing isn't just about what the museum wants. Good marketing puts the museum constituents at the center of the process.

Many museums consider marketing in order to improve public perceptions and eliminate stereotypes or misconceptions. Maybe the marketing effort is to reveal something new about the museum. The New Museum (of Contemporary Art) in Manhattan reopened in 2007 in a new location in a new home. Despite the excitement of the move, there were concerns about visibility and brand—even though they were thirty years old, did people know them? And how can they call themselves "new" when they're thirty years old? To tackle this, museum administrators formed a talented marketing committee of board members and engaged two different firms to first, develop the brand, and second, roll out a marketing blitz. The campaign was a great success, seeing a 600 percent increase in visitation and a 400 percent increase in memberships that first year. Coming out of this concentrated brand activity, administrators focused on sustaining the energy and marketing their core functions of exhibits and programming.[6]

Financial pressures, a changing social and technological environment, or the need for publicity for publicly funded programs may also inspire organizations to "do some marketing." Museums realize there is a limit to the amount of revenue that can be generated from increasing admission fees, so they promote themselves within the community and surrounding area in order to increase interest in their "products," thereby increasing their "volume" (or attendance).

Marketing in reaction to particular needs or circumstances can be useful in addressing those specific cases, but the well-managed museum is one that has a comprehensive marketing plan. Ongoing, strategically designed marketing efforts will produce more effective and lasting results than case-by-case marketing. It is likely that a strategic marketing plan is needed.

History of Marketing Activities

An understanding of the institution's marketing history is vital to development of plans for the future. Former marketing efforts can reveal the commitment the museum has to certain programs or activities, in what ways the museum has shown its appreciation to its audience, and how it has implemented changes in order to better serve this audience. Former activities give clues to what the organization sees as acceptable marketing practices. Some governmental museums, for example, such as state museums, may be prohibited from certain types or forms of marketing.

It's a safe assumption that many marketing histories will show limited and inconsistent efforts, with emphasis on special events and a hodgepodge of unrelated advertisements and mailings and other communications. Museums are often short on financial resources and sustained marketing activity can become costly. Some museums' marketing histories will reveal significant activity and decline, dependent on economic conditions or changes in leadership. In order to have a successful marketing strategy, audience research is needed. It will provide a benchmark of activity so you will know how well the campaign performed.

The Marketing Plan

Museums need to create marketing plans that spell out marketing projects, activities, and costs. A plan that is driven by market research will be considerably more effective than one that has not considered its audience and its competition.

Market research, the process of qualitatively and quantitatively collecting information on audience preferences, can help to identify the needs, desires, and capabilities of the audiences. It may also show you what activities could become greater revenue centers. The research may be collected primarily through interviews, surveys, questionnaires, and focus groups. Comparing these results with a broader study of the museum field and market trends will create a feasible marketing plan.[7] Visitor needs may have gone undetected before this type of study. For example, the research may reveal that 42 percent of a community's population is elderly and visually impaired and does not go to the museum because low light levels in the galleries make it difficult for them to see the items exhibited.

Market research can also identify desires of the visitors as well. Perhaps families do not visit a museum because there is no concession stand or cafe, and perhaps it is not feasible to have one. Collaboration with a nearby restaurant to offer discounts on meals to museum visitors could be beneficial to the museum, the restaurant, and the visitors.

The capabilities of the audience should not be taken for granted. Not all people can reach the museum and enjoy it easily. Lack of bus routes or reliable and convenient parking may be an impediment. With an increase in international travel in your area and new immigrant populations, language barriers may block the museum's message.

Competition can be for time and for money. In your community, where are people spending time? Sports events, movie theaters, national parks are just a few of the activities that draw out people and their spendable income. In the home setting, museums compete with television, online and streaming programming, and other media outlets. When it comes to public funding, museums are competing with their peers, schools, fire and police, and social service agencies.[8] A well-crafted marketing plan will recognize all of these challenges and pick a clear and straight path toward its goals.

A written plan in this critical area is as important as written plans and policies for any other aspect of the museum. Committing the plan to paper makes it easier to identify inconsistencies, unknowns, gaps, and feasibility. More important, the plan helps management and staff focus on new market conditions or key marketing issues. The written plans establish performance goals and set out a timetable for achieving them.[9]

Plans may include sections addressing the following issues:

1. The current marketing situation, which includes relevant background on the market, product offerings, competition, and environmental scan results.[10]

2. Opportunities and issue analysis, which considers threats, opportunities, strengths, weaknesses, and issues the museum will face in the plan's time frame.
3. Goals will include marketing goals (regaining lapsed members, building underserved audiences, and creating a new image) and financial goals (maximizing revenues and full-cost recovery based on admissions). Many marketing campaigns fail because they lack clear goals.

SMART goal setting methodology offers a proven and effective way to set goals. SMART goals are:

- Specific—pinpoint exactly what you want to achieve;
- Measurable—craft a goal that includes numerical measurement;
- Attainable—create a goal that is within reach of your museum;
- Relevant—align goals with your mission, vision, and strategic goals; and
- Time-based—avoid open-endedness and set a timeframe for each goal.[11]

Abstract goals, such as having people know the name of the museum and what the museum does, can be measurable. Perhaps a museum wants to increase its recognition within the community by 15 percent. This increased recognition can be measured through interviews and opinion polls. Most marketing campaigns, no matter how effective in the beginning, lose impact after six months. Museums must keep evaluating and updating their marketing campaign in order to keep the public's attention and to stay consistent with their goals.

4. Marketing strategy includes general positioning and initiatives the museum will pursue related to its product portfolio (offerings, products, and services currently available) and its plans for product and market expansion (deeper penetration into existing market segments, broader geographic base, new market segments, and modifications to attract the existing market). "There may be as many as fifty specific marketing strategies to be implemented," in the plan. These strategies typically align with the five Ps and Cs discussed later in this chapter. Sample strategies include new admission pricing structures that appeal to local families, partnering with lodging businesses and restaurants to attract summer tourists, creating a new young adult evening program that focuses on social needs, and more.[12]

5. Market segmentation is the process of dividing the total market (audience) into relatively homogeneous groups. All markets are

heterogeneous—no single product or service will appeal to all consumers. A blanketed marketing approach that tries to reach people this way will be considerably less effecting (mass marketing). Target marketing requires the understanding of market segments and a marketing plan will have these outlined in the document. There are essentially four clusters that people may be grouped into:

- Geographic—region, size of city/town, population, climate;
- Demographics—age, gender, family size, ethnicity, education, social class, religion;
- Psychographic—activities, interests, values; and
- Behavioralistic—benefits sought, usage rage, brand loyalty, readiness to buy.

   By nature, museums already segment their audiences. Creating programs for adult groups, classroom students, and more are a regular occurrence. Many museums likely have a flyer or brochure designed for social studies teachers so they will bring their students on a field trip. That's segmentation. Identifying more segments is an important part of the marketing plan.[13]

6. Action programs spell out specific programs and steps to be taken by specific staff in specific time periods. What will be done? When will it be done? Who will do it? How much will it cost? What kind of benefit will it generate?

7. Budget figures will identify the amount of money needed to carry out the plan.

8. Controls to ensure that progress is made in achieving the goals set out may include collection and evaluation of data on a regular basis. Each quarter, for example, the museum may want to analyze the information it's been gathering about the number and nature of people affected by a particular marketing strategy. The plan should identify who will take corrective action if elements of the plan prove unsuccessful, and may include contingency plans.[14]

   Smaller museums may have less complexity in the plan, because it's scaled to the amount of staff time available for marketing activities. Or, based on the exhibit or program, the small museum team may choose to stagger activity for a variety of reasons, that is cost to produce, target audience, number of seats available and other factors. Lauren Silberman, deputy director at Historic London Town and Gardens in Edgewater,

Maryland, believes that strategic marketing efforts are beginning to factor more into program planning there. "Now that we're planning our programs up to twelve months out, it's easier to coordinate our marketing. We went through our projected programs and prioritized which ones would receive which levels of treatment: basic, more, and full-out pushes. For example, everything will be added to our website, but only select programs will get press releases, ads, and boosted Facebook posts, and such."[15]

Hassan Najjar, executive director of the Museum Center at 5ive Points in Cleveland, Tennessee, knows his museum's marketing sweet spot well. "Like most things in life you have to diversify and for us that means meeting our audience where they are. We use a mix of newspaper (for the older crowd), paid social media marketing (for the millennial and young professionals set), and billboards (for everyone in between). Our sure thing is our mailing list of members (we know where they live) and a postcard in the mail still reigns supreme."[16]

Incorporating strategies and experience into a marketing plan for the museum will give staff and board a blueprint for improving the museum's exchange with its audiences of something of value. A thorough and well-informed plan will keep the focus on communicating with past and present markets and advocating within the museum so that services continue to evolve to meet the needs of market segments so they will be repeat visitors. And of course, the plan will help increase attendance numbers and revenues, a wish for all museums.[17]

Tactical Marketing

Preparing a marketing plan is a strategic activity whereas tactical marketing outlines the tools and skills needed to accomplish the marketing plan. Traditionally, there are five main elements in preparing a tactical marketing strategy. These are often called "The Five Ps of Marketing"—Product, Place, Price, Promotion, and People—and they are a reflection of the producer's output. Current customer-oriented approaches suggest that the "Five Ps" reflect the seller's, not the buyer's (or customer's or visitor's) point of view. A customer-centered concept features the "Five Cs," which focuses on consumer value.[18]

Marketers may see themselves as selling a product, while customers see themselves buying value. Customers also want the product or service to be conveniently available. More than simply knowing the price, customers want to know their total costs in obtaining and using a product, and they don't want promotion, they want two-way communication. Museum

Text Box 10.1 Case Study: The Case of the Corlis City Rumor Mill

Cindy James recently accepted a job as a public relations officer for the Corlis City Museum of American Art. The museum boasts a hundred-acre campus and over 500,000 objects in its collection. It has been a strong asset to the Corlis City community for 130 years. Currently, the CCMAA has twenty employees and seventy-five volunteers.

Ms. James will replace the newly retired Ed Fogey, who worked for the museum for thirty years and was well known and respected in the community. The museum director and board want Ms. James to foster public relations with Corlis City's twenty- and thirty-something audience, a public that was largely ignored by Mr. Fogey, who favored constituents closer to his age. The city is well known for being home to some of the country's top Internet moguls and software gurus, most of whom are below the age of forty. This generation has a potential for high dollar donations to the museum. They also have young children. In one year, the museum will begin a campaign to raise funds for a new educational component to the museum. The new wing will house a variety of classes and art-related hands-on activities geared toward K-12th graders. For adults, the museum will hold a monthly art history lecture and wine reception to highlight artists in the collection. The museum plans to solicit this younger public for most of the funds.

Two weeks before Ms. James was scheduled to begin work, the museum director, Garrison Grundy, complained to a friend at the local field club that the new software the museum had just purchased was "full of bugs." A local computer guru made the software. One of the guru's competitors overheard the disgruntled Grundy gripe and shared the news with his girlfriend, Ms. Verbatim, who just happened to be a business reporter at the Corlis *Daily News*. The next day a story reporting "serious defects" in the locally produced software cited the museum director's comments. The software maker's mother, Mrs. Chatterly, just happened to be on the museum's board of trustees, and she was not particularly pleased to see her son's new product bashed. Insulted by the director's comments, she decided it was time to share the news that she had walked in on the director and the museum curator, Mrs. Scarletta, in a compromising position in the board room. Soon the community grapevine was buzzing with news of the extramarital affair. In a follow-up newspaper story on the software bugs, the software guru suggested that the director's comments were a smokescreen to take attention away from his inappropriate personal behavior and mismanagement of the museum.

When Ms. James arrived at the museum two weeks later to begin her job as public relations officer, she found the museum staff and board in a state of chaos and finger-pointing. Morale was at an all-time low. Mrs. Scarletta resigned from her job and the director took a sudden three-week vacation without any further comments to the press. Animosity among the board members was growing; some were threatening to resign, while others were torn between their friendships with Mr. Grundy and Mrs. Chatterly, who was loudly demanding they choose sides and fire the director. Board members on both sides of the conflict had made statements to the media regarding the director's behavior.

Older members of the community who were Mrs. Chatterly's friends are considering withdrawing support from the museum. Younger members of the public are writing angry editorials to the local and regional newspapers, with comments ranging from disgust at the unprofessional behavior to distress at the lack of postmodern art in the galleries.

Ms. James has her hands full. What was supposed to be an easy walk to a promising job has turned out to be a public relations nightmare, and it is too late for her to withdraw from her contract. The museum's public image has been tainted and the intra-museum relations are in turmoil.

Using the public relations strategic planning process outline, what steps Ms. James should take to rectify this situation?

1. How will Ms. James control intra-museum conflicts?
2. What should she say to the director or the board member who spread the news about the affair?
3. How should she handle media relations?
4. What should she do to regain support from the museum's older constituency?
5. How will she clear up the image of the museum and establish a relationship with the younger members of the community?

marketing planners may do well to first think through the customer's "five Cs" and then build their own "five Ps" on that platform.

Product/Customer Value

"Understanding the museum product and developing it in line with your users' needs is the task of museum management and a key component in the marketing mix." A product is the object or an "amalgam of services, people, buildings, atmospheres" that a consumer wants.[19] Product is generally defined as a tangible good; however, products can be intangible, as is often the case with museums. And even if a product is tangible, it has intangible elements as well, called quality perception. Tangible goods are easily evaluated for quality by assessing size, shape, texture, fit, and color. Intangible goods like "the museum visit" are often judged on the basis of tangible cues such as physical facilities, equipment, and personnel. If a museum has dirty bathrooms, broken interactives, and curt staff, the visitors' perception of quality will be low, despite excellent programs, labels, and exhibits.[20]

Place/Convenience

Place is defined generally as proximity of customers to product. Museums in many communities are often in the business district or the inner city, away from many residential centers. Marketing has prompted some museums to eliminate place as a restriction on reaching their audience. "Branch" museums in local shopping malls are one example. Museums often reach national audiences though traveling exhibits.

Virtual exhibits and other online offerings are bringing the museum home, so "the place" becomes as close as your smart phone. Special "Met Net" memberships developed by the Metropolitan Museum of Art provide a number of computer-based benefits (members only access to the museum, discounts, plus free downloads of screen savers and online audio features).[21]

Small museums can migrate exhibit text and images online, giving the exhibit life beyond its closing date, reaching people wherever they may reside. At the same time, this online content can enhance mission delivery systems. When the Abbe Museum produced its *Headline News* exhibit in 2010, it was evident that than an online version would be useful for a variety of audiences. Topics explored were "hot button" issues affecting Wabanaki people in Maine that were often reported in the news, including hunting and fishing rights, gaming, stereotypes, and border issues (the Wabanaki homeland extends across the U.S. border into Canada). Online articles about these topics are especially upsetting because of Internet trolls and other negative comments made by online readers. There was an absence of online content that presented clear information. Early in the exhibit's life, a commitment was made by the institution to migrate the content online once the exhibit closed, providing a new source of public information.[22]

In 2015, an article by the Associated Press demonstrated the utility of this website when the Abbe's online content was referenced in an article about the deteriorating relationship between the State of Maine and the Wabanaki.[23]

Price/Customer Cost

Price is the cost to the individual for services or goods. As with many leisure activities, prices do play a factor in museum attendance. When determining price, businesses, including museums, must evaluate the cost in dollars relative to the objectives of the organization as well as to the museum's ability to earn funds. That means if the mission of a children's museum is to serve all children within a community, yet the admission fee is too high for many residents, the mission of the museum is not being fulfilled because of price. Problems often occur when admissions or fees are imposed on previously free services or activities and the audience does not understand why. Psychological costs can also discourage or restrict use of museums or museum programs. Visitors who perceive a museum as being in a "bad" neighborhood may hesitate to attend. Museum hours may be perceived as inconvenient. People may not go to a history museum because "boring old stuff" is a waste of time. The price people pay in time and effort may be a far greater determinant of participation than monetary cost.[24]

Promotion/Communication

Promotion is what non marketers consider "marketing." Promotion or promotional strategy is defined as communicating effectively with and persuading potential customers. Several misconceptions about promotion exist, especially in nonprofit enterprises. Many museums see promotion as commercialistic and unnecessary. Many administrators and staff see promotional campaigns, which spend money on radio and newspaper ads, as unjustifiable to donors, particularly where financial resources are slim.[25]

As museums become more subject to competitive pressures in attracting visitors and raising support, promotion and communication become increasingly important aspects of the marketing plan. The Internet is frequently used as an inexpensive way to communicate with members and potential visitors and to let them talk back. A mix of media and messages can reach varied audiences with an image of the museum that is consistent and effective.[26]

eCommunications

The marketing world has dramatically shifted since the first edition of this book was published. Websites and e-mail marketing was increasingly commonplace in 2003, but social media was only starting to get a toehold in the marketing world. Simply put, the advent of social media has signaled a loss of control over message. One of best publications on this topic, *Marketing in the Groundswell*, offers strategies for making your way in the groundswell, "a social trend in which people use technologies to get the things they need from each other instead of from the company."[27] By getting in the thick of it, embracing the technological advances, and listening to customer insights, organizations will be more likely to succeed in the groundswell.

Fast forward to 2014 and research tells us that Facebook is king, based on a number of users and the users' deep level of engagement, followed by LinkedIn, Pinterest, Instagram, and Twitter.[28] Nancy Schwartz on her excellent marketing blog *Getting Attention!* offers strategies for keeping up with the pace. For example, apply the same market segmentation understanding to social media sites. Older adults use Facebook, while younger adults are using Instagram. Many strategies require payment (but at a scalable level), but the bottom line is, "It's going to be far more effective to use one platform well, rather than use multiple platforms in a half-baked way."[29] And by the time this book is published again, these channels may have changed and new technologies may be leading. Keeping up with the trends and the technologies is as important to marketing efforts as creating a clear brand message is.

Not merely a "sales job," strategic museum marketing can help museums enlarge and diversify their audiences, identify key audience segments and appropriate mechanisms for serving them effectively, retain members, reach program goals, achieve higher quality and broader support, and thrive in a quickly changing world.[30] Many museums lack the resources to create a marketing staff or hire an expert, but they can train their managers and staff members in marketing principles and methods and take on the point of view of visitors and members. A world of tools are available— including printed resources like the model marketing practices of specific museums outlined by Kotler et al. in *Museum Marketing and Strategy* and a continual string of excellent online resources—to help museums assess public perception and create more effective marketing strategies to better serve their audiences.

PUBLIC RELATIONS

From ancient to modern times, museums have served many varied purposes and audiences. John Cotton Dana, a museum icon, championed the idea that museums should be accessible and relevant to people's lives. He believed public programming and community activities were an important part of the work of any museum. In the early twentieth century, museums were among the few sources of information and education outside schools. With limited opportunities for leisure activities, museums were places where the public could spend its time.

Television, mass and electronic media have changed the public's recreational activities. For many people museums hold less of an attraction. Museums need to increase the public's awareness of their presence and reassert their place in community life. Museums, like most businesses, also need to bring in customers to pay their bills. These customers can be paying attendees or they can be donors. For museums to thrive in an ever-changing and increasingly fragmented society, they need to market and promote themselves. One way museums can regain visibility in the community is through public relations.

Public Relations Defined

Public relations is "a strategic communication process that builds mutually beneficial relationships between organizations and their publics."[31] While nonprofits depend on publicity, public relations is built upon marketing. Marketing offers the content for public relations efforts, based on customer research and data.[32]

"PR is charged with trying to develop a successful image for the organization."[33] As such, public relations differs from marketing or advertising. Marketing develops and sells the product (the museum) using advertising, which persuades the public to buy the product. Public relations seek to increase awareness of the product and influence the public's perceptions of and attitudes toward the product.[34] With paid advertising increasing in price and variety, marketing departments and strategies are placing more emphasis on public relations techniques.[35]

Public relations programs can either be active or reactive. An active public relations program allows the museum to control its image and influence how others see it. The reactive public relations program is always putting out fires and coping with complaints and problems and only serves a limited range of the interests of the museum. In a reactive scenario, the environment rather than the museum sets the public relations agenda, crisis defines the museum's image, and the public relations program has little to do with the museum's strategic goals.[36]

Creating a plan that outlines PR activity is a great way to manage media outreach. The plan may outline strategies for contacting the media, developing press kits, a media list, and strategies for gaining visibility in the public. Larger museums may hire a PR firm that will train executives and develop target strategies. The plan can also chart how to react to the unexpected. This may include identifying a point person during times of crisis, setting a timeline for making a public statement, and strategies for harnessing social media.[37]

Kotler et al. offer three categories for organizing PR tasks:

- Image PR—With the intent to shape impressions of a museum, it seeks two goals: revitalize a museum's image and build an image of consumer confidence and trust.
- Routine PR—This involves regular, daily efforts to promote the museum and all of its activities. It has four goals: introduce new offerings, communicate benefits (of membership), raise the visibility of collections, and cultivate new markets.
- Crisis PR—Its primary goal is to protect the museum and the people working there from negative publicity that may damage the museum's image, reputation, and support. And these challenges can arise almost daily which demands prioritized attention.[38] Left unattended, crises can leave a museum in far worse shape than imagined.

The active public relations program provides control over public perception of the museum. The museum can establish its image and develop a full strategy of publicity and promotional programs to enhance that image. By providing a positive image to the media and public, the active public relations program is also better able to manage a crisis.

Incorporating Public Relations

The public relations strategic planning process is key to the development and maintenance of a museum's image and so it must be tied into the museum's overall strategic plan. The museum and its goals drive the public relations program, not vice versa. The museum must clearly identify its goals and use them as a foundation for the public relations program.

Table 10.1 Ps and Cs for a Museum's Strategic Marketing Plan

The Museum's (Marketer's) 5 Ps	The Customer's 5 Cs
Product	Customer value
Place (Distribution)	Convenience
Price	Customer cost
Promotion	Communication
People (Staff)	Courtesy (Hospitality)

Create benefits and value greater than competitor offerings. Build brand loyalty. | Seek great access and low cost.

Source: Adapted from Kotler et al., *Museum Marketing*, 30.

Museum staff need to participate in the public relations process so that all will feel ownership in the publicity activities and understand their roles as representatives of the museum.

The board of trustees and the museum administrator are responsible for the proper stewardship of the museum, including its public relations. Budget, board member or volunteer expertise, levels of activity and programs, and staffing availability will determine the public relations program at each museum. The stage in a museum's life cycle and its reputation in the community will influence public relations budgeting, as well as community size and the level of existing audience interest. Special events and activities may influence public relations budgeting and decisions as well. The particulars of the program are not as critical as the fact that an active program exists.

The position of the public relations professional within the museum is based on the board or executive director's commitment to the importance of public relations. Ideally, the public relations professional can be an executive level position and may be involved in setting direction and policy for the museum. In cases where museums do not have the budget to hire a full time staff member, a volunteer may provide similar service, working closely with the director.

Text Box 10.2 Exercise: Importance of Advocacy

As a museum develops it marketing and public relations department and broadens its network of stakeholders and supporters, it is equally critical to keep museum advocacy at the forefront of conversation and activity. A united museum field tackling issues that affect funding, personnel, donors, education, and more, can have an impact on legislation at the federal, state, and local level. Often, museum boards and staff shy away from advocacy because they are confusing it with lobbying, which is also legal (the museum just needs to be mindful of how much money is spent on lobbying as there is a threshold for nonprofits). Boards and staffs that govern and work for public institutions may have policies that explicitly say they cannot lobby or advocate, but the majority of the museum field—its board members, staff members, volunteers, members, and stakeholders—is free to make a case for their museums.

Led by the American Alliance of Museums, the museum community has stepped up advocacy efforts since the early 2000s. In the face of shrinking funding and museums on the "chopping block" it became critically important for museums it show up on Capitol Hill in Washington, DC, as well as in town council chambers. Every February, AAM coordinates and hosts Museums Advocacy Day, which involves training for appointments with Congressional members and staffs. During these Hill visits, museum staff members have the opportunity to make a case for their museum and advocate for a prepared advocacy agenda that was collectively developed by the museum community.

Visit the AAM website (aam-us.org) and read the numerous resources they have available for museum advocates. Then select a museum in your community and ask the director if he has an economic impact statement or an education impact statement. If he doesn't have one, ask permission to work with him or another staff member to develop them. If you work in a museum, develop statements for your own organization. To supplement these more data-driven statements, develop an "elevator speech" in which you can briefly describe your museum, its purpose, the difference it makes, and why it deserves support. This brief communication should be a message that you use consistently with policy makers, funders, community members, and anybody with whom you find yourself chatting in an elevator.

"One of the biggest mistakes a museum can make is to underestimate the amount of time and planning that goes into a successful public relations."[39] The public relations director will have many ways to serve the museum beyond writing media releases and arranging openings. This professional can be a valuable part of the planning process. Through research and study of the museum's audience and the community in general, the public relations professional can offer insight as to whether goals and objectives of any plan will meet public needs and acceptance. This employee should be involved in all aspects of the museums operation; through involvement, she can identify opportunities for publicity, which will get the museum's message out and increase awareness and visibility.

PR Tools

The variety of public relations tools and the possibilities for their use are as diverse as the museums that can benefit from them. Museums have many different levels of commitment to and expectations from public relations activities. The tools the museum chooses to use will depend on the museum's expectations and staffing abilities. At the Comanche National Museum and Cultural Center, museum director Phyllis Wahahrockah-Tasi cites a long list of tools she uses to help spread news about the museum. "The best way to reach our audiences has been the use of social media (Facebook), U.S. postal service (newsletters and postcards), commercials, a documentary aired on Thanksgiving evening in 2012, newspaper advertisements (local and nationwide Indian), and community involvement (word of mouth). Marketing has been the key to reach our audiences. After years of marketing, the largest audience to attend a museum opening was in September 2012 with approximately 1,200 visitors for a two-hour event."[40]

Events

A planned activity, the marketing team may target key audiences for participation. PR teams help focus a spotlight on the upcoming event through press conferences and grand openings. A heightened level of energy will draw news coverage, bring community members together to engage with the museum, and deliver mission-focused content.[41]

Community Relations

Formally engaging community support is critical as federal and state funding decreases. Many museums will make a concentrated effort to reach out to community groups to seek input and their guidance.

Community relations campaigns will have several goals, including identifying opinion leaders and joining forces, making museum spaces available for community use, holding special open houses and tours for community members, convening community advisory boards to help guide policy and mediate conflicts, and so much more.[42] Community relations can also take an individualized approach.

It is particularly important for the museum director to be seen as being actively involved in the community. The director should consider being a member of the chamber of commerce and one of the local service clubs such as Rotary, Kiwanis, Elks, Lions, Optimists, or Women's Club. If the director has children, it will important that he is seen to be involved with school academic and athletic programs. The director may want to be a member of a local faith-based group. Keeping in mind that no matter where he is and what he is doing, he will be seen as the representative of the museum. This is especially true in smaller communities where the number of people available to participate in community activities is limited. If the museum director wants the support and involvement of the community, he must be seen to support and be involved in the community. And quite frankly, if the community members are to volunteer and support a museum, it is wise to sit at other "tables" and be seen as a community builder. Encouraging all museum staff to engage in community activities is equally wise. At the Abbe Museum in Bar Harbor, Maine, president and CEO Cinnamon Catlin-Legutko sits on numerous boards in her community. Each service opportunity is considered a cultivation step—more people will know about museum events and activities and they will more likely to make charitable gifts to the museum. For example, Catlin-Legutko serves on the board of a housing solutions nonprofit. A long-time low-level donor to her museum became a major donor after serving alongside Catlin-Legutko and seeing her commitment to the community and how the museum fits into the community narrative.

Reaching outside the museum community to find opportunities to work with service groups and others on special projects is a great idea as well. If a local business sponsors an after-school program or summer camp for disadvantaged children, the museum could volunteer its staff to provide a program, or the museum could open its doors to the group for special activities.

The museum benefits from being associated with the other group's public service. A museum might consider sponsoring a kids' sports team and encourage interested staff to volunteer as coaches. These types of activities also help to make the museum relevant in the community's daily life.

Media Relations

A critical activity of any PR department is developing personal relationships with journalists and understanding what they need. Typically, journalists are looking for a great story with wide interest, a little drama, first-person interviews, exclusivity, and clarity. Writing copy is also an excellent pursuit or securing a regular column in the newspaper or feature stories on blogs.

Media Releases

Press releases are the most direct way of communicating with the media. Using a style unique to the format, the release's intent is to inform, not sell. Earned media such as a news article about a museum is as powerful as three or four advertisements. Editorial copy is a very strong third party endorsement of your museum. Making contact with news reporters and news editors is an investment that will generate great dividends. When a museum representative makes contact with the media she should remember that she is in a partnership that benefits not only the museum, but the news outlet as well. Asking questions about media interests in the museum and reporter's goals will guide the content and approach of news releases. Whenever possible include a photograph with the news release. If the newspaper does not have room for the full article it will often print the photograph. Many readers will look at a photograph even if they skip over an article.

Public Service Announcements

Broadcast media continues to offer air time for nonprofit and other public service agencies in the form of public service announcements (PSAs). There is certainly competition for these spots so staying on top of submission deadlines and delivering an engaging PSA will increase your odds of broadcast.

Interviews and Speeches

Public speaking, whether as a subject matter expert in an interview or delivering a talk to Rotary and other service organizations, is a meaningful way for museum leaders and staff to connect with audiences. Larger museums may even have a speakers' bureau and encouraging and enabling staff to get out into the community will reward the museum manifold with new and returning audiences.

Print Materials

Continuing to produce well written and designed brochures and other print materials is a worthwhile PR task. They can provide multiple purposes in addition to public relations—advertising, community relations, and direct marketing.[43]

Buzz

Perhaps the most cost effective public relations tool is word of mouth. It does not cost a thing and its value is beyond measure. Museums should encourage their staff and volunteers to provide the best possible experience to the visiting public. Visitors who have a positive museum experience are more likely to tell their friends and neighbors about their visit and encourage them to attend. They will certainly be quick to post on Facebook or TripAdvisor. Visitors who have a positive experience are more likely to return to the museum.

Museums and Community

Museums continue to grow as important participants in the lives of their communities, and these relationships carry positive public relations benefits. At the turn of the last century, the AAM-sponsored Museums and Community Initiative created opportunities for dialogue between museum and community leaders as well as outside experts on community. The report, *Mastering Civic Engagement,* offers lessons learned and strategies for enhancing this critical interaction and gives the field a benchmark for understanding engagement levels.

National efforts aside, the process of enhancing a museum's image within the community can be as simple as inviting community leaders to exhibit openings and including them in the program. The presence of the mayor, governor, or prominent business leader at a museum event will generate publicity and enhance the stature of the museum. Likewise, the inclusion of local high school band or theater groups in a museum program will bring a new audience—parents and school leaders—to the museum and generate goodwill within the community. Providing staff the opportunity to participate in a speaker's bureau will open new opportunities for the museum to get its message out, and demonstrate support for staff.

Increasing the goodwill of those who already volunteer and donate to the museum will increase their feelings of satisfaction with the museum and may encourage them to volunteer and donate more. Writing thank you notes and special correspondence are good public relations practices that will promote feelings of connection. Holding special recognition ceremonies for board members and volunteers will increase their sense of importance to the organization and will identify them to the community. When the public sees an individual it respects connected to a museum, the museum gains from the positive association.

CONCLUSION

Effective marketing and public relations are vital elements in the museum's success. As with all the aspects of museum operation, the mission and values of the organization and its strategic plan are critical guides for marketing and public relations efforts.

Recent shifts in both marketing strategy and museums' understanding of their roles in our communities have placed the visitor at the center. Visitor desires, needs, and capacities must be considered and married to the museum's programs and services in order for museums to compete successfully against the myriad of leisure time choices now available.

Technology is expanding the ways in which museums can communicate with audiences; social media has expanded the way museums communicate with their audiences. Envisioning marketing and public relations programs

Text Box 10.3 Guiding Questions

1. Consider the media market where you live. How do museums reach audiences in your community? What channels are effective in reaching which segments of museum audiences?
2. Do you consider yourself a museum advocate? If so, how do you advocate for museums in your community? What message do you communicate?
3. How do you find out what's going on in your local museums? What are some of your favorite social media sites? How can you use social media to create greater awareness of the museums you support?

as vehicles through which the museum can have meaningful exchanges with its audiences create deeper levels of engagement that museum professionals will find fulfilling. Appropriately conceived, managed, and communicated, museum marketing and public relations programs can help museums and audiences share something of real value.

NOTES

1. Rentschler and Hede, *Museum Marketing*.
2. Kotler et al., *Museum Marketing*, 21.
3. Lord and Lord, *The Manual of . . .*
4. Ambrose and Paine, *Museum Basics*.
5. Stern, *Marketing Workbook*, 4.
6. Schwartz, "How A Museum . . ."
7. Spencer Pyle, "How to Do . . ."; Kotler et al., *Museum Marketing*.
8. Koontz and Mon, *Marketing and Social Media*.
9. Kotler et al., *Museum Marketing*, 31–32.
10. Edie, "Start Spreading . . ."; Kotler et al., *Museum Marketing*.
11. Kotler et al., *Museum Marketing*; Pilley, "Explaining the Concept . . ."
12. Kotler et al., *Museum Marketing*; Lord and Lord, *The Manual of . . .*
13. Koontz and Mon, *Marketing and Social Media*; "Market Segmentation"; Wind and Bell, "Market Segmentation."
14. Kotler et al., *Museum Marketing*.
15. Silberman, interview.
16. Najjar, interview.
17. Lord and Lord, *The Manual of . . .*
18. Kotler et al., *Museum Marketing*.
19. Ambrose and Paine, *Museum Basics*, 43.
20. Koontz and Mon, *Marketing and Social Media*.
21. Kotler et al., *Museum Marketing*, 339.
22. Abbe Museum, *Headline News*.
23. Associated Press, "Maine Native . . ."
24. Kotler et al., *Museum Marketing*; Stern, *Marketing Workbook*.
25. Ibid.
26. Kotler et al., *Museum Marketing*.
27. Li and Bernoff, *Groundswell*.
28. Duggan et al., "Social Media Update . . ."
29. Schwartz, "Make Social Media . . ."
30. Kotler et al., *Museum Marketing*.
31. PRSA Staff, "Public Relations . . ."
32. Koontz and Mon, *Marketing and Social Media*.

33. Ibid., 261.
34. Andreasen and Kotler, *Strategic Marketing*.
35. Kotler et al., *Museum Marketing*.
36. Andreasen and Kotler, *Strategic Marketing*.
37. Todd, "Business of Nonprofits."
38. Kotler et al., *Museum Marketing*.
39. Ibid., 396.
40. Wahahrockah-Tasi, interview.
41. Kotler et al., *Museum Marketing*.
42. Ibid.
43. Ibid.

COLLECTIONS STEWARDSHIP

Collections are one of the defining characteristics of museums and it is what sets them apart from other nonprofits.[1] While there are a variety of museum types that don't maintain permanent collections that do not have a collections program, namely science museums, a museum usually exists because of its collections. And artifacts communicate a museum's character. Tobi Voigt, chief curatorial officer at the Detroit Historical Society, offers not one but two recent artifact stories that demonstrate the excitement collections stewardship can generate and shows the spectrum of the human condition. "We have 35,000 online records mostly consisting of photographs and postcards. Recently, a woman contacted us to let us know she was using the free online images to help her elderly father who suffers from Alzheimer's and dementia. While his recent short term memory was nearly gone, his long term memory was quite good and he was able to identify places in the old photos and keep his memory fresh."

Another recent story at the Historical Society finds "a volunteer who discovered a small lead bullet while inventorying the coin purse collection. After checking the records the bullet was extracted from the leg of a civil war soldier. Upon further research it was found that we also had a canteen from the same soldier. When we pulled it from the shelf we were shocked to discover a bullet hole going all the way through the canteen, which would have hung from his waist and likely slowed the bullet as it penetrated his leg and likely saved his life."[2]

The collections not only give the museum its character, but they also define its purpose of the museum. It is, therefore, important for a museum to care and manage its collections as effectively as possible (preserving the collection for long-term study and display), staying true to its mission and in keeping with its public trust. To do this, museums develop and operate a collections care program that is guided by a well-articulated collection management policy. The policy is understood by the governing board, staff, and volunteers. This policy defines goals for the development and use of the collection and prepares the museum to face controversial or unexpected eventualities, such as deaccessioning or a disaster endangering the collection.

COLLECTIONS MANAGEMENT POLICY

From an administrative perspective, communication and transparency are important in drafting a collection management policy. Both the staff and board need to agree on all areas of the policy. Although it cannot solve all potential problems, the policy will "define areas of responsibility and set forth guidelines for those charged with making certain decisions . . . completed policy should be approved by the board . . . and once in effect, the policy should serve as formal delegation of responsibilities."[3] Nathan Richie, executive director with Golden History Museums in Golden, Colorado, finds that the policy has improved organizational capacity. "After years of challenging collections management and care issues, a newly approved collections policy is clarifying the museum's value to the community as well as internally, and has inspired sponsorship funds and attracted grant awards for conservation."[4]

Each museum must draw from its own history and the needs of its community and its collections to begin drafting its collection policy. The size and scope of a museum's collections will determine the length and complexity of this policy.

At minimum, there are nine issues that must be covered by comprehensive collection management policies:

- Collection Mission and Scope
- Acquisition and Accessioning
- Cataloging, Inventories, and Records
- Loans
- Collection Access
- Insurance

- Deaccession and Disposal
- Care of the Collection
- Personal Collecting

The policy may also include statements regarding authority, definitions, code of professional conduct, objects in custody, appraisals, intellectual

Text Box 11.1 Exercise: Controversial Collections*

The museum has in its collections firearms used in a notorious series of murders almost sixty years ago. This crime spree, committed by a young "rebel without a cause," not only gripped a region in terror, but later inspired books, movies, and rock'n'roll albums.

As the museum is reopening after a two-year renovation, it plans to exhibit some of the items that have been "under wraps" during the renovation or had not been previously on display. Objects associated with people "notable and notorious" were touted in preliminary public information.

Victims' family members objected to the announcement that the guns would be displayed for the first time. Some of them are museum members and financial supporters. They have asked the museum to remove the objects from the exhibit.

Some staff members say that crime stories attract a younger audience, and the museum shouldn't be censored by outside individuals. They suggest that a Ku Klux Klan hood, peace medals, weapons used in the so-called Indian Wars, a "Whites Only" restroom sign, and a photograph of the burning body of a lynched African American man to be included in the exhibit are also disturbing to the "victims' descendants." Other staff counter that as upsetting as those objects may be, no descendants can point to a given weapon and say, "This killed my aunt and uncle and left my cousin an orphan."

Points to ponder:

1. If you were the exhibit curator, what course of action would you recommend to your director?
2. Should a museum collect material with the intent of keeping it on hold for public access in the future?
3. Are there objects too heinous to collect?

*Exercise contributed by Lynne M. Ireland, 2016.

property, legal and ethical considerations, personal collecting, and a review/ revision schedule for the policy.[5] A collections management policy is so fundamental to museum operations that the American Alliance of Museums has deemed it a core document and its existence in a museum indicates professional practice and excellence.[6]

COLLECTION MISSION AND SCOPE

The collection's purpose and mission determine the nature of the collections. Often, the mission statement will specify themes, subjects, and types of objects, which is known as the scope of collections. The scope may be defined in the collection policy or in the collections plan.[7] Any statutes or legal documents important to the establishment of the museum and maintenance of the collection can be explained in this section. The roles of the board, committees,

Text Box 11.2 Nebraska State Historical Society Acquisition Criteria

1. The material must have clear title.
2. If material is for sale, funding must be available.
3. The Society must have the resources to properly care for the proposed acquisition.
4. The historical significance of the materials (for permanent collections) must be relevant to the Society's mission.
5. Provenance of the materials (for the permanent collection) should be documented.
6. Material for public records must meet the retention schedule.
7. All legal and ethical implications of the acquisition must have been considered and any issues resolved.
8. Acquisition should occur without donor restrictions. Restrictions or conditions may be considered when in the best interest of the Society's fulfillment of its mission. The Board of Trustees must approve permanent restrictions. Use and disposition will be at the discretion of the Society unless otherwise specified.
9. Copyright will be transferred to the Society when possible.
10. Loans, permanent or otherwise, shall not be added to the collections.

Source: Arenz et al., *Nebraska State Historical Society Collections Policy*.

and the staff involved in collection procedures should be explained along with the different types of collections and how they are handled.

Additionally, the museum may have categories within the scope of the collections. Typically the permanent collection is the core collection and it received the highest standard of care. There may be other collections categories, such as education, exhibits, and archive and libraries. Each category may receive an alternate standard of care based on its planned usage.[8]

Questions to consider in defining the scope:

- What is the focus of the collection—discipline; geography; time period; artists, persons, groups of people, or cultures; types or sizes of objects; research; or interpretation?
- What portions of staff time and museum resources are devoted to collecting and collection care?
- What is the state and size of the collection and what resources will it take to support them (record keeping, storage, management, conservation, security, and exhibits)?

ACQUISITION AND ACCESSIONING

Acquisition refers to something obtained by a museum through gifts, purchases, exchanges, transfers, and field collecting. Transfer of ownership occurs through accessioning, which includes transfer of title and the process of recording it as part of the collection.[9] Both acquisition and accessioning are interrelated and should be thoughtful processes that are addressed as such in a museum's collections policy. Before accepting objects, the museum needs to study the question of "title," or ownership, and to avoid stolen objects, improperly excavated (removed illegally) materials from archaeological or paleontological sites, or specimens taken in violation of state, national, or international laws.

A museum's collecting scope should define the types of objects to acquire—their sources, time periods, and geographic origins. Museums such as natural history museums may need to add and define other issues like geological ages, geographic area, taxonomic groups, and cultural representation.

Criteria

The scope of a museum's collection can be developed by considering its mission statement, which will in turn guide a museum to selectively acquire objects.

Another consideration is whether or not the museum has the resources to care for the object for the long term. The cost to the museum must be weighed against the potential benefit of acquiring the object. Costs that a museum should consider include space, staff time for processing and managing the object, overhead (utilities, storage equipment, housekeeping, and other administrative costs), conservation, and insurance.[10] Even if part of this expense is donated, all costs still need to be considered. Criteria used by the Nebraska State Historical Society for acquisitions are described in text box 11.2.

Legal Considerations

An acquisition policy should state that the museum will not violate any local, state, federal, or international laws, treatises, conventions, or regulations.[11] Some of these laws include copyright protection, Visual Artists Rights Act, Endangered Species Act, Marine Mammal Protection Act, Migratory Bird Treaty Act, Bald and Golden Eagle Protection Act, Abandoned Shipwreck Act, Lacey Act, Archaeological Resources Protection Act of 1979, Native American Graves Protection and Repatriation Act, Convention on International Trade in Endangered Species, 1970 and 1972 UNESCO Conventions, 1995 UNIDROIT Convention, 1954 Hague Convention, and the 2011 Convention for the Protection of the Underwater Cultural Heritage, to name a few. The policy also should require the donor to have acquired and possessed the objects legally and ethically. The museum must determine that no archaeological sites, historic sites, natural habitats, or populations were damaged when the object was acquired.[12]

Museums should, under normal circumstances, accept only unencumbered objects, unless their acquisition is in the long-term interest of the museum. The policy needs to have procedures that evaluate encumbrances. Ownership is an important issue to be addressed because if the donor does not have clear title to the object, the museum cannot be positive the object has not been stolen or illegally acquired. If clear title or the right to transfer ownership cannot be established, the museum should not accept the object. Donor restrictions, artist rights, and copyrights must be investigated. The museum must understand what rights it is acquiring and must obtain proper documentation of its rights.[13]

Once a donor's ownership has been verified a museum obtains clear and complete title by having the donor sign a deed of gift. This document should state that the donor is not putting any restrictions on the object and that he or she legally owns the object, and he or she is transferring ownership to the museum.[14]

Text Box 11.3 Case Review: Acquisition Innovation at the Logan Museum of Anthropology

When asked if her museum had an active or passive collections program, the following case study was provided by Nicolette Meister, curator of collections and adjunct assistant professor at the Logan Museum of Anthropology at Beloit College in Beloit, Wisconsin. While her answer was passive, she has been working with alumni and students to create a more active collecting environment that not only meets the museum's collection (and shop buying) needs, but also enriches the student experience in museum studies:

> The generosity of an alumnus and serendipity collided, making possible a recent museum collecting trip to a small village in Chihuahua, Mexico, called Mata Ortiz. Nicolette Meister, curator of collections, and Samantha (Sammi) Kinard, an anthropology major and museum studies minor, traveled to Mata Ortiz in February 2015 with a small group led by alumni Henry Moy, director of the Museum of the Red River in Idabel, Oklahoma.
>
> Mata Ortiz is located about 100 miles south of the U.S.-Mexico border and is the birthplace of a contemporary pottery tradition that has gained international acclaim. The modern tradition has roots in prehistoric archaeological ceramics from the site of Paquimé, which is located nearby and was excavated in the late 1950s and early 1960s by Charles C. Di Peso' (42). Enter Juan Quezada. As a boy, Juan became fascinated by the prehistoric sherds he found throughout the desert and spent the next sixteen years experimenting with local clays and pigments and firing methods. Encouraged and supported by an anthropologist who "discovered" his work, by the mid-1970s Juan was supporting his family by selling his pottery. Juan is considered the self-taught originator of the Mata Ortiz tradition, but he shared his skills with members of his extended family and neighbors. Today, over 400 individuals in a village of just over 1,100 people make pottery for a living. Mata Ortiz pottery is entirely handmade, without a wheel, and is hand painted in fine-line geometric and curvilinear patterns. Families work together to build, fire, and paint pots, and the artistic movement now encompasses many styles and forms distinctive to particular families.
>
> The opportunity to collect pottery from Mata Ortiz resulted from the establishment of a Museum Studies Program acquisition fund by Richard Dexter' (70) in 2013. The fund was established to provide students opportunities to acquire objects for the Logan Museum of Anthropology and Wright Museum of Art. Working with a list of suggestions from museum

(continued)

Text Box 11.3 Case Review: Acquisition Innovation at the Logan Museum of Anthropology (continued)

staff, students in Bill Green's *Introduction to Museum Studies* course submitted proposals for acquisitions to the Logan and Wright museums. Samatha Kinard's proposal to acquire a piece of pottery from Mata Ortiz was the successful Logan proposal. She completed the next step the following semester in Nicolette Meister's *Introduction to Collections Management* class and purchased a polychrome Mata Ortiz jar by Socorro Sandoval from a gallery in Santa Fe, New Mexico. Nicolette had asked Henry for suggestions regarding reputable vendors of Mata Ortiz pottery knowing that the Museum of the Red River was building a substantial collection.

A year later, Henry was planning another trip to Mata Ortiz and invited Nicolette and Sammi to join the group. Sammi quickly made plans to get her first passport. On February 5 they flew to Tucson, Arizona, where they met Henry's group. They made the long drive to Mata Ortiz the following day. Thus began three days of adrenaline-fueled collecting. Purchases were made directly from artists in their homes, in the plaza of the guest house where the group stayed, and at galleries in Mata Ortiz and Nuevo Casas Grandes. Nicolette and Sammi meticulously recorded their purchases and took numerous photographs of the artists and their pottery. They also visited the archaeological site of Paquimé and spent an incredible afternoon with Juan Quezada on his property. In total, the Beloit duo purchased over 120 pots, many of which will be available for sale in the museum's gift store and selected pieces are being added to the Logan's permanent collection.

The trip to Mata Ortiz vividly encapsulates opportunities extended to Beloit students that "put the liberal arts into practice." This trip was made possible through the generous support of the Anthropology Department and Richard Dexter.

While considering the example, can you think of other innovative ways museums can find the resources to move from passive collecting to active?

Source: Meister, "Logan Museum Staff . . ." Additional information about the Logan's collection program are available at https://magazine.beloit.edu/?story_id=246610&issue_id=246440.

Professional Conduct

Museums also must follow IRS regulations regarding appraisals for tax deductions, which require that third-party appraisals be conducted on acquisitions. It is the responsibility of the donor to have this appraisal performed. Museum employees should not conduct appraisals or refer donors to specific appraisers.[15]

While museums need to try to acquire objects that fulfill the breadth and depth of their mission and scope of the collection, they also must be selective. Once an object is accessioned, the museum has a responsibility to properly document, store, conserve, and maintain it. A museum that accepts all objects whether it intends to keep them or not risks losing the trust of the public. Such activities tend to fuel the contention of the U.S. Financial Accounting Standards Board (FASB) that collection materials are assets and should be accounted for as such on financial forms.

As clearly examined and determined in a white paper published by the American Association for State and Local History (AASLH), there are strong reasons to not classify collections as assets, known as capitalization. "Because historical museums and organizations act in public trust, the public interest must be paramount in any decision involving the acquisition, care, interpretation, and use of collections. Therefore, institutional leaders must deliberate carefully before making any decision that might put the collections at risk. Since no accounting standards require that collections be capitalized, any institution that chooses the course of capitalization is making a conscious decision to treat its collections as financial assets, and that decision automatically places those collections at potential risk. AASLH believes that such risk, and therefore the act of capitalizing collections, is inconsistent with the institution's fiduciary responsibility to the collections it maintains and the citizens it serves."[16]

Delegation of Authority

It is good to keep museum governance apprised of accessions. While they have likely delegated the decision-making process to the professional staff, the board of trustees has responsibility for the museum. In smaller museums, with the absence of multiple staff members working in and around collections, it is advisable to have a collections committee approve accessions and a list of these may be found in the committee's minutes, providing a record for the trustees.[17] This varies from one museum to another, but in most cases the director, curator, or collection committee has the authority.

Accessioning

An acquisition policy needs to include procedures for accessioning. Accessioning is the process of entering objects and their proper documentation into the possession of the museum. Not all acquisitions must be accessioned. Accessioning procedures state what records must be completed, where they are stored, and who maintains the records. Each museum has its own record-keeping system, but in most cases a donor file and an accession record is completed. The donor file includes information about the donor and any correspondence with him or her, whereas an accession file may include a brief description, photograph, collecting permits, and any information available about the object or series of objects obtained from a single source. The file may contain condition reports, provenance, as well as the donor or collector information.

Objects added to the collections need to be assigned an accession number. The accession record is the museum's legal record of taking possession of and title to an object. All documents pertaining to an object or group of objects need to have the accession number placed on them.[18] Museums sometimes develop their own numbering systems, so it is important to provide specific directions on how an object should be numbered. The methods used to label objects should be placed in the collection management policy because it is important to have all documents signed and dated.

CATALOGING, INVENTORIES, AND RECORDS

Cataloging

Cataloging is creation of a full collection record. The record will contain full descriptive details about the object, assembly, or lot, cross-referenced to other records and files, such as accession records and donor files. A catalog number is placed on the object associating the record and the object, typically using a trinomial system. Catalog data may be recorded on cards, sheets, ledgers, or computerized databases designed specifically for the museum or purchased off the shelf. Despite the level of computerization involved, backup hard copies of records need maintaining, namely accession records, donor files and receipts, location files, and catalog files.[19]

Because the catalog file is used when working with and inventorying the collection, it is sometimes called the working record. Most museums give each object a separate catalog number along with the accession number for record-keeping purposes. From the information given on the catalog record, anyone should be able to locate the object, know what it looks like, and find related records or files.[20] Often objects are photographed to document the condition, color, and appearance of the object. And photographs help with locating objects without handling them. Digital images of objects are easily integrated into the collections database for enhanced visual management.[21] This level of digitization and technology better enables collection catalogs to be hosted online, an increasingly common decision that museums are choosing. Online catalogs invite broader audiences to view the collections, making them more accessible and online collections databases promote research opportunities.

Inventories

Museums need to establish uniform methods to inventory the objects in the collection and their records. Complete, partial, and random inventories should be undertaken routinely. A complete inventory locates all objects in the collection and reviews the records to make sure all documents are present and in good order. Because most museums have large collections, there is usually not enough time, staff, or money to do a comprehensive inventory every year, so it is normally done every five years. A partial inventory may be initiated when big changes are made to gallery and storage spaces, such as renovation or reinstallations. A random inventory, on the other hand, can be done more often because it entails finding randomly-selected objects in the collection and checking their records. Inventories allow the museum to track the status of objects and their records in the collections. If any objects are missing, they can be located or reported as missing to the proper authorities. The curator, collection manager, or registrar is responsible for completing inventories.[22]

Records

Three other types of records need to be mentioned—photographs, condition reports, and conservation reports. Other records, such as collecting permits and field or collection notes used mainly in natural history or archaeological collections, need to be stored by individual museums according to the requirements as stated in their collection policy. The same is true for historical documentation of items, such as archival materials or other paper documents.[23]

Photographs

Photographs can document the condition of an object and give a visual description of it. Most museums take photographs of each object when it is accessioned and these photographs are placed with the accession file and uploaded to the database. For condition and conservation treatment reports, photographs show more detail, including all sides of the object and close-ups of specific parts of the object.[24]

Condition Reports

Condition reports document an object's state of preservation whether it is a new acquisition, an incoming loan, or a returning loan. These allow the museum to note any damage and they protect the museum from liability for damage already present on loaned or borrowed objects. Most condition reports include a name and description of the object, the examiner, the dates it was examined, a description of any physical, chemical, or biological damage, and any potential damage to the object. Photographic documentation should be included in condition reports.[25]

Conservation Treatment Reports

Any time an object is altered by a conservator, the work is documented using a conservation treatment report. This report should include the condition of the object, recommended storage, how the object should be and was repaired, information on how cleaning was undertaken, photographs of treatment stages, and any other important information observed or done to the object. This information is to be kept in the accession or catalog file.[26]

LOANS

Even with the largest collections, a museum may have inadequate objects for an exhibit or for research study and will decide to borrow other objects from a private individual or another institution. Objects also can be received on loan for conservation or research purposes. Whether the loan is incoming or outgoing, a clear loan policy and loan agreement stating the rules and procedures for loans will eliminate any potential problems.[27]

Incoming Loans

A museum should never accept a loan without a written contract that clearly states the rights and responsibilities of each party. Each incoming loan should have an agreement that covers specific issues, such as insurance, loan criteria, care and use of objects, duration of the loan, the dates and method for return of the loan, and proper packing methods.

In most cases, it is advantageous to have the loan insured because it can resolve the lender's claims and protects the museum from possible liability. The borrowing museum may carry the insurance, the lending museum may, or the insurance may be waived. A certificate of insurance should be part of the loan agreement. The lender should provide a value for the object based on fair market value, or in the case of field-collected specimens, the value can be based on the replacement cost.

Borrowing objects is a great responsibility and therefore only certain persons should be allowed to request a loan. Usually the director or board of trustees must give final approval for a loan request but in some types of museums, such as natural science museums, the curator has the authority to make requests. Once the loan has been requested, authority needs to be given to a registrar or curator to receive, open, inspect the loan, and keep all records. It is also important to specify who within the lender museum should be notified in case of damage. One person needs to be responsible for notifying the insurance company of damage and negotiating a settlement.

The reasons for museums to request loans vary. A museum needs to state clearly the purposes for which it will request a loan, whether for exhibition, research, education, or photography. Loans need to comply with international, federal, state, and local regulations concerning wildlife specimens and the Native American Grave Protection and Repatriations Act (NAGPRA), among others.

How the object can be used and any special care it requires should be detailed in the loan agreement. This can cover anything from photography to the wording of the credit line on the exhibit labels. Any intent to photograph or reproduce the object for cataloging, educational, or publicity purposes needs to be stated, along with any fumigation or examination the borrower may wish or be required to do. The requesting museum also should state that it will not repair or restore any object without the written permission of the lender and the employment of a conservator with appropriate expertise. The transportation method and expense responsibility for an object need to be specified in the agreement. The lender should provide the borrower with instructions on repacking the object for return.

The length of the loan needs to be clearly stated, with the provision that the borrower may terminate the loan at any time. The usual length of a loan is six months; long-term loans vary by agreement, but usually do not exceed three years. Provisions for returning a loan need to be stated clearly, with specific dates for pickup or shipping. If the loaned object is to be returned to the lender by the borrower, written notification of the object's return should be given to the lender. When the object is successfully returned, a return receipt should be signed by the lender and returned.[28]

Outgoing Loans

Outgoing loans are similar to incoming loans, with the roles reversed. Generally, a museum will not lend to an individual, because its collection is for public, not private, use. Most museums will request that the object be maintained in the same environmental conditions as in its home institution, which individuals normally cannot provide. Most museums will make loans only to similar educational or nonprofit organizations. The authority to approve loans is typically given to the governing board, but in larger museums, the professional staff or director may be able to approve loans of objects of certain value or classes. It is best to set a definite loan period and state who is responsible for returning the object. It is important for the lending museum to assign a person, usually a registrar in larger museums, to monitor outgoing loans and their termination dates so there is no question about the return of the object. [29]

Temporary Custody

In some cases, such as conservation, identification, or study, objects are left in the temporary care of the museum. When this occurs, a temporary custody receipt should be signed. It is important to outline a way of monitoring these materials and a way for them to be processed expeditiously. Documentation needs to be permanently retained on objects under temporary custody just as for other loaned or accessioned objects.[30]

Many states have passed laws regarding unclaimed loans and undocumented collections. In general, these laws state that after the objects have been abandoned by the owner in the care of the museum for a specific period of time (usually five to seven years), with proper notification (usually a public notice published in certain newspapers), the museum may claim the object as a donation. In Indiana, for example, under the Museum Property Law (IC32-34-35), there is a simpler process. If the item was found on museum property after July 1, 1989, the museum only needs to hold the property for ninety days before it becomes official museum property.[31] In other states like Nebraska the process is much more cumbersome and lengthy (seven years).

Long-Term or Permanent Loans

There are no standard definitions for the terms "long-term" and "permanent" loans, but as used here, long-term loans are those made for an extended, but specific, period of time (likely five to ten years), whereas objects on permanent loan are for the use of the holding museum as long as it desires. In permanent loans, the original museum or owner has not relinquished title, so the object must be returned when the holding museum no longer has a use for the object. Many museums do not accept long term or permanent loans as the museum is committed to offering care for something it doesn't own, at the expense of the rest of the collections care needs. Although some museums will not accept long-term or permanent loans, others will take them under specific circumstances. If this is the case, the collections committee and the governing board must approve the loan agreement.[32]

Long-term loans may involve the lending of one or a few objects that are needed by an institution for a long-term temporary exhibit. Museums, when they have duplicates of objects, may choose to make such loans to assist another museum's programs. Some examples of permanent loans are those made by the U.S. Fish and Wildlife Service of preserved specimens of endangered species, such as sea otters and whooping cranes, to museums. These are given to the museums for their collections and use, but the Service retains title and the agency's catalog numbers must be maintained on the specimens along with the museum's catalog number. The Service audits the specimens on an irregular schedule.

ACCESS TO THE COLLECTION

Access to the collection includes how to provide access to collections, availability of objects and records for study or research, and access for disabled staff and visitors. Legal and ethical considerations are involved in all aspects of making the museum accessible and should be included when planning policies about access to the collections of the museum. Collections are not physically open to members of the general public;

therefore, the hours that the collections are available for use may vary from the museum's public visiting hours. The collections are available for research and for preparation of exhibits during the hours the collection staff is available.[33] As previously mentioned, online collections catalogs promotes greater access, but the museum will likely make decisions about what content to offer online.

Availability of Objects and Records

Museums can limit who has access to the collections and their records by establishing criteria for using the collection for research, exhibition, student projects, photography, and loans. It is legitimate to restrict access for the reasons of security and preservation of the collection. Careful documentation and monitoring of users must be done. This insures the safety of the collection and provides data for collection use reports. Authority to determine the use of the collection is usually given to the department chair or curator of a particular collection but the governing board may choose to have the final say. Part of the criteria for access to the collection should be that the user provides an adequate reason for using the collection and proves competence in handling the objects in the collection. Museums also may establish different levels of access for various users. For example, students may require more supervision while museum professionals may require less, although theft by professionals can be an issue. Guidelines for the handling of objects should be given to all users and an explanation of the collection arrangement may be needed by new users.[34]

Besides having access to the collection itself, a user may need to have access to the records of a particular object. Procedures and restrictions for this should also be included in the policy. An example of a restriction is not giving the specific locality of an endangered species, fossils, or archaeological materials because the user may go to that location for financial gain.[35] Some states such as Nebraska, for example, have laws pertaining to access to information on sensitive localities and identities and contact information of donors; therefore, state and federal laws need to be examined when determining this specific section of the policy.

Access to the collection should be in accordance with the Americans with Disabilities Act of 1992 and the Rehabilitation Act of 1973. Access involves a multitude of issues and criteria and procedures need to be clearly stated and documented by the museum in collection policies. Consultation with representatives of a disabled population can create access responsive to the needs of the artifacts and constituents alike.

INSURANCE

Because most museum's permanent collections are considered irreplaceable and insurance compensates only for the monetary loss, many museums choose not to insure their collections or may insure only parts of them, such as an important piece of art. Insurance should be a last resort for a museum because instead of anticipating reimbursement, a museum should be looking toward prevention. This is where risk management becomes important. A museum should seek security measures to prevent loss or damage through the use of controlled access, proper storage, exhibit procedures, crowd control, security guard training, inventory, and record procedures.

If insurance is found to be necessary, the museum should identify the type of risks it must cover in order to negotiate intelligently with the insurance company. Some risks that may be covered are hazards like fire, water damage, transportation, and packing. Zoos, arboretums, and other museums with living collections will need to seek special policies and should look at similar institutions to determine how to set up a policy. Insurance is a difficult decision, but museums need to evaluate carefully the need for insurance and the type of coverage they need for their collection. Unfortunately, there are no standard insurance policies for museums; however, some insurance companies have specialized in coverage designed for museums and related organizations.[36]

DEACCESSION

Deaccessioning is the process used to remove legally and permanently accessioned objects from the museum's collection. Deaccessioning is used to improve the quality and integrity of the collection in respect to the museum's mission. Deaccessioning may be used to reshape the collection by allowing unneeded objects to be removed, freeing needed space and funds. As with accessioning, deaccessioning should be a thoughtful process. If not handled properly deaccessioning can endanger the museum's reputation and public trust.

At the Kentucky Historical Society (KHS), administrators have gone to great lengths to make deaccessioning a normal part of operations. Trevor Jones, director of historical resources, conveys their view: "This (deaccessioning) process is still too slow and cumbersome for museums. Museums have painted themselves into a corner by making it really easy to accept things but very hard to get rid of them once they are accessioned. This is not sustainable and if we continue taking in 500 objects for everyone we deaccession we will soon be buried in stuff. At KHS we have items ready for deaccession approval at every single board meeting. It's important to teach board members that collections management means that pieces come in and also that others leave. Starting this process was rocky (we hadn't deaccessioned successfully since the 1980s), but now it's humming along—but it still takes too much time and isn't designed to cope with the volume of pieces we will need to dispose of in the coming years."[37]

Delegation of Authority

As with the accession policy, the deaccession policy needs to specify the persons who can give approval for deaccessioning of an object and who will keep the deaccessioning records. In general, the curator or person in charge of the collection is allowed to make recommendations for deaccessioning and then the director, or more appropriately, the governing board, makes the final decision based on the given criteria.[38] Some museums choose a more layered approach to deaccessioning. For example, if an object is valued at less than $500, the deaccession can be recommended by the curator and approved by the department chairperson; if the object is valued at between $501 and $10,000, the director must approve deaccessioning; and anything valued at more than $10,000 must be approved by the governing board. This method saves time, especially when small quantities of objects, having minimal market or research value, are being deaccessioned. No matter how a museum delegates authority, it should be clearly stated in the policy. All deaccession records must be kept on file permanently by the appropriate person, usually a registrar in larger museums.[39]

Criteria

The first step in the deaccession process should be a search of the museum's records to determine if it holds title to the object or if there were any stipulations placed on the object that prohibit deaccessioning. If there are restrictions, it may be necessary to go to court and show that the donor's wishes are impossible to fulfill. Once it is determined that an object can be deaccessioned, this action needs to be justified. A set of criteria must be established to help guide deaccession decisions. The deaccession criteria used by the Indianapolis Museum of Art are presented in text box 11.4.

Text Box 11.4 Indianapolis Museum of Art Deaccession Criteria

1. Objects that are not appropriate for the permanent, study, or Lilly House collections or are not consistent with the goals of the Museum.
2. Objects that are determined to be below the level of quality necessary to advance the museum's mission or possess little potential for research, scholarship, or educational purposes.
3. Objects that have been forged or misrepresented by the seller. A forgery is defined as a work that was intentionally made or sold for the purpose of defrauding buyers, or that has been altered in any way toward the same end. For ethnographic art, this definition also includes objects not made or used in their traditional contexts. Forgeries do not include studio work, copies, imitations, and similar works made without deceitful intent and sold in good faith by a reputable dealer. Objects misrepresented by the seller include forgeries and objects with falsified provenance.
4. Duplicate and redundant objects. An example would be two prints of the same state. The Museum shall retain the superior example. Condition and source shall also be considered. Redundant works include objects that are either duplicates, or similar variants, such as slightly different states of the same print. They also include works closely related in subject and style by the same artist or school but varying in quality, condition, and interest. In such instances, the Museum shall retain the superior example.
5. Objects damaged or deteriorated beyond reasonable repair.
6. Items for which the Museum is not able to provide proper storage or care.

Source: Indianapolis Museum of Art, "Deaccession Policy."

Methods and Procedures for Disposal

Deaccessioning is not to be confused with disposal. Deaccessioning represents a change in status in the museum records, while disposal refers to the permanent, physical removal of the item from the collection. Deaccessioned items may be exchanged with or transferred to another museum or educational institution, donated, used in destructive analysis for research, sold, destroyed, or discarded. Most museums set priorities among these methods and list them in the deaccession policy.

While deaccessioning is a highly charged topic in the museum field, disposal practices are even more controversial. This is especially true if the museum chooses to use the proceeds from the sale for general operating expenses, which is in conflict with the American Alliance of Museum Code of Ethics:[40]

> Disposal of collections through sale, trade or research activities is solely for the advancement of the museum's mission. Proceeds from the sale of nonliving collections are to be used consistent with the established standards of the museum's discipline, but in no event shall they be used for anything other than acquisition or direct care of collections.[41]

If proceeds are used in a different manner, the collection appears as a cash reserve to be used anytime it is needed. This is the reason that many museums give detailed outlines on how the object should be sold and how the proceeds from the sale should be used.[42] The sale of a deaccessioned object must be conducted as a public sale such as an auction or online.

Whatever method is chosen, the public does need to be notified of the plan to deaccession and all records (with the possible exception of the donor record) relating to the process should be available to the public. The deaccession policy should state whether or not the donor is to be notified. If there are no restrictions on the object and the donor has no legal interest in it, then the museum has no legal requirement to notify the donor.[43]

The code of professional conduct of many museums prohibit staff and board members from acquiring items deaccessioned from the museum's collections even at public sales. In fact, some museums extend this prohibition to the immediate family of the museum's staff and board members. Deaccessioning can be an emotional action and the museum must avoid any conflict of interest or even the appearance of a conflict of interest.

CARE OF THE COLLECTION

All museums are responsible for providing care for their collections as well as for the health and safety of their staff and visitors. Each museum should tailor its collection management plans to fit its own collections and situation. Issues involving emergency preparedness, integrated pest management, and health and safety will be important parts of any collection

Text Box 11.5 Case Review: Security of Collections

Threats to the security of collections can come from a variety of sources, but theft is high among those that the museum must protect itself against. The thief can be a member of the staff, such as the collections manager who stole more than three hundred coins from the American Numismatic Association Money Museum, or the curator of World War I artifacts at the National Air and Space Museum, who sold artifacts to war memorabilia dealers.* "Insider" theft may involve a researcher, such as the professor from the University of Scranton, who stole antique ceramic and glass from a number of museums and donated them to other museums, particularly the Peabody Museum of Salem, Massachusetts, where he became a board member; or unknown outsiders such as the two thieves dressed as policemen who stole thirteen objects worth approximately $200 million from the Isabella Stewart Gardner Museum in Boston in March 1990 that remains unsolved a quarter of a century later.** Obviously, stealing of museum objects is illegal and the perpetrators can be prosecuted, but museums have an even higher ethical standard to meet, which is to prevent theft of objects by any agent.

*Benzel, "Insider Pleads Guilty . . ."; Johnston, "A Professor Helps . . ."
**Honan, "The Trusted Museum Insider . . ."; Crimesider Staff, "New Development in Infamous . . ."

management plan; however, because these issues extend beyond collection areas in the museum, they are covered in chapter 9 on facilities. Only a brief discussion of the important issues for preventive conservation is covered here.[44] Numerous funding sources for museums, including collections care, are described in chapter 5.

Preventive conservation is a field of practice that is concerned with the condition of the overall collection rather than the condition of individual objects. Primary emphasis is placed on environmental and storage conditions. Topics that can be included within preventive conservation are environmental monitoring,[45] climate control, design of storage equipment,[46] use of inert storage materials,[47] building construction, facilities management, security systems, fire protection, emergency preparedness, integrated pest management, housekeeping, fluid preservatives,[48] storage supplies,[49] and health and safety issues.[50] Personnel involved in collections care need to be thoroughly familiar with the latest developments in the rapidly evolving field of preventive conservation.

Temperature and relative humidity are the two most important environmental conditions for museum collections and should be monitored at all times. Temperature has a direct effect on relative humidity and can be controlled; achieving a stable collection storage temperature around 70°F +/–2°F is a good goal. Stability is important. The most damage occurs when relative humidity shows repeated changes over the daily cycle or if rapid changes occur over a period of a few days. However, over the past few years, museum professionals have made these targets less rigid and the demand on climate control systems to maintain these levels has a negative impact on the environment. Instead, the trend is to focus on a stable environment and determine a range of tolerance for fluctuations.[51]

To promote a stable environment, collections storage areas are ideally located away from other museum activity areas. Storage equipment should be constructed of nonreactive materials that exclude vibrations, light, dust, pests, and pollution. Storage materials need to be alkaline buffered. Many collection professionals have found ethafoam to be an ideal storage material with multiple uses, from packing or cushioning material, to use as a cover for reactive surfaces.[52]

COLLECTIONS PLANNING

With a collections policy approved by governance and in force, turning to a collections planning process is an excellent way to maximize resources and be strategic about collections management and care. By definition, a collections plan "guides the content of the collections and leads staff in a coordinated and uniform direction over time to refine and expand the value of the collections in a predetermined way. Plans are time-limited and identify specific goals to be achieved. They also provide a rationale for those choices and specify how they will be achieved, who will implement the plan, when it will happen, and what it will cost."[53]

At the plan's core is its intellectual framework, which outlines the vision for the collection and helps the staff and other stakeholders work in a unified manner. Establishing the framework begins with assessing the museum's mission, analyzing current collections, and looking critically at collections use. A plan that provides a response to these data, offers a vision and plan of attack, and outlines evaluation strategies that will strengthen the museum's core, the collection, and the museum's institutional capacity.[54]

CONCLUSION

Trevor Jones easily describes the importance of collections and their care. "Collections are the sail that propels our organization forward. They provide the basis for our programs, serve as the foundation of our research efforts, and provide us multiple touch points for a wide variety of stakeholders. Our collections are essential to our success."[55] Developing, implementing, and enforcing clear policies and procedures related to collections stewardship will ensure that the museum will keep moving forward, relying on collections to engage audiences and to record the human condition.

Text Box 11.6 Guiding Questions

1. Describe a museum artifact that left an impression on you. Why? What does this mean?
2. Museums are charged with the preservation of their collections and with making them accessible for aesthetic, educational, informational, research, and recreational purposes. Are these intents contradictory? How should policies ensure balance between public access and collections preservation?
3. Are collections the defining characteristic of museums? What does a museum lose or gain if it doesn't have a collection?

NOTES

1. Miller, "Collections Management."
2. Voigt, interview.
3. Malaro and DeAngelis, *A Legal Primer*, 47.
4. Richie, interview.
5. American Alliance of Museums, *Collections Management.*
6. American Alliance of Museums, *Core Documents Verification*.
7. Miller, "Collections Management."
8. Clark, "Do You Really Want . . ."
9. Simmons, *Things Great and Small.*
10. Carnell and Buck, "Acquisitions and Accessioning"; Miller, "Collections Management"; Simmons, "Storage in Fluid . . ."
11. Buck and Gilmore, *Museum Registration Methods*; Simmons, "Storage in Fluid . . ."

12. Malaro and DeAngelis, *A Legal Primer*; Phelan, *Museum Law*.

13. Reibel, *Registration Methods*; Simmons, *Things Great and Small;* Simmons, "Collections Management Policies."

14. Simmons, *Things Great and Small*.

15. Malaro and DeAngelis, *A Legal Primer*; Miller, "Collections Management."

16. American Association for State and Local History, *Ethics Position Paper*.

17. Reibel, *Registration Methods*; Simmons, *Things Great and Small*.

18. Carnell and Buck, "Acquisitions and Accessioning."

19. Miller, "Collections Management."

20. Ibid.

21. Hankins, "Photography."

22. McCormick, "Inventory."

23. Longstreth-Brown and Buck, "Types of Files"; Demeroukas, "Condition Reporting."

24. Ibid.

25. Demeroukas, "Condition Reporting."

26. The Institute of Conservation, "Introduction to Conservation . . ."

27. Freitag et al., "Loans."

28. Malaro and DeAngelis, *A Legal Primer*; Reibel, *Registration Methods*; Freitag et al.,"Loans."

29. Freitag et al., "Loans"; Reibel, *Registration Methods*.

30. Buck, "Initial Custody and Documentation."

31. Butler-Clary, "Implementing Indiana's . . ."; Harris, "Indiana's Museum . . ."

32. Clark, "Do You Really . . ."

33. Clark, "Do You Really . . ."; Simmons, *Things Great and Small*.

34. Simmons, *Things Great and Small*.

35. Ibid.

36. Tarpey et al., "Insurance."

37. Jones, interview.

38. Simmons, *Things Great and Small*.

39. Morris and Moser, "Deaccessioning."

40. The AAM Code of Ethics is under review at the time of publication and will have revised language regarding direct care.

41. American Alliance of Museums, *Code of Ethics for Museums*.

42. The Accreditation Commission of the American Alliance of Museums requested the formation of a Direct Care Task Force to determine how museums are defining direct care and to consider the ethical considerations of the results. While an important statement in the Code of Ethics for Museums, "direct care" does not have a universally accepted definition. A white paper is expected in the spring of 2016 hopes to formally define "direct care."

43. Morris and Moser, "Deaccessioning."

44. Blanchegorge, "Preventive Conservation . . ."; de Guichen, "Preventive Conservation . . ."; Duckworth et al., *Preserving Natural Science*; Howie, *The Care and Conservation*; Krebs, "A Strategy for Preventive . . ."

45. Weintraub and Wolf, "Environmental Monitoring."

46. Hatchfield, "Wood and Wood Products"; Moore and Williams, "Storage Equipment"; von Endt et al., "Evaluating Materials . . ."

47. Baker, "Synthetic Polymers"; Burgess, "Other Cellulosic Materials"; Hatchfield, "Wood and Wood Products."

48. Simmons, "Storage in Fluid Preservatives."

49. Baker, "Synthetic Polymers"; Burgess, "Other Cellulosic Materials."

50. Grzywacz, "Air Quality Monitoring."

51. Carrlee, "Collections Care Basics"; Swain and Buck, "Storage."

52. Ibid.

53. Gardner and Merritt, *The AAM Guide*.

54. Meister and Hoff, "Collections Planning."

55. Jones, interview.

12

INTERPRETATION, EXHIBITS, AND PROGRAMMING

In the broadest sense, interpretation is, as described by Anna Bright, interpretation officer at the British Museum, "everything we do that helps visitors make sense of our collection."[1] This includes exhibitions, education programs, and evaluation. At the core of interpretation is communication—objects, photographs, landscapes, works of art—and they all have something to say. It's up to museum professionals to translate these communication pathways to a variety of audiences.[2]

In 1984, the American Association of Museums (now the American Alliance of Museums) issued *Museums for a New Century*, which identified education as the "primary" purpose of museums. This report was followed in 1992 by *Excellence and Equity: Education and the Public Dimension of Museums*, which urged museums to place education at the center of their public service roles. In response AAM revised its accreditation criteria and granting agencies and foundations started to provide increased funding for projects that made the museum's collections publicly accessible. Museums were to develop, expand, and use objects and the unique learning opportunities they present to serve their audiences. The landmark report states that museums are "institutions of public service and education, a term that includes exploration, study, observation, critical thinking, contemplation, and dialogue."[3]

The learning that occurs in museums and similar places is termed "informal learning." According to Judy Diamond et al., informal learning differs from formal learning, which occurs primarily in schools, because it is "voluntary . . . has no established sequence or curriculum . . . can occur in a variety of settings . . . [and] is ubiquitous." As such it is "personal and individualized. People choose whether or not to visit informal institutions." Informal learning often involves social interaction, especially with family or peers, which involves a large element of play.[4] Within museums, informal learning occurs primarily through self-led and guided tours of exhibits and planned educational programs.

It can be argued that since 1992, museums have been challenged to find the balance in combining "intellectual rigor with the inclusion of a broader spectrum of our diverse society."[5] But as the world has changed and competition for the public's attention has grown, developing content that is relevant and engaging has become paramount. Museum leaders like Nina Simon and her seminal publication *The Participatory Museum* have propelled new thinking and inspired museum workers to reinvent how programs and exhibits are developed and designed. Simon defines a participatory museum as a "place where visitors can create, share, and connect with each other" during their visit. In the end, each visitor has an individualized museum that she co-produced, offering diversity and a created experience that is formed "with" a visitor.[6]

Research developed by the Cultural Policy Center, Reach Advisors, and AAM's Center for the Future of Museums, among others, has pointed to the U.S.'s rapidly changing demographics and expected generational differences to push for a new kind of museum learning experience. Not only do museum board and staff compositions need to be diverse to reflect their communities and contemporary society, museums must create content—exhibits, programs, and initiatives—that reflect the interests and perspectives of their communities. Museums are places for life-long learning and they must develop interpretation that matters to twenty-first century audiences.[7]

EXHIBITS

Visitors expect to see exhibits when they go to a museum. Whether it's a permanent or temporary exhibit, or a blockbuster traveling exhibit, people populate museums to see what the curators, designers, fabricators, and educators have created. When done well, the exhibit development process considers the visitor's perspectives and expectations, while ensuring the long-term preservation of the exhibited objects.[8]

John Falk and Lynn Dierking believe that museum visitors come for the same reasons that they use other media—for information, personal identity, reinforcement of personal values, social interaction, and entertainment and relaxation. These reasons are not mutually exclusive, and information may not necessarily be the most important reason for visiting a museum.[9] This makes for a demanding environment; a museum is best prepared and ultimately successful by formalizing an interpretive plan, exhibit policy, and a clear exhibit planning and development process.

Interpretive Planning

Practiced by the National Park Service (formally since 1995) and numerous historic sites and museums across the United States, interpretive planning is about deciding which interpretive messages will be carried throughout the organization, via exhibits, educational programs, marketing, and other forms of communication. Naturally the interpretative plan aligns with the mission and vision of the organization, and serves as a strategy document. It's about making decisions and creating a plan of action that meets the financial resources of the museum and responds to the visitors' interests and desires.[10] An excellent idea is to develop an interpretive plan first, allowing policy, planning, and process to flow out of the themes and messages the plan presents.

Created through a collaborative process that includes a variety of stakeholders (management, interpretive specialists, subject matter experts, community members, academics), the structure of the plan depends on the museum and its mission. The plan typically includes two elements, the foundation and the action plan:

- Foundation presents the conceptual framework.
- Significance statements for the geographic area represented
- Interpretive themes
- Audience analysis
- Visitor experience objectives
- Action plan describes how the plan will be implemented.
- Necessary actions, listed by priority
- Decisions on how to convey themes to visitors
- Evaluation strategies[11]

Interpretive planning offers a platform for creating program- and exhibit-based experiences that deepen visitor engagement and create personal

Text Box 12.1 Harwood Museum of Art Exhibit Policy

Exhibitions at the Harwood Museum of Art reach for the museum's vision "to bring Taos arts to the world and world arts to Taos" by serving as portals between the museum's audiences and the dynamic, global world of the visual arts. Exhibitions stimulate dialogue by introducing new ideas into the community, by inspiring new and diverse audiences to participate in the Harwood, by engaging museum audiences with works of art that they might otherwise never have seen, by interpreting the museum's diverse collection from multiple perspectives, and by creating opportunities to initiate and share new scholarship related to the museum's collection.

GUIDING PRINCIPLES

- Audience—Exhibitions at the Harwood focus on clearly defined audiences. Each exhibition takes into consideration the museum's strategic goals for audience cultivation, is aligned with those goals when possible, and is informed by research documenting the needs and interests of the exhibition's target audience(s).
- Education—A strong interpretive element is integrated into the design of all exhibitions. Whenever possible, interpretive elements are interactive and/or multi-sensory. Educational programs aligned with the exhibition's target audience(s) are presented in conjunction with exhibitions. The museum strives to offer some type of educational publication (gallery guide, catalog, etc.) with exhibitions. When possible and appropriate, educational resources and programs weave a common thread between exhibitions simultaneously on view in the museum.
- Evaluation—Each exhibition is informed by clearly articulated curatorial goals and learning outcomes, and those goals and outcomes are measured with appropriate evaluation protocols.
- Community Engagement—Exhibitions foster and are shaped by community collaborations whenever possible, in the form of both collaborating institutions contributing content to the exhibition and educational programs developed in collaboration with organizations serving the exhibition's targeted audiences.

- Social Concerns—The museum's exhibition portfolio includes exhibitions relating to contemporary local, regional, national, and international social concerns.
- Quality—Exhibitions at the Harwood are comprised of significant works of art that demonstrate a high level of aesthetic quality.
- Balance—The museum presents a balanced portfolio of exhibitions, demonstrating diversity in audiences served, artists represented (local, regional, national, gender, ethnicity, contemporary, historic) and types of exhibitions (traveling, museum-originated, collection-based, juried).
- Documentation—Each exhibition is visually documented, and that documentation—along with educational materials produced for the exhibition—is preserved in an exhibition archive that is accessible to museum audiences.
- Design—Each exhibition integrates high-quality exhibition design that is visually pleasing, that effectively communicates the exhibition's message, and that facilitates meaningful aesthetic experiences for all of the museum visitors.

The Harwood Museum of Art invites artists, independent curators, scholars, and community members to submit exhibition proposals for the consideration of the Museum's Exhibitions Committee.

Source: Harwood Museum of Art, "Exhibition Policy."

meaning. This plan, whenever possible, should be approved by museum leadership as it charts the course for future exhibit and program-related themes and messages.

Exhibit Policy

Exhibits are essential to museum operations and identity and as such, the public will gauge the success or failure of a museum by the quality of its exhibits (TripAdvisor reviews have broken many a museum administrator's heart). An exhibit policy is one way that leadership can ensure a "creative and visitor-responsive exhibition program." As a management tool, the exhibit policy determines "the objectives of the exhibition program, the philosophy of presentation; and the number, frequency, size, and scope of temporary exhibitions."[12] The policy may also include conservation guide-lines for collections on display. The Harwood Museum of Art in Taos, New Mexico, offers its exhibit policy on the website, emphasizing the objectives of the exhibit program (text box 12.1). It demonstrates a balance between academia and visitor interests, with a keen eye on museum mission and policy.

Exhibit Planning and Development

Barry Lord presents two kinds of exhibits that are typically found in muse-ums that many think are oppositional. Research-based exhibits are driven by museum curators and their interest in advancing knowledge of the field. Market-driven exhibits are the result of public interest and demand, as well as timely content (unfolding events). But he argues for the audience-responsive approach, which is a combination of the two, "public interest is always relevant to the direction of socially responsible research."[13] This is good advice for planning an exhibition schedule that will accomplish strate-gic goals and attract a variety of audiences.

When creating a plan, it quickly becomes obvious that the exhibit staff does not create exhibitions alone. There are five key areas that must work in tandem to implement an exhibit plan and they must be feasible for the organization. Considerations include the collections (objects), space (galler-ies), timing, staff, and cost.[14]

Collections

Concerns about the availability and preservation of the collection should be as much of an issue for the exhibits staff as it is for the collections staff. There are important questions to be answered: What are the best items to tell the story of the exhibit? What is the condition of the object? Can it withstand permanent exhibition, or any exhibition time at all? Will this item be secure in the exhibit?

According to Heather Maximea, "very few objects displayed ... are immune to damage from vandalism or accident and are most vulnerable to theft." [15] Security of the objects displayed is critical and whenever pos-sible and appropriate, seeking out the advice of a security professional is advisable.[16]

Security measures involve locking cases, adding weight or fastening cases to the floor to prevent tipping, keeping a record of what objects are on exhibit and where they are, installing a security system, and having a strolling guard or other staff member in the exhibit space.[17] If the museum has a security or facility manual, be sure to include procedure for reporting security issues.

Conservation is a major concern when objects leave the storage environment for the unknown of the exhibit floor. Threats appear from materials used in case construction, light and humidity levels, improper mounts, pests, and human negligence. The safest route is to create microenvironments in which the objects can spend time in the so-called limelight without suffering any adverse effects. Exhibition policy and planning should outline ways to neutralize as many threats as possible, but must also allow the visitor access to the object and exhibit. Each area needs to avoid natural light and have a listing of acceptable values, such as five-foot-candles for dyed textiles, UV filters placed on lighting, consideration of use of LED lighting, relative humidity of 40 to 50 percent, and buffering to prevent off-gassing of materials. Maintenance schedules, including case inspection, should be regular procedure. All measures to preserve the collection must be taken seriously and to preserve the objects, as well as the public trust given to museums.[18]

"Public trust cannot be undervalued," says David Dean; "Properly presented exhibitions confirm public trust in the museum as a place for conservation and careful presentation. Potential donors of objects or collections will be much more inclined to place their treasures in institutions that will care for the objects properly, and will present those objects for public good in a thoughtful and informative manner."[19]

Space Considerations

"Don't squish me." "I feel like a sardine." "I'm getting claustrophobic." "I can't breathe." These are not the words museum staff members want to hear in an exhibit area. It is essential that enough space is allocated for exhibits. There must be space for the artifacts and space for visitors to view them comfortably, whether there are many in a large school group or an individual using a wheelchair.

Museums commonly exhibit objects in two ways—permanent exhibits and temporary or special exhibits. "Permanent" exhibit is technically a misnomer as they are planned to last ten to fifteen years while some have lasted well beyond that date, but not forever.[20] They can set the character of an institution, becoming in some cases an icon or signature image for a museum (as "Archie" the mammoth has become for the University of Nebraska State Museum in Lincoln, Nebraska, or the dinosaur *SUE the*

Table 12.1   Characteristics of a Good Exhibit

Museums Are	Good Exhibits Are
Free choice experiences—visitors decide which exhibits or sections of exhibits they will see	Built for success—make the trip worthwhile by creating situations where the visitor is likely to see the point or complete the task
Physical spaces—visitors walk through and are surrounded by the exhibits	Strongly dimensional—they have objects, props, and other three-dimensional components, and also make use of the total environment, including the visitor path
Open to a broad audience—visitors bring a wide variety of abilities, knowledge, and learning styles	Relevant and accessible to the general visitor and support diverse interests and learning styles
Multimodal—exhibits engage different senses (sight, sound, touch) and have different types of expression	Engaged with multiple modalities and take full advantage of the different senses employed during a visit
Nonlinear—visitors do not take a predetermined route, but choose their own path	Clearly organized—the structure transparent, easy to follow, and can be understood in any order
	Strongly focused—present and reinforce a single clear message
Temporal experiences—the visitor sees different parts of the museum or exhibit over time; however, most visitors have an informal "time budget" and generally spend twelve to twenty minutes in a gallery	Designed so individual components can stand alone, and don't require the visitor to have seen something else first; however, together they create a cumulative effect
Social experiences—visitors often come with family and friends	Designed to accommodate more than one user, designed to encourage conversation and/or group activity

Source: Dillenberg and Klein, "Creating Exhibits."

T. Rex at the Field Museum in Chicago, Illinois). Yani Herreman offers that instead of thinking of long-term exhibits as permanent, "since these are planned as part of a core concept structure, storyline or discourses within a museum, it would be better to call these 'core' exhibitions."[21] And many smaller museums, have no interest in permanent exhibitions, electing to have rotating exhibits that last one to two years. The cost of the exhibit can be spread over time, but replacement or refurbishment costs may be incurred over its life cycle.[22] These activities are to be included in a five-year exhibit schedule alongside the timelines for new exhibits.

Museums cannot live by permanent exhibits alone. Temporary or special exhibits (traveling exhibits included) can maximize use of space. They provide a chance for change and for sustaining visitor interest and attracting new visitors. The time frame for temporary exhibits is generally six months to five years.

"Blockbuster" shows have become part of the temporary exhibit world. "Blockbuster" refers to shows that attract significant attention, such as the "King Tut" exhibit that started the modern "blockbuster" craze. The field has started to issue "dire warnings" that the time of the blockbuster exhibit has passed. The drain on staff resources is immense and other worthy, mission-aligned projects are neglected. But they can be a boon for income and visitation.[23] Tobi Voigt, chief curatorial officer at the Detroit Historical Society, opines that it's time for the modern blockbuster exhibit to take on a new life:

> I think we need to redefine the concept of "blockbuster." An exhibit doesn't have to be all sparkle and no substance to be a blockbuster these days. The key, especially for history museums, is finding exhibit topics that are important and relevant to the general public AND the museum. We have a few exhibits that are very popular, but I call them "history lite" because they capitalize on nostalgia and provide minimal historical content. But we are now planning an exhibit to commemorate the 50th anniversary of the 1967 civil unrest in Detroit. This is a blockbuster topic, because it is still so relevant in our community and we are engaging the community in its creation. However, we plan to create the exhibit in a way that meets our educational goals and mission. It's a heck of a lot of work, but if we can pull it off, this is what I want to call the new "blockbuster."[24]

In addition to hitting the right exhibition note with the public, the museum must also consider inclusive exhibit design. The museum visitor brings with him a host of interests and characteristics, and sometimes physical limitations. With the passage of the Americans with Disabilities Act, museums must provide equal access for visitors with disabilities to public programs and spaces, including exhibits. By focusing on details such as audio descriptions, items for tactile examination, adequate lighting, height of display cases, and readability of text, exhibit staff members can broaden audiences. Additional considerations include better circulation pathways and broadened presentation of content to accommodate a variety of learning styles.[25] The Smithsonian Guidelines for Accessible Exhibition Design outlines specifics for these components, as well as proper language for symbols and inoffensive terminology. Museums are finding that the guidelines do not create design problems, as much as they create a better visitor experience for all.[26]

Timing

An exhibit schedule considers all the resources available to the museum and it considers long-range opportunities and obstacles for new exhibits. Ideally, the schedule will include five years of exhibit projects and openings, allowing for sufficient advance planning. The schedule will include, at a topical level, the themes, locations, and budget. It will also create time estimates for all of the stages of exhibit production—research, design, fabrication, installation—and chart the phases to ensure successful project completion.[27] Museum leadership either attends these planning team meetings or is positioned to make the final decision on which exhibitions go on the schedule, making sure the exhibits align with mission and financial capacity (budget).

Staff

How grants, sponsorships, gifts, and general museum dollars are spent on exhibits will ultimately become the responsibility of the museum director and the museum's board. They must spend money wisely in the creation of

Text Box 12.2 Exercise: Evaluation of Exhibits

At a local museum with which you are familiar and where you have received permission, evaluate visitors' use of one of the important exhibit galleries. You should make your observations over a period of at least four hours. Try to be inconspicuous while observing so that you do not change visitor behavior.

Sketch the floor plan of the exhibit gallery and trace the routes individual visitors or groups of visitors take through the gallery. Record how long visitors spend at each of the exhibits in the gallery. Record any intragroup or intergroup interactions you observe, especially as these interactions relate to the exhibits.

Write a two-page summary of your observations to be given to the museum. What part of the gallery seemed to be of most interest to visitors? Why do you think this is true? What part of the gallery seemed to be least interesting to visitors? Can you give reasons why this area seemed to be of the least interest? What could the museum do to enhance the visitors' experience in this gallery? What recommendations can you make to the museum as it plans future exhibits?

good exhibits. Exhibits are a critical investment. And they are responsible for raising the funds, working closely with a development or advancement department.

The tasks that relate directly to exhibit planning and production include scheduling and contracting for exhibitions, contracting for services, production and resource management, documentation and registration, and publicity and marketing. It is incredibly wise to adopt a project management strategy to keep the team moving forward, promote communication, and to deliver the exhibit on time without over-taxing resources. For each exhibit, a project plan is designed that includes project status reports, budget updates (income and expense), a timeline of required tasks, and task assignments. It acts as a tracking document and provides a quick reference that shows the exhibit's current stage of development.

In some museums, the curator will act alone in developing exhibit content, but more often in recent years exhibits have been created by a team of museum staff members—educators, curators, collection managers, marketers, exhibit designers, cultural and community advisory groups, and more. Members of the exhibit team may change with every exhibit and they are responsible for a wide range of tasks—determining themes and messages, selecting objects for the proposed exhibit, determining how they will be displayed, and keeping the exhibit within budget. A successful team also needs the full backing and support of the museum director.

Cost

Exhibits are among the most expensive public programs the museum produces, and, as the most visible of programs, exhibits can attract monetary support. This support can take the form of corporate sponsorship of exhibits, whether they are "blockbusters" or small displays. When you consider just art museums, each year corporations contribute $1 billion to art museums and a significant portion of this is to support exhibitions. In 2007, the Association of Art Museum Directors published a white paper, outlining how to manage the relationship between art museums and corporate sponsors. Useful to the entire museum field, it provides a series of questions to ask when entering a relationship with a corporate sponsor. Some corporations, because they are motivated by marketing exposure, may want to influence content, showcase products or services in a museum context, or have business practices that are oppositional to museum's mission and purpose. Managing these conflicts of interest ensures public trust.[28]

Despite these considerations, corporations may say they are not involved in the exhibition, but the public still sees the connections. This is especially evident with the surge in fashion exhibitions in the 2000s. It began with Giorgio Armani's $15 million contribution to the Guggenheim capital campaign in 1999 followed in the same year by the show "Giorgio Armani" at the museum that got the public's attention. Fast forward to today, fashion sponsors are donating far less and demanding much more involvement, as the fashion industry grows more corporate and popular. Examples include the Met's Alexander McQueen exhibit in 2011, the Jean Paul Gaultier exhibit of 2013 that traveled across the United States, and the more subtle connections—clothing and accessory store Nordstrom sponsoring The Brooklyn Museum's *Killer Heels: The Art of the High-Heeled Shoe* and Macy's sponsoring *The Rise of the Sneaker Culture* exhibit.[29] Taking it even one, concerning step further, exhibitions are also being curated by sponsors, from their corporate collections. The economic downturns of the 2000s have precipitated this loosening of restrictions because corporations like Bank of America and JPMorgan Chase are offering their collections as ready-made exhibits for little to no cost. For small institutions, this is an ideal solution and their audiences get to see the works of art icons like Warhol and the Wyeth family.[30]

The principles at the core of museum ethics should serve as a guide—honesty, transparency of all dealings, independence, and "preventing at all costs both the perception and the reality of conflict of interest."[31] The museum must remember that as the corporation benefits from the museum's reputation, for good or bad, of the corporation will reflect on the museum.

Another source of revenue comes from the private sector. When museums approach individual givers, they must learn what a potential donor's interests are and match them to the appropriate exhibition or program. A careful consideration of the museum's mission and its commitment to intellectual integrity will ensure an appropriate mesh of donor wishes and museum needs. Museums that offer donors significant input into program content will find themselves subject to constituent criticism at the least, if not editorial castigation in the media.[32] Much the same considerations should be made when approaching foundations. Generally, local foundations will be more interested in the programs of a local museum than foundations in other regions of the country. The exception to this rule is large foundations, such as the Ford Foundation or the Fidelity Foundation, that provide grants nationwide.

Although exhibits are expensive, they also help to support the institution financially by giving people a reason to visit the museum; therefore, exhibits should be treated with respect and an eye to the future. Exhibitions provide a highly visible justification for a museum's existence and its expectation for continued support.

All of these aspects of exhibit policy and procedure have one thing in common. They focus on visitors who after all, are the reason we are doing this. Visitors should be the first and last thought no matter what kind of challenges arise. A good exhibit policy and plan will reflect the importance of keeping visitors in mind during every step of the planning process. With visitors foremost in mind, museums have the best chance of ensuring that all of these components will work together and produce the best possible product.

PROGRAMMING

While collections are the core around which most museums are built, education generally is regarded as the primary purpose of all museums. The educational function is what gives the collection meaning. "Much of the world knows our museums through our programs . . . our programs are powerful tools."[33] This responsibility includes presenting a diversity of perspectives through a wide range of media in order to increase the modes of understanding for as many people as possible. It also requires consideration of physical, language, and other barriers that may affect visitors' understandings. Alexandra Rasic, director of public programs at the Homestead Museum in City of Industry, California, shares that mission-central efforts like educational programs and exhibits are part of their daily conversations, making them a critical function of the museum. "Our world revolves around programming and exhibits. We have been making a greater effort to align the two by creating more of a flow, seasonally and programmatically, that aligns with exhibit changes in our (historic) houses. The more in alignment exhibits and programming are, more comfortable things feel. It's like holding hands."[34]

The work of the museum educator includes a long list of educational activities—serving on exhibit teams, docent training, tours (self-guided and guided), teacher training, field work, school programs, special programs and events, museum theater, demonstrations, teaching kits, publications, online programs, and classes/workshops.[35] Museums tend to focus more attention on the school-age visitor but with the average age of the population of the

Text Box 12.3 Exercise: "Indians Behind Glass"—Museum Exhibits of Native People[1]

Whose story gets told in museums, who gets to tell it, and what objects are used to tell the story are sources of long-standing tension between indigenous peoples and museums. Natural history museums in the United States have been criticized for some exhibitions of Native Americans and their cultural and utilitarian objects. Statements such as "there are Indians in the Museum of Natural History, and there aren't any other kinds of people" are typical of this controversy.[2]

This was the backdrop for a situation that faced the director of the University of Michigan Museum of Natural History in 2009–2010.[3] The museum had received complaints from members of the Anishinabe and Potawatomi tribes after some of their children had visited the museum's exhibits on a school field trip. The exhibits in question were fourteen miniature dioramas depicting "tiny figurines of Great Lakes and other American Indian people cooking around a fire, putting up a teepee in a snowy wood, and kneeling on staked-out leather hides to scrape and cure them."[4] The complaints from the tribal members about the exhibits were that "it sounded like we were an ancient people and that we didn't exist anymore" and "by displaying American Indian cultures alongside dinosaur fossils, gemstones and taxidermied animals, dioramas make their subjects seem less than fully human."[5]

How did Native American material come to be displayed in natural history museums? As scientists were scouring the near and far reaches of North America during the nineteenth century collecting representatives of fauna, flora, and fossils, they were taking notes and collecting cultural and utilitarian objects of native people who also seemed to be as endangered as the plants and animals. They created exhibits because it was believed that disease, loss of land and culture, government schools, and warfare would erase the natives and their cultures. The scientists were wrong, but many of the exhibits they created remain on public display.

The director of the University of Michigan Museum of Natural History resisted removing the dioramas at first, but decided after studying the issues involved to remove them in early 2010. Predictably, some opposed this decision, such as the fourth-grade teacher who wrote, "We cannot take our students back into time to experience firsthand the life of our country's natives ... the dioramas offer a wonderful visual aid."[6]

At much the same time as the university was grappling with the decision on the Native American dioramas, exhibits were being constructed at the Ziibiwing Center of Anishinabe Culture and Lifeways in Mt. Pleasant, Michigan. The tribe decided to make their displays open, without glass, and using life-sized mannequins. They used tribal members to model the mannequins and to voice the recordings in the museum. The objects used in the exhibits were authentic and along with photographs and modern artworks produced by tribal members showed the tribe's current culture.[7]

Anishinabes were following a path the Makah tribe from the Olympic Peninsula of Washington followed in the 1970s. The impetus for them to build a tribal museum or cultural center was the recovery of artifacts and the remains of six longhouses from part of a village buried by a coastal landslide about 500 years earlier. The resulting museum exhibits began with a scale model of the buried village and proceeded with what pre-contact tribal members did season by season. The museum used artwork, text panels, and artifacts to tell this story. Finally, the exhibits concluded with a full-sized replica of a longhouse that allowed visitors to walk into the interior and explore.[8] All of the exhibits in this tribal museum lacked life-sized mannequins, which was a decision made by the Makah Tribal Council. Wax noted the difficulty American Indians have in using mannequins because of their "ambiguous counterpoint to the savage mannequins held at bay behind the plate glass of the museum display."[9]

As a museum professional, you should keep in mind that all objects and artifacts in museum collections have been stripped of their context. They have been removed from their original settings. Natural history museums have tried to return context for Native American objects in their exhibit programs by recreating the original settings within dioramas as they have done for plants, animals, and even gemstones and fossils. This approach does not appear to have satisfied many of the visitors to these museums, but there must be ways to overcome these issues. Other types of museums—history, art, anthropology, and tribal—have successfully exhibited Native American objects with little controversy. With these ideas in mind, please complete the following exercises.

Exercises (discussion and in writing):

1. Are there different philosophical or contextual bases underlying the exhibition of Native American objects in history, art, anthropology, or tribal museums?

(continued)

Text Box 12.3 Exercise: "Indians Behind Glass"—Museum Exhibits of Native People¹ (continued)

2. Should all nontribal museums stop exhibiting Native American cultural and utilitarian objects?
3. What are the pros/cons of using miniatures in Native American exhibits?
4. What are the pros/cons of using life-sized mannequins in Native American exhibits?
5. What does "glass in museum exhibits" mean? Is there a way to dispel this problem?
6. Are there no other people behind glass in American museums other than Native Americans?
7. What peoples are behind glass in museums in Europe, Australia, and Asia? Do you discern any patterns?
8. Did the director at the University of Michigan Museum of Natural History do the right thing? Defend your response in two pages or less stating the philosophical basis of your response.
9. Assume that you are the director of a museum planning new cultural exhibits, would you be willing to have your staff collaborate with or cede total authority to the people whose culture is being exhibited? After discussion, write a work plan detailing who will be responsible for each part of project, including conceptualization, planning, exhibit design, case design, modeling, object selection, label writing, construction, installation, and opening.

NOTES

1. Exercise contributed by Hugh H. Genoways, 2015.
2. LaVaque-Manty, "There are Indians . . ."
3. Brown, "Removing Dioramas . . ."; Diep, "The Passing of . . ."; Miller, "Native American . . ."; Zhu, "Natural History . . ."
4. Diep, "The Passing of . . ."
5. Ibid.
6. Brown, "Removing Dioramas . . ."; Miller, "Native American . . ."; Zhu, "Natural History . . ."
7. Diep, "The Passing of . . ."
8. Ibid.
9. Ibid.

United States steadily rising, museums cannot afford to ignore nonschool audiences.[36]

In many institutions, it is the responsibility of the education program to find and develop new audiences such as working adults, the retired traveling public, or audiences with special needs. And the education program, along with the visitor services staff are to be mindful of the diversity of their audiences and adopt inclusive language. When working with children and families, it is especially important to ensure a sensitive and calm learning environment. Table 12.2 offers guidelines for working with family-inclusive language that reflects the nature of twenty-first century families, which is defined by the individuals involved who "may or may not be biologically related, share the same household, or be legally recognized. Inclusive language doesn't make assumptions about the relationships between people."[37]

With such a broad scope of possible activities filling crucial roles in the community, the importance of creating museum policies regarding education programs seems clear. Thinking of education as "learning" creates a focus on the visitor, the learner. To do this, the educators must keep these four factors in mind when developing policy and programs, identifying audiences, and evaluating results:

- "Museums work best as informal rather than formal educational institutions."
- "Informal education is most successful at affective learning—although some cognitive learning is also always involved."
- "The outcome of affective learning is reflected in a change in attitude, valuation, or interest, rather than the formal cognition of information or data."
- "Affective learning works best when the experience is fun."[38]

Policy and Guidelines

In most museums, the educational function is delegated to a public programs or education staff member or department. Through its programs and through the voices of individual staff and volunteers, this department speaks to the public for the museum as a whole. Educators work closely with the public and they are the resident experts on the museum's audiences. This perspective is incredibly valuable in the development of exhibits and programs; providing policy and guidelines for accessing this information is critical.[39]

Table 12.2 Family-Inclusive Language

Avoid	Why?	Instead
"parents" "mom" "dad" "mom and dad"	Not everyone accompanying a child is a parent. Grandparents, step-parents, and nannies may not identify as parents. Not all children have a mom and dad.	"grownup" "adult" "caregiver"
"son" "daughter"	The children in someone's care could be grandchildren, nieces, nephews, godchildren, etc. You may also not want to assume the gender of a child.	"children"
"extended family"	The term is usually meant to include grandparents, aunts, uncles, and cousins but for folks of many cultures this isn't "extended" family—it's just family.	"family"
"family resemblance"	We're conditioned to look for similar features in family members so you may see resemblances where there are none. Many families include stepparents, adoptive parents, or parents who conceived with donated eggs or sperm. Inversely, don't assume that a child who doesn't look like their caregiver is adopted—many multiracial children resemble one parent more than the other.	Keep it to yourself.
"members of a household"	Families don't always live together. For example, families with divorced parents or incarcerated parents.	"family members"

Source: Excerpted from Middleton, *Including the 21st Century Family.*

Further, guidelines clarify the goals of public programs and describe the steps to meet those goals; the scope of the particular programs and the role of individuals within the programs should be defined. The policies and guidelines will help focus the efforts of the staff to meet the specific needs of the community and institution. Program policies and guidelines should include relevant job descriptions for paid and volunteer staff, the expectations regarding the conduct of the staff, and the training provided for the staff and volunteers. Policies should address the overall goals of the program as well as addresses specific issues of accessibility, diversity, and outreach. A means of evaluating the program should also be provided. Ideally this evaluation will provide opportunities for feedback from both the staff and the community.[40]

Text Box 12.4 Program Management Checklist

PLANNING

- Determine the audience.
- Set institutional objectives and educational goals.
- Choose a format.
- Select presenters.
- Decide on a staffing plan.
- Plan the publicity.
- Create a supply list.
- Make a contingency plan.
- Develop a budget and determine funding sources.
- Decide on an evaluation plan.

EXECUTING

- Train staff.
- Set up (signs, seating, supplies, etc.).
- Hold the program.
- Clean up

ASSESSING

- Gather feedback.
- Analyze data to measure program outcomes against goals and objectives.
- Record thoughts for next time.

Source: Martin, "The Nuts and Bolts . . . ," 131.

Guidelines for professional conduct are also critical. As basic as such issues may seem, if there is no policy, there can be no enforcement. The AAM provides guidelines for professional conduct for museum staff. The best time to create codes of conduct and job descriptions is before a problem arises.

Certain expectations can be made regarding the experience and abilities of paid staff members. If they have been properly trained for the position of educator, they will have familiarity with educational method and theory, an understanding of the practices of education in an informal setting, and some education experience as well as an appropriate background in the relevant subject matter of the museum. For volunteers, however, expectations of previous experience or background are not appropriate. A thorough training program should be implemented for all volunteers, especially those who will be interacting with the public.

Many education programs have a mission statement that builds on the general mission of the institution, but addresses the specific goals of the education program. Defining the goal of the education program will provide focus for paid and volunteer staff members. Education in a museum setting is about the exploration of concepts, the shaping of opinions, and the stimulation of ideas. David Carr stated that "Flexibility, openness, diversity of interpretations are essential for the creation of a situation where multiple kinds of becoming are possible. . . . The museum that embodies mindfulness naturally attracts minds."[41] The mission of the education program should be used as a tool to nurture an attitude of mindfulness in the educational staff. For them, the most important characteristic is an attitude that nurtures learning. Carr's statement, "Learners learn from learners," should be the motto of any museum education department.[42] This is equally important whether that staff is composed of a part-time coordinator with a few loyal volunteers or a department with many paid professionals.

EVALUATION

Museums, like all publicly funded institutions, are under increasing pressure to show outcomes, not merely output. Stephen Weil and John Falk, in separate articles published in the summer 1999 issue of *Dædalus*, emphasize the importance of museums being able to document that learning is occurring in their programs. Weil states, "the demand is that the American museum provide some verifiable added value to the lives of those it serves in exchange for their continued support."[43] In Weil's view, the museum's portion of this social contract is to provide educational experiences. Museums must be able to provide evidence from outcome-based evaluations that they are fulfilling this social contract. Falk believes that museums have provided learning experiences all along, but have failed in the documentation of this learning through erroneous assumptions and approaches to learning assessment.[44] He points out that immediate assessments may miss the most important part of the museum learning process: "It may take days, weeks, or months for the

Text Box 12.5 Exercise: Field Trips and the Twenty-First Century Student

It has been stated time and again the educational value of museum field trips is clear—students learn skills in numeracy and literacy, but they also benefit from exposure to arts and culture. This is especially true when disadvantaged students are less likely to visit a museum otherwise. Unfortunately, the field trip is a shrinking educational opportunity in U.S. schools. The Field Museum in Chicago, Illinois, historically welcomed more than 300,000 students each year; now, the number has dropped below 200,000. Arts organizations in Cincinnati, Ohio, reported a 30 percent drop in student attendance between 2002 and 2007. And the American Association of School Administrators found that more than half of schools eliminated field trips in 2010–2011. Financial pressures and performance standards have kept students in the classroom more, and when they do go on field trips, they are designed more as reward field trips rather than an extension of learning environment (amusement parks get selected over museums). While there isn't a great deal of data available about the impact of field trips on student learning, one recent study demonstrated that field trips positively impact critical thinking skills, display stronger historical empathy (the ability to understand and appreciate what life was like in a different time and place), develop higher tolerance, and are students more like to visit cultural institutions in the future.*

When asked how her museum has adapted to decreases in classroom field trips, Janet Stoffer, director of education at the National Czech and Slovak Museum and Library (NCSML), Cedar Rapids, Iowa, demonstrated a well-oiled machine of docents and staff working together, following policy to improve a situation. "The NCSML staff and docents listen to teachers and observes students while onsite to see what works and does not work. Staff and docents communicate openly about these observations, and adjust accordingly. Additionally, the NCSML staff asks a lot of questions of teachers. The formation of the Elementary Education Advisory Committee has greatly contributed to the future success of NCSML educational programming for school groups."** This type of active listening and proactive educational programming will serve a museum well when planning for classroom field trips.

At a local museum that you are familiar with and you have received permission, evaluate their classroom or field trip programs. Review the descriptions on line and ask permission to observe a field trip experience.

(continued)

> Interview a museum educator and possibly the director to find out how they are adapting to (or not) the changes in the field trip landscape.
>
> Write a two-page summary of your observation to be given to the museum. What ideas do you have to improve the field trip experience? How might they connect with students outside to the classroom and deliver similar content? What recommendations can you make to the museum as it plans for future programs?
>
> °Greene, "The Educational Value . . ."
> °°Stoffer, interview.

experience to be sufficiently integrated with prior knowledge for learning to be noticeable even to the learner himself, let alone measurable."[45]

Providing for the evaluation of programs most often falls into the responsibilities of the education department. The evaluation of museum programs should provide opportunities for feedback from both the staff and the community. Stacy Klingler and Conny Graft outline instructions on how to design, implement, and present an evaluation study. They discuss three main types of evaluations that any department should incorporate into its evaluation process.

- Front-end evaluation occurs before the program or exhibit is still being defined, allowing for changes, if needed.
- Formative evaluation or prototyping happens when an affordable, pilot version of the program is offered to test effectiveness.
- Summative evaluation is scheduled for after the program or exhibit is produced to gather feedback, or lessons learned.[46]

A good evaluation program helps the institution achieve strategic goals and make decisions or course corrections. It also aids in securing funding; donors want to know the impact of their giving and this is best measured through formal evaluation techniques

CONCLUSION

Regardless of its mission, size, or emphasis, a museum will be known to its audiences through its public programs. "Great museum exhibitions offer

Text Box 12.6 Case Review: Abbe Museum's Decolonization Initiative

Museum professionals must keep in mind that the very act of placing another culture on display is continuing the idea of "different." There is no way around this. There are no easy solutions, nor is there a catch-all formula for avoiding conflict in portraying the "Other." Diversity and inclusion policies will help to give a more appropriate voice to museums. However, because no museum staff can reflect the range of cultural diversity of our nation, or probably even its own community, alternative methods have been sought to inform cultural exhibits and public programs.

Working in tandem with its interpretive planning process, the Abbe Museum in Bar Harbor, Maine, launched a Decolonization Initiative and Task Force. The initiative was an outgrowth of the board of trustees' 2012 annual retreat, facilitated by Jamie Bissonette Lewey (Abenaki), where trustees and staff studied the concept and meaningfulness of sovereignty to Indigenous people. To quote Lewey, "The understanding of what is encompassed in the idea of sovereignty and how it is achieved is crucial in the building of relationships between Native and non-Native people." An outcome of the retreat was a commitment from trustees and the staff to (1) better understand Wabanaki culture, history and values, (2) examine the Abbe's museum practices at every level to see whether, in what ways, and to what extent they reflect those values, and (3) take steps toward practices that embody this commitment. During its initial convening, the task force considered the scope of its work, and identified key concepts that underpin the discussions board and staff were having. These include, but are not limited to sovereignty (cultural and legal), culture, decolonization, colonization, racism, jargon, and museum history.

The task force found the scholarly work of Amy Lonetree (Ho-Chunk) especially useful in helping them understand what it means to decolonize a museum. Through her writings, the task force focused on her recommendations: (1) collaborate with tribal communities, members and advisors, (2) incorporate truth-telling—present exhibits or programs focused on the difficult stories of colonization, and (3) present Native voice and perspective.* Since 2012, the Abbe has focused on these strategies in its exhibition program and the new core exhibit *People of the First Light*, opened in May 2016, reflects these recommendations.

(continued)

Text Box 12.6 Case Review: Abbe Museum's Decolonization Initiative (continued)

COLLABORATION

- Abbe Museum staff held listening sessions in Wabanaki communities to gather ideas from community members about what should be included in an exhibit about the Wabanaki.
- Wabanaki community curators and content specialists are central to the creation of exhibit content.
- Wabanaki artists participated in the design of the exhibit.

TRUTH-TELLING

- The exhibit acknowledges that the Wabanaki and their ancestors have been in this place for at least 12,000 years. (This is presently contested by a group of archaeologists working in Maine.**)
- This exhibit makes it abundantly clear that there are Wabanaki people in Maine today, and that they have always been here.

PERSPECTIVE

- All content is credited, so that it will always be clear to the visitor whose voice is being shared.
- Wabanaki curators and artists are fully involved in the creation and design of the exhibit.

As the exhibit's project plan came together, so too did the Abbe's current strategic plan. The concept and practice of decolonization has risen in prominence at the Abbe and is now the museum's vision: The Abbe Museum will reflect and realize the values of decolonization in all of its practices, working with the Wabanaki Nations to share their stories, history, and culture with a broader audience.*** The task force is now a standing committee of the board that includes key staff members and content specialists. Through this vision, the Initiative extends beyond exhibits and considers collections management and care, governance and staffing, research, policy development, and more. The Abbe Museum will continue to develop decolonizing protocols that support and include Indigenous communities. With any museum working cross-culturally and with diversity and inclusion policies, a heightened level of sensitivity and respect is required. The Abbe example and Lonetree's research offer a methodology for institutionalizing inclusive practices in a museum setting.

°Lonetree, *Decolonizing Museums.*
°°Some archaeologists working in Maine have interpreted significant changes in the archaeological record occurring about 3,800 years ago as evidence of a population replacement. Based on their interpretation of the archaeological record, they argue that contemporary Wabanaki communities are not culturally affiliated (as it relates to NAGPRA) with any artifacts or human remains older than approximately 3,000 years before present. This is not the perspective of Native people and other anthropologists and archaeologists working in Maine.
°°°The Abbe's current strategic plan is available at abbemuseum.org.

visitors transformative experiences that take them outside the routines of everyday life."[47] Museums also have the potential to offer a valuable alternative to people who feel oversaturated with mass media and the products of entertainment conglomerates. Through creative and effective public programs, museums can give visitors safe public spaces for recreation, learning, and sociability as well as enchanting, celebrative, and transforming experiences.[48] This is a great privilege.

Text Box 12.7 Guiding Questions

1. In what ways do permanent, temporary, or blockbuster exhibits work together in a museum? Or don't they?
2. If you work in a museum, as classroom visitation has dropped, what has your museum done to adapt?
3. Describe an educational program that excited you. Why? What were the elements that made it so successful to you?

NOTES

1. Bright, "Small Objects . . ."
2. Hague and Keim, "Preparing an Outstanding . . ."

3. Committee on Education, *Excellence in Practice*; American Association of Museums, *Excellence and Equity*.

4. Diamond et al., *Practical Evaluation Guide*, 11–13.

5. American Association of Museums, *Excellence and Equity*.

6. Simon, *The Participatory Museum*.

7. American Association of Museums, *Demographic Transformation*.

8. Lord and Piacente, *Manual of Museum*.

9. Falk and Dierking, *The Museum Experience*.

10. Brochu, *Interpretive Planning*.

11. National Park Service, *Interpretive Planning*.

12. Lord and Piacente, *Manual of Museum*, 110–11.

13. Lord, "Where Do Exhibition . . . ," 24.

14. Herreman, "Display, Exhibits and Exhibitions."

15. Maximea, "Exhibition Facilities," 89.

16. Ibid.

17. Dean, *Museum Exhibition*.

18. Dean, *Museum Exhibition*; Dillenburg and Klein, "Creating Exhibits . . . "

19. Dean, *Museum Exhibition*, 2.

20. Maximea, "Exhibition Facilities."

21. Herreman, "Display, Exhibits and Exhibitions," 92.

22. Maximea, "Exhibition Facilities."

23. Lord and Lord, *The Manual of* . . .

24. Voigt, interview.

25. Thompson and Thompson, "Universal Design and Diversity."

26. Smithsonian Accessibility Program, *Smithsonian Guidelines for Accessible Exhibition Design*.

27. Herreman, "Display, Exhibits and Exhibitions."

28. American Association of Museum Directors. "Managing the Relationship . . ."

29. Farago, "The Degas Wears Prada."

30. Pogrebin, "And Now . . ."

31. Lord, "Quid Pro Show," 79.

32. Balzar, "And the Next Item . . ."

33. Martin, "The Nuts and Bolts . . .," 100.

34. Rasic, interview.

35. Brüninghaus-Knubel, "Museum Education . . . "; Johnson, "Museum Education . . . "

36. Falk and Dierking, *The Museum Experience*.

37. Middleton, "Including the 21st Century Family."

38. Lord and Lord, *The Manual of* . . . , 136–37.

39. Brüninghaus-Knubel, "Museum Education. . . "

40. Dean, *Museum Exhibition*.

41. Carr, "The Need for the Museum," 34.

42. Carr, "The Need for the Museum," 35.

43. Weil, "From Being about . . . ," 244.

44. Falk, "Museums as Institutions . . . "

45. Falk, "Museums as Institutions . . . ," 260.

46. Klingler and Graft, "In Lieu of . . . "

47. Kotler et al., *Museum Marketing*, 5.

48. Ibid.

EPILOGUE

Now you know everything there is to know about museum administration, right? While the scope of the book is large and wide, its depth only goes so far. It is up to you to fill your baskets, your buckets, your briefcases full of experience and perspectives. The longer you work in the field, as you would any profession, the more you will know and the more you will give back.

Throughout this book you've read ideas and reflections from administrators across the field and from all museum types. And you've been exposed to the range of tools available to help make museums work and in so doing, to change lives in the communities they serve. One of the questions asked was, "What advice would you give to a museum employee, looking to move up administration ladder, or a graduate student who wants to lead a museum?" While there were many notable responses, Bob Beatty, chief of engagement of the American Association for State and Local History, gave the most inspiring and motivational response:

> First, it is worth it to pursue the goal of leadership. No, it's not easy, and as Shakespeare wrote in Henry IV, "Uneasy lies the head that wears a crown," but it's important to take the mantle of leadership if you are called to do it.
>
> Second is this: always keep your saw sharp. Don't settle on old ideas or understandings. Constantly grow and learn. You can learn much more from the folks who are working for you than from the folks for whom you are working. Be self-reflective as you go forward.

Last, just because you've gotten in this position does not mean you leave the "meat" of your discipline behind. Stay engaged and connected with content. It's easy to forget that's why we're here in the first place when you're dealing with budgets and human resources and fundraising and the like. Present a program at least once or twice a year. Write and research. And give a tour every now and again. It reminds you of why we do what we do.

There's really nothing else to say, huh? Good luck. Keep your head up, your eyes forward, and your brain learning. The museum field needs the best and the brightest to lead it through the twenty-first century and strong administrative skills and practices will form the bedrock of our future.

APPENDIX I

Exercise: Museum Plan

As a member of a group, plan a museum of a predesignated type (art, history, anthropology, natural science). Your museum has an annual budget of $650,000 and has just been given a newly renovated structure of 40,000 square feet on one level. Your plan should include at least the elements listed below.

For those using this book as textbook, this is a semester-long project. For those readers that are using this book as an individual or as a member of a small group of staff, follow along with this exercise as you read through the book. Try your hand at writing these documents as examples that you can use as models at a later time. Or use this list of documents and information in the following chapters to create these documents for your institution:

- Mission statement and symbol
- Bylaws
- Strategic plan
- Budget (benefits are 24.32 percent of salaries)
- Personnel policies
- Collection policies
- Public program policies
- Multicultural statement
- Staffing
- Marketing plan

- Floor plan
- Development plan
- Code of professional museum conduct (two-page limit)

The total document should not exceed fifty pages, double-spaced, typed. You will find the book *Organizing Your Museum: The Essentials,* edited by Sara Dubberly, particularly useful to you in this project.

WORKS CITED

PREFACE

Rosenthal, Ellen. Interview by author. E-mail, October 19, 2015.

CHAPTER I

Alexander, Edward P. *The Museum in America: Innovators and Pioneers*. Walnut Creek, CA: AltaMira Press, 1997.

Alexander, Edward P., and Mary Alexander. *Museums in Motion: An Introduction to the History and Functions of Museums*. Lanham, MD: AltaMira Press, 2008.

American Alliance of Museums. Accessed October 28, 2015. www.aam-us.org.

American Association for State and Local History. Accessed October 28, 2015. www.aaslh.org.

American Public Garden Association. Accessed October 28, 2015. www.publicgardens.org.

Association of Zoos and Aquariums. Accessed October 28, 2015. www.aza.org.

Coleman, Laurence Vail. *The Museum in America: A Critical Study*, vol. 2. Washington, DC: American Association of Museums, 1939.

Danilov, Victor J. *Museum Careers and Training: A Professional Guide*. Westport, CT: Greenwood Press, 1994.

Fleming, David. "Leadership." In *Management in Museums*, edited by Kevin Moore, 93–132. New Brunswick, NJ: Athlone Press, 1999.

Harper, Douglas. "Administration." Online Etymology Dictionary. Accessed November 14, 2015, www.etymonline.com/index.php?term=administration.

Hein, Hilde H. *The Museum in Transition: A Philosophical Perspective*. Washington, DC: Smithsonian Institution Press, 2000.

International Council of Museums. "ICOM Statutes." Accessed October 28, 2015, http://icom.museum/the-vision/museum-definition/.

Institute for Museum and Library Services. Accessed October 28, 2015, www. imls. gov.

National Council for Public History. Accessed October 28, 2015, www.ncph.org.

Parr, A. E. "Is There a Museum Profession?" *Curator: The Museum Journal* 3 (1960): 101–6.

Ruthven, Alexander Grant. *A Naturalist in a University Museum*. Ann Arbor, MI: Privately published, 1931.

Society for American Archivists. Accessed October 28, 2015, www.archivists.org.

Steiner, Rochelle. Interview by author. E-mail, October 24, 2015.

Vaughan, Janet. Interview by author. E-mail, November 4, 2015.

Weil, Stephen E. "The Ongoing Pursuit of Professional Status: The Progress of Museum Work in America." *Museum News* 67 (1988): 30–34.

CHAPTER 2

Abbe Museum. Accessed November 14, 2015, www.abbemuseum.org.

American Alliance of Museums. Accessed February 13, 2016, www.aam-us.org.

———. "Developing a Mission Statement." Accessed November 14, 2015, www. aam-us.org/docs/continuum/developing-a-mission-statement-final.pdf?sfvrsn=2.

American Association for State and Local History. Accessed February 13, 2016, www. aaslh.org.

Anderson, Gail. *Museum Mission Statements: Building a Distinct Identity*. Washington, DC: American Association of Museums, 1998.

Bailey, Dina. Interview by author. E-mail, January 25, 2015.

George, Gerald, and Carol Maryan-George. *Starting Right: A Basic Guide to Museum Planning*. Lanham, MD: AltaMira Press, 2012.

Hoagland, K. E. *Guidelines for Institutional Policies and Planning in Natural History Collections*. Washington, DC: Association of Systematics Collections, 1994.

Institute for Museum and Library Services. Accessed October 28, 2015, www. imls. gov.

Internal Revenue Service. "Tax Exempt Status for Your Organization." *Internal Revenue Service, Department of the Treasury, Publication* 557, 2013.

Lent, Amy. Interview by author. January 26, 2015.

Lord, Gail Dexter, and Barry Lord. *The Manual of Museum Management*. Lanham, MD: AltaMira Press, 2009.

Lynch-McWhite, Wyona. Interview by author. E-mail, January 29, 2015.

Malaro, Marie C., and Ildiko P. DeAngelis. *A Legal Primer on Managing Museum Collections*. Washington, DC: Smithsonian Institution Press, 2012.

Merritt, Elizabeth E. *National Standards and Best Practices for U.S. Museums*. Washington, DC: American Association of Museums, 2010.

Nebraska Revised Statute 21-1921. *Nebraska Legislature*. Accessed November 14, 2015, http://uniweb.legislature.ne.gov/laws/statutes.php?statute=s2119021000.

NOLO Law for All. "How to Form a Nebraska Nonprofit Corporation." Accessed November 14, 2015, www.nolo.com/legal-encyclopedia/forming-nonprofit-corporation-nebraska-36074.html.

Phelan, Marilyn E. *Museum Law: A Guide for Officers, Directors, and Counsel*. Lanham, MD: Rowman and Littlefield, 2014.

Rasic, Alexandra. Interview by author. E-mail, January 28, 2015.

Robert, Henry M. *Robert's Rules of Order, Newly Revised*. Cambridge, MA: Da Capo Press, 2011.

Robinson, Andy. *Great Boards for Small Groups: A 1-Hour Guide to Governing a Growing Nonprofit*. Medfield, MA: Emerson and Church, 2006.

———. "Going for Consensus, Not Robert's Rules." GuideStar, last modified February 2008, www.guidestar.org/rxa/news/articles/2008/going-for-consensus-not-roberts-rules.aspx.

Silberman, Lauren. Interview by author. E-mail, January 25, 2015.

Skramstad, Harold, and Susan Skramstad. 2012. "Mission and Vision Again? What's the Big Deal?" In *Small Museum Toolkit: Leadership, Mission, and Governance*, edited by Cinnamon Catlin-Legutko and Stacy Klingler. Lanham, MD: AltaMira Press, 2012.

Stroh III, Scott M. Interview by author. E-mail, January 27, 2015.

Wolf, Thomas. *Managing a Nonprofit Organization*. New York: Free Press, 2012.

Zeitlin, Kim Arthur, and Susan E. Dorn. *The Nonprofit Board's Guide to Bylaws: Creating a Framework for Effective Governance*. Washington, DC: National Center for Nonprofit Boards, 1996.

CHAPTER 3

Allison, Michael, and Jude Kaye. *Strategic Planning for Nonprofit Organizations: A Practical Guide for Dynamic Times*. Hoboken, NJ: John Wiley and Sons, 2015.

Barry, Bryan W. *Strategic Planning Workbook for Nonprofit Organizations*. Saint Paul, MN: Fieldstone Alliance, 1997.

Bryson, John M. "The Future of Public and Nonprofit Strategic Planning in the United States." *Public Administration Review*, December 2010.

———. *Strategic Planning for Public and Nonprofit Organizations: A Guide to Strengthening and Sustaining Organizational Achievement*. San Francisco: Jossey-Bass, 2011.

Bryson, John M., and Farnum K. Alston. *Creating and Implementing Your Strategic Plan: A Workbook for Public and Nonprofit organizations*. San Francisco: Jossey-Bass, 2011.

Catlin-Legutko, Cinnamon. "DIY Strategic Planning." *Small Museum Toolkit: Leadership, Mission, and Governance*, edited by Cinnamon Catlin-Legutko and Stacy Klingler, 77–96. Lanham, MD: AltaMira Press, 2012.

———. Interview, November 15, 2015.

Durel, Anita. Interview by author. E-mail, October 10, 2015.

"A Guide to Strategic Planning." The Kresge Foundation. Last update June 30, 2011. http://kresge.org/sites/default/files/A_Guide_to_Strategic_Planning.pdf.

Kotler, Neil G., Phillip Kotler, and Wendy I. Kotler. *Museum Marketing and Strategy: Designing Missions, Building Audiences, Generating Revenue and Resources*. San Francisco: Jossey-Bass, 2008.

La Piana, David. *The Nonprofit Strategy Revolution*. New York: Fieldstone Alliance, 2008.

Logan, Burt, e-mail message to author, January 21, 2016.

Lord, Barry, and Gail Dexter Lord. *The Manual of Museum Management*. Lanham, MD: AltaMira Press, 2009.

Lord, Gail Dexter, and Kate Markert. *The Manual of Strategic Planning for Museums*. Lanham, MD: AltaMira Press, 2007.

McNamara, Carter. *Field Guide to Nonprofit Strategic Planning and Facilitation*. Minneapolis: Authenticity Consulting, 2003.

"Mission, Vision, and Values." Boston Children's Museum. Accessed December 23, 2015. www.bostonchildrensmuseum.org/about/mission-vision-values.

Mittenthal, Richard A. "Ten Keys to Successful Strategic Planning for Nonprofit and Foundation Leaders." TCC Group. Last modified 2002. www.tccgrp.com/pdfs/per_brief_tenkeys.pdf.

Najjar, Hassan. Interview by author. E-mail, November 19, 2015.

Pakroo, Peri. "Create a Strategic Plan for Your Nonprofit." NOLO Law for All. Accessed November 15, 2015. www.nolo.com/legal-encyclopedia/create-strategic-plan-nonprofit-29521.html.

Phillips, Will. *Why Plans Fail*. San Diego, CA: Qm2, 1995.

Skramstad, Harold, and Susan Skramstad. "Mission and Vision Again? What's the Big Deal?" In *Small Museum Toolkit: Leadership, Mission, and Governance*. Lanham, MD: AltaMira Press, 2012.

CHAPTER 4

AccountingEdu.org "Fund Accountancy." Accessed November 15, 2015, www.accountingedu.org/fund-accountancy.html.

American Association for State and Local History. *Financial Policies and Procedures Manual*, 2012.

"Analyzing Financial Information Using Ratios." Nonprofits Assistance Fund. Last accessed November 15, 2015. https://nonprofitsassistancefund.org/resources/item/analyzing-financial-information-using-ratios.

Batic, Eloise. Interview by author. E-mail, February 9, 2015.

Boland, Amy. "The Importance of Operating Reserves for Nonprofits." Nonprofit Accounting Basics. Last modified August 13, 2012. www.nonprofitaccountingbasics.org/financial-management-reserves/importance-operating-reserves-nonprofits.

Coley, Hillary. "Accounting and Bookkeeping: Accounting 101." Nonprofit Accounting Basics. Last modified June 3, 2009. www.nonprofitaccountingbasics.org/accounting-bookkeeping/accounting-101.

Dropkin, Murray, Jim Halpin, and Bill La Touche. *The Budget-Building Book for Nonprofits: A Step-by-Step Guide for Managers and Boards*. San Francisco: Jossey-Bass, 2007.

Durel, John, and Will Phillips. *Strategic and Inclusive Budgeting*. Baltimore: QM2, 2004.

Foley, Elizabeth Hamilton. "Budgeting Practices." Nonprofit Accounting Basics. Last modified July 28, 2010. www.nonprofitaccountingbasics.org/reporting-operations/budgeting-practices.

———. "The Budgeting Process." Nonprofit Accounting Basics. Last modified July 28, 2010. www.nonprofitaccountingbasics.org/reporting-operations/budgeting-process.

———. "Budgeting Terms and Concepts." Nonprofit Accounting Basics. Last modified July 28, 2010. www.nonprofitaccountingbasics.org/reporting-operations/budgeting-terms-concepts.

———. "Internal Reports." Nonprofit Accounting Basics. Last modified June 21, 2009. www.nonprofitaccountingbasics.org/reporting-operations/internal-reports.

Granger, Brenda. "The Good, the Best, and the IRS: Museum Financial Management Solutions and Recommendations." In *Small Museum Toolkit: Financial Resource Development and Management*, edited by Cinnamon Catlin-Legutko and Stacy Klingler, 1–26. Lanham, MD: AltaMira Press, 2012.

———. Interview by author. E-mail, February 9, 2015. "GW, Corcoran, National Gallery Complete Agreements." *GW Today*, August 21, 2014. Accessed November 15, 2015. http://gwtoday.gwu.edu/gw-corcoran-national-gallery-complete-agreements.

Harvard Business School. *Finance for Managers*. Boston: Harvard Business School Press. 2002.

Ho, Carl. "Five Internal Controls for the Very Small Nonprofit." *Blue Avocado: A Magazine of American Nonprofits.* Accessed November 15, 2015. http://blueavocado.org/content/five-internal-controls-very-small-nonprofit.

Kennerley, Brent. "Maintaining Sufficient Reserves to Protect Your Not-For-Profit Organisation." *Perspective.* Grant Thorton LLP. Summer 2011. Accessed November 15, 2015. www.grantthornton.co.nz/Assets/documents/sectors/sufficient-reserves-article.pdf.

Klingler, Stacy, and Laura Roberts. "Technical Leaflet #268: Building Better Budgets." *History News* (Autumn 2014).

———. "Technical Leaflet #269: Improving Financial Management" *History News* (Winter 2015).

Lord, Barry, and Gail Dexter Lord. *The Manual of Museum Management*. Lanham, MD: AltaMira Press, 2009.

McLean, Chuck, and Suzanne E. Coffman. "Why Ratios Aren't the Last Word." *Guidestar* (June 2004). Last accessed November 15, 2015. www.guidestar.org/rxa/news/articles/2004/why-ratios-arent-the-last-word.aspx.

McGlone, Peggy. "Secrecy Breeds Anxiety over the Future of the Corcoran's Gallery of Art." *The Washington Post,* January 10, 2015. Accessed November 15, 2015. www.washingtonpost.com/entertainment/museums/secrecy-breeds-anxiety-over-the-future-of-the-corcoran-gallerys-art/2015/01/08/7e351b7a-94f0-11e4-aabd-d0b93ff613d5_story.html.

Miller, Shawn H. "Donor Imposed Restrictions." Last modified June 6, 2009. www.nonprofitaccountingbasics.org/contributions/donor-imposed-restrictions.

Montgomery, David. "Corcoran Gallery: Why Don't Donors Give?" *The Washington Post,* July 20, 2012. Accessed November 15, 2015. www.washingtonpost.com/entertainment/museums/corcoran-gallery-why-dont-donors-give/2012/07/19/gJQAJkNGyW_story.html.

Montgomery, David, and Maura Judkis. "Judge Approves Corcoran Gallery of Art Plan to Partner with National Gallery, GWU." *The Washington Post*, August 18, 2014. Accessed November 15, 2015. www.washingtonpost.com/lifestyle/style/judge-approves-corcoran-gallery-of-art-plan-to-partner-with-national-gallery-gwu/2014/08/18/18eefdbc-2326-11e4-8593-da634b334390_story.html.

National Council of Nonprofits. "Does Your Nonprofit Need to Have an Independent Audit?" Accessed February 14, 2016. www.councilofnonprofits.org/nonprofit-audit-guide/need-independent-audit.

———. "Federal Law Audit Requirements." Accessed February 14, 2016. www.councilofnonprofits.org/nonprofit-audit-guide/federal-law-audit-requirements.

Phelan, Marilyn E. *Museum Law: A Guide for Officers, Directors, and Counsel.* Lanham, MD: Rowman and Littlefield, 2014.

Skramstad, Harold, and Susan Skramstad. *A Handbook for Museum Trustees.* Washington DC: American Association of Museums, 2003.

Stroh III, Scott. Interview by author. E-mail, February 10, 2015.

Washington, Schermeen L. "Audit vs Review vs Compilation." Nonprofit Accounting Basics. Last modified October 17, 2008. www.nonprofitaccountingbasics.org/audit/audit-vs-review-vs-compilation.

———. "Interpreting an Audit." Nonprofit Accounting Basics. Last modified October 17, 2008. www.nonprofitaccountingbasics.org/audit/interepreting-audit.

Wolf, Thomas. *Managing a Nonprofit Organization.* New York: Simon and Schuster, 2012.

Yerdon, Lawrence. Interview by author. E-mail, February 9, 2015.

CHAPTER 5

Adams, Henry. "What Happened to the Blockbuster Art Exhibition?" *The Conversation*, December 2, 2014. Accessed November 15, 2015. http://theconversation. com/what-happened-to-the-blockbuster-art-exhibition-34644.

American Alliance of Museums. "Standards Regarding Developing and Managing Business and Individual Donor Support." Accessed November 15, 2015. www. aam-us.org/resources/ethics-standards-and-best-practices/financial-stability.

Anderson, Heather. *2015 Abbe Museum Development Plan*. Abbe Museum, 2015.

Andrews, Tanya. *Children's Museum of Tacoma FY16 Development Team Plan*. Children's Museum of Tacoma, 2015.

Brophy, Sarah. "Technical Leaflet #257: Is Your Site Grant-Ready? How to Prepare to Attract Grants." *History News* (Winter 2012).

Catlin-Legutko, Cinnamon. "Fearless Fundraising." In *Small Museum Toolkit: Financial Resource Development and Management*, edited by Cinnamon Catlin-Legutko and Stacy Klingler, 27–56. Lanham, MD: AltaMira Press, 2012.

Council on Federations. Accessed November 15, 2015. www.cof.org/content/ foundation-basics.

deLearie, Lynn. "Who Moved My Funder?" Fundraising for Nonprofits Blog. Last updated June 14, 2012. http://managementhelp.org/blogs/ fundraising-for-nonprofits/2012/06/14/who-moved-my-funder/.

"DMA Friends." Dallas Museum of Art. Accessed November 15, 2015. www.dma. org/visit/dma-friends.

Durel, Anita. Interview by author. E-mail, March 17, 2015.

Durel, John. *Building a Sustainable Nonprofit Organization*. Washington, DC: AAM Press, 2010.

Foundation Center. Accessed November 15, 2015. http://foundationcenter.org.

Gregg, Gail. "From Bathers to Beach Towels." *ARTnews* (April 1997): 120–23.

GuideStar. Accessed November 15, 2015. www.guidestar.org.

Hannon, Kerry. "Family Foundations Let Affluent Leave a Legacy." *New York Times*. February 10, 2014. Accessed November 15, 2015. www.nytimes. com/2014/02/11/your-money/family-foundations-let-affluent-leave-a-legacy. html?_r=0.

Hope Consulting. *Money for Good II: Driving Dollars to the Highest-Performing Nonprofits*. Guidestar. 2011. Accessed March 12, 2016. www.multivu.com/ players/English/52621-guidestar-and-hope-consulting-money-for-good-II/flex-Swf/impAsset/document/6791d726-d81b-4095-9fba-977dc438e3e0.pdf.

Hruska, Benjamin. "Oh, Just Write a Grant and Fix the Building: Landing Grants to Support Your Institution." In *Small Museum Toolkit: Financial Resource Development and Management*, edited by Cinnamon Catlin-Legutko and Stacy Klingler, 57–80. Lanham, MD: AltaMira Press, 2012.

"Hyundai Capital America Becomes Corporate Sponsor of MoMA." Hyundai Capital, February 17, 2015. Accessed November 15, 2015. https://

ir.hyundaicapitalamerica.com/2015-02-17-Hyundai-Capital-America-Becomes-Corporate-Sponsor-of-MoMA.

Independent School Management. "Fund Raising. Development. Advancement. What Does It All Mean?" *The Source* 9, no. 2. (2010). Accessed November 15, 2015. https://isminc.com/article/fund-raising-development-advancement-what-does-it-all-mean.

Indiana University Lilly Family School of Philanthropy. *Giving USA 2015: The Annual Report on Philanthropy for the Year 2014.* Indianapolis: Giving USA Foundation.

Institute for Museum and Library Services. Accessed November 15, 2015. www.imls.gov.

Janus, Kathleen Kelly. "Three Ways to Engage Millennial Donors." *Stanford Social Innovation Review*, July 14, 2014. Accessed March 12, 2016. http://ssir.org/articles/entry/three_ways_to_engage_millennial_donors.

Johnson, Steve. "More Museums Skip Admission." *Chicago Tribune*, July 25, 2014. Accessed November 15, 2015. www.chicagotribune.com/entertainment/museums/ct-free-museums-20140725-column.html#page=1.

Kamp, David. "The King of New York." *Vanity Fair,* April 2013. Accessed November 15, 2015. www.vanityfair.com/culture/2013/04/king-tut-exhibit-new-york.

Knight, Christopher. "Metropolitan Museum of Art to Shrink Staff." *Los Angeles Times* Blog, March 12, 2009. Accessed November 15, 2015. http://latimesblogs.latimes.com/culturemonster/2009/03/metropolitan-mu.html.

Kotler, Neil G., Phillip Kotler, and Wendy I. Kotler. *Museum Marketing and Strategy: Designing Missions, Building Audiences, Generating Revenue and Resources*. San Francisco: Jossey-Bass, 2008.

Lord, Gail Dexter, and Barry Lord. *The Manual of Museum Management*. Lanham, MD: AltaMira Press, 2009.

Love, Jay. "Should the Pareto Principle Apply to Fundraising?" *GuideStar* Blog (October 23, 2014). Accessed November 15, 2015. http://trust.guidestar.org/2014/10/23/should-the-pareto-principle-apply-to-fundraising/.

Lynch-McWhite, Wyona. Interview by author. E-mail, March 17, 2015.

Metropolitan Museum of Art Store. Accessed November 15, 2015. http://store.metmuseum.org.

National Endowment for the Arts. Accessed November 15, 2015. www.arts.gov.

National Endowment for the Humanities. Accessed November 15, 2015. www.neh.gov.

National Science Foundation. Accessed November 15, 2015. www. nsf.gov.

NonProfit Gateway. Accessed November 15, 2015. www.npogateway.com.

Phelan, Marilyn E. *Museum Law: A Guide for Officers, Directors, and Counsel*. Lanham, MD: Rowman and Littlefield, 2014.

Poderis, Tony. "Check out Your Organization's Fund-Raising." *Raise-Funds* Blog. Accessed November 15, 2015. www.raise-funds.com/1998/check-out-your-organizations-fund-raising-readiness- and-learn-the-secret-of-fund-raising-success/.

Prince, Russ Alan, and Karen M. File. *Seven Faces of Philanthropy: A New Approach to Cultivating Major Donors*. San Francisco: Jossey-Bass, 1994.

Quimby Family Foundation. Accessed November 15, 2015. http://quimbyfamily-foundation.org.

Richie, Nathan. Interview by author. E-mail, March 18, 2015.

Rudnitksi, Jill. Interview by author. E-mail, May 26, 2015.

Schorr, Melissa. "What Make Millennials Give to Charity?" *Boston Globe Magazine*, October 28, 2015. Accessed March 12, 2016. www.boston-globe.com/magazine/2015/10/28/what-makes-millennials-give-charity/0nkxv2YCmzYuteWiBN1FIM/story.html.

Schwarzer, Marjorie. "Schizophrenic Agora: Mission, Market and the Multi-Tasking Museum." *Museum News* 78 (1999): 40–47.

Seiler, Timothy L. "Plan to Succeed." In *Achieving Excellence in Fundraising*, edited by Eugene R. Tempel, Timothy L. Seiler, and Eva E. Aldrich, 10–17. San Francisco: Jossey-Bass, 2011.

Sharpe Group. "Millennial Donors Rising?" *Give and Take*. Accessed March 12, 2016. http://sharpenet.com/give-take/millennial-donors-rising/.

Simon, Nina. "Is There a Formula for Free Admission?" *Museum 2.0* Blog. Accessed November 15, 2015. http://museumtwo.blogspot.com/2015/01/is-there-formula-for-free-admission.html.

Smith, Erin Geiger. "Children's Museums Brand Exhibits with Corporate Sponsorship." *Wall Street Journal*, November 12, 2014. Accessed March 12, 2016. www.wsj.com/articles/childrens-museums-brand-exhibits-with-corporate-sponsorship-1415826288.

Tempel, Eugene R., Timothy L. Seiler, and Eva E. Aldrich. *Achieving Excellence in Fundraising*. San Francisco: Jossey-Bass, 2011.

Tenenbaum, Jeffrey S., and George E. Constantine. "Corporate Sponsorship: The Final Regulations." Venable LLP (May 1, 2002). Accessed November 15, 2015. www.venable.com/corporate-sponsorship--the-final-regulations-05-01-2002/.

Wellen, Jim. "Moves Management Explained." JWA Consulting Blog. Last updated October 28, 2015. http://jwaconsulting.net/moves-management-explained/.

Wolf, Thomas. *Managing a Nonprofit Organization*. New York: Simon and Schuster, 2012.

CHAPTER 6

Anderson, Katie. "Marry Me! The Relationship between the Director and the Board." In *Small Museum Toolkit: Leadership, Mission, and Governance*, edited by Cinnamon Catlin-Legutko and Stacy Klingler, 77–96. Lanham, MD: AltaMira Press, 2012.

Anonymous. "A Tiger Escaped Today . . . and I'm on the Zoo Board." *Blue Avo-cado: A Magazine of American Nonprofits*, 2015. Accessed January 26, 2016. www.blueavocado.org/node/961#sthash.Odq5HD5s.dpuf.

Batey, Eve. "Taunting Allegations Raised Again After Another SF Zoo Tiger Attack Report Comes To Light." *San Francisco Appeal*, February 14, 2011. Accessed January 26, 2016. http://sfappeal.com/2011/02/tiger-taunting-allegations-raised-again-after-another-sf-zoo-tiger-attack-report-comes-to-light/.

Condrey, Stephen E. *Handbook of Human Resource Management in Government.* San Francisco: Jossey-Bass, 2010.

Ellis, Susan J. "The Organizational Chart." *Non-Profit Times*, September 2, 2014. Accessed November 15, 2015. www.thenonprofittimes.com/news-articles/organizational-chart/.

Fagan, Kevin, Cecilia M. Vega, John Coté, and Marisa Lagos. "Tiger Grotto Wall Shorter than Thought, May have Contributed to Escape and Fatal Attack." *San Francisco Chronicle*, December 27, 2007. Accessed January 26, 2016. www.sfgate.com/news/article/Tiger-grotto-wall-shorter-than-thought-may-have-3232519.php.

Fletcher, Sara. "5 Reasons Why Emotional Intelligence Is Critical for Lead-ers." Lead Change Group Blog, May 30, 2012. http://leadchangegroup.com/5-reasons-why-emotional-intelligence-is-critical-for-leaders/.

Gastil, John W. *Democracy in Small Groups: Participation, Decision Making and Communication.* Philadelphia: Efficacy Press, 2014.

George, Gerald, and Carol Maryan-George. *Starting Right: A Basic Guide to Museum Planning.* Lanham, MD: AltaMira Press, 2012.

Goforth, Teresa. "'Thousands of Small Good Actions': Successful Museum Gov-ernance." In *Small Museum Toolkit: Financial Resource Development and Management,* edited by Cinnamon Catlin-Legutko and Stacy Klingler, 97–116. Lanham, MD: AltaMira Press, 2012.

Goleman, Daniel, Richard Boyatzis, and Annie. McKee. *Primal Leadership: Learn-ing to Lead with Emotional Intelligence.* Boston: Harvard Business Review Press, 2002.

Hoff, Jackie. Interview by author. E-mail, June 1, 2015.

Jones, Trevor. Interview by author. E-mail, June 5, 2015.

Karlgaard, Rich, and Michael S. Malone. *Team Genius: The New Science of High-Performing Organizations.* New York: HarperCollins, 2015.

Kouzes, James M., and Barry Z. Posner. *Leadership Practices Inventory: Partici-pant's Workbook.* San Francisco: Pfeiffer, 2003.

———. *The Leadership Challenge: How to Make Extraordinary Things Happen in Organizations.* San Francisco: John Wiley and Sons, 2012.

Lencioni, Patrick. *The Five Dysfunctions of a Team.* San Francisco: Jossey-Bass, 2002.

———. *Overcoming the Five Dysfunctions of a Team: A Field Guide.* San Fran-cisco: Jossey-Bass, 2005.

Lord, Allyn. Interview by author. E-mail, June 3, 2015.

Lord, Gail Dexter, and Barry Lord. *The Manual of Museum Management*. Lanham, MD: AltaMira Press, 2009.

Male, Richard. "Nonprofit Weaknesses Start with Leadership." *Chronicle of Philanthropy*. February 10, 2013. Accessed November 15, 2015. philanthropy.com/article/Nonprofit-Weaknesses-Start/155399.

Martin, David M. "Organisation Charts." *The A-Z of Employment Practice*. London: Thorogood Publishing, 2004.

Miller, Patricia L. "Are You Being Served? Attracting and Keeping Volunteers." In *Small Museum Toolkit: Organizational Management*, edited by Cinnamon Catlin-Legutko and Stacy Klingler, 62–79. Lanham, MD: AltaMira Press, 2012.

Murphy, Patricia Anne. "Human Resources Administration: Building an Effective Team." In *Small Museum Toolkit: Organizational Management*, edited by Cinnamon Catlin-Legutko and Stacy Klingler, 31–61. Lanham, MD: AltaMira Press, 2012.

Renz, David O. "Leadership, Governance, and the Work of the Board." In *The Jossey-Bass Handbook of Nonprofit Leadership and Management*, edited by David O. Renz and Robert D. Herman, 125–56. San Francisco: Jossey-Bass, 2011.

Right Management and Chally Group. *Why Global Leaders Succeed and Fail: Insights from CEOs and Human Resource Professionals*, 2011. Accessed November 15, 2015. www.right.com/wps/wcm/connect/961094e6-0299-4e9b-939d-97dbb38b82d5/Chally_Leadership_Study.pdf?MOD=AJPERES.

Rosenthal, Ellen. Interview by author. E-mail, October 19, 2015.

Russell, Lou. *10 Steps to Successful Project Management*. Alexandria, VA: ASTD, 2007.

Schall, Eric. "Liability Trends for Nonprofit Organizations." Nonprofit Risk Management Center, 2003. Accessed November 15, 2015. www.nonprofitrisk.org/library/articles/trendb09002000.shtml.

Schonfeld, Roger, and Mariët Westermann. *The Andrew W. Mellon Foundation Art Museum Staff Demographic Survey*. New York: Andrew W. Mellon Foundation, 2015.

Skramstad, Harold, and Susan Skramstad. *A Handbook for Museum Trustees*. Washington DC: American Association of Museums, 2003.

Strauss, William, and Neil Howe. *The Fourth Turning: What the Cycles of History Tell Us about America's Next Rendezvous with Destiny*. New York: Broadway Books, 1997.

———. *Generations: The History of America's Future, 1854 to 2069*. New York: HarperPerennial, 1991.

Taylor, Paul. "The Next America." Philadelphia: Pew Research Center, April 10, 2014. Accessed March 13, 2016. www.pewresearch.org/next-america/#Two-Dramas-in-Slow-Motion.

Trio, Robert. Interview by author. E-mail, June 2, 2015.

Tyler, Kathryn. "Job Worth Doing: Update Descriptions." *HR Magazine* 58 (January 1, 2013): 47–49.

U.S. Department of Labor. *Testing and Assessment: An Employer's Guide to Good Practices.* Washington, DC: Employment and Training Administration, 2000.

Wolf, Thomas. *Managing a Nonprofit Organization.* New York: Simon and Schuster, 2012.

Wolfenden, Elizabeth. "How to Write a Diversity Statement for an Employer." *Houston Chronicle.* Accessed March 13, 2016. http://smallbusiness.chron.com/write-diversity-statement-employer-15410.html.

Zemke, Ron, Claire Raines, and Bob Filipczak. *Generations at Work: Managing the Clash of Veterans, Boomers, Xers, and Nexters in Your Workplace.* New York: AMACOM, 2000.

CHAPTER 7

American Alliance of Museums. *Code of Ethics.* Washington, DC: American Association of Museums, 2000.

———. "Updates." Task Force on Direct Care. Accessed November 15, 2015. www.aam-us.org/resources/ethics-standards-and-best-practices/direct-care-task-force.

Andrei, Mary Anne, and Hugh H. Genoways. "Museum Ethics." *Curator: The Museum Journal.* 40 (1997): 6–12.

Austin, Dan. "Detroit Museum of Art." Historic Detroit.Org. Accessed December 8, 2015. http://historicdetroit.org/building/detroit-museum-of-art/.

Bailey, Dina. Interview by author. E-mail, November 8, 2015.

Corley, Cheryl. "Chicago's Famed Field Museum Struggles to Dig Out of a Hole." NPR: Morning Edition (online story), May 6, 2013. Accessed November 15, 2015. www.npr.org/2013/05/06/180855132/cash-crunch-prompts-controversial-sales-at-chicagos-field-museum.

DeAngelis, Ildiko Pogany. "Collections Ethics." In *Museum Registration Methods,* edited by Rebecca A. Buck and Jean Allman Gillmore, 399–407. Washington, DC: American Association of Museums, 2010.

Detroit Institute of the Arts. *A Brief History of the Detroit Institute of Arts.* Accessed December 29, 2015. www.phillipsoppenheim.com/pdf/DIA-Addendum%20-%20A-Brief-History-of-the-Detroit-Institute-of-Arts.pdf.

Edson, Gary. *Museum Ethics.* London: Routledge, 1997.

Feldscher, Kyle. "Gov. Rick Snyder on Judge's Approval of Detroit Bankruptcy Plan: 'Michigan's Largest City is Stronger.'" MLive Media Group, November 1, 2014. Accessed December 29, 2015. www.mlive.com/lansing-news/index.ssf/2014/11/gov_rick_snyder_on_judges_appr.html.

Gallagher, John, and Mark Stryker. "Battle Brewing over Detroit Museum Collection." *USA Today,* May 26, 2013. Accessed December 29, 2015. www.usatoday.com/wlna/news/nation/2013/05/26/detroit-museum-collection/2362291/.

Genoways, Hugh H. "To Members of the Museum Profession." In *Museum Philosophy for the Twenty-first Century,* edited by Hugh H. Genoways, 221–34. Lanham, MD: AltaMira Press, 2006.

Genoways, Hugh H., and Mary Anne Andrei. "Codes of Professional Museum Conduct." *Curator: The Museum Journal* 40 (1997): 86–92.

Gillers, Heather, and Jason Grotto. "Hard Times at the Field." *Chicago Tribune,* March 8, 2013, 1, 10–11.

Heddaya, Mostafa. "11th-Hour Appraisal Imperils Detroit Institute of Arts 'Grand Bargain.'" *Hyperallergic,* August 28, 2014. Accessed December 29, 2015. http://hyperallergic.com/145937/11th-hour-appraisal-imperils-detroit-institute-of-arts-grand-bargain/.

Hein, Hilde S. *The Museum in Transition: A Philosophical Perspective.* Washington, DC: Smithsonian Books, 2000.

ICOM. Code of Ethics, 2004. Accessed November 15, 2015. http://icom.museum/the-vision/code-of-ethics/.

Institute of Museum Ethics. Accessed November 15, 2015. Museumethics.org.

Kennedy, Randy. "Detroit Institute of Arts Meets Bankruptcy Plan Fund-Raising Goal." *New York Times,* January 6, 2015. Accessed November 15, 2015. http://artsbeat.blogs.nytimes.com/2015/01/06/detroit-institute-of-arts-meets-bankruptcy-plan-fund-raising-goal/?ref=topics&_r=0.

Kennedy, Randy, Monica Davey, and Steven Yaccino. "Foundations Aim to Save Pensions in Detroit Crisis." *New York Times,* January 13, 2014. Accessed November 15, 2015. www.nytimes.com/2014/01/14/us/300-million-pledged-to-save-detroits-art-collection.html.

Kennicott, Phillip. "Detroit Institute of Arts Fire Sale: The Worst Idea out of Motor City since the Edsel." *Washington Post,* October 2, 2013. Accessed December 29, 2015. www.washingtonpost.com/entertainment/museums/detroit-institute-of-arts-fire-sale-the-worst-idea-out-of-motor-city-since-the-edsel/2013/10/03/e95e842a-217b-11e3-b73c-aab60bf735d0_story.html.

Lewis, Geoffrey. "The Role of Museums and the Professional Code of Ethics." Running a Museum: A Practical Handbook. Paris: ICOM, 2004. Accessed November 15, 2015. http://icom.museum/uploads/tx_hpoindexbdd/practical_handbook.pdf

Lord, Gail Dexter, and Barry Lord. *The Manual of Museum Management.* Lanham, MD: AltaMira Press, 2009.

Lovin, Robin W. "What Is Ethics?" In *Writing a Museum Code of Ethics,* 15–20. Washington, DC: American Association of Museums, 1994.

Macdonald, Robert R. "Ethics: Constructing a Code for All of America's Museums." *Museum News* 71 (May–June 1992): 62–65.

Malaro, Marie. *Mission Ethics Policy.* Washington, DC: Smithsonian Institution Press, 1994.

Marstine, Janet. "Introduction." Defining Museum Ethics Conference, 2008. Accessed on November 15, 2015. http://museumethics.org/2011/10/defining-museum-ethics-agenda/.

Merryman, John Henry. "Museum Ethics." Legal Issues in Museum Administration (ALI-BABA Course of Study), 2006. Stanford, CA: American Law Institute. Accessed November 15, 2015. www.law.harvard.edu/faculty/martin/art_law/museum_ethics.html.

Najjar, Hassan. Interview by the author. E-mail, November 19, 2015.

National Park Service. "Code of Ethics." *NPS Handbook I: Collections.* Washington, DC: National Park Service, 2006.

Rhodes, Steven. *Oral Opinion on the Record: In re City Detroit Bankruptcy Judge Steven Rhodes*, 2014. Detroit, MI. Accessed December 29, 2015. www.mieb.uscourts.gov/sites/default/files/notices/Oral_Opinion_on_Detroit_Plan_Confirmation_Judge_Rhodes_FINAL_for_Release.pdf.

Robinson, Aaron. "A Furor over Sales by the Petersen Museum." *New York Times*, July 26, 2013. Accessed November 15, 2015. www.nytimes.com/2013/07/28/automobiles/collectibles/a-furor-over-sales-by-the-petersen-museum.html.

Rose, Joel. "Philadelphia Museum Sells Objects to Get a Face-Lift." NPR: All Things Considered, January 5, 2011. Accessed November 15, 2015. www.npr.org/2011/01/05/132678420/in-philadelphia-a-museum-fundraising-controversy.

Schuette, Bill. *Opinion No. 7272: Conveyance or Transfer of Detroit Institute of Arts Collection*, 2013. Attorney General Office, Lansing, MI. Accessed December 29, 2015. http://media.mlive.com/news/detroit_impact/other/AGO%207272.pdf.

Stryker, Mark. "Detroit Rising: The DIA's $170 Million Challenge." *Detroit Free Press*, November 22, 2015. Accessed December 29, 2015. www.freep.com/story/entertainment/2015/11/21/dia-after-grand-bargain-detroit-bankruptcy/75113624/.

———. "Fight over DIA Value Resumes in Court Next Week." *Detroit Free Press*, September 25, 2014. Accessed December 29, 2015. www.freep.com/story/news/local/2014/09/25/dia-art-detroit-bankrutpcy-trial-valuation/16184545/.

Tempel, Eugene R. "Ethical Frameworks for Fundraising." In *Achieving Excellence in Fundraising*, edited by Eugene R. Tempel, Timothy L. Seiler, and Eva E. Aldrich, 395–412. San Francisco: Josey-Bass, 2011.

Walsh, David. "Detroit Institute of Arts on Track to Become Wholly Owned Corporate Subsidiary." World Socialist Web Site, July 17, 2014. Accessed December 29, 2015. www.wsws.org/en/articles/2014/07/17/diad-j17.html.

Wolf, Thomas. *Managing a Nonprofit Organization.* New York: Free Press, 2012.

CHAPTER 8

Americans with Disabilities Act of 1990. Accessed November 15, 2015. www.ada.gov/pubs/adastatute08.htm.

Association of Science-Technology Centers. "Accessible Practices." Accessed November 15, 2015. www.astc.org/resource/access/index.htm.

Benjamin, Jenny. Interview by author. E-mail, September 8, 2015.

Birkhold, Matthew H. "NOTE: Tipping NAGPRA's Balance Act: The Inequitable Disposition of "Culturally Unidentified" Human Remains under NAGPRA's New Provision." *William Mitchell Law Review* 37, no. 4 (2010–2011): 2046–96.

Board Source and Independent Sector. "The Sarbanes-Oxley Act and Implications for Nonprofit Organizations." GuideStar, 2003. Accessed November 15, 2015. www.guidestar.org/Articles.aspx?path=/rxa/news/articles/2003/sarbanes-oxley-act-and-implications-for-nonprofit-organizations.aspx.

"Civil Penalties Increased for Violation Americans with Disabilities Act." *ADA News.* May 5, 2014. Accessed November 15, 2015. www.ada.org/en/publications/ada-news/2014-archive/may/civil-penalties-increased-for-violating-americans-with-disabilities-act.

Cohen, Rick. "Sarbanes-Oxley: Ten Years Later." *Nonprofit Quarterly,* 2012. Accessed November 15, 2015. https://nonprofitquarterly.org/2012/12/30/sarbanes-oxley-ten-years-later/.

Daehnke, Jon, and Amy Lonetree. "Repatriation in the United States: The Current State of the Native American Graves Protection and Repatriation Act." *American Indian Culture and Research Journal* 35 (2011): 87–97.

"Disability Statistics." Cornell University. Accessed November 15, 2015. www.disabilitystatistics.org.

Dongoske, Kurt. E. "The Native American Graves Protection and Repatriation Act: A New Beginning, Not the End, for Osteological Analysis—A Hopi Perspective." *American Indian Quarterly* 20 (1996): 287–96.

Echo-Hawk, Walter. "The Native American Graves Protection and Repatriation Act: A Legislative History." *Arizona State Law Journal* 24 (1992): 74–76.

Ferguson, Thomas J., Roger Anyon, and Edmund J. Ladd. "Repatriation at the Pueblo of Zuni: Diverse Solutions to Complex Problems." *American Indian Quarterly* 20 (1996): 251–73.

Fletcher, V., B. Siegel, and R. Bloomer. "Going Beyond: What Does Universal Design Look Like?" *Museum* (March–April 2011): 40–45.

Green, Julius, and Seth Moskowitz. "Revised Form 990: The Evolution of Governance and the Nonprofit World." *Tax Advisor.* August 1, 2009. Accessed November 15, 2015. www.thetaxadviser.com/issues/2009/aug/revisedform990theevolutionofgovernanceandthenonprofitworld.html.

"Introduction to the ADA." Information and Technical Assistance on the American with Disabilities Act. Accessed November 15, 2015. www.ada.gov/ada_intro.htm.

Killheffer, Robert K. J., and Amy Guip. "Reburying the Past: Controversy over Native American Artifacts and Remains." *Omni* 17 (1995): 30–36.

Lind, Robert C., Robert M. Jarvis, and Marilyn E. Phelan. *Art and Museum Law: Cases and Materials.* Durham, NC: Carolina Academic Press, 2002.

Lonetree, Amy. *Decolonizing Museums: Representing Native America in National and Tribal Museums.* Chapel Hill: University of North Carolina Press, 2012.

Lord, Allyn. "Not Above the Law: Museums and Legal Issues." In *Small Museum Toolkit: Financial Resource Development and Management*, edited by Cinnamon Catlin-Legutko and Stacy Klingler, 81–141. Lanham, MD: AltaMira Press, 2012.

Majewski, J. "Accessibility for People with Disabilities: Razing the Problems." *Public Garden* (July 1993): 8–9.

Malaro, Marie C., and Ildiko Pogany DeAngelis. *A Legal Primer on Managing Museum Collections*. Washington, DC: Smithsonian Institution Press, 2012.

McManamon, Francis P., and Larry V. Nordby. "Implementing the Native American Graves Protection and Repatriation Act." In *Technical Information Service's Forum: Native American Collections and Repatriation*, 60–82. Washington DC: American Association of Museums, 1991.

Merrill, William L., Edmund J. Ladd, and T.J. Ferguson. "The Return of The Ahayu:da: Lessons for Repatriation from Zuni Pueblo and The Smithsonian Institution." *Current Anthropology* 34 (1993): 523–51.

NAGPRA Review Committee. *Annual Report to Congress 2014*. Accessed November 15, 2015. www.nps.gov/nagpra/REVIEW/Reports_to_Congress/RTC_May2015.pdf.

National Park Service. "Frequently Asked Questions." National NAGPRA. Accessed November 15, 2015. www.nps.gov/nagpra/FAQ/INDEX.HTM#How_many.

———. National NAGPRA Online Database. Accessed November 15, 2015. http://grantsdev.cr.nps.gov/Nagpra/Summaries/default.cfm.

Native American Graves Protection and Repatriation Act. 1990. Accessed November 15, 2015. www.nps.gov/history/local-law/FHPL_NAGPRA.pdf.

New England ADA Center. ADA Checklist for Existing Facilities. Accessed November 15, 2015. www.adachecklist.org/checklist.html.

Newsom, Bonnie. "Cultural Affiliation and NAGPRA: A Case Study from Maine." Paper presented at the World Archaeological Congress, Dublin, Ireland, 2008.

Nonprofit Risk Management Center. *Protecting Your Nonprofit and the Board*, 2015. Accessed November 15, 2015. www.nonprofitrisk.org/library/articles/insurance01021999.shtml.

Phelan, Marilyn E. *Museum Law: A Guide for Officers, Directors, and Counsel*. Lanham, MD: Rowman & Littlefield, 2014.

Platt, G., Jr. "The Repatriation Law Ends One Journey—But Opens A New Road." *Museum News* 70 (1991): 91.

"The Principles of Universal Design." NC State University, 1997. Accessed November 15, 2015. www.ncsu.edu/ncsu/design/cud/about_ud/udprinciplestext.htm.

Ranco, Darren, and Julia Clark. "The Abbe Museum: Seeking a Collaborative Future through Decolonization." In *Interpreting Native American History and Culture at Museums and Historic Sites*, edited by Raney Bench, 57–67. Lanham, MD: Rowman & Littlefield, 2014.

Riding In, James. "Graves Protection and Repatriation: An Unresolved Universal Human Rights Problem Affected by Institutional Racism" In *Human Rights in Global Light: Selected Papers, Poems, and Prayers, SFSU Annual Human Rights*

Summit, 2004–2007. San Franscisco, CA: Treganza Museum Anthropology Papers 24 and 25, 2007–2008.

Rose, Jerome C., Thomas J. Green, and Victoria D. Green. "NAGPRA is Forever: Osteology and the Repatriation of Skeletons." *Annual Review of Anthropology* 25 (1993): 23–51.

Sackler, E. "Three Voices for Repatriation." *Museum News* 71 (1992) 58–61.

Salmen, John P. S. *Everyone's Welcome: The Americans with Disabilities Act and Museums*. Washington, DC: American Association of Museums, 1998.

Silk, Thomas. "Model Document Retention Policy for Nonprofits." *Blue Avocado: A Magazine of American Nonprofits*. Accessed November 15, 2015. http://blueavocado.org/content/model-document-retention-policy-nonprofits.

———. "Model Whistleblower Policy for Nonprofits." *Blue Avocado: A Magazine of American Nonprofits*, Accessed November 15, 2015. http://blueavocado.org/content/model-whistleblower-policy-nonprofits.

Strand, John. "20 Years and Counting: James Pepper Henry's Multifaceted View of NAGPRA." *Museum* 89 (2010): 50–57.

Tabah, A. "Native American Collections and Repatriation." In *Technical Information Service's forum: Native American Collections and Repatriation*, 5. Washington, DC: American Association of Museums, 1993.

Thompson, Raymond H. "Dealing with the Past and Looking To the Future." *Museum News* 70 (1991): 37–40.

U.S. Department of Justice: Civil Rights Division: Disability Rights Section. *2010 ADA Standards for Accessible Design*, September 15, 2010. Accessed November 15, 2015. www.ada.gov/regs2010/2010ADAStandards/2010ADAstandards.htm#designconstruction.

———. *ADA Update: A Primer for Small Business*, 2010. Accessed November 15, 2015. www.ada.gov/regs2010/smallbusiness/smallbusprimer2010.htm#readilyachievable.

———. *Expanding Your Market: Maintaining Accessibility in Museums*, 2009. Accessed November 15, 2015. www.ada.gov/business/museum_access.pdf.

———. Information and Technical Assistance on the Americans with Disabilities Act. Accessed November 15, 2015. www.ada.gov/.

U.S. General Accounting Office. *Native American Graves Protection and Repatriation Act: After Almost 20 Years, Key Federal Agencies Still Have Not Fully Complied with the Act*, July 28, 2010. Accessed November 15, 2015. www.gao.gov/products/GAO-10-768.

U.S. Library of Congress. *Copyright Office*. Accessed November 15, 2015. www.loc.gov/copyright.

World Health Organization. *World Report on Disability*, June 2011. Accessed November 15, 2015. www.who.int/disabilities/world_report/2011/report/en/.

Zimmerman, Larry J. "Epilogue: A new and different archaeology?" *American Indian Quarterly* 20 (1996): 297–307.

CHAPTER 9

Ambrose, Timothy, and Crispin Paine. *Museum Basics*. New York: Routledge Press, 2012. Kindle edition.

Artim, Nick. "An Introduction to Fire Detection, Alarm, and Automatic Fire Sprinklers." Northeast Document Conservation Center. Accessed November 15, 2015. www.nedcc.org/free-resources/preservation-leaflets/3.-emergency-management/3.2-an-introduction-to-fire-detection,-alarm,-and-automatic-fire-sprinklers.

Bailey, Dina. Interview by author. E-mail, November 8, 2015.

Ball, Cynthia, Audrey Yardley-Jones, and Betty Walsh. *Help! A Survivor's Guide to Emergency Preparedness*. Edmonton, Alberta: Museums Alberta, 2001.

Brown, Donn W. *Facility Maintenance: The Manager's Practical Guide and Handbook*. New York: American Management Association, 1996.

Byers, Rachel. "Green Museums and Green Exhibits: Communicating Sustainability through Content and Design." MA thesis, University of Oregon, December 2008.

Canadian Conservation Institute. "Emergency Preparedness for Cultural Institutions: Introduction." *Canadian Conservation Institute Notes* 14, no. 1(1995): 1–2.

Carrlee, Scott. "Collections Care Basics." In *Small Museum Toolkit: Stewardship—Collections and Historic Preservation,* edited by Cinnamon Catlin-Legutko and Stacy Klingler, 1–41. Lanham, MD: AltaMira Press, 2012.

Catlin-Legutko, Cinnamon. Interview. E-mail November 15, 2015.

Cockerline, Neil, and Melinda Markell. "Technical Leaflet #248: The Handling and Exhibition of Potentially Hazardous Artifacts in Museum Collections." *History News* (Fall 2009).

Conn, Donia. "Protection from Light Damage." Northeast Document Conservation Center. Last modified 2012. www.nedcc.org/free-resources/preservation-leaflets/2.-the-environment/2.4-protection-from-light-damage.

Faulk, W. "Are You Ready When Disaster Strikes?" *History News* 48 (1993): 4–11.

Gallimore, Janet. Interview by author. E-mail, October 25, 2015.

Grover, Andrea. Interview by author. E-mail, September 15, 2015.

Hargraves, Ruth. *Cataclysm and Challenge: Impact of September 11, 2001, on our Nation's Cultural Heritage*. Washington, DC: Heritage Preservation, 2002.

Hatchfield, P. "Wood and Wood Products." In *Storage of Natural History Collections: A Preventive Conservation Approach*, edited by Carolyn L. Rose, Catharine A. Hawks, and Hugh H. Genoways, 283–90. York, PA: Society for the Preservation of Natural History Collections, 1995.

"Hazardous Materials in Museum Collections." *Museums and Galleries of NSW*. Accessed November 15, 2015. http://mgnsw.org.au/sector/resources/online-resources/risk-management/hazardous-materials-museum-collections/.

Hemmerlein, Tamara. "Good Visitor Services, Or 'Put Down the Pencil and Put on a Smile!'" In *Small Museum Toolkit: Reaching and Responding to the Audience,* edited by Cinnamon Catlin-Legutko and Stacy Klingler, 121–40. Lanham, MD: AltaMira Press, 2012.

Herskovitz, Robert, Timothy Glines, and David Grabitske. *Building Museums: A Handbook for Small and Midsize Organizations.* St. Paul: Minnesota Historical Society Press, 2012. Kindle edition.

Hillberry, J. D. "Architectural Design Considerations." In *Storage of Natural History Collections: A Preventive Conservation Approach*, edited by Carolyn L. Rose, Catharine A. Hawks, and Hugh H. Genoways, 103–22. York, PA: Society for the Preservation of Natural History Collections, 1995.

Ishii, Mie, Takayoshi Moriyama, Masahiro Toda, Kohtaro Kohmoto, and Masako Saito. "Color Degradation of Textiles with Natural Dyes and of Blue Scale Standards Exposed to White LED Lamps: Evaluation of White LED Lamps for Effectiveness as Museum Lighting." *Journal of Light and Visual Environment* 32 (2008): 8.

Keller, S. R., and D. R. Wilson. "Security Systems." In *Storage of Natural History Collections: A Preventive Conservation Approach*, edited by Carolyn L. Rose, Catharine A. Hawks, and Hugh H. Genoways, 51–56. York, PA: Society for the Preservation of Natural History Collections, 1995.

Kotler, Neil G., Phillip Kotler, and Wendy I. Kotler. *Museum Marketing and Strategy: Designing Missions, Building Audiences, Generating Revenue and Resources.* San Francisco: Jossey-Bass, 2008.

Linnie, J. M. "Integrated Pest Management: A Proposed Strategy for Natural History Collections." *Museum Management and Curatorship* 15 (1996): 133–43.

Liston, David. *Museum Security and Protection: A Handbook for Cultural Heritage Institutions.* New York: Routledge, 1993.

Lord, Barry, Gail Dexter Lord, and Lindsay Martin. *Manual of Museum Planning: Sustainable Space, Facilities, and Operations.* Lanham, MD: AltaMira Press, 2012.

Lord, Gail Dexter, and Barry Lord. *The Manual of Museum Management.* Lanham, MD: AltaMira Press, 2009.

Lord, Gail Dexter, and Kate Markert. *The Manual of Strategic Planning for Museums.* Lanham, MD: AltaMira Press, 2007.

Makos, K. A., and E. C. Dietrich. "Health and Environmental Safety." In *Storage of Natural History Collections: A Preventive Conservation Approach*, edited by Carolyn L. Rose, Catharine A. Hawks, and Hugh H. Genoways, 233–52. York, PA: Society for the Preservation of Natural History Collections, 1995.

Matthews, Tonya. Interview by author. E-mail, September 15, 2015.

Miller, Naomi J., and Jim R. Druzik. "Demonstration of LED Retrofit Lamps at an Exhibit of 19th Century Photography at the Getty Museum." U.S. Department of Energy, Pacific Northwest National Laboratory Technical Report. Pacific Northwest National Laboratory, Richland, WA, 2012.

Minnesota Historical Society. *Historic Housekeeping Handbook*, June 2000. Accessed November 15, 2015. www.mnhs.org/preserve/conservation/reports/manual-0102.pdf.

National Park Service. "Biological Infestations." *Museum Handbook, Part 1: Museum Collections*. Washington, DC: National Park Service, U.S. Department of the Interior, 2014.

———. "Emergency Planning." *Museum Handbook, Part 1: Museum Collections*. Washington, DC: National Park Service, U. S. Department of the Interior, 2000.

———. "Identifying Museum Insect Pest Damage." *Conserve O Gram*. Washington, DC: National Park Service, U.S. Department of the Interior, 2008.

———. "Museum Housekeeping." *Museum Handbook Part 1: Museum Collections*. Washington, DC: National Park Service, U.S. Department of the Interior, 1998.

———. The Secretary of Interior's Standards. *Technical Preservation Services*. Washington, DC: National Park Service, U.S. Department of the Interior. Accessed November 15, 2015. www.nps.gov/tps/standards.htm.

The National Trust. *The National Trust Manual of Housekeeping*. St. Louis: Elsevier Butterworth-Heinemann, 2006.

Nicholson, Claudia. "Can You Hand Me That Wrench? Managing Museum Operations." In *Small Museum Toolkit: Organizational Management,* edited by Cinnamon Catlin-Legutko and Stacy Klingler, 1–30. Lanham, MD: AltaMira Press, 2012.

Occupational Safety and Health Administration. "Hazard Communication Standard: Safety Data Sheets." OSHA Brief. Accessed November 15, 2015. www.osha.gov/Publications/OSHA3514.html.

Ogden, Sherelyn. "Temperature, Relative Humidity, Light, and Air Quality: Basic Guidelines for Preservation." Northeast Document Conservation Center. Accessed November 15, 2015. www.nedcc.org/free-resources/preservation-leaflets/2.-the-environment/2.1-temperature,-relative-humidity,-light,-and-air-quality-basic-guidelines-for-preservation.

Patkus, Beth Lindblom. "Integrated Pest Management." Northeast Document Conservation Center. Accessed November 15, 2015. www.nedcc.org/free-resources/preservation-leaflets/3.-emergency-management/3.10-integrated-pest-management.

Phelan, Marilyn E. *Museum Law: A Guide for Officers, Directors, and Counsel*. Lanham, MD: Rowman & Littlefield, 2014.

Reilly, Julie. *Are You Prepared? A Guide to Emergency Planning*. Omaha: Nebraska State Historical Society, 1997.

Sebor, A. J. "Heating, Ventilating, and Air-conditioning Systems." In *Storage of Natural History Collections: A Preventive Conservation Approach*, edited by Carolyn L. Rose, Catharine A. Hawks, and Hugh H. Genoways, 135–46. York, PA: Society for the Preservation of Natural History Collections, 1995.

Stewart, Niki Ciccotelli. Interview by author. E-mail, September 17, 2015.

Strang, Thomas J. K. "Controlling Insect Pests with Low Temperature." *Canadian Conservation Institute Notes* 3, no. 3 (1997). Accessed November 15, 2015. http://canada.pch.gc.ca/eng/1439925170155.

Strang, Thomas, and Rika Kigawa. "Agent of Deterioration: Pests." Canadian Conservation Institute. Last modified September 6, 2013. www.cci-icc.gc.ca/resources-ressources/agentsofdeterioration-agentsdedeterioration/chap06-eng.aspx#pest-parasites1.

Sutton, Sarah. *Environmental Sustainability at Historic Sites and Museums.* Lanham, MD: Rowman & Littlefield, 2015.

Texas A&M AgriLife. "Biological Collections Grant Awarded!" 2015. Accessed November 15, 2015. http://brtc.tamu.edu/biological-collections-grant-awarded/.

Tremain, David A. "Developing an Emergency Response Plan for Natural History Collections." New York: American Museum of Natural History. Accessed November 15, 2015. www.museum-sos.org/htm/strat_developing_an.html.

U.S. Department of Homeland Security. *Active Shooter: How to Respond.* Accessed November 15, 2015. www.dhs.gov/xlibrary/assets/active_shooter_booklet.pdf.

U.S. Department of Labor. "Hazard Communication Standard: Safety Data Sheets." Accessed November 15, 2015. www.osha.gov/Publications/OSHA3514.html.

Voelker, Gary, Jessica Light, and Ben Marks. "A Conservation Imperative: Replacement of Bird and Mammal Specimen Cases at Texas A&M: Abstract." 2015. Accessed December 31, 2015. www.nsf.gov/awardsearch/showAward?AWD_ID=0954113&HistoricalAwards=false.

Wahahrockah-Tasi, Phyllis. Interview by author. E-mail, November 7, 2015.

Wilcox, U.V. "Facility Management." In *Storage of Natural History Collections: A Preventive Conservation Approach*, edited by Carolyn L. Rose, Catharine A. Hawks, and Hugh H. Genoways, 29–41. York, PA: Society for the Preservation of Natural History Collections, 1995.

Wilson, J. Andrew. "Fire Protection." In *Storage of Natural History Collections: A Preventive Conservation Approach,* edited by Carolyn L. Rose, Catharine A. Hawks, and Hugh H. Genoways, 57–79. York, PA: Society for the Preservation of Natural History Collections, 1995

———. "Technical Leaflet #206: Protecting Cultural Heritage Properties from Fire." *History News* (1999).

CHAPTER 10

Abbe Museum. *Headline News.* 2010. Accessed November 15, 2015. www.abbe-museum.org/headline-news/Introduction/HeadlineNewsIndex.html.

Ambrose, Timothy, and Crispin Paine. *Museum Basics.* New York: Routledge Press, 2012. Kindle edition.

American Association of Museums. *Mastering Civic Engagement: A Challenge to Museums.* Washington, DC: American Association of Museums, 2002.

Andreasen, Alan R., and Phillip T. Kotler. *Strategic Marketing for Nonprofit Organizations.* Englewood Cliffs, NJ: Prentice Hall, 2008.

Associated Press. "Maine Native American Tribes Say Trust Is Deteriorating." *New York Times*, November 15, 2015. Accessed December 31, 2015. www.nytimes. com/2015/11/16/us/maine-native-american-tribes-say-trust-is-deteriorating. html?emc=etal&_r=0.

Bucolo, M. "Model Museum Practice: Museums and E-Communications." In *Museum Marketing and Strategy: Designing Missions, Building Audiences, Generating Revenue and Resources.* San Francisco: Jossey-Bass, 2008.

Duggan, Mary, Nicole B. Ellison, Cliff Lampe, Amanda Lenhart, and Mary Madden. "Social Media Update 2014." Pew Research Center. January 9, 2015. Accessed November 15, 2015. www.pewinternet.org/2015/01/09/ social-media-update-2014/.

Edie, Kara. "Start Spreading the News: Marketing and Communication." *Small Museum Toolkit: Reaching and Responding to the Audience,* edited by Cinnamon Catlin-Legutko and Stacy Klingler, 1–36. Lanham, MD: AltaMira Press, 2012.

Koontz, Christie, and Lorri Mon. *Marketing and Social Media: A Guide for Libraries, Archives, and Museums.* Lanham, MD: Rowman & Littlefield, 2014.

Kotler, Neil G., Phillip Kotler, and Wendy I. Kotler. *Museum Marketing and Strategy: Designing Missions, Building Audiences, Generating Revenue and Resources.* San Francisco: Jossey-Bass, 2008.

Li, Charlene, and Josh Bernoff. *Marketing in the Groundswell.* Boston: Harvard Business Press, 2009.

Lord, Gail Dexter, and Barry Lord. *The Manual of Museum Management.* Lanham, MD: AltaMira Press, 2009.

"Market Segmentation." NetMBA. Accessed November 15, 2015. www.netmba. com/marketing/market/segmentation/.

Najjar, Hassan. Interview by author. E-mail, November 19, 2015.

Pilley, Marjory. "Explaining the Concept of SMART Goals." Bright Hub Project Management. Last modified October 24, 2014. www.brighthubpm.com/ methods-strategies/79127-explaining-the-concept-of-smart-goals-with-examples/.

PRSA Staff. "Public Relations Defined: A Modern Definition for the New Era of Public Relations." *Public Relations Society of America* Blog, April 11, 2012. Accessed November 15, 2015. http://prdefinition.prsa.org.

Rentschler, Ruth, and Anne-Marie Hede. *Museum Marketing: Competing in a Global Marketplace.* New York: Routledge, 2007.

Schwartz. Nancy E. "How a Museum Re-Branded Itself to Boost Visitors by 600%." *Getting Attention!* Blog. Accessed November 15, 2015. http://gettingattention. org/articles/129/branding/museum-branding-case-study.html.

———. 2015. "Make Social Media Matter More: Part I." *Getting Attention!* Blog. Accessed November 15, 2015. http://gettingattention.org/2015/01/ nonprofit-social-media-pew/.

Silberman, Lauren. Interview by author. E-mail, October 12, 2015.

Spencer Pyle, Lesley. "How to Do Market Research: The Basics." *Entrepreneur,* September 23, 2010. Accessed November 15, 2015. www.entrepreneur.com/ article/217345.

Stern, Gary J. *Marketing Workbook for Nonprofit Organizations*. St. Paul, MN: Amherst H. Wilder Foundation, 2001.

Todd, Sarah. "Business of Nonprofits: Create a PR Plan for Your Nonprofit." *Savannah Morning News*, July 24, 2009. Accessed November 15, 2015. http://savannahnow. com/column/2009-07-24/business-nonprofits-create-pr-plan-your-nonprofit.

Wahahrockah-Tasi, Phyllis. Interview by author. E-mail, November 7, 2015.

Wind, Yoram, and David R. Bell. "Market Segmentation." In *The Marketing Book*, edited by Michael Baker and Susan Hart, 222–42. Oxford: Butterworth-Heinemann, 2007.

CHAPTER II

Ambrose, Timothy, and Crispin Paine. *Museum Basics*. New York: Routledge, 2012. Kindle edition.

American Association for State and Local History Standing Committee on Standards and Ethics. *Ethics Position Paper #1: The Capitalization of Collections*. Nashville, TN: American Association for State and Local History, 2003.

American Alliance of Museums. *Code of Ethics for Museums, 2000*. Accessed November 15, 2015. www.aam-us.org/resources/ethics-standards-and-best-practices/code-of-ethics.

——— *Core Documents Verification*. Accessed November 15, 2015. www.aam-us. org/resources/assessment-programs/core-documents.

——— 2012. *Developing a Collections Management Policy*. Accessed November 15, 2015. www.aam-us.org/resources/resource-library/cs/collections-management.

Arenz, Deborah, Cindy Drake, Paul Eisloeffel, et al. *Nebraska State Historical Society Collections Policy*. April 6. 2012. Accessed November 15, 2015. www. nebraskahistory.org/museum/collect/collections_policy.pdf.

Baker, M. T. "Synthetic Polymers." In *Storage of Natural History Collections: A Preventive Conservation Approach*, edited by Carolyn L. Rose, Catharine A. Hawks, and Hugh H. Genoways, 305–23. York, PA: Society for the Preservation of Natural History Collections, 1995.

Benzel, Lance. "Insider Pleads Guilty in Stealing 300 Coins from Money Museum." *Gazette*. January 12, 2012. Accessed March 13, 2016. http://gazette.com/insider-pleads-guilty-in-stealing-300-coins-from-money-museum/article/131652%20 January%2012,%202012.

Blanchegorge, Eric. "Preventive Conservation on a Day-to-day Basis: The Antoine Vivenel Museum in Compiègne." *Museum International* 51 (1999): 16–21.

Buck, Rebecca A. "Initial Custody and Documentation." *Museum Registration Methods*, edited by Rebecca A. Buck and Jean Allman Gilmore, 38–43. Washington, DC: American Association of Museums, 2010.

Buck, Rebecca A., and Jean Allman Gilmore. *Collections Conundrums: Solving Collections Management Mysteries*. Washington, DC: American Association of Museums, 2007.

————, eds. *Museum Registration Methods*. Washington, DC: American Association of Museums, 2010.

Burgess, H. D. "Other Cellulosic Materials." In *Storage of Natural History Collections: A Preventive Conservation Approach,* edited by Carolyn L. Rose, Catharine A. Hawks, and Hugh H. Genoways, 291–303. York, PA: Society for the Preservation of Natural History Collections, 1995.

Butler-Clary, Karen. "Implementing Indiana's Museum Property Law." *Collections Advisor* 37 (November 2014). Accessed November 15, 2015. www.indiana-history.org/our-services/local-history-services/connect/collections-advisor-1/all-issues-by-date/2014.11%20IN%20Museum%20Property%20Law.pdf.

Carnell, Clarisse, and Rebecca Buck. "Acquisitions and Accessioning." *Museum Registration Methods,* edited by Rebecca A. Buck and Jean Allman Gilmore, 38–43. Washington, DC: American Association of Museums, 2010.

Carrlee, Scott. "Collections Care Basics." In *Small Museum Toolkit: Stewardship: Collections and Historic Preservation,* edited by Cinnamon Catlin-Legutko and Stacy Klingler, 1–41. Lanham, MD: AltaMira Press, 2012.

Clark, Julia. "Do You Really Want That Bust of Jesus, and What Should We Do with the Pump Organ in the Other Room? Or, Why You Want a Good Collections Management Policy." In *Small Museum Toolkit: Stewardship: Collections and Historic Preservation,* edited by Cinnamon Catlin-Legutko and Stacy Klingler, 86–107. Lanham, MD: AltaMira Press, 2012.

Crimesider Staff. "New Development in Infamous 1990 Boston Art Heist." *CBS News,* August 11, 2015. Accessed March 13, 2016. www.cbsnews.com/news/new-development-in-infamous-1990-boston-art-heist/.

de Guichen, Gael. "Preventive Conservation: A Mere Fad or Far-Reaching Change?" *Museum International* 51 (1999): 4–6.

Demeroukas, Marie. "Condition Reporting." *Museum Registration Methods,* edited by Rebecca A. Buck and Jean Allman Gilmore, 223–32. Washington, DC: American Association of Museums, 2010.

Duckworth, W. Donald, Hugh H. Genoways, and Carolyn L. Rose. *Preserving Natural Science Collections: Chronicle of our Environmental Heritage.* Washington, DC: National Institute for the Conservation of Cultural Property, 1993.

Freitag, Sally, Cherie Summers, and Judy Cline. "Loans." *Museum Registration Methods,* edited by Rebecca A. Buck and Jean Allman Gilmore, 120–32. Washington, DC: American Association of Museums, 2010.

Gardner, James B., and Elizabeth E. Merritt. *The AAM Guide to Collections Planning.* Washington, DC: American Association of Museums, 2004.

George, Gerald, and Carol Maryan-George. *Starting Right: A Basic Guide to Museum Planning.* Lanham, MD: AltaMira Press, 2012.

Grzywacz, C. M. "Air Quality Monitoring." In *Storage of Natural History Collections: A Preventive Conservation Approach,* edited by Carolyn L. Rose, Catharine A. Hawks, and Hugh H. Genoways, 197–209. York, PA: Society for the Preservation of Natural History Collections, 1995.

Hankins, Scott. "Photography." *Museum Registration Methods*, edited by Rebecca A. Buck and Jean Allman Gilmore, 277–85. Washington, DC: American Association of Museums, 2010.

Harris, John. "Indiana's Museum Property Law." In *Museogram*. Indianapolis: Association of Indiana Museums, 1989.

Hatchfield, P. "Wood and Wood Products." In *Storage of Natural History Collections: A Preventive Conservation Approach*, edited by Carolyn L. Rose, Catharine A. Hawks, and Hugh H. Genoways, 283–90. York, PA: Society for the Preservation of Natural History Collections, 1995.

Honan, William H. "The Trusted Museum Insider Who Turned Out to Be a Thief." *New York Times*, December 19, 1991. Accessed March 13, 2016. www.nytimes.com/1991/12/19/arts/the-trusted-museum-insider-who-turned-out-to-be-a-thief.html.

Howie, F. M. *The Care and Conservation of Geological Materials: Minerals, Rocks, Meteorites, and Lunar Finds*. Oxford, UK: Butterworth-Heinemann, 1992.

Indianapolis Museum of Art. "Deaccession Policy." 2008. Accessed November 15, 2015. www.imamuseum.org/sites/default/files/Final_IMA_Deaccession_policy.pdf.

Institute of Conservation, The. "Introduction to Conservation Reports: Treatment Reports." *Conservation Register*. Accessed November 15, 2015. www.conservationregister.com/PIcon-ConservationReports.asp.

Johnston, David. "A Professor Helps to Catch Smithsonian's Curator-Thief." *New York Times*, February 17, 1996. Accessed March 13, 2016. www.nytimes.com/1996/02/17/us/a-professor-helps-smithsonian-catch-the-curator-thief.html.

Jones, Trevor. Interview by author. E-mail, October 9, 2015.

Kozak, Zenobia. "How Do We Select a Collections Management System?" *Museum* (January/February 2013).

Krebs, Magdalena. "A Strategy for Preventive Conservation Training." *Museum International* 51 (1999): 7–10.

Longstreth-Brown, Kittu, and Rebecca Buck. "Types of Files." In *Museum Registration Methods*, edited by Rebecca A. Buck and Jean Allman Gilmore, 150–54. Washington, DC: American Association of Museums, 2010.

Lord, Gail Dexter, and Barry Lord. *The Manual of Museum Management*. Lanham, MD: AltaMira Press, 2009.

Malaro, Marie C., and Ildiko Pogany DeAngelis. *A Legal Primer on Managing Museum Collections*. Washington, DC: Smithsonian Institution Press, 2012.

McCormick, Maureen. "Inventory." In *Museum Registration Methods,* edited by Rebecca A. Buck and Jean Allman Gilmore, 307–13. Washington, DC: American Association of Museums, 2010.

Meister, Nicolette B. Interview, October 5, 2015.

———. "Logan Museum Staff and Student Travel to Mexico to Purchase Mata Ortiz Traditional Pottery." *Terrarium*, February 21, 2015. Accessed November 15, 2015. www.beloit.edu/campus/museummondays/?story_id=433244.

Meister, Nicolette B., and Jackie Hoff. "Collections Planning: Best Practices in Collections Stewardship." In *Small Museum Toolkit: Stewardship: Collections and Historic Preservation,* edited by Cinnamon Catlin-Legutko, and Stacy Klingler, 108–31. Lanham, MD: AltaMira Press, 2012.

Miller, Patricia L. "Collections Management: Know What You Have, Know Why You Have It, Know Where You Got It, Know Where It Is." In *Small Museum Toolkit: Stewardship: Collections and Historic Preservation,* edited by Cinnamon Catlin-Legutko and Stacy Klingler, 63–85. Lanham, MD: AltaMira Press, 2012.

Moore, B. P., and S. L. Williams. "Storage Equipment." In *Storage of Natural History Collections: A Preventive Conservation Approach,* edited by Carolyn L. Rose, Catharine A. Hawks, and Hugh H. Genoways, 255–67. York, PA: Society for the Preservation of Natural History Collections, 1995.

Morris, Martha and Antonia Moser. "Deaccessioning." In *Museum Registration Methods,* edited by Rebecca A. Buck and Jean Allman Gilmore, 100–107. Washington, DC: American Association of Museums, 2010.

Phelan, Marilyn E. *Museum Law: A Guide for Officers, Directors, and Counsel.* Lanham, MD: Rowman and Littlefield, 2014.

Reibel, Daniel B. *Registration Methods for the Small Museum.* Lanham, MD: AltaMira Press, 2008.

Richie, Nathan. Interview by author. E-mail, October 5, 2015.

Rose, Carolyn L., and Amparo R. de Torres, eds. *Storage of Natural History Collections: Ideas and Practical Solutions.* Pittsburgh, PA: Society for the Preservation of Natural History Collections, 1992.

Simmons, J. E. "Collections Management Policies." In *Museum Registration Methods,* edited by Rebecca A. Buck and Jean Allman Gilmore, 24–29. Washington, DC: American Association of Museums, 2010.

———. "Storage in Fluid Preservatives." In *Storage of Natural History Collections: A Preventive Conservation Approach,* edited by Carolyn L. Rose, Catharine A. Hawks, and Hugh H. Genoways, 161–86. York, PA: Society for the Preservation of Natural History Collections, 1995.

———. *Things Great and Small: Collections Management Policies.* Washington, DC: American Association of Museums, 2006.

Swain, Lynn, and Rebecca Buck. "Storage." In *Museum Registration Methods,* edited by Rebecca A. Buck and Jean Allman Gilmore, 293–99. Washington, DC: American Association of Museums, 2010.

Tarpey, Sean, Patricia Hayes, and Deborah Peak. "Insurance." In *Museum Registration Methods,* edited by Rebecca A. Buck and Jean Allman Gilmore, 353–59. Washington, DC: American Association of Museums, 2010.

Voigt, Tobi. Interview by author. E-mail, October 8, 2015.

von Endt, D. W., W. D. Erhardt, and W.R. Hopwood. "Evaluating Materials Used for Constructing Storage Cases." In *Storage of Natural History Collections: A Preventive Conservation Approach,* edited by Carolyn L. Rose, Catharine A. Hawks, and Hugh H. Genoways, 269–82. York, PA: Society for the Preservation of Natural History Collections, 1995.

Weintraub, S., and S. J. Wolf. "Environmental Monitoring." In *Storage of Natural History Collections: A Preventive Conservation Approach*, edited by Carolyn L. Rose, Catharine A. Hawks, and Hugh H. Genoways, 187–96. York, PA: Society for the Preservation of Natural History Collections, 1995.

CHAPTER 12

American Alliance of Museums. *Collections Management*. Washington, DC: American Alliance of Museums. Accessed March 13, 2016. www.aam-us.org/resources/resource-library/cs/collections-management.

———. *Core Documents Verification*. Washington, DC: American Alliance of Museums. Accessed March 13, 2016. www.aam-us.org/resources/assessment-programs/core-documents.

American Association of Museums. *Demographic Transformation and the Future of Museums*. Washington, DC: American Association of Museums, 2010. Accessed January 10, 2016. www.aam-us.org/docs/center-for-the-future-of-museums/demotransaam2010.pdf?sfvrsn=0.

———. *Excellence and Equity: Education and the Public Dimension of Museums*. Washington, DC: American Association of Museums, 1992.

American Association of Museum Directors. "Managing the Relationship between Art Museum and Corporate Sponsors." Association of Art Museum Directors, 2007. Accessed November 15, 2015. https://aamd.org/sites/default/files/document/Corporate%20Sponsors_clean%2006-2007.pdf.

Balzar, J. "And the Next Item Up for Bids: The Smithsonian." *Los Angeles Times*, June 6, 2001.

Bright, Anna. "Small Objects Telling Big Stories." British Museum Blog, August 26, 2011. Accessed November 15, 2015. http://blog.britishmuseum.org/tag/interpretation/.

Brochu, Lisa. *Interpretive Planning*. Fort Collins, CO: National Association for Interpretation, 2003.

Brown, Kevin. "Removing Dioramas Provokes Debate: Rethinking Role of Natural History Museum, Portrayal of Native Americans." Montage: University of Michigan Blog, 2009. Accessed January 9, 2016. www.montage.umich.edu/2009/10/dioramas-debate/.

Brüninghaus-Knubel, Cornelia. "Museum Education in the Context of Museum Functions." In *Running a Museum: A Practical Handbook*. Paris: ICOM, 2004.

Carr, David. "The Need for the Museum." *Museum News* 78 (1999): 31–35, 56–57.

Committee on Education. *Excellence in Practice: Museum Education Principles and Standards*. Washington, DC: American Association of Museums, 2005. Accessed November 15, 2015. www.aam-us.org/docs/default-source/accreditation/committee-on-education.pdf?sfvrsn=0.

Dean, David. *Museum Exhibition: Theory and Practice*. New York: Routledge,1996.

Diamond, Judy, Jessica J. Luke, and David H. Uttal. *Practical Evaluation Guide: Tools for Museums and Other Informal Educational Settings.* Lanham, MD: AltaMira Press, 2009.

Diep, Francie. "The Passing of the Indians behind Glass." *The Appendix: Futures of the Past* 2 (2014). Accessed January 9, 2016. http://theappendix.net/issues/2014/7/the-passing-of-the-indians-behind-glass.

Dillenburg, Eugene, and Janice Klein. "Creating Exhibits: From Planning to Building." *Small Museum Toolkit: Interpretation—Education, Programs, and Exhibits,* edited by Cinnamon Catlin-Legutko and Stacy Klingler, 71–99. Lanham, MD: AltaMira Press, 2012.

Falk, John H. "Museums as Institutions for Personal Learning. *Dædalus* 128 (1999): 259–75.

Falk, John H., and Lynn D. Dierking. *The Museum Experience Revisited.* Walnut Creek, CA: Left Coast Press, 2013.

Farago, Jason. "The Degas Wears Prada." *New Republic*, September 16, 2013.

Greene, Jay P., Brian Kisida, and Daniel H. Bowen. "The Educational Value of Field Trips." *Education Next* (Winter 2014): 78–86.

Hague, Stephen G., and Laura C. Keim. "Preparing an Outstanding Concert: How to Plan and Implement Interpretation." In *Small Museum Toolkit: Interpretation—Education, Programs, and Exhibits,* edited by Cinnamon Catlin-Legutko and Stacy Klingler, 1–25. Lanham, MD: AltaMira Press, 2012.

Harwood Museum of Art, "Exhibition Policy." Accessed November 15, 2015. http://harwoodmuseum.org/exhibition_policy.

Herreman, Yani. "Display, Exhibits and Exhibitions." *Running a Museum: A Practical Handbook.* Paris: ICOM, 2004.

IUPUI and Institute for Museum and Library Services. *Shaping Outcomes: Making a Difference in Libraries and Museums.* Accessed November 15, 2015. www.shapingoutcomes.org/index.htm.

Johnson, Anna. "Museum Education and Museum Educators." In *The Museum Educator's Manual: Educators Share Successful Techniques*, edited by Anna Johnson, Kimberly A. Huber, Nancy Cutler, Melissa Bingmann, and Tim Grove, 7–14. Lanham, MD: AltaMira Press, 2009.

Klingler, Stacy, and Conny Graft. "In Lieu of Mind Reading: Visitor Studies and Evaluation." *Small Museum Toolkit: Reaching and Responding to the Audience,* edited by Cinnamon Catlin-Legutko and Stacy Klingler, 37–74. Lanham, MD: AltaMira Press, 2012.

Kotler, Neil G., Phillip Kotler, and Wendy I. Kotler. *Museum Marketing and Strategy: Designing Missions, Building Audiences, Generating Revenue and Resources.* San Francisco: Jossey-Bass, 2008.

LaVaque-Manty, Danielle. "There are Indians in the Museum of Natural History." *Wicazo Sa Review* 15 (2000): 71–89.

Lonetree, Amy. *Decolonizing Museums: Representing Native America in National and Tribal Museums.* Chapel Hill: University of North Carolina Press, 2012.

Lord, Barry. "Where Do Exhibition Ideas Come From?" In *Manual of Museum Exhibitions*, edited by Barry Lord and Maria Piacente, 23–24. Lanham, MD: AltaMira Press, 2014.

Lord, Barry, and Maria Piacente. *Manual of Museum Exhibitions*. Lanham, MD: Rowman & Littlefield, 2014.

Lord, Gail Dexter, and Barry Lord. *The Manual of Museum Management*. Lanham, MD: AltaMira Press, 2009.

Lord, R. "Quid Pro Show: Museums That Take Corporate Shillings Risk Looking Like Corporate Shills." *Pittsburgh City Paper*, December 27, 2000.

Martin, Rebecca. "The Nuts and Bolts of Program Management." In *Small Museum Toolkit: Interpretation—Education, Programs, and Exhibits*, edited by Cinnamon Catlin-Legutko and Stacy Klingler, 100–32. Lanham, MD: AltaMira Press, 2012.

Maximea, Heather. "Exhibition Facilities." In *Manual of Museum Exhibitions*, edited by Barry Lord and Maria Piacente, 99–117. Lanham, MD: AltaMira Press, 2009.

Middleton, Margaret. "Including the 21st Century Family." Incluseum Blog. July 7, 2014. Accessed March 13, 2016. http://incluseum.com/2014/07/07/including-the-21st-century-family/.

Miller, Janet. "Native American Dioramas at University of Michigan Exhibit Museum of Natural History to be Removed." *Ann Arbor News*, September 18, 2009. Accessed January 9, 2016. www.annarbor.com/news/native-american-dioramas-at-u-m-exhibit-museum-of-natural-history-to-be-removed-jan-4/.

National Park Service. *Interpretive Planning Tools for Heritage Areas, Historic Trails and Gateways*. Chesapeake Bay Office/National Park Services. U.S. Department of the Interior, 2010.

Pogrebin, Robin. "And Now, and Exhibition from Our Sponsor." *New York Times*, August 21, 2009. Accessed November 15, 2015. www.nytimes.com/2009/08/23/arts/design/23pogr.html?_r=0.

Rasic, Alexandra. Interview by author. E-mail, October 8, 2015.

Simon, Nina. *The Participatory Museum*. Santa Cruz, CA: Museum 2.0, 2010.

Smithsonian Accessibility Program. *Smithsonian Guidelines for Accessible Exhibition Design*. Accessed November 15, 2015. www.si.edu/Accessibility/SGAED.

Stoffer, Janet. Interview by author. E-mail, October 5, 2015.

Thompson, Craig, and Phillip Thompson. "Universal Design and Diversity." In *Manual of Museum Exhibitions*, edited by Barry Lord and Maria Piacente, 322–34. Lanham, MD: Rowman & Littlefield, 2014.

Voigt, Tobi. Interview by author. E-mail, October 8, 2015.

Wax, Dustin. 2006. "In the Flesh in the Museum." Savage Minds: Notes and Queries in Anthropology Blog, August 10, 2006. Accessed January 9, 2016. http://savageminds.org/2006/08/10/in-the-flesh-in the museum/.

Weil, Stephen E. "From Being about Something to Being for Somebody: The Ongoing Transformation of the American Museum." *Dædalus* 128 (1999): 229–58.

Zhu, Jasmine. "Natural History Museum Removes Dioramas Amidst Contro- versy." *Michigan Daily*, September 14, 2009. Accessed January 9, 2016. www. michigandaily.com/content/natural-history-museum-removes-dioramas-amid- controversy/.

EPILOGUE

Beatty, Bob. Interview by author. E-mail, October 19, 2015.

INDEX

Blue Avocado, 172
board-director-staff interactions, 164–66
board members, 167–68
Boomers, 156
Boston Children's Museum, 53
Boston Museum of Fine Arts, 132
Bright, Anna, 309
British Museum, 189, 309
Brooklyn Historical Society, 47
Brophy, Sarah S., 233
Bryson, John, 42–43; on strategic
  planning, 44, 46
budget management, 3; AASLH, 76;
  accounting in, 83–90; accounting
  software in, 87–88; cash flow, 77;
  cuts, 82–83; financial
  statements, 78–82; long-range
  planning, 74; measurement, 76–78;
  mismanagement, 91; monitoring,
  71–73; in practice, 78;
  reports, 78–82; reserve levels, 80;
  team, 74–75; timing, 76–77
budgets: adjusting, 70; amending, 70–71;
  annual, 62; balancing, 70, 78;
  board approval of, 70; capital, 62;
  cycle, 65–68; defining, 62;
  direct costs, 64; evaluation of,
  70–71; fund types, 62–63; Indiana
  Historical Society, 66; indirect costs,
  64; line-item, 65; marketing and, 264;
  monthly status report, 86;
  operating, 62; performance, 62;
  plan creation, 68–69; preparing,
  68–71; priorities in, 69–70;
  program, 67; resource
  allocation, 69;
  terminology, 62; zero-based, 69
Buffet, Warren, 122
building funds, 228–29
Burt's Bees, 121
Bush, George H. W., 20
buzz, 278
bylaws: Article I, 28; Article II, 28;
  Article III, 28–29; Article IV, 30;
  Article IX, 31; Article V, 30; Article
  VI, 31; Article VII, 31; Article VIII,
  31; Article X, 31–32

Canadian Museums Association (CMA),
  180
CAP. *See* Conservation Assessment
  Program
capital budgets, 62
capital campaign, 100
capital funds, 62
capital needs, 96
careers, 1, 2
Carnegie Museum, 213
carpet beetles, 245
Carr, David, 328
Carrlee, Scott, 231
cash flow management, 77
casual givers, 104
cataloging, 292–93
Catalog of Federal Domestic Assistance,
  123
catering services, 134
Catlin, George, 186
Catlin-Legutko, Cinnamon, 46–47, 102,
  276
Center for Civil and Human Rights, 177
CEOs, 166
certified public accountant (CPA), 78
CFO. *See* chief financial officer
chairpersons, 29–30
Characteristics for Excellence, 37–38
charitable gift annuity, 115
charitable lead trust, 115
charitable remainder annuity trust, 115
charitable remainder unitrust, 115
chart of accounts, 84
chief financial officer (CFO), 74–75
Children's Museum of Houston, 108
Children's Museum of Tacoma, 135
Christie's, 108
Civil Rights Act, 202
Claremont Graduate University, 18
cloth moths, 245
CMA. *See* Canadian Museums
  Association
coaches, 162
Coca-Cola Foundation, 122
cockroaches, 245
code of ethics: AAM, 180, 197, 302;
  AAMD, 180; CMA, 180; enforcement,

ABOUT THE AUTHORS AND REVISER

Hugh H. Genoways is professor emeritus and former director of the University of Nebraska State Museum and former editor of the journals *Museum History Journal* and *Collections: A Journal for Museum and Archives Professionals*. He is the editor with Mary Anne Andrei of *Museum Origins: Readings in Early Museum History and Philosophy*, editor of *Museum Philosophy for the Twenty-First Century*, and co-author of *Museum Administration: An Introduction* and *Preserving Natural Science Collections: Chronicle of Our Environmental Heritage*. He served as president of the Nebraska Museums Association from 1990 to 1992.

Lynne M. Ireland is deputy director of the Nebraska State Historical Society and former Chair of the Council of the American Association for State and Local History. She is coauthor *of Museum Administration: An Introduction* and contributor to *Zen and the Art of Local History* and *Leadership Matters*. She has served as president and is currently secretary of the Nebraska Museums Association.

Cinnamon Catlin-Legutko is president and CEO of the Abbe Museum in Bar Harbor, Maine, and has worked in museums for more than twenty years, serving as a museum leader since 2001. Prior to joining the Abbe in 2009, she was the director of the General Lew Wallace Study and Museum in Crawfordsville, Indiana, where she led the organization to the

National Medal for Museum Service in 2008. She is coeditor and contributor to the *Small Museum Toolkit* and contributor to *Zen and the Art of Local History*. She is the former treasurer of the American Association of State and Local History, and is currently on the board of the American Alliance of Museums.